# Adolescent Literature

# as a Complement to the Classics

## Volume Three

# Adolescent Literature
# as a Complement to the Classics

## Volume Three

Edited by Joan F. Kaywell
University of South Florida

Christopher-Gordon Publishers, Inc.
Norwood, MA

# Credits

Every effort has been made to contact copyright holders for permission to reproduce borrowed material where necessary. We apologize for any oversights and would be happy to rectify them in future printings.

**Chapter One:**

"Values Profile." Copyright 1996 by the National Council of Teachers of English. Reprinted with permission.
Student comments reprinted with permission.

**Chapter Three:**

"Something Permanent" reprinted by permission of Cynthia Rylant
Student comments reprinted with permission.

**Chapter Nine:**

From **Cool Salsa** by Lori M. Carlson, Editor. Collection Copyright 1984 by Lori M. Carlson. Reprinted by permission of Henry Holt & Co., Inc.

Christopher-Gordon Publishers, Inc.
480 Washington Street
Norwood, MA 02062

Printed in the United States of America

10 9 8 7 6 5 4 3 2 1      02 01 00 99 98 98 97

ISBN: 0-926842-61-7

# Dedication

*Dr. John Powell*
*and*
*The Whitmore Family: "Mom," "Dad," Gale, Debbie,*
*Richard, Judy, and Genevieve*

# Acknowledgments

My first thanks must go to my best friend, Susan Maida. I couldn't have done it without you! I also want to thank two more of my dearest friends, Jeannie and Ben Borsch, who encouraged me every step of the way. Jeannie, thanks for noting all the comma splices, helping me "find myself," and sharing in some wonderful laughter. Special thanks are extended to Heidi M. Quintana and David Wellens for helping me with the bibliography, especially those ISBN's.

I am indebted to Peter Lowe (Peter Lowe International), Paul Archer (principal), Annelle Tuminella (teacher), Joanna Garcia (actress), and all of the 1995-1996 class of eighth graders of Corpus Christi Catholic School for their willingness to participate in the "Project of Significance." The eighth graders are as follows: Sean Affleck, Meg Baker, Corey Beahon, George Boyd, Chris Cavalcanti, Melissa DaSilva, Robyn Davison, Marianna DeAmbrose, Keith Downer, John Duda, Michael Flatau, Adam Guyer, Carrie Hughes, Tara Keaton, Rena Rodriguez, Lauren Lanza, Jenny Locander, Kara Lyons, Katie Peterson, Mark Pilarczyk, Greg Pizzo, Samantha Ritchie, Kristen Russo, Christine Satorre, Richard Smyth, Michelle "Miki" Stark, Clare Tagliarino, Jon Tozier, Amy Trefzer, Kara Von Pusch, Ian Walters, Jennifer Webster, and Sarah Yodzis.

Next, I'd like to thank my colleagues who agreed to write chapters: Janet "my B.B." Allen, Sissi Carroll, Kelly Chandler, Leila Christenbury, Pam Cole, Pat Daniel, Bonnie Ericson, Ted Hipple, Rosemary Ingham, Jeff Kaplan, Teri Lesesne, John Moore, Lois Stover, and Connie Zitlow. A special thanks is extended to Sue Canavan, the Executive Vice President of Christopher-Gordon Publishers, for her never-ending faith in me. Also, thanks, Sue, for teaching me how to eat lobster like a native!

And finally, I'd like to thank my family, friends, and various faculty and staff at the University of South Florida for supporting me and giving me the time and encouragement necessary to complete this task, especially Stephen Kaywell, Christopher Maida, Scott Seifreit, Ed Steiner, Pat Virgil, and Craig Wooley.

# Table of Contents

# Preface

*Adolescent Literature as a Complement to the Classics, Volume 3* is based on two assumptions: (1) The classics comprise the canon of literature that is mostly taught in our schools; and (2) most teachers are familiar with adolescent literature, or young adult novels, but are unsure how to incorporate their use in classrooms. This book provides the necessary information so that teachers may confidently use young adult novels in conjunction with commonly-taught classics.

Why should teachers try to get students to read more when it is already difficult getting them to read the required material? I'll tell you. Part of the problem, as most teachers are fully aware, is that the classics are often too distant from our students' experiences, or the reading level is too difficult. Students often question why they have to study something, read the Cliff's notes, or watch the movie version of the required classic. As a result, not only are students not reading the classics, but they are not reading much of anything!

By using young adult (YA) novels in conjunction with the classics, teachers can expose students to reading that becomes relevant and meaningful. Additionally, the reading levels of most young adult books are within a range of ease that most students can master. Reading, as with any type of human development, requires practice. The problem that occurs in our schools, however, is that we often place our students into reading practice that **we** require, a practice our students view as forced, meaningless, and too difficult. To make my point, let me draw an analogy to the developmental process of eating.

Just like a newborn baby has to be fed milk, a newborn reader needs to be read to. Babies begin with baby foods that are easily digested; something too solid will cause the baby to reject it. So too with reading. Young readers need to start with easy readers, ones that are easily consumed. Eventually, young children desire foods that have a little more substance—vegetables, eggs, and some palatable meats. Similarly, young readers might find delight in such books as Nancy Drew or Hardy Boys mysteries. Just as children regurgitate and learn to hate certain foods if forced too early to consume them, so will novice readers learn to hate certain books, or books in general, if forced to read books that are beyond their capabilities. As children reach adolescence, they will consume vast quantities of "hamburgers" in the form of adolescent literature—if we let them. Some hamburgers, as we all know, are better than others; the same is true for YA novels.

Like concerned parents, we want our children to eat a proper diet, so we make them eat balanced meals, much like the way we want our children to read certain books. Ideally our children will learn to appreciate fine cuisine in the form of the classics. Some may find the experience too much for their stomachs to handle and so will turn up their noses at lobster newburg and *A Tale of Two Cities* and order something a bit lighter. Others, unfortunately, may never even get exposed to that level, but they still survive, unaware of what they are missing. Some of our students, however, will learn to enjoy and appreciate the delicacies of fine literature. It's all in the presentation, and adolescent literature can help make our teaching of the classics more appealing.

Now you are probably saying, "I am sold on exposing my students to adolescent literature, but why **this** book?" First, some of the biggest names in the field of adolescent literature have contributed chapters: Sissi Carroll, research editor for *The ALAN Review*; Leila Christenbury, the current editor of *English Journal*; Ted Hipple, one of the founders of ALAN (the Assembly on Literature for Adolescents); Lois Stover (the former Adolescent Literature Column Editor for *English Journal*); among others.

Second, all chapters stand alone, but an experienced teacher can easily adapt the strategies employed in one chapter to fit his or her particular situation. For example, a teacher may not be required to teach *The Grapes of Wrath* but may choose to incorporate the multi-text strategy to whatever classic is required. Or, a teacher might be required to teach the aforementioned novel but could choose to approach its teaching under the strategies suggested for teaching *Of Mice and Men* with poetry and photographs. In other words, several different approaches are suggested so that a teacher who likes a certain strategy could omit the suggested novels and insert ones of choice. Because young adult novels are frequently out of print, there are enough suggestions and other resources listed to assist teachers and their students with their search for complementary novels. Single novels that are out of print are often found in used bookstores.

Third, this book is on the cutting edge, incorporating all of the latest research in reader response theory, whole language, student ownership, and collaborative learning. Each chapter is written so that each student from the least to the most talented can learn at his or her optimum level. Each student is a vital contributor to the class, and each student gets exposed to the classics in meaningful, relevant ways. The acquisition of multiple texts, parental involvement, and censorship issues are also addressed. The book is written for middle and high school English teachers; however, university professors who teach preservice teachers and graduate students may also find this text valuable.

Finally, Volume Three often refers to the previous two volumes; both successful in their own rights. At the fall 1995 NCTE convention, it was reported that *Adolescent Literature as a Complement to the Classics* is among the top ten language arts methods texts used in the country. With that kind of popularity, something must be right!

# Organization

The first chapter focuses on the classic *Fahrenheit 451* and the problems with censorship and the importance of books. The unit described in **Chapter One** begins with introductory reading and response activities that engage students and their parents. Next, the students' reading experiences are extended by reading seven related young adult (TA) novels in reading circles where small groups of students read the same book while other groups in the class are reading different books. Reading circle books are categorized in two different ways: challenged books and books about adolescents who value literacy. This is followed by the whole class's reading of *Fahrenheit 451* with several novel response activities.

The next two chapters focus on Steinbeck's *The Grapes of Wrath* and *Of Mice and Men.* In **Chapter Two,** students read *The Grapes of Wrath* and participate in a thematic study with five YA novels; universal brotherhood (Bridgers' *All Together Now*), good versus evil (Crutcher's *Chinese Handcuffs*), power of nature (Paulsen's *Hatchet*), poverty and its effects (Wolff's *Make Lemonade*), and life goes on (Gibbon's *Ellen Foster*). The study of *Of Mice and Men,* in **Chapter Three,** is enhanced by pairing it with Cynthia Rylant and Walker Evan's *Something Permanent,* a YA book of poetry and photographs of the Depression. Several activities are suggested as well as a list of related young YA literature titles appropriate for independent reading. Lastly, using Rylant and Evans's work, students design class booklets of student-generate poetry and images—"Something Permanent" for the 1990s.

Not only does **Chapter Four** pair narrative poetry with YA literature for thematic study, but several activities are included that help students develop their understanding of and appreciation for literary elements. Form Service's "The Cremations of Sam McGee" to Hobb's *The Big Wander* to teach setting, and from Eliot's "The Love Song of J. Alfred Prufrock" to Wolff's *Make Lemonade* to teach point of view, teachers and students will find this chapter both thorough and enjoyable.

**Chapter Five** and Six show how the Bard can be appealing to the most- to least-skilled student. Students practice literary criticism in their study of Shakespeare's *The Tempest* in Chapter Five. This is accomplished through studying the intertextual relationships between Shakespeare's classic play, Dorris's *Morning Girl*, Covington's *Lizard,* and Oneal's *In Summer Light.* This chapter, especially designed for advanced students, dispels the myth that YA literature is for poor readers. **Chapter Six** asks students to consider race, racism, and specifically, interracial romance in their study of *Othello, The Moor of Venice* and several fiction, nonfiction, classic, and YA works. By combining Shakespeare's *Othello* with YA literature, most students can deeply experience and respond to this important and removing tragedy.

**Chapter Seven** and Eight focus on *home* and young adults' developing their "sense of place" in the world. Through several innovative prereading strategies, students study the concept of home before reading about the African-American members of the community in Meyer's YA book, *White Lilacs,* and the Younger family in Hansberry's classic play, *A Raisin in the Sun.* A series of extension and exploration activities complete chapter Seven, making it a self-contained unit. **Chapter Eight** begins with prereading activities, moves into the selection and reading of YA novels which carry the theme of belonging, and ends with students reading and responding to *Jane Eyre.* Several YA titles are included, but the six featured are Cushman's *The Midwife's Apprentice,* Pfeffer's *Nobody's Daughter,* Taylor's *Walking Up a Rainbow,* Kirkpatrick's *Keeping the Good Light,* Pullman's *The Ruby in the Smoke,* and Speare's *The Witch of Blackbird Pond.*

**Chapter Nine** is a dream come true for English teachers having to include world literature in their curriculum. The themes embodied in *Don Quixote*—of idealism, friendship, and responsibility—are connected to the protagonists' voices in Hodge's *For the Life of Laetitia,* Casteneda's *Imagining Isabel,* and Velasquez's *Juanita Fights the School Board.* An extensive annotated bibliography of contemporary YA books from Hispanic, Chicano, and various Latino cultures, organized by their thematic connections with *Don Quixote,* is also included.

In **Chapter Ten,** students all listen to Crutcher's *Staying Fat for Sara Byrnes* to help them identify with the characters in *A Tale of Two Cities.* Then students choose among several YA novels that fall into two primary thematic categories—family members demonstrating love and sacrifice, and people sacrificed by the system. Students use double entry learning logs to record their insights.

**Chapter Eleven** is a six week unit on war divided into three phases: prereading materials and activities, activities during the reading of *A Farewell to Arms,* and postreading materials and activities. Poems and picture books such as "Song Vu Chine," Maruki's *Hiroshima, No Pika,* and Tsuchiya's *Faithful Elephants* introduce this thematic unit. Annotations of several YA novels dealing with the Vietnam War, political unrest overseas, and nuclear war are also included. Students will acquire a slightly different perspective on wars that what they may have encountered in their United States' history books.

The study of *Dracula* in **Chapter Twelve,** begins with students freewriting about everything they know about this famous literary character. Then, students read and view several adaptations of the Dracula story through YA novels (from Pike to Peel) and film (from Brooks to Laemmle) before reading "the original" to see how the stories were modified. Several activities are included.

**Chapter Thirteen** leads students from survival to success, culminating in a "Project of Significance." After students participate in survival activities, they choose from five "classic" reading options. Survival classics, ranging from most to least difficult, include *Robinson Crusoe, Lord of the Flies, The Diary of a Young Girl, The Call of the Wild,* and "The Cremations of Sam McGee," "To Build a Fire," and "The Open Boat." Accompanying each reading option, are annotated YA novels and contemporary movies that complement the reading of the classic(s). The unit ends with the explanation and results of a "Project of Significance."

The last chapter, **Chapter Fourteen,** ends the book on a happy note. The humor of James Thurber is often lost on young adults who simply cannot relate to his degree of sophisticated humor. Domestic strife, as found in so much of Thurber's work, is the stuff of many YA novels, where the protagonists are often teenagers. Chapter Fourteen invites students to read several YA funny novels about animals, romances, family relationships,, and school, in order to help them learn to laugh.

A complete reference bibliography follows that includes author's complete names and books' ISBN numbers. Two indexes are included: "Authors and Titles" and "Subject."

# 1

# Exploring Censorship, Exploring the Future: *Fahrenheit 451* and Young Adult Literature

*Bonnie O. Ericson*

## Introduction

*Catcher in the Rye. Huckleberry Finn. The Giver. Romeo and Juliet. The Cay. The Grapes of Wrath. The Chocolate War.* These are just a few of the classic and young adult (YA) literature selections that have been and are increasingly being challenged as choices for our students' classroom reading. English teachers are generally familiar with censorship issues, both the direct form in which a book is challenged by an individual or group, and the more indirect or "better part of valor" form, which leads a teacher to opt for the path of least resistance and select a book less likely to be challenged. (See Note at the end of this chapter.)

Adolescents, on the other hand, may be oblivious to censorship issues, taking for granted the freedom that they enjoy when reading fine literature in their classes. So, when first reading Ray Bradbury's *Fahrenheit 451*, students' initial responses may include several "borings," a "so what," and even groans from those who prefer to avoid any book that could be labeled science fiction. Additionally, as they begin *Fahrenheit 451*, students may experience difficulty making connections with a middle-aged protagonist who has a bad marriage and an odd job; later, they may become frustrated with numerous references to books they've never heard of or read. Why, then, select *Fahrenheit 451* for your class? For one thing, it is quite readable once students become involved. The vocabulary and sentence structures aren't difficult; and, at 180 pages, the book is not lengthy. More significant reasons to select Bradbury's classic, however, are the timely and crucial themes (power of books, education, censorship, etc.), some haunting prose, and the potentially beneficial possibilities for parental involvement. I believe that *Fahrenheit 451* is an outstanding choice for 9th or 10th grade classes, and that introducing the book with reading circles of a related work of YA literature will result in students' genuine engagement with the characters and themes in both books.

I have included in this chapter several activities that call for parental involvement. We English language arts teachers must reach out to parents or guardians more often and in ways that involve them in the everyday classroom activities of their daughters and sons if we are to develop mutual trust. Such trust is a requirement for defusing the censorship problem, for improving the public's image of schools, and for increasing the achievement of our students. Therefore, at the beginning of this unit I send home a letter to parents that briefly explains the reading choices, the main class activities, and the ways all parents are invited to participate.

## Introductory Activities

There are two short selections I share with students before they begin their group reading. The first is an excerpt from Bill Moyers' introduction to Haba's *The Language of Life: A Festival of Poets*, a powerful story about poet Jimmy Santiago Baca. Like Malcolm X years earlier, Baca finds escape from a life of poverty and violence through books and literacy. Read this marvelous selection aloud to your students or provide copies for classroom use. Then ask for their thoughts about the power of books, writing, and education. What would their lives be like without books? Why would some groups or governments concern themselves with limiting access to books?

I also share with students a short piece by Phyllis Levitt (1994) entitled "Douse the Lit Matches Aimed at Literature." She concludes, "Instead, let us teach the children to read critically. Let us teach them standards of taste and appreciation so they can reject what is intellectually, philosophically, theologically, politically, and aesthetically against the principles they hold dear." (p. 12). After discussing what she means in this statement, explore with students how teachers and schools should select the books they teach. Are teenagers capable of developing standards of taste and appreciation? And what are the "principles they hold dear"? Invite students to interview their parents for their ideas about these questions. Then have them share the parents' answers and the parents' responses to students' ideas as part of an ongoing discussion. If possible, also invite several parents to the class to participate in the discussion.

Reading circles allow small groups of students to read the same book while other groups in the class are reading different books. Reading circles shift the responsibility for reading and responding to the students. At the same time, students' ownership of their reading tends to increase, in part because they've been given responsibility, and in part because they have been given a voice in selecting what they will read. Successful reading circles require book choices with compelling characters and interesting plots. Often, the books that meet these criteria can be classified as adolescent or young adult (YA) literature (although you don't need to use that label with your students).

## Reading Circles with Seven Young Adult Novels

Annotated below are the books I use for introducing *Fahrenheit 451*. Each focuses on adolescents making a difference in a future world or involves contemporary teens dealing with the censorship issue. All the books also raise genuine questions worth consideration by students and their parents, questions that will be raised again in reading the Bradbury work.

### *No Kidding* by Bruce Brooks (207 pp.)

Sam is a 13-year-old of the future. Despite his age, he is the one making all the plans and decisions. His mother, like the majority of adults, is an alcoholic. Sam on a number of occasions has committed her to one of the many institutions for those battling alcoholism. He also monitors his younger brother Ollie's life with foster parents, trying to decide whether to make Ollie's situation permanent. Sam's planning and schemes are all intended to lead to the survival of his family. But will these plans work? And what about Sam's needs?

### *Invitation to the Game* by Monica Hughes (192 pp.)

In the year 2134, Lisse and her friends graduate from high school only to learn that there are no jobs for them. The government does provide them with a place to live, but learning to survive in their new urban environment is filled with challenges. They learn about and are eventually invited to "The Game," which takes them to another world. The world of The Game is a beautiful one, and they all seem to have particular skills which allow them to survive its dangers. Is The Game only a computer simulation designed to pacify the unemployed? Is The Game some kind of sinister trick, or is it something much more important?

### *Andra* by Louise Lawrence (240 pp.)

What a find this book is! Andra, too, lives in a world of the future. Following a nuclear holocaust, hers is a subterranean world. People live below the surface of the planet, without sunlight, trees, animals or birds. After an accident, Andra receives a brain graft to restore her vision. The piece of brain is from a male teen who died in 1987. Strangely, Andra also receives some of his memories, including memories of life on the planet's surface.

Like Jonas in Lois Lowry's *The Giver,* Andra studies with an elderly mentor, reading voraciously to compile facts about life on the surface. Time for life underground is running out, and a planet that can support life has been located. Will Andra's free spirit get her into terrible trouble, or is she the key to the future? Or will political intrigues bring unexpected conclusions?

### *The Giver* by Lois Lowry (208 pp.)

This stunning book is set in a future society in which there is no color, no music, no imperfection, no pain or suffering. Babies are born and raised at an infant center until they're a year old, then are given to families, all of which have one boy and one girl. All 12-year-olds are assigned a life's work, and the elderly are "released" in a joyful ceremony. Jonas, the central character, is to become the Receiver—the only person who knows all from the past. He is taught by the former Receiver, now the Giver. But Jonas can't accept how much has been sacrificed for the sake of happiness and order. What will he do? If reading circles aren't a possibility, consider reading this remarkable book aloud to your entire class. (See *Adolescent Literature as a Complement to the Classics,* Volume Two, Chapter 11 for additional information on pairing this YA novel with Orwell's classic, *Brave New World.*)

### *The Day They Came to Arrest the Book* by Nat Hentoff (160 pp.)

Nat Hentoff's book captures both sides of the censorship argument. Friendships are strained when *The Adventures of Huckleberry Finn* is challenged by African-American parents after a social studies teacher assigns the book to her class. Occasionally didactic, the book will nevertheless draw readers into the conflict. Who will win when the Board of Education votes on whether or not to retain Mark Twain's classic? Are there "winners" at all? Or is this a single battle in a larger, exceptionally complex war whose outcome is still uncertain?

### *Memoirs of a Bookbat* by Kathryn Lasky (215 pp.)

Harper is a 14-year-old who is recounting events in the recent years of her life, events that find her on a bus on the way to live with her grandmother. Harper's parents become involved with a conservative religious group that saves their marriage, but their involvement has other effects, too. Harper finds herself hiding her beloved books from her parents and their friends because her parents believe these books will have a negative influence on her. The books and her friend Gray help her cope with her increasingly difficult situation, but her younger sister seems completely in agreement with her parents. What does Harper's future hold now? Has she made the right decision?

### *The Last Safe Place on Earth* by Richard Peck (176 pp.)

Todd lives on Tranquillity Lane and attends Walden Woods High School. It seems idyllic, the "last safe place on earth." But when his younger sister Marnie is strangely afraid of Halloween and *The Diary of Anne Frank* is challenged by a group of junior high parents, Todd and his family must respond. At the same time, Todd's sophomore English class is reading and discussing *Fahrenheit 451,* making Peck's book practically made-to-order as a reading circle selection. What does Todd's class think of the book, and what points do they make in their discussions? Can Todd help his friend Laurel, or does she even need his help? What say should a small group of parents have in the selection of what an entire class reads, and what happens when parents disagree?

## Reading Circles with Controversial Young Adult Novels

Other directions could be taken in selecting YA literature to read with *Fahrenheit 451.* For example, students could read books that have been challenged. These could include, among others: *A Hero Ain't Nothin' But a Sandwich* by Alice Childress; *I Am the Cheese* and *The Chocolate War* by Robert Cormier (See *Adolescent Literature as a Complement to the Classics,* Volume One, Chapters 11–13); *The Crazy Horse Electric Game* and *Stotan!* by Chris Crutcher; *The Drowning of Stephan Jones* and *Summer of My German Soldier* by Bette Greene; *The Outsiders* by S.E. Hinton; *The Giver* by Lois Lowry; *Fallen Angels* by Walter Dean Myers; *The Catcher in the Rye* by J.D. Salinger (See *Adolescent Literature as a Complement to the Classics,* Volume One, Chapter 4); and *The Pigman* by Paul Zindel.

If you choose to read challenged books, I would eventually ask students (and their parents) to discuss the positive and negative aspects of the books. Students then can form and defend a position on whether or not the book is appropriate and valuable for reading by high school students.

## Reading Circles with Young Adult Novels Valuing Literacy

Yet another thematic connection is the value of reading, writing, and education. Adolescent books focusing on literacy include Barbara Barrie's *Adam Zigzag* (192 pp.); Sandra Forrester's *Sound the Jubilee* (183 pp.); Merle Hodge's *For the Life of Laetitia* (213 pp.); Kathryn Lasky's *Memoirs of a Bookbat* (215 pp.); Gary Paulsen's *Nightjohn* (96 pp.); Zipha Keatley Snyder's *Libby on Wednesday* (196 pp.); and Virginia Euwer Wolff's *Make Lemonade* (200 pp.). If you were to include books such as these, I'd certainly want students to picture what their lives would be like if they possessed minimal versus excellent reading and writing skills. I'd also ask students to develop and discuss their individual literacy timelines. In other words, have students note the important literacy moments or events in their past as well as predictions about their literacy futures. What educational futures do students envision, and what can they be doing now in order to realize those futures?

## Acquiring Multiple Text Copies

A common question asked when organizing reading circles is how to obtain sets of multiple copies of the different titles needed. Teachers I know have had success with one or a combination of the following:

1. Ask for donations from local businesses or community groups.
2. Write grants. (The ALAN Foundation welcomes innovative grant proposals concerning YA literature.)
3. Get copies from school and public libraries.
4. Recycle donations of old books at used or new bookstores.
5. Conduct fund-raisers specifically for books.
6. Spend book club (Troll, Scholastic, etc.) bonus points.
7. Ask students to purchase the books.

There's no doubt that it takes time and energy to build these sets of books for reading circles, but I'm convinced the results will support the effort.

Whichever types of thematic connections you opt to pursue for introducing *Fahrenheit 451*, and however you build your sets of books, students benefit from careful structuring of the reading and response activities—introducing the reading circle books, completing activities at three points in reading, and participating in mixed-book group discussions.

## Introducing the Reading Circle Books and Organizing the Groups

Place students in groups of six or seven. Provide each group with one copy each of the six or seven choices to be read for the class. Give students five minutes to examine each of the books. They may observe the front and back covers, note any preview on the book jacket interior, and read at the beginning or even in the middle of the book. Teachers may opt to conduct a book pass, a strategy made popular by Tchudi and Mitchell (1989, pp. 139–140). Once students have had the opportunity to examine all the books, they independently select their first two or three choices and form groups.

Next, develop a calendar for reading based on the particular classes you're working with. Many classes are capable of quickly reading these books, and class time can be given for group responses. Other classes need a longer amount of time, as well as class time both for reading and the response activities. I have had success with scheduling the group meetings in thirds—after reading the first 50 pages, the first half of the book, and the entire book. At these three points, students meet and discuss the reading as they complete an activity.

The activity choices encourage different types of responses. The Values Profile, for example, leads students to a close examination of characters, while the storyboard results in a focus on plot. It is important to display the activity results so that students may become curious about some of the other groups' books. Additionally, I ask that students show their parents the book their group will be reading. Parents are invited to read the book and to participate in the mixed-book group discussion, which will occur after the reading and various activities are completed.

## Reading Circle Activities

## Activities Following Completion of the First 50 Pages

Each reading circle group selects one of the following two activities to complete— the storyboard or the bubble sheet.

### Storyboard

Students discuss and agree on the four most important events in the book so far. Using four separate pieces of paper, students draw each scene, then provide each drawing with an appropriate quotation from the book. The four pieces are then displayed in sequence.

### Bubble Sheet (modified from Sanchez, 1995)

Students select a key scene from the first 50 pages of the book that involves three or more characters. On a sheet of paper, they draw face and shoulder representations of all the characters, along with a large cartoon-style bubble for each of the characters' thoughts. They should label the drawings and head the page with the title and author of the book. The group then discusses what the thoughts of each character would be at that particular moment in the book. They write in the thoughts for all the characters,

thus increasing their awareness of multiple perspectives. Students also write an explanation of why they chose the particular scene they did.

## Activities Following Completion of Half the Book

Each reading circle group selects one of the following two activities to complete—
the Values Profile or the question web.

### Values Profile (based on Johannessen, 1996)

See Figure 1.1.

### Question Web

Students work together to create a cluster of questions they have about the reading
or of questions they think are important to discuss in order to understand the book and
the book's connections to their lives. After their group develops a cluster of 12–15
questions, each student selects one to write about. Stress with the students that their
choice should be a question they really are wondering about, and that writing will be
their opportunity to explore different possible answers. Once students have written
responses, they share with their groups their question choices and what they wrote.
Others in the group react to the written responses—agreeing, questioning, and adding
ideas. To close, the group discusses and lists three or four insights about the book that
have resulted from their writing and discussing.

## Discussion Following Completion of the Entire Book

Each reading circle group examines the questions in Figure 1.2 and determines
which four or five questions are most crucial in developing an understanding of the
group's book. Students explore their answers to these questions in preparation for the
mixed-book groups; they may also add a question for the mixed-book groups to consider.

# Mixed-Book Group Discussions

A highlight of the reading circles is the mixed-book group discussion. These mixed-
book groups consist of five or six students who have all read different books. Parents
or guardians who have read a book are also invited to participate in these discussions.
For parents who have read the book but are unable to attend the class, students should
be encouraged to discuss the handout questions (See Figure 1.2) with their parents
prior to the discussions. Then all students can incorporate parental responses. Each
student presents a summary of his or her book, then the group discusses the questions
as they apply to the different books.

Once students and parents have addressed these questions in mixed-book group
discussions, they may share some of the highlights with the whole class. Additionally,
parents who participate should have time to view the displayed group response
storyboards, question webs, etc.

**Figure 1.1**
**Values Profile for**

_____

(Insert Author and Title of Book)

**Values**

1.  Achievement
2.  Approval of others
3.  Beauty
4.  Creativity
5.  Family
6.  Friendship
7.  Honesty
8.  Independence/freedom
9.  Justice
10. Knowledge

11. Love
12. Loyalty
13. Physical appearance
14. Pleasure
15. Power
16. Religious beliefs
17. Self-respect
18. Skills
19. Tradition
20. Wealth
21. Other: _____

**Values Most**

**Directions.**   Identify 2-3 characters to analyze using the values listed above. What does each character value most? List his or her top three values, and include an example from the book that influenced your decision.

**Character One:** _____

Values    1. _____    2. _____    3. _____

Example for 1: _____

_____ (page(s):   )

Example for 2: _____

_____ (page(s):   )

Example for 3: _____

_____ (page(s):   )

**Character Two:** _____

Values    1. _____    2. _____    3. _____

Example for 1: _____

_____ (page(s):   )

Example for 2: _____

_____ (page(s):   )

Example for 3: _____

_____ (page(s):   )

**Character Three:** _____

Values    1. _____    2. _____    3. _____

Example for 1: _____

_____ (page(s):   )

Example for 2: _____

_____ (page(s):   )

Example for 3: _____

_____ (page(s):   )

Figure 1.1 continued on next page

Figure 1.1 continued

**Values Least**

**Directions.** Using the values listed above and the characters you have selected to study, identify what each character values least. List her or his bottom three values, and include an example from the book that influenced your decision.

**Character One:** _____

Values     1. _____     2. _____     3. _____

Example for 1: _____

_____ (page(s):   )

Example for 2: _____

_____ (page(s):   )

Example for 3: _____

_____ (page(s):   )

**Character Two:** _____

Values     1. _____     2. _____     3. _____

Example for 1: _____

_____ (page(s):   )

Example for 2: _____

_____ (page(s):   )

Example for 3: _____

_____ (page(s):   )

**Character Three:** _____

Values     1. _____     2. _____     3. _____

Example for 1: _____

_____ (page(s):   )

Example for 2: _____

_____ (page(s):   )

Example for 3: _____

_____ (page(s):   )

# Introducing *Fahrenheit 451*

With the completion of the mixed-book discussions, it is time to move to *Fahrenheit 451*. Ask students about their visions of the future, review with them the connections they saw in the reading circle books, and note that similar issues will emerge during their reading of Bradbury's classic.

*Fahrenheit 451* was published as a novel in 1953, having first appeared in a short story version in 1950. Those were the days of the Cold War threat, tract housing, and the first computers. Students' reading of *Fahrenheit 451* will be enriched if they have a bit of background. To this end, student pairs could be given a day to do research in the school library on a single topic. They could be asked to create a single page visual representation and definition or explanation, which could then be briefly explained to

---

**Figure 1.2**

**Discussion Questions for Mixed-Book Groups**

1.  How would you describe the societies portrayed in your books? What are the characters' daily lives like? If the book takes place in the future, how does the future seem connected to the present day?

2.  What are families like in the books? Would you like to live in such families? Why or why not?

3.  How are children treated? The elderly? Those with handicaps or different views? What benefits and problems do you see with these treatments?

4.  What part, if any, does technology play in the lives of the characters? Does the technology seem plausible, given current technological developments?

5.  What is the role of books, reading, and censorship in these books? How does literacy work in the societies portrayed?

6.  What seem to be the predominant images in these books? Colors? Music? Other? What is the impact of these images?

7.  What symbols seem to play a role? What is the impact of these symbols?

8.  Why do you think the author wrote his or her book? What was each trying to say? What has he or she said to you? How self-serving was the author?

9.  What connections do these books seem to have with each other?

10. Which books would you recommend for next year's class? What are the reasons for your recommendations?

11. Other _____

     _____

---

the class and displayed for others to see. Possible topics include the following: the Cold War, Joseph McCarthy, Hollywood blacklisting and blackballing, the first televisions, Univac and early computers, roles of females in the early 1950s, roles of males in the early 1950s, "Dover Beach" by Matthew Arnold, *Uncle Tom's Cabin* by Harriet Beecher Stowe, *Hamlet* by William Shakespeare, phoenix, irony, salamander, censorship, and Daedelus.

## Reading and Responding to *Fahrenheit 451*

Ray Bradbury's book is divided into three parts: "The Hearth and the Salamander," "The Sieve and the Sand," and "Burning Bright." For all three parts, students read in a manner and at a pace that is appropriate. At least some of the time, I use a readers' theater approach, with individual students reading aloud the words of Guy, Clarisse, Mildred, Captain Beatty, and Faber. I also have students do some small group "read-arounds," in order to actively involve as many students as possible. Additionally, homework reading is often appropriate.

## Reading Journals

For each section of the book, students write responses or reading reactions twice a week in their reading journals. These entries become the basis for ongoing group or class discussions. For most classes, I recommend a divided page format. Students select a key quotation to write in the left column; in the right column, they comment on it. If students aren't quite sure how to begin their comments, "Response Starters" (See Figure 1.3) may be helpful.

---

**Figure 1.3**

**Response Starters**

1. I noticed _____

2. I suppose _____

3. I don't see how/that _____

4. Why did _____

5. I wonder _____

6. I can't believe _____

7. I know the feeling _____

8. If I were _____, I'd _____

9. I'm having trouble with _____

10. The main thing the author seems to be saying here is _____

---

Why have students keep reading journals? First, the responses make powerful springboards to discussion, particularly in small groups at the beginning of class. Further, teachers can readily determine if students are completing their reading; more importantly, teachers can determine if students are having difficulties with interpretations, based on a quick perusal of reading journal entries. Finally, these journals are a way to involve parents or guardians. Simply ask parents to respond each weekend in the reading journal to either their own reading of the book, or to what their son or daughter has written. I'd suggest you provide parents with Okura's "Response Starters" (See Figure 1.4).

Following Figure 1.4 is a list of discussion questions and response activities for each of the three sections. I present ideas I have found successful. In addition to their reading journal responses, I urge you to offer those choices to your students which fit their abilities and interests.

---

**Figure 1.4**

**Response Starters**

1.  I'm proud of you for making such a good observation about
    _____. I think _____
    _____

2.  Tell me more about _____

3.  I like what you said about _____

4.  What do you think about _____

5.  What do you think _____ should do?

---

# Part One: "The Hearth and the Salamander"

## Questions for Discussion

1.  What are your impressions of the society portrayed in *Fahrenheit 451*? For what reasons would you like to be living at this time? For what reasons would you not want to be living at this time? Could such a society really exist?

2.  What books are in your home, and what members of your family read these books? For what reasons do they read? What would replace these books if they were banned and burned?

3.  How would you describe the relationship between Mildred and Guy? What do you think will happen to them?

4.  What symbols seem to be present in this segment? What might the hearth, salamander, phoenix, dog, and books symbolize? What present-day uses of these symbols can you think of? Which of these do you believe to be the most effective and important use of symbolism in the book, and why?

5.  Some critics have noted Bradbury's use of irony: firemen who burn books and a dog who kills people. What do you think is the effect of these, and other, ironies?

6.  Bradbury also refers to several works of literature. Near the end of this part, he refers to *Hamlet* and *Uncle Tom's Cabin*. What is the effect of these references for you?

7.  What do you believe to be the three most important scenes from Part One? Explain.

## Individual Response Activities

### Create a Symbol

Draw a symbol for one of the main characters and write a paragraph of explanation. (Some students may also want to create symbols for themselves.)

### Create a Venn Diagram

Compare and contrast present-day society and Bradbury's future society in your diagram of overlapping circles. (See *Adolescent Literature as a Complement to the Classics*, Volume One, Chapter 12 for a sample Venn Diagram.)

### Write a Letter

Write the letter Montag might have written to Mildred explaining his feelings about what happened the night she almost died.

## Part Two: "The Sieve and the Sand"

## Questions for Discussion

1. What caused Montag to decide to take responsibility and start acting on his beliefs? What might the consequences be? Do you think he's right?

2. Why did Montag read "Dover Beach" to his wife and her friends? Why did they react the way they did? (I also display the entire poem on an overhead projector and ask students which lines connect with the book.)

3. What is Captain Beatty's philosophy of life? Do you think he wanted to die? Explain.

4. How are Montag, Beatty, and Faber alike and different? What would each approve of and be troubled by in today's society?

5. Some readers have criticized Bradbury's work because it is "sexist." They have asked Bradbury to make changes in the book to update it. What do you think about these charges? How do you suppose Bradbury has responded?

6. If you had to choose a single word to describe this book so far, what word would you choose? Explain.

## Individual Response Activities

### Values Profile

Complete a Values Profile for Montag, Beatty, and Faber (See Figure 1.1). Then write a paragraph describing which character you find most interesting and explain why.

### Bubble Sheet

Complete a Bubble Sheet (See Reading Circle Activities, Activities Following Completion of the First 50 Pages and Bubble Sheet).

### Pantoum

Using phrases from a single passage or several passages, use the format of a Pantoum to write your own poem (See Figure 1.5).

## Part Three: "Burning Bright"

## Questions for Discussion

1. Why do authors write about the future? Why are there movies and television series about the future? How does Bradbury's vision of the future compare with those you've seen in other books and in movies? How does it compare with your own vision of the future?

2. Is the ending of the book depressing or hopeful? Or is it something else? Explain.

**Figure 1.5**

**The Pantoum**

The Pantoum is an ancient poetic form from Indonesia. Create found poems by using phrases from a passage or passages in a book you are reading and following the form of the Pantoum. A brief excerpt from Chapter 11 of Lois Lowry's *The Giver* is the basis for the Pantoum below. In the passage, Jonas receives his first memory from The Giver.

| Line | Text | Pattern |
|------|------|---------|
| | | "The Giver's Memory" |
| 1 | One ride on one sled | |
| 2 | Dots of cold | |
| 3 | Balance, excitement, peace | |
| 4 | Total silence | |
| 5 | Dots of cold | 5 repeats 2 |
| 6 | Whirling torrent of crystals | |
| 7 | Total silence | 7 repeats 4 |
| 8 | Visible breath | |
| 9 | Whirling torrent of crystals | 9 repeats 6 |
| 10 | Cold air swirling | |
| 11 | Visible breath | 11 repeats 8 |
| 12 | Featherlike feelings | |
| 13 | One ride on one sled | 13 repeats 1 |
| 14 | Cold air swirling | 14 repeats 10 |
| 15 | Featherlike feelings | 15 repeats 12 |
| 16 | Balance, excitement, peace | 16 repeats 3 |

3. What do you think the future holds for Montag and his new friends?

4. Who are the Guy Montags, Clarisses, Mildreds, and Captain Beattys of today's world?

5. Do you think censorship is ever warranted? How do you respond to the issue of censorship of books? Of music?

6. What are the connections between this book and the reading circle book you read?

7. Develop five or six criteria for what makes a good book for class reading. Share the criteria with parents or guardians and revise the criteria based on parental comments. Then evaluate your reading circle book and *Fahrenheit 451* with these criteria. Which is the superior book, and why?

## Response Activities

### View a Video

View the video of *Fahrenheit 451*, starring Julie Christie and Oskar Werner. Discuss how successful the movie is in capturing the characters and mood of the book.

### Select and Memorize

Montag's new friends have all memorized parts or all of some of the literary classics. If you were to choose a book to "become" in order to save it for posterity, what book or story or poem from your own reading would you select? Select and practice a passage from the book and present it to the rest of the class. You may audiotape your reading and possibly add sound effects. Alternatively, ask others in the class to assist you in doing a choral reading version.

## Writing Assignment Ideas

### Controversial Issue

Describe the issue of censorship in schools and school libraries, including information about some books that have been challenged and why. Explain why some groups favor and other groups oppose censorship. Then take a stand on this issue and support your position.

### Biographical Sketch

Faber had an important impact on Montag. He was a friend, a mentor, and a supporter. Jonas, Andra, and other reading circle book characters also were influenced strongly by another person. Choose someone who has had an impact on you, such as a friend, coach, or family member. In an essay, describe what that person is like, using at least two anecdotes about the person.

### Reflective Essay

Select a concept or topic addressed in *Fahrenheit 451* and in your reading circle book: literacy, friendship, technology, etc. Write an essay in which you reflect on this topic, discussing it in terms of the books and of your own experiences.

### Analysis

Compare and contrast a literary device or aspect found in the reading circle book and *Fahrenheit 451*. For example, color plays an important role in both *The Giver* and *Fahrenheit 451*, yet the roles and symbolism in the two books are quite different. You might compare and contrast symbols, irony, characters, conflict, etc.

## Conclusion

If we English teachers desire active involvement on the part of our students' parents, then it is our responsibility to seek out and invite that involvement. Parental inclusion is one important thread running through the ideas presented in this chapter. Another thread is the importance of student choice. Throughout this chapter, students have been asked to select their reading circle books and response activities both for the reading circle book and for *Fahrenheit 451*.

We teachers, of course, make many choices in our teaching. One of the most crucial is to provide our students with important and compelling literature, including both classic and contemporary works, even when some aspects of the books may be open to challenge. Perhaps as a result of activities and discussion revolving around *Fahrenheit 451* and related works of adolescent literature, students and their parents will more fully recognize and support teachers' thoughtful, informed literature selections for classroom reading.

Note: Teachers interested in furthering their knowledge about censorship are encouraged to read *What Johnny Shouldn't Read: Censorship in America* (DelFattore, 1992), *Banned in the U.S.A* (Foerstel, 1994), *Censorship: A Threat to Critical Reading* (Simmons, 1994), and "Censorship Matters" (McCracken, 1994). Additionally, *The ALAN Review* devoted its entire Winter, 1993 issue to censorship, and the April, 1993

"Booksearch" column of *English Journal* discusses "Books Worth Teaching Even Though They Have Proven Controversial." Teachers involved in a censorship dispute can get assistance from the National Council of Teachers of English (NCTE) and the International Reading Association (IRA).

# References

Allen, J. S. (1995). Exploring the individual's responsibility in society in *The giver* and *Brave new world*. In J.F. Kaywell's (Ed.), *Adolescent literature as a complement to the classics*. Volume Two. Norwood, MA: Christopher-Gordon Publishers, Inc., pp. 199–212.

Barrie, B. (1994). *Adam Zigzag*. New York: Delacorte Press.

Booksearch. (1993, April). Books worth teaching even though they have proven controversial. *English Journal, 82* (4), pp. 86–89.

Bradbury, R. (1953). *Fahrenheit 451*. New York: Ballantine Books.

Brooks, B. (1989). *No kidding*. New York: HarperKeypoint.

Bushman, K. P. & Bushman, J. H. (1993). Dealing with the abuse of power in *1984* and *The chocolate war*. In J. F. Kaywell's (Ed.), *Adolescent literature as a complement to the classics*. Volume One. Norwood, MA: Christopher-Gordon Publishers, Inc., pp. 215–222.

Censored. (1993, Winter). *The ALAN Review, 20* (2).

Childress, A. (1982). *A hero ain't nothing but a sandwich*. New York: Avon Books.

Cormier, R. (1986). *The chocolate war*. New York: Pantheon.

Cormier, R. (1977). *I am the cheese*. New York: Pantheon.

Crutcher, C. (1987). *The crazy horse electric game*. New York: Greenwillow Books.

Crutcher, C. (1986). *Stotan!* New York: Dell Laurel-Leaf.

DelFattore, J. (1992). *What Johnny shouldn't read: Textbook censorship in America*. New Haven: Yale University Press.

Foerstel, H. N. (1994). *Banned in the U.S.A.: A reference guide to book censorship in schools and public libraries*. Westport, CT: Greenwood Press.

Forrester, S. (1995). *Sound the jubilee*. New York: Lodestar Books.

Greene, B. (1991). *The drowning of Stephan Jones*. New York: Bantam.

Greene, B. (1973). *Summer of my German soldier*. New York: Dial Press.

Haba, J. (Ed.). (1995). *The language of life: A festival of poets*. New York: Doubleday.

Hentoff, N. (1982). *The day they came to arrest the book*. New York: Delacorte Press.

Hinton, S. E. (1989). *The outsiders*. New York: Dell.

Hipple, T. (1993). *Catcher* as core and catalyst. In J. F. Kaywell's (Ed.), *Adolescent literature as a complement to the classics*. Volume One. Norwood, MA: Christopher-Gordon Publishers, Inc., pp. 61–78.

Hodge, M. (1993). *For the life of Laetitia*. New York: Farrar, Straus, & Giroux.

Hughes, M. (1990). *Invitation to the game*. New York: Simon & Schuster.

Johannessen, L. R. (January, 1996). Conflict with authority: James Hanley's 'The Butterfly.' *Notes Plus, 13* (3), pp. 10–14.

Lasky, K. (1996). *Memoirs of a bookbat*. San Diego: Harcourt Brace.

Lawrence, L. (1991). *Andra*. New York: HarperCollins.

Levitt, P. (September, 1994). Douse the lit matches aimed at literature. *Council Chronicle*. Urbana, IL: National Council of Teachers of English, pp. 1–2.

Lowry, L. (1993). *The giver*. Boston: Houghton Mifflin.

McCracken, N. (1994, Winter). Censorship matters. *The ALAN Review, 21* (2), pp. 39–41.

Myers, W. D. (1988). *Fallen angels*. New York: Scholastic.

Okura, S. (1996). Unpublished class handout. Grant High School, Los Angeles Unified School District.

Paulsen, G. (1993). *Nightjohn*. New York: Dell Laurel–Leaf.

Peck, R. (1995). *The last safe place on earth*. New York: Delacorte Press.

Poe, E. A. (1993). Alienation from society in *The scarlet letter* and *The chocolate war*. In J.F. Kaywell's (Ed.), *Adolescent literature as a complement to the classics*. Volume One. Norwood, MA: Christopher-Gordon Publishers, Inc., pp. 185–194.

Salinger, J. D. (1951). *Catcher in the rye*. Boston: Little Brown Company.

Samuels, B. G. (1993). The beast within: Using and abusing power in *Lord of the flies*, *The chocolate war*, and other readings. In J. F. Kaywell's (Ed.), *Adolescent literature as a complement to the classics*. Volume One. Norwood, MA: Christopher-Gordon Publishers, Inc., pp. 195–214.

Sanchez, R. (December, 1995). Bubble reading: The active read aloud. *Notes Plus, 13* (2), pp. 9–10.

Simmons, J. S. (Ed.). (1994). *Censorship: A threat to critical reading*. Newark, DE: International Reading Association.

Snyder, Z. K. (1991). *Libby on Wednesday*. New York: Dell.

Tchudi, S. & Mitchell, D. (1989). *Explorations in the teaching of English*. New York: Harper & Row.

Wolff, V. E. (1993). *Make lemonade*. New York: Scholastic.

Zindel, P. (1983). *The pigman*. New York: Bantam.

## Film Cited (Available on Home Video)

Allen, L. M. (Producer). (1966). *Fahrenheit 451*. Universal City, CA: MCA Universal.

# 2

# A Study of Themes: *The Grapes of Wrath* and Five Young Adult Novels

*Ted Hipple*

## Introduction

A distressingly large number of fine American novels enjoy a far better literary reputation than their curricular one; that is, everyone, teachers included, says "what a wonderful novel," but few, teachers again included, recommend its being required in English classes. Among the novels I'm thinking of are several by Hemingway (*A Farewell to Arms* (See Chapter 11 of this text), *The Sun Also Rises, For Whom the Bell Tolls*), many by Faulkner (*Absalom, Absalom*; *Light in August*; *The Sound and the Fury*) and works like *Moby Dick* and *An American Tragedy*. The reasons for their limited use in schools are many: their difficulty, their language or depictions that teachers may feel will arouse the wrath of local censors, their length. Whatever the cause, a case can be made that students are being deprived of monumentally valuable reading experiences, opportunities that would be enhanced by the guidance of a skilled teacher who could help students with these admittedly demanding novels.

Of all the novels that suffer this fate, the one whose case troubles me most is *The Grapes of Wrath* by John Steinbeck. Oh, it is taught here and there, an advanced placement entry in, say, suburban Cleveland, on a recommended list in Pasadena, but it hardly commands the classroom attention of many other novels, including, also by Steinbeck, *The Pearl* and *Of Mice and Men* (See Chapter 3 of this text). And its appearances in schools are well behind those of, say, *Huckleberry Finn* (See *Adolescent Literature as a Complement to the Classics*, Volume One, Chapter 3), *The Great Gatsby* (See *Adolescent Literature as a Complement to the Classics*, Volume One, Chapter 9), *The Scarlet Letter*, (See *Adolescent Literature as a Complement to the Classics*, Volume One, Chapter 11), *The Red Badge of Courage* (See *Adolescent Literature as a Complement to the Classics*, Volume Two, Chapter 2), and *A Separate Peace* (See *Adolescent Literature as a Complement to the Classics*, Volume Two, Chapter 8).

I would like to argue that *The Grapes of Wrath* ought to be required reading for every kid in every high school, from the future Cal Tech grad to the biggest "simpleton in pimpledom"—to use John Ciardi's felicitous name for those students who often operate a bit beyond the reach of their mental supply lines. Both deserve to get as much as they can from this American masterpiece, a novel that ranks, in my judgment, with all of those I have so far mentioned. It is, bluntly put, too significant a reading experience to deny it to any student.

There are troubles with teaching *The Grapes of Wrath*—double troubles when it is required reading. Noting its language, the censors will attack it with a vehemence usually reserved for *The Catcher in the Rye* (See *Adolescent Literature as a Complement to the Classics,* Volume One, Chapter 4). Teachers will note its length—581 pages in the Penguin paperback version I'm using for this chapter—and wonder how they can possibly get their students to read it all. Other teachers will wonder about how a Depression Era novel can be made relevant to today's teens. Still others will worry about some of its themes—the notion that we are all in this world together and must help each other, or Jim Casy's ponderings about religion and his conclusion that it may not amount to much when it comes to putting food in the belly of a starving baby.

To be sure, these kinds of problems are formidable, but I believe that the power of the novel—its exhibition of language used well, its characters, its plot lines, its ideas, its sheer force and humanitarian appeal—will overcome these pedagogical obstacles. What will be left will be a literary experience students have rarely had before and will rarely have afterwards. I think the study of this novel can change their reading lives.

And there's another reason I want to recommend *The Grapes of Wrath* for classroom use. It is a novel that spins off in many different directions, particularly in its adaptability to other novels. For this chapter, I am going to limit my discussion of these other novels to young adult (YA) literature (a favorite genre of mine), but I could mention almost any literary work—from Shakespeare to "Peanuts," from the movie version of *Schindler's List* to a television sit-com. *The Grapes of Wrath* illuminates them all, and can be itself illuminated by them.

Comes now (at what may be long last) the structure of this chapter. I'm going to talk some about *The Grapes of Wrath* (my assumption is that you have read it), particularly some of its themes. Then I'm going to try to suggest how these same literary themes are also found in good YA novels, if not to the same degree of excellence Steinbeck attained, at least to a level that makes them worth classroom study. The adolescent novels I'll be using are *All Together Now* by Sue Ellen Bridgers, *Chinese Handcuffs* by Chris Crutcher, *Hatchet* by Gary Paulsen, *Make Lemonade* by Virginia Euwer Wolff, and *Ellen Foster* by Kaye Gibbons.

This is not a methodological chapter. I'm not going to suggest specific classroom activities, though I hope that by inference teachers can identify things they would want to do with *The Grapes of Wrath* and, say, *Make Lemonade*. I do, however, want to suggest what I think would be good overall ground rules. First, all students will be expected to read *The Grapes of Wrath*. I'll return in a moment to the difficult but important question of how to get them to read it. There will be about five or six copies of each of the other five novels in the classroom library, and each student will read at least two of them and relate them to the core novel. This will be a longish literature unit, several weeks maybe, but it may pay handsome dividends.

# Reading *The Grapes of Wrath*

## In-class Silent Reading

First, how to get students to read a novel the size of *The Grapes of Wrath*. One useful technique may be simply to ask them to read the first 100 pages and provide a period or two of class time for them to do much of this reading. By page 100 Tom Joad, paroled from prison for killing a man, has met Preacher Casy; has returned to his family's Oklahoma farm, only to find it deserted and virtually haunted by the ghostlike Muley; has discovered that most of the sharecroppers are leaving the area for the promised land of California; and has finally become reunited with his family (who are at his uncle's farm).

By then, too, readers will have read several general chapters, those usually referred to as "intercalary" chapters. These are enormously powerful, both in themselves and in their capacity to set the stage. Chapter One describes the ruinous droughts and dust storms; Three is the famous turtle chapter (to which I'll return later). Chapter Five describes how the distant and heartless bankers have taken over the land and, with their huge and equally heartless machines, have raped it. The banks have driven off the sharecropping families, some of whom have worked the land for generations, have been born on it, have buried parents and children on it, and now have to leave it. Seven describes the unscrupulous used car dealers who sell the sharecroppers—now thought of as "Okies"—oil- and gas-guzzling automobiles with frayed tires and weak batteries that have little chance of making the cross-continental trip. If students read these first hundred pages, I think most of them will finish the book. Unfortunately, that's a big if for some.

## In-class Oral Reading

A second technique is to read parts of the book aloud. Spend some time with the truly excellent *Better Than Life* (1994) by Daniel Pennac, and learn anew the joys of reading aloud to students of all ages and abilities. An alternative, of course, is to use an audiobook, but these proceed page by page and I'd suggest you skip around. I'd recommend reading Chapter Three, the turtle essay, first. You'll recall part of it: The turtle is struggling across the hot pavement of a dusty roadway. One oncoming driver sees the turtle and swerves to miss it. A second swerves to hit it. The idea is simple yet profound: Some people are decent to creatures less fortunate than they; others are not. Then follow that chapter with Chapter Seven about the unscrupulous used car salesmen with their Rotary Club pins and their church membership, and note how evilly they treat the unsophisticated and impoverished sharecroppers. Follow that reading with Chapter Fifteen, another intercalary chapter. This chapter is about the kindnesses offered to a struggling and penny-careful Okie family on Route 66 by people just a slight bit better off themselves—a cafe manager, his hard-talking waitress Mae, and two truck drivers. The cognitive fit of these three chapters will be evident to even weaker students and will, I think, whet their appetites to read more of this engaging book.

# Examination of Similar Themes Found in *The Grapes of Wrath* and Several Young Adult Novels

Once students have read *The Grapes of Wrath*, it is time to examine some of its many provocative themes. Here I am going to take several of them, one by one, and for each I describe, I will mention a YA novel in which the same theme is explored. You and your students can do the same sort of analysis.

## The Theme of Universal Brotherhood

### *The Grapes of Wrath*

One of the dominant and expanding themes of *The Grapes of Wrath*, perhaps its most significant, is the notion that we're all in this together—almost a kind of transcendental oversoul idea. It is first explored, uncertainly but with a touch of elegance, by Preacher Casy:

> 'And I got thinkin', on'y it wasn't thinkin', it was deeper down than thinkin'. I got thinkin' how we was holy when we was one thing, an' mankin' was holy when it was one thing. An' it only got unholy when one mis'able little fella got the bit in his teeth and run off his own way, kickin' an' draggin' an' fightin'. . . . But when they're all workin' together . . . one fella kind of harnessed to the whole shebang—that's right, that's holy.'
>
> (p. 105)

This theme of universal brotherhood runs throughout the novel, in the Joad chapters as well as in the intercalary ones, but some characters are reluctant to embrace it the way Casy does. Tom Joad, ever the individualist, a you-take-care-of-you and I'll-take-care-of-me kind of guy, finally accepts that Casy has been right all along when, in California, he leaves the family to strike out and help others. He tells Ma,

> '[Casy] says one time he went out in the wilderness to find his own soul, an' he foun' he didn't have no soul that was his'n. Says he foun' he jus' got a little piece of a great big soul. Says . . . his little piece of a soul wasn't no good 'less it was with the rest, an' was whole.'
>
> (p. 534)

Two pages later, Tom announces his plans to subjugate his me-first tendencies and join the larger brotherhood. Again to Ma, he says, " 'I'll be ever'where—wherever you look. Wherever they's a fight so hungry people can eat, I'll be there. Wherever they's a cop beatin' up a guy, I'll be there' " (p. 536).

Ma herself sees her obligations not to the larger human race, but to the family. Early in the novel Steinbeck writes of her: "She seemed to know that if she swayed the family shook, and if she ever really deeply wavered or despaired the family would fall, the family will to function would be gone" (p. 96). Later, when Noah leaves, Ma's first thought is about the family; she worries that it is "falling apart" (p. 278).

But then even Ma senses that she is part of a larger whole. When the Joads get some work and are able to buy food, a number of the other Okies in the campground are envious and hungry, as are their children who gather near the Joad tent and watch Ma cook. Her heart breaks, but her first instinct is to feed her own family. Later, however, she relents and says to the starving neighbor children, "'You little fellas go an' get you each a flat stick an' I'll put what's lef' for you'" (p. 331).

At the end of the novel, it is Ma Joad who persuades Rose of Sharon, the most self-centered of all the characters and the one least interested in anyone else's well being, to give of herself—literally—and suckle the dying old man they meet in a barn. Ma's energy for this ennobling action comes from her full awareness that she is not simply a part of the family. She is, as John Donne put it, "involved in mankind," cognizant of Donne's further truth that she should never ask for whom the bell tolls; it tolls for her. Her knowledge is revealed in her quote: " 'Use' ta be the fambly. It ain't so now. It's anybody' " (p. 569). Steinbeck's overriding theme comes into full fruition here. Despite being out of money, shelter, and food, the Joads may be viewed with, if not incautious optimism, then at least a bit of hope. Cradling the old man to her pregnancy-swollen breasts, Rose of Sharon "looked up and across the barn, and her lips came together and smiled mysteriously" (p. 581). Readers can make a case that the Joads will prevail.

### *All Together Now* by Sue Ellen Bridgers (192 pp.)

An adolescent novel that explores this same theme of universal brotherhood is *All Together Now*. Dwayne, a retarded 33-year-old adult with the mind of a 12-year-old, is at the center of a small North Carolina town's consciousness. Dwayne is harmless, yet his mental limitations plague his politically ambitious brother Alva and Alva's shrewish wife Marge. In anger, Dwayne takes his sister-in-law's car and drives it around the dirt racing track at the edge of town. Alva has him arrested for auto theft but is convinced to drop the charges.

At that same race track a little later, Dwayne gets into a fistfight. Though he hates violence, Dwayne enters the fight to help his friend Taylor. This time, Alva says "enough is enough" and threatens to have Dwayne taken to jail and then to a live-in mental institution that Dwayne dreads. Led by Taylor's mother, Jane Flanagan, and spurred on by the novel's moral center, 12-year-old Casey, the whole town comes to Dwayne's rescue. Dwayne hurts no one, they argue. He is beloved in the neighborhood and will be taken care of by everyone in the town. Alva finally relents and lets Dwayne remain at home.

This small town solidarity, one Bridgers describes by saying that "the whole town acts almost as a character in the novel" (Hipple, 1990, p. 52), demonstrates the same sort of universal brotherhood Steinbeck writes about. People do better when they act as a part of the whole. The treatment of this theme in *The Grapes of Wrath* and *All Together Now* permits rich comparisons.

# The Theme of Good Versus Evil

## *The Grapes of Wrath*

A second theme Steinbeck explores in *The Grapes of Wrath* is good versus evil. Perhaps, as mentioned earlier, the best treatment occurs early on in the turtle chapter where one driver swerves to miss the turtle as it crawls across the highway but a second swerves to hit it. These same human characteristics appear in the used car chapter and the cafe chapter.

They also appear elsewhere. The impersonal, uncaring bankers who take the land from the sharecroppers embody a kind of evil that the uneducated Okies cannot quite understand. Where is the person they can confront, can argue with, can beat up if necessary? That same sense of helplessness greets them in California when the landowners never appear themselves, but send foremen and henchmen to do their dirty work for them. What makes the evil particularly pernicious is that some of the Okies are literally starving as wages go below what a family must have to maintain itself. They simply do not earn enough to buy decent food, to get to the next farm for another few days' work, to afford medical care or protected shelter. Steinbeck writes of this situation: "There is a crime here that goes beyond denunciation. There is a sorrow here that weeping cannot symbolize" (p. 449).

But not all the evil is disembodied. The used car salesmen have esteemed places in the community, earned by their duplicitous techniques as they demand and get outrageously inflated prices for cars with worn tires and dead batteries. Their counterparts in California mistreat the Okies, even those at a government-run work camp where they attempt to break up an evening dance. This evil feels more vicious when some of it is perpetrated by other Okies—themselves displaced, hungry, and, impoverished—who have been promised money by the local residents if they can incite a riot so that the police can close up the camp. They are thwarted in their attempt—this time.

Yet there are those who try to do right, even though their circumstances limit what they can do. The coffee shop waitress provides a powerful example. She lies that nickel candy is really two-for-a-penny candy so that two hungry little migrant boys (their breath held as they stare longingly at the peppermints) can each have one. Another "right moment" occurs among the Okies while they are traveling to the promised land of California. In intercalary Chapter Nineteen, a little boy has died of "black-tongue. Comes from not gettin' good things to eat" (p. 306). Those commenting on his death learn that his family does not have the money to bury him. "'Well, hell,'" someone says. "And hands went into pockets and little coins came out. In front of the tent a little heap of silver grew. And the family found it there" (p. 307).

## *Chinese Handcuffs* by Chris Crutcher (220 pp.)

Many of Chris Crutcher's novels explore the theme of good versus evil, a theme as common in adolescent literature as it is in adolescent life. Crutcher's *Chinese Handcuffs* centers on the stories of Dillon Hemingway and Jennifer Lawless, both loners, athletes, and members of dysfunctional families. Dillon is struggling to understand the breakdown and eventual suicide of his older brother, Preston. In posthumous letters written to Preston, Dillon explores the question of why and how some people crumble when they face evil in themselves and the world while others choose to look for good.

Dillon comes face to face with evil when he at long last learns the secret that his friend Jennifer is hiding. Jennifer has for years been abused by her step-father T.B., who, readers learn, is the devil incarnate and who abused children in a previous marriage as well. T.B. threatens to kill the young Jennifer's dog if she tells on him, then kills it anyway even though she does not tell. Telling, Jennifer believes, would do no good. Though T.B. beats Jennifer's hapless mother, she stays with him and refuses to believe anything bad about him. Further, Jennifer feels trapped by her fear that if she runs away, T.B. will abuse her younger sister.

The climax comes when Dillon decides, on his own and against Jennifer's wishes, to take action on her behalf. He puts himself and particularly Jennifer at considerable risk should he fail, but in the end he pulls it off, and T.B. is out of the Lawless family's life forever. Dillon's courageous actions and his desire to do good are in sharp contrast to T.B.'s evil. And along the way, Dillon comes to understand more about the nature of good and evil through his interactions with other people in his life. Kathy Sherman, Jennifer's basketball coach, exemplifies good as she risks losing her job in order to stand by Jennifer and Dillon. At the other end of the spectrum stands Mr. Caldwell, the high school principal, who wreaks an unjustifiable and power-driven vengeance on Dillon whenever he can. On still another level, Dillon's father—a war veteran who refuses to talk about his experiences as a soldier killing people in Vietnam—finally provides Dillon with a powerful example of honor, integrity, and the value of life, aspects of good that Dillon has never really recognized in him before.

At the end of the novel, Dillon is at last able to let go of his brother's decision to kill himself. Just as Jennifer is at last able to move forward, away from T.B.'s evil, Dillon is ready to come to terms with the fact that although not all evil can be fixed, it is possible to find a lot of good in oneself if you know how to look for it.

Crutcher's novel reminds readers of Shakespeare's truth in Antony's speech over the body of the assassinated Caesar: "The evil that men do lives after them; the good is oft interred with their bones" (p. 495). T.B.'s actions devastate a family and specifically a teenager, Jennifer Lawless. In a totally uncompromising way, Crutcher explores this evil. While a happy ending is implied—at least T.B. is out of Jennifer's life—the evil he has caused will linger on and continue to do its damage. Jennifer will have to have therapy and, readers can only hope, will some day overcome the effects of T.B.'s evil.

## The Theme of The Power of Nature

In Stephen Crane's *Red Badge of Courage*, youthful recruit Henry Fleming is amazed at the apparent indifference Nature has for the carnage of the Civil War battle he has been in. Yet this indifference must not be confused with inaction. As Emerson notes, "Nature is reckless of the individual. When she has points to carry, she carries them." So it is in *The Grapes of Wrath*. Nature has points to carry and, by them, this novel is driven.

### *The Grapes of Wrath*

Both the opening and the closing pages of *The Grapes of Wrath* reveal Nature at her most powerful and life-shaping. For decades the sharecroppers have lived on their Oklahoma farms, doing better some years than others, never rich, but always managing. Then along come the droughts, year after year, and, in their wake, the dust storms. The small landowners cannot survive the meager yield their farms produce, and they sell them to the conglomerates who choose to farm them with their giant machines. The sharecropper is done for.

What's left, then, for many of the families—too many, as it turns out—is a migration to California, a trip that Nature makes difficult. With their life's collection—furniture, pots and pans, farm tools, bags of clothing, dogs and cats too loved to be left behind—piled on a cutdown car made into a truck, the Okies move west—west into the setting sun, the hot sun of Oklahoma and Texas and New Mexico and Arizona and on to Death Valley in eastern California. More than a few die on this trip, including both Grampa and Granma Joad.

At the end of this novel, Nature deals the Joads another cruel blow. Those left in the family—Ma, Pa, Uncle John, Rose of Sharon (who has just given birth to a stillborn child), and the two kids Ruthie and Winfield—have been living in a boxcar on an abandoned railroad siding amid the cold rains, which continue relentlessly. Soon the water level has risen so much that cold water is pouring into the boxcar and they have to leave. In a daring effort, with Pa carrying Rose of Sharon, they make their way over the creek forming outside their railroad home and move to a cold barn offering little shelter. But, Steinbeck seems to imply when Rose of Sharon suckles the starving man, there is enough shelter—just enough. Nature can takes its shots, indifferent or not; the Joads will survive.

### *Hatchet* by Gary Paulsen (195 pp.)

Few novels written for adolescents offer a clearer picture of the power of Nature than Gary Paulsen's *Hatchet*, an enormously popular novel with young readers and with students of YA literature. In a survey I conducted (Hipple, 1992) among professionals in the field of adolescent literature—middle school and high school teachers, librarians, and university professors alike—this novel was picked as the best of the decade of the 1980s; it has maintained that kind of popularity ever since. *Hatchet* is an exciting tale, all the more because Brian's adversary is not a malevolent teacher, a bully down the block, or even his own stupidity, but, instead, the forces of Nature.

The book begins with Brian as the only passenger in an airplane flying him to Alaska to join his father, who has recently divorced Brian's mother. The pilot suffers a heart attack, and Brian manages to crash-land the plane in a lake and make his way to a deserted island. Then Nature, simply doing her thing, takes over. Brian and Nature first collide over insects:

> He had come through the crash, but the insects were not possible. He coughed them
> up, spat them out, sneezed them out, closed his eyes and kept brushing his face,
> slapping and crushing them by the dozens, by the hundreds. But as soon as he

cleared a place, as soon as he killed them, more came, thick, whining, buzzing masses of them. Mosquitoes and some small black flies he had never seen before. All biting, chewing, taking from him.

(pp. 36–37)

Happily, direct sunlight drives the bugs away.

Next comes the wrong kind of berries. A very hungry Brian finds some and unwittingly eats them voraciously. They make him sick, with strength-draining vomiting and diarrhea. And from then on, for several more days, it is, as they say, one damned thing after another: a bear, a thunderstorm, a porcupine, a wolf, a skunk, a moose, a tornado. Yet Brian learns from these encounters. He learns to avoid making mistakes, a lesson Paulsen uses frequently in this adventure novel.

Finally, Brian prevails. A tornado washes the downed plane up from the depths of the lake, and Brian is able to get to it. Brian secures supplies that augment those he has hacked out of nature with his little hatchet, the one tool he had with him when the plane first crashed. So secure has he made his wilderness existence that, when he is at last found, he is able to ask his rescuer, " 'Would you like something to eat?' " (p. 191)

(For another take on the battles between Brian and Nature, readers can be guided to *The River*, Paulsen's sequel to *Hatchet*.)

## The Theme of Poverty and Its Effects

Readers, it seems to me, often overlook economic conditions as a theme worth exploring in a work of literature; yet these very readers themselves worry about the upcoming mortgage payment, their ability to buy a new car or take a vacation, their salary increases, and so on. Students worry about whether their part-time jobs will pay for the gasoline they need and about the cost of the upcoming prom. We need, I think, to suggest to students that money often drives the characters in a piece of literature and that money—more precisely in *The Grapes of Wrath*, the lack of it—is worth examining.

### The Grapes of Wrath

Steinbeck dramatizes the effects of poverty throughout this powerful novel. At the outset, the sharecroppers who leave the land do so because they can no longer make a living on it. Between the devastation of the dust storms and the takeovers by the impersonal and hard-hearted bankers, the farmers have no choice but to move West and hope that the fliers they have seen about the riches awaiting them in California are true. Money becomes a factor, not only in the decision to move West, but in its initial implementation. Can the Okies afford a car to make the trip? Chapter Seven, the intercalary chapter on the selling of junk vehicles by the rich to the impoverished, contrasts the arrogance of monied greed with the despair of humble poverty; monied greed wins again.

Not all the possessions of the tenants leaving the land will go on their cars-turned-trucks, and they have to sell plows and horses and harnesses and wagons and the like. When what they are offered first insults, then embitters them, they can sense again, as they did on the car lot, that the new life they hope to lead has rough beginnings. Not only do they have to leave the home where grandparents lived, where children were born and raised, where dreams had at least a chance of coming true, but they have to do so with little money and diminishing optimism. But a bit of pride remains, and they tell those who buy for-next-to-nothing what, in addition to farm implements and livestock, they are getting for their contemptible dollars:

> 'You're not buying only junk, you're buying junked lives. And more—you'll see— you're buying bitterness. . . . There's a premium that goes with this pile of junk, . . . a packet of bitterness to grow in your house and to flower, some day. We could have saved you, but you cut us down, and soon you will be cut down and there'll be none of us to save you.'
>
> (pp. 112–113)

The threat: What goes around comes around.

The migrants, however, have hope: "'Maybe we can start again, in the new, rich land—in California, where the fruit grows. We'll start over'" (p. 113). Soon, though, the trip west begins to take its financial toll. The overpriced cars need parts and repairs. Campgrounds that opened along Route 66 demand payment for space. The food brought along for the trip hasn't gone as far as anticipated. Nowhere is this situation more dramatically described than in the diner in Chapter Fifteen. Mae, a hard-boiled waitress with, as it turns out, a heart of gold, refuses at first to sell a loaf of bread to an Okie; she wants to sell "san'widges." When she finally relents about selling the bread, she says she must have 15 cents; the Okie only has ten cents. In response to the traveler's request to cut off ten cents' worth, her boss Al exclaims, "'Goddamn it, Mae. Give 'em the whole loaf'" (p. 205).

The scenario takes on a special poignancy moments later when Mae sells the nickel candy at two-for-a-penny to the farmer's two boys in the episode mentioned earlier. This generosity of Mae, who, presumably, is barely above the poverty line herself, contrasts sharply with that of the car salesmen and sets the stage for what confronts the migrants when they reach the promised land.

Money is a factor there, too. The private campsites demand too much. Gas is expensive, but you have to get to where there's work. Trouble is, once you get there, the wages become negotiable and your eagerness to pick oranges for 20 cents a bag is undercut by someone who will do it for 15 and he, in turn, is ignored because someone else will do it for a dime. Get hired in one of the private places, where you live in a company shack, and you'll be paid in company scrip, deducted from which is the exorbitant rent. The scrip is usable only at the store set up by the owners of the field. Here is an excellent place to resurrect an enormously popular Tennessee Ernie Ford song of the 1950s, "Sixteen Tons," where miners had to spend their money at the company store. For a more contemporary example of a usurious system, have students watch the PG-13 movie *City of Joy*, starring Patrick Swayze, based on the novel with the same title.

Steinbeck illuminates poverty and its effects generally through the intercalary chapters and specifically through what happens to the Joads. They buy a broken down truck, sell their goods for less than they hoped—even less than first offered when the buyer successfully bluffed them and said he wouldn't take their stuff at any price—and begin the migration west. But trepidation sets in at the cost of the travel. Despite the constant worries about not having enough money for their cross-country odyssey, they do ultimately get to California.

Once there, the Joads realize very quickly that rumors of too many workers, too few jobs, and too little and rapidly decreasing wages are true. The effects are far-reaching, including, though not for the Joads, actual starvation and death. The negative consequences for the Joads include the continuing disintegration of the family. Noah leaves before they even get to California, Granma dies as they enter the state, Connie runs away from the pregnant Rose of Sharon without even a goodbye, and Preacher Casy is arrested. Finally, Tom Joad himself must go. He has hit a company cop and, having already violated Oklahoma parole by leaving the state, has no choice but to strike out on his own. Shortly thereafter, the novel ends with the Joad family struggling against the onset of winter, penniless.

Thus, poverty and its effects form the moral center of this novel and merit classroom exploration. Steinbeck's sympathies are clear: "Our people [the migrants] are good people; our people are kind people. Pray God some day kind people won't all be poor. Pray God some day a kid can eat" (p. 308).

### *Make Lemonade* by **Virginia Euwer Wolff (200 pp.)**

Virginia Euwer Wolff has written an important YA novel in *Make Lemonade*. Fourteen-year-old LaVaughn responds to a "Babysitter Needed Bad" (p. 4) note on the school bulletin board. She meets Jolly, a 17-year-old with two kids, Jeremy and Jilly, and no husband or parents to help her care for them. Jolly's previous babysitter has quit, and unless she gets a replacement soon, Jolly will lose her own job. Though LaVaughn must first clear things with her no-nonsense mother, she is given permission to take the work and goes again to Jolly's apartment to begin. Jolly's poverty is coupled with dirtiness at first. LaVaughn provides readers with this description.

> Here's how it was at Jolly's house:
> The plates are pasted together with noodles
> and these rooms smell like last week's garbage
> and there isn't a place I can put my books to study for school
> except places where something else already is.
> The mirror is smeared with toothpaste.
> The kitchen floor has the creamed spinach spilled a month ago.
> I pull up a corner of the living room curtain and smell it:
> you'd die.
> You can't imagine the things that live
> down the plugged drain.
> Stuck in the high-chair corners are margarine
> and rotting banana goo. . . .
>
> (p. 23)

LaVaughn takes a deep breath and cleans the house.

But LaVaughn soon realizes that dirt isn't the only, or even the main, problem Jolly must confront; it is poverty. She makes too little money and then loses her job when she spurns the sexual advances of her boss. Yet Jolly refuses to take welfare, fearing that if she does so, she risks losing her children. Without income, she cannot pay LaVaughn. LaVaughn chooses to stay on without pay to help Jolly and the two children to whom she has become attached. It is a struggle.

An episode where LaVaughn dips into money her mother has forced her to save for college in order to buy shoes for the kids reveals just how intense the poverty is. LaVaughn observes, "I look at the shoe prices and I think how Jeremy grows too fast for his mother's money. . . Jeremy's shoes cost what Jolly would pay me for 6 hours of sitting" (p. 79).

In spite of absent fathers who Jolly says can " 'go rot' " (p. 70), Jolly believes she is okay. LaVaughn persists in pointing out the family's plight, saying "'No, you're not. You're not doing okay. The kids need their vegetables, you got maybe six squares of toilet paper left, every time the rent comes due there's a panic—'" (p. 87). Ultimately, additional schooling for Jolly and some public assistance funding suggest a brighter future, and the novel ends on a slightly upbeat note.

But Wolff's point has been made, abundantly so. Poverty wins, at least in the short run, and more than likely over the longer haul, too. This comparison of contemporary poverty with the Depression Era poverty of Steinbeck's novel can fuel some worthwhile classroom discussion about the effects of being poor, no matter where, when, or how you live. Moreover, both Steinbeck and Wolff manage to make their stories of poverty universal. Steinbeck uses intercalary chapters to discuss general conditions. Wolff deliberately avoids naming a place—inner cities, she suggests, have enough sameness that one can do for any of the others. Wolff also provides no clues about the ethnicity of LaVaughn or Jolly—any ethnic group mired in poverty can, she suggests, symbolize any other.

## The Theme of Life Goes On

It is a common theme in literature, the idea that life goes on no matter what. Scarlet O'Hara won't think about that today; she'll think about it tomorrow, because tomorrow is another day. Faulkner's acceptance speech on his receiving the Nobel Prize included his beliefs that "man will not merely endure; he will prevail" (p. 601). As these two examples suggest, this theme often finds expression through protagonists in American literature commonly studied in schools; Hester Prynne, Henry Fleming, and Huck Finn survive and, it can be hoped, prevail. There are, to be sure, exceptions such as Edna Pontellier, Willy Loman, and Sister Carrie's Hurstwood, but the generalization is supportable.

### The Grapes of Wrath

True to this pattern, *The Grapes of Wrath* speaks often and consistently of this theme, in both the general chapters and in those devoted to the Joads. Again, in the turtle essay, the turtle struggles mightily to get up onto the highway and traps a head of wild oats in its shell in the effort. Its trek across the highway is hastened when a driver hits the turtle and flips it tiddly-wink style over to the other side. There another mighty struggle ensues—the turtle is on its back. But it does at long last right itself and move along. As it does so, the wild oats fall out of the shell, and three spearhead seeds stick into the ground. As the turtle crawls away, it drags dirt over the seeds. And life will indeed go on.

Steinbeck's most explicit expression of his agreement with Faulkner (or the latter's with him; Steinbeck wrote his novel before Faulkner won the Nobel Prize) that man will not merely endure but will prevail is found in Chapter Fourteen:

> This you may say of man—when theories change and crash, when schools, philosophies, when narrow dark alleys of thought, national, religious, economic, grow and disintegrate, man reaches, stumbles forward, painfully, mistakenly sometimes. Having stepped forward, he may slip back, but only half a step, never the full step back. This you may say and know it and know it.
>
> (p. 193)

To put a new twist on this same principle, you might look at it this way: Man might bend, but he will not break. Near the end of the novel, Steinbeck describes the women watching their men:

> The women stood silently and watched. And where a number of men gathered together, the fear went from their faces, and anger took its place. And the women sighed with relief, for they knew it was all right—the break had not come; and the break would never come as long as fear could turn to wrath.
>
> (p. 556)

For the Joads, too, life goes on. It's a cliché from a John Wayne movie—"a man's gotta do what a man's gotta do"—but clichés earn their currency from truths embodied in them, and the Joads do what the Joads gotta do. They leave their land. They reject the role adopted by Muley, who refuses to go west with his family and stays in Oklahoma, a crazed, ferret-like creature of the night inhabiting empty cabins and deserted fields. The Joads struggle to get to California and, when Granma dies just as they cross the border, they let her be buried in a pauper's grave. They cannot afford the 40 dollars required for the nice funeral they all know Granma would have wanted. The family makes and breaks camp as necessary, working when they can, eating when they work. They do what they have to do.

What Casy and Tom have to do is to fight for the cause, and readers can sense that ultimately they will win because they will not break. Oh, Casy may be killed and Tom may kill his killer, but then Tom will move on to help others, to be around "'wherever's they's a fight so hungry people can eat . . . '" (p. 536). And what Rose of Sharon has to do is to suckle the dying man in the barn. Through her, life will go on. Her gesture brings the theme squarely into the reader's consciousness.

### *Ellen Foster* by Kaye Gibbons (126 pp.)

Kaye Gibbons' first novel won critical acclaim and popular readership for a variety of reasons: the beauty of her language, the humor of the telling, but perhaps most of all, the indomitability of her 11-year-old heroine, Ellen Foster. Ellen tells her own story, beginning with this sentence: "When I was little I would think of ways to kill my daddy" (p. 1). Her daddy is a rotter, a weak, malicious alcoholic who abuses his wife and would be equally abusive to Ellen if she let him.

Ellen's ill mother cannot hold out and dies early in this brief novella, leaving Ellen, her father, her mama's mama, and her aunts. Mostly it is Ellen and her father. Like the Okies, she does what she has to do, stealing her father's bootlegging money to pay the electric bills and buy food, staying clear of him when he is in his drunken rages, surviving. Ellen meets life head on. When her drunken father brings home his cronies, she hides or lights out for the home of her little "colored" friend Starletta. When Ellen and her father are alone in the house, she shoves a chair under her doorknob. Interspersed with these chapters is Ellen's later life with her "new mama" in a foster family.

Midway through the novel Ellen's father dies, in effect having drunk himself to death, and Ellen is shifted between, among others, her two aunts and her mama's mama. Throughout, Ellen is the unwelcome one, the unloved one, much like the Joads and their fellow Okies once they arrive in California. Life is never easy. Ellen shares with Ma Joad a certain homespun but insightful philosophy. She says of her life, "Down the path in the darkness I gather my head and all that is spinning and flying out from me and wonder Oh you just have to wonder what the world has come to" (p. 38). But she perseveres, saying, "I just lived to see what would happen next" (p. 72). And, a little later, "I just did the best I could with what I had to work with" (p. 77).

Finally Ellen, wise beyond her years, spunky, and determined, decides after the death of her mama's mama that neither aunt is for her. Better that she be in a foster home, even down to taking the name. Her choice of a foster home is revelatory:

> Now was the time to get old Ellen squared away for a fresh start. And that is what I did. That is why I think I am somebody now because I said by damn this is how it is going to be and before I knew it I had a new mama. And I looked her over plenty good too before I knew she was a keeper.
>
> (p. 95)

For Ellen Foster, life goes on. She confronts three deaths—her mother's, her father's, and her grandmother's. She deals with the rejection of both her aunts. As a white girl, she violates local taboos by being friends with a black girl and her family. And she chooses her future by marching up to the door of her future foster family saying, "Here I am, take me in" (p. 116).

## Conclusion

Thematic studies in literature classes are useful for a variety of reasons. Students can profitably learn that literature, though often based on the lives of specific people in specific circumstances confronting specific problems, is nonetheless a repository for larger ideas. Thematic examinations can produce lively classroom experiences as students discuss and debate various meanings and their significances. Thematic studies facilitate comparisons and contrasts between and among works. As this brief discussion I hope has illustrated, a classic like *The Grapes of Wrath* can shed light on, and be itself illuminated by, adolescent novels.

Let me reiterate the plan once more. Each student will be expected to read *The Grapes of Wrath*, the core novel of the unit. Additionally, each student will be expected to read at least two of the five additional novels. Heightened classroom interest may result in many students reading more than two, with some perhaps reading all five. Teaching activities will be at times on one novel, at times on several. It is worth noting that just as *All Together Now* may have something to say about *The Grapes of Wrath*, and vice versa, so also may the Bridgers novel be used in conjunction with the other adolescent novels—*All Together Now* being compared with *Hatchet*, for example. The English class, its teacher, *The Grapes of Wrath*, and some YA novels can all come together, like that town in Bridgers' novel or Jim Casy's great big soul—into one dynamic and worthwhile whole.

# References

Alvine, L. & Duffy, D. (1995). Friendships and tensions in *A separate peace* and *Staying fat for Sarah Byrnes*. In J.F. Kaywell's (Ed.), *Adolescent literature as a complement to the classics*. Volume Two. Norwood, MA: Christopher-Gordon Publishers, Inc., pp. 163–174.

Bridgers, S. E. (1990). *All together now*. New York: Bantam.

Cole, P. B. (1995). Bridging *The red badge of courage* with six related young adult novels. In J.F. Kaywell's (Ed.), *Adolescent literature as a complement to the classics*. Volume Two. Norwood, MA: Christopher-Gordon Publishers, Inc. pp., 21–39.

Crane, S. (1981). *The red badge of courage*. Mahwah, NJ: Watermill Press.

Crutcher, C. (1991). *Chinese handcuffs*. New York: Dell.

Faulkner, W. (1950). Nobel Prize acceptance speech. In R. Anderson, J. M. Brinnin, J. Leggett, G. Q. Arpin, & S. A. Toth's (1993), *Elements of literature*. Fifth Course. Orlando, FL: Holt Rinehart Winston, p. 601.

Gibbons, K. (1987). *Ellen Foster*. New York: Random House.

Higgins, J. & Fowinkle, J. (1993). *The adventures of Huckleberry Finn*, prejudice, and adolescent literature. In J. F. Kaywell's (Ed.), *Adolescent literature as a complement to the classics*. Volume One. Norwood, MA: Christopher-Gordon Publishers, Inc., pp. 37–59.

Hipple, T. (1993). *Catcher* as core and catalyst. In J. F. Kaywell's (Ed.), *Adolescent literature as a complement to the classics*. Volume One. Norwood, MA: Christopher-Gordon Publishers, Inc., pp. 61–78.

Hipple, T. (1992, November). Have you read? *English Journal*, *81* (7), p. 91.

Hipple, T. (1990). *Presenting Sue Ellen Bridgers*. Boston: Twayne Publishers.

Lapierre, D. (1985). *City of joy*. Garden City, NY: Doubleday.

Mitchell, D. (1993). Exploring the American dream: *The great Gatsby* and six young adult novels. In J. F. Kaywell's (Ed.), *Adolescent literature as a complement to the classics*. Volume One. Norwood, MA: Christopher-Gordon Publishers, Inc., pp. 143–161.

Paulsen, G. (1988). *Hatchet*. New York: Puffin.

Paulsen, G. (1991). *The river*. New York: Dell.

Pennac, D. (1994). *Better than life*. Toronto: Coach House Press.

Poe, E. A. (1993). Alienation from society in *The scarlet letter* and *The chocolate war*. In J.F. Kaywell's (Ed.), *Adolescent literature as a complement to the classics*. Volume One. Norwood, MA: Christopher-Gordon Publishers, Inc., pp. 185–194.

Shakespeare, W. (1599). *Julius Caesar*. In G. Kearns's (1984), *Appreciating literature*. New York: Macmillan, pp. 438–535.

Steinbeck, J. (1939). *The grapes of wrath*. New York: Penguin.

Wolff, V. E. (1993). *Make lemonade*. New York: Scholastic.

## Film Cited (Available on Home Video)

Eberts, J. & Joffe, R. (Producers). (1992). *City of joy*. Burbank, CA: TriStar Pictures.

## Song Cited

Ford, T. E. (1955). Sixteen tons. In *Sixteen tons*. Nashville, TN: Capital Records.

# Helping Students to Find *Something Permanent* in Steinbeck's *Of Mice and Men*

*Kelly Chandler*

## Introduction

Unlike many American classics, John Steinbeck's *Of Mice and Men* is accessible to almost all of the readers in my heterogeneously grouped English 10 classes. Most sophomores, regardless of their ability or experience, identify strongly with George and Lennie's friendship and cheer for them to obtain a little piece of the American dream. Some of the students are so invested in the characters that they rush into my classroom to protest the tragic conclusion when they finish the book. "I can't believe how it ended, Ms. Chandler," one girl told me last year. "I wanted to throw that book!"

Given these claims of success, you might wonder why I have chosen to write about this novel and the possibilities that open up for students when it is paired with Cynthia Rylant and Walker Evans's *Something Permanent*, an unusual book of poetry and photographs for young adults. It might seem unnecessary, perhaps even redundant, to provide that kind of support and scaffolding for students who are already having a positive experience with a text. In the next few pages, however, I hope to demonstrate how and why teachers might consider using these two books together.

Just because most of my students can navigate the text with relative ease does not necessarily mean that they take away everything they might from their reading experience. Although *Of Mice and Men* meets with favorable reviews from most students, each year I have a cadre of resistant readers who are unable or unwilling to connect with the book. Furthermore, I believe that all students' transactions with *Of Mice and Men* can be further enriched when *Something Permanent* is used to help them develop more active reading strategies.

Experienced along with *Of Mice and Men*, Rylant's poetry and Evans's photographs provide a fuller sense of the historical context, help students to visualize Steinbeck's setting and characters more concretely, and treat similar themes in a different genre. The inclusion of several teenage voices also helps to connect the themes of Great Depression literature to the concerns of contemporary adolescents. Lastly, the book's unique combination of photographs and poetry serves as a powerful model for student artists and writers.

This chapter describes a unit combining the two texts and expands on my rationale for doing so. Some daily activities are suggested, as well as a list of related young adult (YA) literature titles appropriate for independent reading by adolescents. The last section demonstrates how Rylant and Evans's work can be used as a springboard for students' creative efforts as they design class booklets of student-generated poetry and images: their own versions of *Something Permanent* for the 1990s.

## The Pair of Core Texts

### *Of Mice and Men* by John Steinbeck (128 pp.)

George Milton and Lennie Small have no one but each other as they travel around California seeking work during the Depression. George looks out for Lennie, a powerful but intellectually feeble man who does not know his own strength. Whenever they share a quiet moment, Lennie insists that George tell him the story of the little place they're saving to buy, where they will farm a couple of acres and Lennie will tend the rabbits. When they begin working on a ranch just outside of Salinas, it seems like their dreams are just within reach. But a disastrous turn of events involving the boss's daughter-in-law shatters their hopes for the future and forces George to make a horrible decision. His final act of friendship toward Lennie both engages and enrages student readers, causing them to debate the nature of justice and morality as well as the limits of personal responsibility.

### *Something Permanent* by Cynthia Rylant & Walker Evans (64 pp.)

During the 1930s, photographer Walker Evans was hired by the Farm Security Administration (FSA) to travel across America and document the effects of the Great Depression. Collaborating with writer James Agee, he became famous for his work in *Let Us Now Praise Famous Men*, a book about the lives of tenant farmers in rural Alabama. Sixty years later, he is the posthumous partner of Cynthia Rylant, a noted author for young adults.

For *Something Permanent*, Rylant wrote brief narrative poems—none more than 25 lines in length—to accompany a selection of Evans's FSA photographs. The combination is arresting. Stark black and white images are set off by spare blank verse about parents struggling to make ends meet, young people yearning for adventure, and children hoping for things to get better. Issues are raised about maintaining dignity in the face of hardship and about the power of family, friendship, and love to sustain us.

## Why Pair the Texts?

As mentioned previously, I see three primary ways that experiencing *Something Permanent* can enrich readers' experiences with *Of Mice and Men*: by providing a richer historical context for the novel, by helping students to visualize as they read, and by providing a connection between issues of the 1930s and the 1990s.

## Providing a Historical Context

Although the effects of the Great Depression permeate *Of Mice and Men*, the time period is rarely discussed directly by either Steinbeck or the characters. Its influence is subtly treated—too subtly for some students to appreciate. Before I began pairing these two texts, I was appalled by how many of the students were unable to discuss the novel's setting in anything but superficial terms. It was clear to me that I needed to provide more background information for them about the story's context, but I did not want to spend a great deal of time introducing historical content.

*Something Permanent*, which illustrates the impact of the Depression on a variety of different characters, gives students multiple perspectives to compare and contrast with George's and Lennie's experiences. They also become more motivated to investigate the history on their own after reading the poems.

## Helping Students Visualize What They Read

There is a growing amount of evidence suggesting that highly engaged readers actively visualize the setting, characters, and events of books, while less successful readers do not (Wilhelm, 1996). Reading an illustrated text like *Something Permanent* develops my students' schema about the Great Depression. Although most of the sophomores empathize with George and Lennie, they see both the characters and their context in rather generic terms—if they can visualize them at all. Since many of my students were born in Maine and have rarely left the state, they have very little prior knowledge about other places to bring to their reading.

In addition, most texts set before the 1950s tend to be lumped together by my sophomores in a broad, general category of "a long time ago." Although most of Evans's photographs were taken on the Eastern seaboard, not in California, the Depression-era clothing, furnishings, and tools are still consistent with Steinbeck's work. The photographs, therefore, provide students with pictures of real people and places from the 1930s—images that are then available in their memory banks while they're reading *Of Mice and Men*. I like to have students experience *Something Permanent* before viewing the PG-13 movie version of *Of Mice and Men,* starring John Malkovich and Gary Sinise.

## Connecting Issues of the 1930s with the 1990s

Lastly, students can connect the stories in *Something Permanent,* particularly those about or told by young people, to their own experiences. The book helps them to see that some crucial things—longing, family friction, and poverty—have remained constant over the past 60 years. The plight of the young man in "Traveler" who "swore to God he'd get out [of town] / by 16, 17 at the latest / and when twenty hit, / and him still there, / it hit hard . . ." (p. 25) strikes a chord with students. Many of my students have this same fear about never escaping their small town.

And when Rylant writes in "Filling Station" about the brown boy whose mother "was walking through that / house stark naked and / trying to hang dinner plates on the / clothesline" (p. 34), students whose parents have embarrassed or let them down can empathize and perhaps find some strength to endure. Because the voices of teenagers are among the chorus that Rylant creates, *Something Permanent* has a credibility and a capacity to move students that *Of Mice and Men* alone—no matter how engaging it is—cannot have.

# Pairing the Texts

## Length of Unit

I recommend setting aside about six weeks for the entire unit, during which students will read and discuss the two core texts, write a number of poems using Rylant's work as a model, compile a class booklet of poetry and images, and read independently a third book set during the Depression. My classes meet every other day for 80 minutes. During the first half of the unit, I generally set aside one day a week to discuss *Of Mice and Men* directly, then spend the other day—or two days, depending on the sequence—working on *Something Permanent.* The mock trial, which serves as the novel's final assessment piece, requires about a week. Poetry workshop and the compilation of the class booklet can usually be accomplished in two to three more weeks, provided that students are willing to spend some study halls or after-school sessions scanning in their pictures and completing layout work.

## Reading Aloud and Sketching

Begin the *Of Mice and Men* unit by reading aloud the first few pages. This section is the most descriptive of the novel, lacking the dialogue and action of the subsequent chapters, and it can turn off less patient readers. If I am able to hook students on the two distinctive characters of Lennie and George, whose relationship begins to reveal itself fairly quickly, then I'm confident that most of them will be willing to take it from there. I also want to be able to discuss the foreshadowing that Steinbeck employs and help students make predictions about what will happen later. By modeling this kind of questioning and reflecting behavior as a reader, I hope to counteract the passive conception of reading that many of my students possess.

Reading aloud frees up my less proficient readers to visualize, predict, and question by lessening the task of decoding print (Allen, 1995). When finished, ask students to make some of those visualizations tangible by sketching both the riverbank and the ranch where George and Lennie take a job. Students share their sketches and compare them in small groups, discussing why they depicted the scenes as they did and resolving contradictions between their perceptions and the text. I occasionally ask students to sketch subsequent scenes as we progress through the novel, and many of them also draw when they begin to produce their own poetry.

After these initial activities, I divide the book into thirds and ask students to read each section by a specified date. The rest of the novel is completed independently, although I do have audiotapes available for those students who need more support.

## Experiencing and Discussing Selected Poems and Photographs

Begin the study of *Something Permanent* by reading aloud the short poem "Stories" and showing students the photo that accompanies the text.

> So what are you gonna do
> while you're waiting for
> a little work,
> 'cept find someone else
> who's waiting, too,
> and swap some stories.
> Hell, story's the only thing that's free in the world.
>
> (p. 53)

I discuss with the students why I think this poem expresses one of the primary themes of the book—of the unit, in fact—and talk about how we will be sharing and "swapping" the stories told by Rylant, Evans, and Steinbeck, as well as the stories of our own lives, through the discussion of literature and the writing of poetry.

Then I select several evocative poems such as "Hitchhiker" (p. 9), "Bed" (p. 22), and "Mule" (p. 39) to read aloud and respond to as a whole class. We talk about how the text and the photographs work together, discuss themes that run across all three pieces, and formulate beginning answers to the essential question, "What do the poems and photographs of *Something Permanent* tell us about life during the Great Depression?"

After this whole-class discussion, divide students into groups of four or five students in order to discuss a poem and photograph among themselves and then present their ah-ha's to the class. "Photograph" (p. 5), "Traveler" (p. 25), "Grave" (p. 41), and "Land" (p. 58) are examples of poems that raise particularly interesting issues about the Depression and that are particularly accessible to students who are reading in collaborative groups.

## Writing Poems from Photographs

From the beginning of the unit, my students and I are not just consumers of poetry; we are also producers of it. One of the things that fascinates students most about *Something Permanent* is the way Rylant knits a story from a single thread in the photograph: an overturned plate on a baby's grave, laundry flapping behind some tenements, a bicycle outside a diner. I want my students to recognize the importance of these details of daily life, to see how telling they can be if we pay attention to them as readers and writers. So, after we have read a few of the poems together and examined their relationship to the accompanying photographs, I ask them to try to create this effect on their own. This activity also serves as an in-class warm-up for creating their contemporary version of *Something Permanent*.

Cover up the poems on several pages and ask pairs of students to write using one of Evans's photographs as a prompt. Students may choose a number of photos to work from, but those accompanying "Rocker" (p. 19), "Traveler" (p. 24), "Filling Station" (p. 35), and "Cafe" (p. 57) have been my students' favorites. The only requirement is to generate a poem that maintains the flavor of the time period and the style of Rylant's narrative poetry.

In about 20 minutes, with a little coaching and coaxing, most students are able to draft some sort of a poem that tells a story in a few words. Then, with the class sitting in a circle, the pairs read their drafts aloud to their peers for feedback. The students are often surprised by how different all of the poems are, even when they are inspired by the same photograph.

Since students are reading *Of Mice and Men* simultaneously, themes from the novel often find their way into this assignment, as the following example of student work demonstrates (See Example 3.1). Whitney and Brianna have chosen to write about a picture of three men sitting in front of a gas station (p. 35). They imagine that the men, all unemployed, are offered a ride out of town, which they refuse.

---

**Student Example 3.1**

Whitney and Brianna's poem concludes with these haunting lines:

> But they turn down the offer,
> Because they know better times will come,
> And soon the hard times will be a distant memory.
> As lonely as they may seem,
> They've got themselves,
> And that's all they need,
> Until the better times come.

---

Their emphasis on the men's friendship and dogged optimism about the future suggest that they have internalized some of the characters' attitudes in *Of Mice and Men*.

Later on in the unit during writers' workshop, consider using some of the pairs' drafts for mini-lessons. This will depend on the strengths and weaknesses of the poems that individuals are producing for the class booklet. I have included a sample revision activity using a first-draft response to the photograph on p. 57. (See Figure 3.1).

## Writing Poems from *Of Mice and Men*

Students also take the previous assignment one step further by writing poems from or with images that are based on events and characters in *Of Mice and Men*. In addition to crafting the poem, they must also determine how to illustrate it with a drawing, magazine cut-out, or photograph. Possible approaches might include a picture of a tack room with a lonely first-person poem by Crooks, a movie poster with a regretful la-

---

**Figure 3.1**

**"River Hill Cafe" Re-Visioning Activity**

**River Hill Cafe**

> I saw it for only a moment.
> We passed by swiftly.
> In the back of the pickup,
> I wanted to say stop,
> But we had no money,
> And I didn't know the man.
> There was only one person
> Sitting inside.
> I wished I was him,
> As we swiftly passed by.

**Instructions for Pairs**

1.  Add lines or words that will show more about who the narrator is.
2.  Add lines or words that will tell more about how the narrator ended up in the back of the pickup.
3.  Add lines or words that will tell more about the person in the cafe.
4.  Generate 3-4 other possible titles.
5.  Make any other additions or changes that you think will improve the poem.
6.  Be ready to share your ideas.

---

ment from Curley's wife, or a photograph of rabbits in a hutch accompanied by a description of George and Lennie's dream. Students are able to devise dozens of others.

This activity asks readers to elaborate on small, interesting details in the novel. Students also consider the perspectives of characters other than the two primary ones and explore further the relationship between text and image that *Something Permanent* introduces.

## Role-playing from *Of Mice and Men* and *Something Permanent*

Another way of building on these strategies of detail elaboration and gap filling is to ask students to write and perform dramatic role-plays for scenes that are missing or beyond the scope of either text. As Wagner and Moffett (1992) explain, drama requires students to "think on their feet, make spontaneous decisions, exercise independence, and respond to the unexpected in a flexible, creative way" (p. 94). These are the same qualities I want my students to demonstrate as readers, which is why I ask them to improvise from texts.

Both *Of Mice and Men* and *Something Permanent* leave numerous unanswered questions about which students can speculate through drama. What does Curley say to his wife when they're back at the ranch house after George and Lennie come to town? Do the two young lovers in Rylant's "Hitchhikers" (p. 8) make it to Pittsburgh and get married? What have George and Lennie been doing since they fled Weed? How did the woman in "Land" (p. 59) feel when she first came to the farm, and with whom did she come? Some of the best conversations take place when students choose to enact the same situation in very different ways.

## Conducting a Mock Trial

Instead of insisting that students write an essay exam or a final paper about *Of Mice and Men*, I ask them to participate in a mock trial of George for the murder of Lennie. I find that this final assessment piece is less intimidating and more fun for the majority of sophomores. The mock trial is also more consistent with the kinds of visualization, written improvisation, and role-play activities that we pursued during the rest of the unit. Participation in the trial requires students to know the book well, to make reasonable conjectures, and to develop a convincing, rational argument—all desirable outcomes in themselves.

Divide students into defense and prosecution teams, then allow each side to decide who will play the roles of attorneys and witnesses. The teams meet at the beginning of the preparation time, usually for two full class periods, to plan their overall strategy. Then, pairs of students break off to script and rehearse testimony. Most roles, including the lawyers, are double or triple cast so that almost everyone can have speaking parts. For example, one student might make the opening statement and question only one witness, while another might do two cross-examinations. The role of Slim might be played by one student during direct examination and another during the cross examination. Since the groups also create some roles for expert witnesses—for example, a ballistics specialist, a criminal psychologist, or a resident of Weed—they get a chance to use some of the elaboration and gap-filling strategies they develop during the poetry writing exercises.

Part of a class period is devoted to reviewing courtroom procedure and going over some legal vocabulary. Our focus, however, is on using the novel creatively and consistently, so students' prior knowledge of the law from movies and television is usually sufficient for our purposes.

I also choose two students to share the role of judge. I usually pull names from a hat since more students volunteer for the part than I can accommodate. During the preparation time, I help these two to develop assessment criteria for the performance, then they present that information to their classmates. This way, all students know what is expected of them ahead of time. In addition to keeping order during the performance and instructing the jury (usually students from another class or grade), the judges help me grade their peers using the rubric they develop. Trial participants also have the opportunity to self-assess their performance.

The higher stakes of an invited audience and the theatricality of the event make the mock trial a fitting conclusion for our *Of Mice and Men* study. The rest of the unit, about three weeks, is devoted to exploring a novel of choice and writing poetry about the 1990s based on Rylant's model.

# Extending the Core Texts

## Independent Reading

After everyone has the same "gene pool" of common ideas and themes from *Something Permanent* and *Of Mice and Men*, I ask students to read a third book set during the Depression. Spreading the available books out in the room for perusal and doing short booktalks will help students select texts that are appropriate for them in terms of their personal interests and reading abilities.

Individuals who are interested in exploring more of John Steinbeck's work may choose to read *The Grapes of Wrath* (See Chapter 2 of this text). Students who particularly appreciated the photographs in *Something Permanent* (64 pp.) might investigate *Let Us Now Praise Famous Men* (471 pp.). Those who are interested in how the Depression affected members of different ethnic groups may choose Forrest Carter's *The Education of Little Tree* (227 pp.) or Mildred Taylor's *Roll of Thunder, Hear My Cry!* (276 pp.). Depending on their interests, students sometimes choose to read in pairs or in small collaborative groups.

During the three weeks that students are writing, revising, and laying out their poetry in class, homework mostly consists of this independent reading, accompanied by journal responses. The period it takes to assemble the booklet is usually ample time for them to complete their texts, although I sometimes negotiate a later due date for the longer works. I would not suggest burdening students with a substantial project on their independent book since they are likely to be invested in their work on the booklet. For me, they generally write a short essay discussing connections between the two core books and their independent choice.

## Suggested Books for the Booktalks

### *Let Us Now Praise Famous Men* by James Agee & Walker Evans (471 pp.)

Evans's photographs animate Agee's 1936 narrative about the daily lives of tenant farm families in Alabama. The book may be difficult for some adolescent readers because of its unconventional text structure and length, but its gritty realism and evocative photographs make it well worth offering as a choice.

### *The Education of Little Tree* by Forrest Carter (216 pp.)

An orphaned Cherokee boy is raised by his grandparents in the mountains, where he learns many important life lessons along the way. This is one of the few books my sophomores read that makes them literally cry—in class—and laugh aloud!

### *8 Plus 1* by Robert Cormier (192 pp.)

This collection of autobiographically inspired short stories is set in the "Frenchtown" section of an industrial New England city during the 1930s. Each story is preceded by a brief explanation of its origins from one of YA literature's luminaries.

### *Fried Green Tomatoes at the Whistle Stop Cafe* by **Fannie Flagg (403 pp.)**

This bittersweet and funny contemporary novel moves back and forth between the 1980s and the 1930s. First, there is the story of Evelyn Couch, a bored housewife, and Mrs. Threadgoode, the nursing home resident whom she befriends. Then, there is the Depression-era story of Idgie and Ruth, two young women who own the Whistle Stop Cafe. Many of your students will have seen the popular PG-13 movie version *Fried Green Tomatoes*, starring Kathy Bates and Jessica Tandy.

### *No Promises in the Wind* by **Irene Hunt (223 pp.)**

An aspiring teenage musician, Josh, sets out on his own when his father loses his job and there is no longer enough money to feed the family. Josh doesn't plan on being accompanied by his 10-year-old brother, Joey. Their hardship-filled journey and the family reconciliation give this YA novel suspense and tenderness.

### *To Kill a Mockingbird* by **Harper Lee (284 pp.)**

In this classic, Scout Finch learns powerful lessons about justice, racism, and integrity during the summer that her father defends a black man unfairly accused of raping a white woman (See *Adolescent Literature as a Complement to the Classics*, Volume One, Chapter 1).

### *A Day No Pigs Would Die* by **Robert Newton Peck (156 pp.)**

When he must sacrifice his beloved pet pig for the good of his Shaker family, young Rob is forced to grow up quickly and confront the nature of duty. This loss, however, is just a rehearsal for the events that follow. This is another YA novel that prompts both belly-laughs and tears.

### *The Grapes of Wrath* by **John Steinbeck (502 pp.)**

This classic novel, explored at length by Ted Hipple in this text (pp. 19–34), details the Joad family's migration from their foreclosed fields in Oklahoma to search for a better life in California. A much more challenging text than *Of Mice and Men* in terms of length and complexity, it is worth the effort for students who are interested in one of the most important fictional chronicles of the Depression.

### *Roll of Thunder, Hear My Cry!* by **Mildred Taylor (276 pp.)**

The Logan family struggles to hold onto their land as white racists try to wrest it from them. Narrated by Cassie, a bright and spunky 10-year-old, this YA novel moves quickly and is appealing to both boys and girls. *Let the Circle Be Unbroken* (432 pp.), the sequel to *Roll of Thunder, Hear My Cry!,* is also appropriate. (See *Adolescent Literature as a Complement to the Classics*, Volume One, Chapter 10).

## Generating and Connecting Themes

After students have read both of the core texts, ask them to brainstorm a list of themes that they feel are represented in the books then display their lists using an overhead projector. My sophomores generated the following list of "Themes of Literature About the 1930s": poverty, desperation, optimism, finding comfort, making do, friendship, love, dreams, holding onto each other, endurance, not getting too attached, and simplicity. Discuss each potential entry, suggesting evidence from either text to support its inclusion, then reproduce the list on butcher paper to post in the classroom. Students may add to this list as other themes come to mind later. Students often draw from this list when they are writing their essays about common themes in the three books they've experienced.

In addition to the Depression themes, my sophomores generate a list of themes that they feel are "Themes Representative of the 1990s." Last year's list included violence, family, friendship, peer pressure, drugs and alcohol, environmental awareness, pollution, stress, love, sex, racism and sexism, homophobia, the power of advertising, exercise and health awareness. This list becomes a reference guide for students as they decide which pieces to include in their booklets. Each class tries to include poems that deal with a wide variety of the issues they brainstormed.

We also compare the two lists of themes and discuss which ones have remained constant from generation to generation. This activity reminds students that literature written during and about another time can be relevant to their own lives.

## Writing Their Own Poetry

With its symbiotic relationship between text and image, *Something Permanent* can serve as a powerful model for students—demonstrating, in a sense, that there is not as much distance between the "classic" and the everyday creative effort as one might think. After they have experienced Rylant's work and generated a list of possible ideas for 1990s poetry, students are ready to begin work on their own booklets.

The requirements for this part of the unit are simple: Draft at least three poems with corresponding images, revise and edit these poems during writing workshop, assist others with their work, and submit at least one piece and picture to the class booklet. Students also sign up for jobs related to the production of the booklets that range from designing a cover to scanning photographs and drawings, from laying out pages to typing and editing poems. Class time is spent writing, conferencing, and sharing poems in progress. See Figure 3.2 for a checklist to help students keep track of the process. Like Rylant, about half of the kids write their poems beginning with an image, often a personal photograph. The others write the poem first and then find a picture to go along with it.

Students are more enthusiastic about this project than any other writing assignment I give them during the course of the year. They appreciate the opportunity to write about things that are close to them and welcome the chance to bring their daily lives into the classroom. They also recognize the value of having a model. "I enjoyed reading the poems from *Something Permanent*," Tanya wrote in her unit evaluation. "It helped me develop ideas to write my own poems." According to Eric, "analyzing the *Something Permanent* poetry . . . enabled the class to look a little deeper than normal into poetry that has a lot of different themes." Several other students com-

---

**Figure 3.2**

**Writing Workshop Checksheet**

Your Name: _____

Directions: You must turn in this completed checksheet with your submission for the class booklet. Initialize the spaces when each item is finished.

1.   _____   Rough draft completed, with picture

2.1  _____   Poem read by _____
                                    (student #1's signature)

Comments:

2.2  _____   Poem read by _____
                                    (student #2's signature)

Comments:

3.   _____   Revise and/or edit, using comments from peers

4.   _____   Conference with _____
                                    (teacher signature)

5.   _____   Edit, using comments from teacher

6.   _____   Type poem and save on class disk as "S.P. [your name]"

7.   _____   Give picture labeled with your name to team to be scanned

8.   _____   Complete author bio and turn it in to team to be typed

---

mented that their exposure to authentic photographs from the Depression encouraged them to use pictures from their own collections to illustrate their poetry.

Several of the poems in the class booklets demonstrate a clear debt to Rylant's spare and moving style. Ryan's fine example (See Student Example 3.2) is paired with a magazine cutout of a man flanked by his faithful hound.

In addition to borrowing from Rylant, many students take their topics from those that appeared on our "Themes for the 1990s" brainstorming list. Many of them write

---

**Student Example 3.2**

**Again**

Again outside the cornfields,

Where the woods get heavy,

There lies a small log cabin,

Where stands a dog and an old man.

They've been together for two years,

And are the best of friends.

As the sun rises upon the cabin,

The two lonely companions stand and look.

Another day is coming,

Just like today and tomorrow,

Again they'll be there to watch.

---

about everyday things such as pets, friends, and relationships. They also choose to deal with weighty issues including politics, abuse, suicide, and drunk driving. For example, Eric's poem "Escape" was inspired by a wry *Newsweek* cartoon in which a white politician points to a Hispanic family and tells a Native American in traditional dress, "It's time to reclaim America from illegal immigrants!" Eric transcends the political rhetoric implied by the cartoon to write an empathetic piece about Mexican border-crossers (See Student Example 3.3).

In the past, I must confess, I was wary about teaching poetry to my students. I frequently read it to them and always allowed it as an alternative medium for completing other projects, but I rarely asked everyone in my classes to experiment with writing it. Most, though certainly not all, of the student-generated poems I saw before we read

---

**Student Example 3.3**

**Escape**

So they stream to

The land of opportunity,

Dodging the watchmen

Who wear night vision glasses,

And climb over

Cast iron fences that separate

Two very different lands.

---

*Something Permanent* could be divided into two categories: love and death. Occasionally, the two would intersect: "I love her so much I could die." After reading Rylant's work and experimenting with writing poetry related to Steinbeck's novel, the quality and variety of students' pieces increased dramatically. Their comfort level with and enthusiasm for writing poetry also increased. Students began to recognize that poetry can chronicle social issues as well as personal emotions, and that the most compelling poems—like Rylant's—often connect the two.

## Conclusion

For many of my sophomores, reading *Something Permanent* marks the first time that they have experienced poetry as accessible and comprehensible. Additionally, for many it is the first time they have paid attention to photographs as works of art rather than just mementos. They connect the themes of the poetry and pictures to their own lives and the lives of their families, then they borrow the model to express their own ideas and experiences. This kind of rare cross-fertilization between reading and writing—the ideal in an English class as far as I'm concerned—is made possible by the approachability of Rylant and Evans's book.

My students' abilities to question, reflect on, and extend *Of Mice and Men* have also been enhanced by the pairing of these two works. The activities I have designed around both core texts allow me to integrate all of the language arts—reading, writing, speaking, listening, and viewing—in a way that I have frequently talked about but often been unable to accomplish. Less verbal students whose learning styles lean more to the kinesthetic or the visual are considerably more successful with *Of Mice and Men* than these kinds of students were before I discovered *Something Permanent*. Complementing the novel with a different kind of text, and encouraging response to both books in less traditional ways, has invited those who were silent before to join the classroom conversation. What could be a more convincing reason to try a new approach and use adolescent literature to complement the classic *Of Mice and Men*?

## References

Agee, J. & Evans, W. (1973). *Let us now praise famous men.* Boston: Houghton Mifflin.

Allen, J. (1995). *It's never too late: Leading adolescents to lifelong literacy.* Portsmouth, NH: Heinemann.

Carroll, P. S. (1993). *Their eyes were watching God* and *Roll of thunder, hear my cry.* Voices of African-American Southern women. In J. F. Kaywell's (Ed.), *Adolescent literature as a complement to the classics.* Volume One. Norwood, MA: Christopher-Gordon Publishers, Inc., pp. 163–183.

Carter, F. (1986). *The education of Little Tree.* Albuquerque, NM: University of New Mexico Press.

Cormier, R. (1980). *8 plus 1.* New York: Pantheon.

Ericson, B. O. (1993). Introducing *To kill a mockingbird* with collaborative group reading of related young adult novels. In J. F. Kaywell's (Ed.), *Adolescent literature as a complement to the classics*. Volume One. Norwood, MA: Christopher-Gordon Publishers, Inc., pp. 1–12.

Flagg, F. (1988). *Fried green tomatoes at the Whistle Stop Cafe*. New York: McGraw-Hill.

Hunt, I. (1987). *No promises in the wind*. New York: Berkley Publishing Group.

Lee, H. (1960). *To kill a mockingbird*. New York: Warner Books.

Moffett, J. & Wagner, B.J. (1992). *Student-centered language arts, K–12*. Fourth edition. Portsmouth, NH: Boynton Cook.

Peck, R. N. (1972). *A day no pigs would die*. New York: Alfred A. Knopf.

Rylant, C. & Evans, W. (1994). *Something permanent*. San Diego: Harcourt Brace.

Steinbeck, J. (1939). *The grapes of wrath*. New York: Penguin.

Steinbeck, J. (1970). *Of mice and men*. New York: Bantam.

Taylor, M. (1981). *Let the circle be unbroken*. New York: Bantam.

Taylor, M. (1976). *Roll of thunder, hear my cry!* New York: Puffin.

Wilhelm, J. (1996). *"You gotta be the book": Teaching engaged and reflective reading with adolescents*. New York: Teachers College Press.

## Films Cited (Each Available on Home Video)

Avnet, J. & Kerner, J. (Producers). (1991). *Fried green tomatoes*. Universal City, CA: MCA Universal.

Smith, R. & Sinise, G. (Producers). (1992). *Of mice and men*. Culver City, CA: Metro-Goldwyn-Mayer.

# Enlivening Canonical Narrative Poetry with Young Adult Literature

*Pamela Sissi Carroll*

## Introduction

When I began looking through popular literature textbooks for narrative poems offered for readers at grade levels 6–12, I quickly realized three things. My first realization was that the writing of narrative poems seems to be part of the literary past. Many of the narrative poems I found were written by poets who were born in the 1800s, and few written after 1950 are published in currently popular literature texts. My second realization was that the narrative poems included in textbooks are, by an overwhelming majority, written by male authors, most of whom are white. My third realization, though, was that memory had served me correctly: Few reading experiences are more fun than settling into a narrative poem to participate in the speaker's story.

Following is a sampling of the poems and poets that are regularly included in literature textbooks. Introducing each poem title is an indication of the grade level textbook in which it is frequently included.

**6th Grade**  "The Cremation of Sam McGee" by Robert Service
"The Walrus and the Carpenter" by Lewis Carroll

**7th Grade**  "The Highwayman" by Alfred Noyes
"The Charge of the Light Brigade" by Alfred, Lord Tennyson

**8th Grade**  "Paul Revere's Ride" by Henry Wadsworth Longfellow
"The Raven" by Edgar Allan Poe

**9th Grade**  "Fifteen" by William Stafford
"Out, Out —" by Robert Frost

**10th Grade** "The Road Not Taken" by Robert Frost
"Ex-Basketball Player" by John Updike

**11th Grade** "The Death of the Hired Man" by Robert Frost
"The Love Song of J. Alfred Prufrock" by T.S. Eliot

**12th Grade** translated excerpts from the epic poem *Beowulf* by author unknown
translated excerpts from *The Canterbury Tales* by Geoffrey Chaucer

Regardless of the publishers' determinations of reading levels and grade appropriateness, there is no reason to restrict the teaching of the poems to the grade levels that correspond with textbook designations. Experienced teachers of middle and high school English know that the student's independent or instructional reading achievement level should be a consideration, particularly when a young reader selects a sophisticated text. These reading levels must be considered in light of the reader's interest in approaching a particular work. A young student who believes that the reading of "The Raven" will be entertaining and interesting, perhaps because of previous literary experiences with Gothic literature, is likely to be less confounded or frustrated by Poe's challenging use of language than will be the older student who is forced to read the poem because it appears in her or his textbook and in the teacher's lesson plan book. And the reverse also seems to be true when one is referring to narrative poetry and, within limits, to young adult (YA) literature.

Poems and novels that are often taught to younger readers hold appeal, for a different set of reasons, to older, more sophisticated students. While young readers enjoy narrative texts because they delight in the stories within them, older readers approach narratives—poems and novels—because they are interested in making personal connections with the story or because they are interested in considering the poem or novel as a work of art. High school seniors, for example, will read and respond to "The Cremation of Sam McGee" differently than will 6th graders, particularly if the seniors have had previous experience with the poem. The quality of the seniors' reading experience will depend not on a pre-determined reading level but on the readers' interest in the poem and their willingness to engage in the reading event. As teacher-readers, we can easily test this theory by asking ourselves, "As an adult, have I ever enjoyed— really enjoyed—reading a YA book?" If we answer, "Yes," then we understand the appeal of universal themes and recognizable circumstances to readers of all ages. The stages of literary appreciation, as determined by Margaret Early's research on reading development, are clearly outlined by Nilsen and Donelson in *Literature for Today's Young Adults* (pp. 48–58).

Pairing narrative poems with contemporary YA literature, especially YA literature written by and about people of varied cultures and both genders, offers teachers a means for bringing the narrative poems of the secondary school canon to life. Such pairings have the potential for appeal to a wide range of readers—the kind of range we find in today's middle and high schools.

# Themes and Story Lines in Canonical Narrative Poems and Contemporary Young Adult Literature

Why would a teacher want to pair canonical narrative poetry with YA literature? A primary reason is that both genres offer teachers vehicles through which readers' responses to literature can be expressed, reflected on, discussed, defended, crystallized, and occasionally revised. The stories that are at the center of narrative poems, like the stories in well-written YA literature, have the potential to attract and hold the attention of adolescent readers. Following are a few examples of possible pairings that center around common themes or issues.

## Historical Events

Alfred, Lord Tennyson's "The Charge of the Light Brigade" and Henry Wadsworth Longfellow's "Paul Revere's Ride" present compelling accounts of historical events; so do Melba Patillo Beals's *Warriors Don't Cry* (336 pp.), a non-fiction account of her participation as an African-American student in the 1957 integration of Central High School in Little Rock, Arkansas, and Walter Dean Myers's riveting *Fallen Angels* (320 pp.), a novel about 17-year-old Richie's escape from Harlem into a more terrible world as a soldier in the Vietnam War.

## The Fantastic and Strange

Lewis Carroll's "The Walrus and the Carpenter" and Edgar Allan Poe's "The Raven" offer escape from the real world into an anthropomorphized one that is both fantastic and strange. Jane Yolen's *The Dragon's Boy* (128 pp.) tells the story of Artos's meeting with a magical dragon who offers friendship and gold, jewels, or wisdom; Laurence Yep's multiple prize-winning *The Rainbow People* (208 pp.) introduces adolescent readers to the mystery and majesty of Chinese culture through 20 short stories. Jon Scieszka's hilarious *Your Mother Was a Neanderthal* (80 pp.) will have students rolling with laughter as they follow the "Time Warp Trio" into the Stone Age and back again.

## Tragic News

Robert Frost's "The Death of the Hired Man" and Alfred Noyes's "The Highwayman" touch a reader's conscience with tragic or violent tales that resemble the news stories one might read or hear about daily. The stories in these poems are similar to the stories in Hadley Irwin's *So Long at the Fair* (160 pp.), which deal with what happens when high school senior Joel's best friend and love, Ashley, commits suicide; and Paul Zindel's *A Begonia for Miss Applebaum* (176 pp.), about a pair of friends who face the death by cancer of their favorite and eccentric teacher. Jacqueline Woodson's Coretta Scott King Award-winning poetic novel, *I Hadn't Meant to Tell You This* (155 pp.) could also be a news story today. Woodson takes a tender look at the silent suffering Lena endures at the hands of her abusive father and her attempts to make herself—a white girl in a black school—invisible. Things change when she befriends Marie, another girl who has lost her mother.

## Individuality Versus Conformity

William Stafford's "Fifteen" and T.S. Eliot's "The Love Song of J. Alfred Prufrock" offer readers a means of affirming their individual humanity by recognizing that others have desires and feelings like their own. Caroline Cooney's *The Party's Over* (192 pp.) explores Hallie's life once her friends leave to attend college and she is no longer the center of attention. Chris Lynch's *Shadow Boxer* (224 pp.) deals with George's struggle to protect his younger brother, Monty, from the life of a boxer—a career that claimed their father's life. Both novels lead readers to consider the collision or the intersection of personal and universal questions. Haitian-born Joanne Hyppolite's *Seth and Samona* (121 pp.) introduces young adolescent readers to the world of two unusual friends. Seth is Haitian, and Samona, who is African American, is part of a family that "just acts weird 'cause they want to" (p. 6). Their adventures and loyalty to each other demonstrate the value of friendship, family, and heritage. Francesca Lia Block's quirky novella *Weetzie Bat* (88 pp.), like its popular sequels, presents the more sophisticated adolescent reader with an unusually free-spirited group of teens who, despite their anti-establishment lifestyles and irreverent perspectives, have concerns about self-identity and purpose in life. Maria Hinojosa's *Crews* is a shocking and, in parts, poignant account of gang life, as told to the writer by members of youth gangs in New York City.

In the most general sense, the novels and the poems paired above can be used to enhance each other during the study of thematic units. In some cases, students might read and study the YA novel first in order to gain insight into the kind of story they will read in the parallel poems. In other cases, students might read the poems first as an introduction to kind of the story they will follow in the YA novel. The potential benefit of these pairings, however, certainly exceeds the general suggestions outlined above.

## Literary Elements, Narrative Poems, and Young Adult Books

In addition to exploring themes, narrative poetry and YA literature can also be used in tandem to teach, reinforce, and enhance students' understanding of literary elements such as plot, character, setting, point of view, tone and style. Readers who consider ways that these separate elements are interwoven into a literary piece will be more fully engaged in the literary experience than will readers whose response to a work of literature relies solely on their initial, overall impression of the piece.

As teachers, many of us believe in the importance of devoting instructional attention and time to literary elements. In some literature classes, the elements serve as curricular underpinnings. Sometimes, though, as well-meaning teachers and as readers who are more experienced than our students, we treat knowledge of the literary elements as an end in itself. We sometimes assume that a student who can define or, better yet, identify the parts of a "plot" or the perspective of "point of view" will enjoy reading a novel more than a student who cannot. Unfortunately, if we consider our jobs completed when students demonstrate that they have memorized the definitions of poetic terms and can properly scan lines, we do little to help them learn to enjoy engaging in reading events. We need to go further. We need to help students learn how and why, as readers, the attention they give to specific literary elements can inform, shape, and enhance their reading experiences. When they are able to recognize, then synthesize, the interplay of the literary elements while they read—to make sense of whatever it is that they read—for themselves, students are more likely to have satisfying experiences with literature. And they are more likely to become readers for life than if they are reading merely to answer someone else's questions about texts.

In the section below, I will suggest pairings of often-anthologized narrative poems and YA books in ways that take advantage of the strong presence of one of the specific literary elements in each. Attention is divided between each of five literary elements: plot, characterization, setting, point of view, and tone and style. For each literary element, narrative poems and YA books that clearly manifest the element are listed. The YA books are annotated briefly and an indication of the target audience (MS for middle grades and HS for high school) is listed. Finally, for each literary element, suggestions for teaching are offered. The suggestions share one common feature: Each incorporates the pairing of one of the canonical, narrative poems and one of the YA books listed under the particular literary element.

## Literary Works that Focus on Plot

Narrative poems that can be used to study plot include "The Highwayman" by Alfred Noyes; "The Charge of the Light Brigade" by Alfred, Lord Tennyson; and excerpts from *Beowulf*. Annotations of recommended YA titles follow.

### *Wizard's Hall* by Jane Yolen (144 pp.)

Thornmallow, usually known as Henry, becomes an unlikely hero. Going against his wishes, he goes to Wizard Hall and learns to be a wizard. (MS)

### *A Voice in the Wind* by Kathryn Lasky (224 pp.)

The telepathic Starbuck twins, Liberty and her brother July, befriend a Native American and discover an ancient tragedy during an adventure in New Mexico. (MS)

### *Indio* by Sherry Garland (292 pp.)

In this work of historical fiction, 14-year-old Ipa Tah Chi's family and village, in what is now Mexico and the southwest United States, are ruined by Spaniard conquistadors during the 1500s. The novel presents the demise of the native Indio and the rise of the Mexican. (HS)

### *April and the Dragon Lady* by Lensey Namioka (214 pp.)

April, a high school junior, is torn between the pressures of finding her niche as a normal American teen among peers and the expectations her traditional Chinese grandmother has for her and for others in the family. April eventually realizes that her grandmother is a cunning and manipulative woman who insists on seeing the world from one perspective. (MS/HS)

## Ideas for Teaching Plot

"The Highwayman," a narrative poem about two lovers in 18th-century England, has been popular among readers since the early 20th century. *April and the Dragon Lady* is a YA novel which features a modern teen protagonist who has problems making choices about friends, family, and her future. April's problems are similar to ones most adolescents face. These texts seem, on their surfaces, to have little in common. Yet the author of each creates tensions that give the texts momentum, tensions that encourage the reader to become involved in the text. For this reason, the two can be paired for a focus on plot. Following are suggestions for a sequence of lessons, using these two texts as examples.

The teacher reads "The Highwayman" aloud (and dramatically) while students follow along with their printed versions of the poem. Ask students to highlight any words, phrases, or lines that indicate that a person is involved in some kind of action in the story of the poem. For instance, they might highlight, "And the highwayman came riding" in line four, and "And he rode with a jeweled twinkle" in line ten.

From the highlighted passages, students work individually or in small groups to list the events of the "story" within the poem. The lists will include approximately 35 points of action. The exact number may slightly vary because of individual interpretations of which passages denote action and which are merely descriptive. Regardless of the final number derived by any group, the group's conversations are likely to be productive as each group works toward consensus.

While still in small groups, students use their list of events to identify the points that they would feature if they were developing a television show using the story of this poem. At this point, it may be helpful for students to narrow down the number of important features to a manageable number, perhaps limited to ten or less.

Groups use the condensed list as a reference during the creation of a modified script or, for more graphically-inclined and visually-stimulated students, a storyboard. Either of these can be developed in order to present the poem as a television show (See Figure 4.1).

---

### Figure 4.1

### Preparing A Television Script

*Directions to prepare the script:*

Divide several sheets of legal-sized paper in half, lengthwise. On the left side of the paper, write lines of dialogue and narrative comments from the poem. On the right side of the paper, parallel to the copied words, write stage directions.

*Directions to prepare the storyboard:*

Select important points of action from the poem. Add corresponding dialogue or narrative comments, using stick figures to draw what the scene should roughly look like when it is staged or filmed.

---

To "test" the quality of the script or storyboard, the group can give it to peers from another class, one in which "The Highwayman" has not been studied. If those peers can follow the script to act out the important scenes of "The Highwayman, " the group can consider itself a successful team of script writers. Many students enjoy this type of assessment "test" and are willing to videotape it. The videotapes enable students to participate in self-evaluations, as well as to enjoy the fact that they rewrote a poem into a "made-for-television" version.

This set of activities—highlighting the main points of action, listing those highlights, condensing the list into essential features, then using those features to create a version of the literary work in a different genre and a different medium—can also be used to enhance the reading of *April and the Dragon Lady* and focus on the novel's strong plot and sub-plots. In order to sustain a focus on plot while they read and enjoy the novel, students should list the main events of each section in a reading response journal. Students will have to be especially careful to denote actions that involve more than one character simultaneously. For example, they will have to find ways to explain what the grandmother was doing during the time that her family thought that she had gotten lost while they were having a picnic on the mountain.

When they complete their lists of action points in *April and the Dragon Lady*, students work in groups to identify the essential plot features. Students then create and present an original script or a storyboard for the novel. It is important for students to consider the implications of varied interpretations of texts that emerge through the different scripts and storyboards.

As an alternative assignment, especially if time is restricted, the teacher might assign a different part of the plot to each small group of students. When each group has developed a script or storyboard for its section of the plot, groups can dramatize and, if possible, videotape their particular section of the novel. Each student must be accountable for a specific job in producing a video. Insist that at least one student serve as a technical advisor to the teacher. This student keeps the teacher abreast of what students are doing, both in class and outside of class time, regarding their literature-related projects.

## Literary Works that Focus on Characterization

Narrative poems that can be used to study characterization include "The Death of the Hired Man" by Robert Frost, "Ex-Basketball Player" by John Updike, and "Fifteen" by William Stafford. Annotations of recommended YA titles follow.

### *I Hadn't Meant to Tell You This* by Jacqueline Woodson (115 pp.)

Poor, white, and motherless, 12-year-old Lena finds herself in a school for black girls from the rich side of town. Marie defies her popular crowd by befriending Lena, and Lena pours out truths about her sexually abusive father to Marie. (MS)

### *Keeping Christina* by Sue Ellen Bridgers (288 pp.).

Hardly anyone recognizes the fact that Christina, whom Annie has befriended, is a chronic liar. Annie struggles with what she knows but does not want to believe: Christina is using Annie's family for her own twisted purposes, and only Annie, with the help of her mother, can rid the family of Christina's negative presence. (MS/HS)

### *Clover* by Dori Sanders (192 pp.)

Clover is a 10-year-old black girl living in rural South Carolina. Her father dies the day he marries a white woman, a person whom Clover does not know and whose actions and attitudes she cannot understand. Despite Clover's misgivings and the family's skepticism, she and her stepmother develop mutual respect and, finally, a close bond. (MS)

### *Maniac Magee* by Jerry Spinelli (240 pp.)

Jeffrey Lionel Magee, soon known as "Maniac," becomes legendary around his new town. Maniac is a sports hero who never really joins a team. He is different because he is not afraid of anything, even the racial tension that, until he fights it, has kept kids in Two Mills divided by color for years. Finally, Maniac finds a place where he is wanted, a place where he is at home. (MS/HS)

## Ideas for Teaching Characterization

Although many pairings are possible and may lend themselves to the activity set described below, I will pair "Ex-Basketball Player" with *I Hadn't Meant to Tell You This* as an example of an activity that focuses on characterization.

Give students a copy of "Ex-Basketball Player" on which they can write and draw. First, read the poem aloud and then have students read it silently. After asking for their initial responses to the poem, ask students to zero in on the descriptions of Flick Webb. Have students, either in small groups or in pairs, circle the clues or details that describe Flick's character. Next, ask them to generate a list of questions that they might have about Flick. Use this list to guide the discussion regarding the effectiveness of Updike's characterization of Flick. For some classes, the teacher may need to model this part of the discussion by giving students examples of questions such as these: What does Flick look like? What is his life like today? What was his life like in the past? What do his hands tell us about him? Following the discussion, ask students to select one of the following options.

1. Imagine that you are short story writer who has decided to use Flick as the central character in a short story about a former athlete in your region. Build a story around the details that Updike has provided.

2. Imagine that you are a sports writer for your local newspaper and that Flick graduated from your high school. You have decided to do a feature on him as a part of a "Where Are They Now?" series. Write a note to your editor in which you explain the following: Where you will go to find more information on Flick, with whom you will talk and what kinds of questions you will ask, and what you expect to learn about Flick.

3. Imagine that you are Flick Webb and that you are speaking to a room filled with elementary school students. Some of these students have heard of you because they are the children of your former high school basketball teammates. Using the details that Updike provides as well as the ones he hints at in the poem, write your responses to the children's honest and pointed questions about your life. Responses may be written in the form of an interview, with the child's question followed by your response.

As an extra touch, students may want to include newspaper and magazine photographs that illustrate their short stories, feature articles, or interviews.

Following this sequence of activities that deal with characterization in the poem, students will be better prepared to consider characterization in the short novel *I Hadn't Meant to Tell You This*. Because this novel is told from a first person point of view, readers will need to be reminded that the pictures they develop of the characters are limited to the perspective of the narrator, Marie, who is also one of the central characters of the novel. Again, ask students to identify passages that help them get a sense of Lena's and Marie's characters: What does each girl looks like? How do they act? What do their actions say about them?

This novel lends itself well to having pairs of students work together as they focus on finding three types of characterization clues: passages in which physical descriptions are given, passages in which actions provide clues about personality, and passages in which other characters discuss either Marie or Lena. One student in each pair identifies passages that present information about Marie, while the other student can look for the same three types of clues about Lena.

After they have collected clues, students continue working in pairs to create a poem modeled loosely on Updike's "Ex-Basketball Player." The poem should present either Marie or Lena in a particular physical setting representing both then and now. Have students incorporate specific details from the novel and, drawing on what they understand about the characters as adolescents, imagine what each will be like as an adult. The primary challenge is for students to develop an image of either Marie or Lena as a young woman which is consistent with the characterization presented in the novel.

This pairing of poem and novel to improve the study of characterization can be enhanced by having the class watch *Hoop Dreams,* a 1995 documentary that chronicles the lives of two promising basketball players. This PG-13 movie, which has won popular and critical acclaim, presents a troubling record of both boys' struggles with academic, athletic, adult, and social pressures. After viewing the film, have students discuss what it reveals about the two stars and their support groups of family, coaches, teachers, and friends. By having students discuss the features of the stars' lives that the makers of the documentary chose to ignore, students' understanding of the choices that writers and others make when they create or report on characters may be improved. This activity may also help them consider the different choices Marie and Lena make, and the impact of each girl's environment on her choices.

## Literary Works that Focus on Setting

Narrative poems that can be used to study setting include "The Cremation of Sam McGee" by Robert Service, "Paul Revere's Ride" by Henry Wadsworth Longfellow, and "The Road Not Taken" by Robert Frost. Annotations of recommended YA titles follow.

### *The Big Wander* by Will Hobbs (181 pp.)

Fourteen-year-old Clay and his big brother, Mike, set out on an adventure through the Southwest to find their uncle, an ex-rodeo star of mythic proportions. Mike quickly abandons the search and returns home, leaving Clay to fend for himself. Clay heads into Monument Valley where he finds his uncle, becomes involved in a scheme to save wild horses from unscrupulous men, and meets Sarah, who shares his enthusiasm for the natural world. (MS)

### *Canyons* by Gary Paulsen (184 pp.)

Brennen, a 15-year-old, discovers a skull with a bullet hole in it. The skull eventually connects him to the spirit of Coyote Runs, a young Apache who was training to become a warrior when he was killed a century ago by soldiers. Brennen's task is to return the skull to its sacred burial place, beyond the canyons to the desert north of El Paso, and to evade those who would keep him from completing his mission. Paulsen uses alternating narrators, Coyote Runs' voice from the 1800s and Brennen's from the present, to deliver an adventure story in which geography and topography are treated almost as if each is a character. (MS/HS)

### *White Lilacs* by Carolyn Meyer (237 pp.)

Rosa Lee, a young black girl, must confront the prejudices that drive the whites of her town to force her black community to relocate so that a park can be built on their land. The temporal as well as the geographic setting of this book make it ideal for study in social studies as well as in language arts classes. The novel is based on an actual historical event that occurred in the South in 1921. (MS/HS)

### *Your Mother Was a Neanderthal* by Jon Scieszka (80 pp.)

Sam, Fred, and Joe, better known as the Time Warp Trio, leave their daily grind of math class, including their normal tricks with drinking straws, to take a trip back to prehistoric time. The trio battle nudity, dinosaurs, and their own growing list of time-travel mistakes. (MS)

## Ideas for Teaching Setting

Occasionally, a story is propelled not by its characters or even its themes but by its setting. Such is the case with "The Cremation of Sam McGee," a popular narrative about a man from Tennessee who freezes to death while searching for gold in the Yukon Territory and whose companion promises to cremate him so that he will not spend eternity encased in ice. Students who have never experienced frigid climates often cannot comprehend the bone-chilling cold of the Yukon. These students may have a difficult time making sense of this narrative poem, which is driven by its icy setting.

An instructional focus on its geographic setting may provide students with a basis for understanding the poem. Teachers can create a "cold air blitz" through the use of films and videos, both fiction and non-fiction, that feature icy settings. Excerpts from the lighthearted *Cool Runnings*—a PG movie about a Jamaican bobsled team—or the more serious *Alive*—an R-rated movie based on the true story of a rugby team that survives a plane crash in the Andes Mountains—may help to provide such an atmosphere.

Teachers can also use excerpts from YA novels that use icy settings. Two contemporary literary works that are especially appropriate are Gary Paulsen's novel *Hatchet* (195 pp.)—about Brian's struggle as the lone survivor of a plane crash in the Canadian wilderness—and John McPhee's non-fiction essay "Survival in the Forty-Ninth" (5 pp.)—the account of how Leon Crane survived a plane crash in the Yukon, lived for about two and one-half months in an abandoned trapper's cabin, then found his way to help. Each of these literary works mirrors both the geographic and the temporal setting of "The Cremation of Sam McGee."

These experiences, enhanced if possible by a guest speaker who has spent time in the northern wilderness, will help prepare students to make sense of the narrative poem. A more developed example on how to focus on setting by pairing "The Cremation of Sam McGee" with *The Big Wander* follows.

*The Big Wander* also poses problems of comprehension if students are unfamiliar with Monument Valley, the setting around which Hobbs develops this novel. Before assigning the reading of this novel or any other work that depends heavily on a reader's ability to visualize a setting, the teacher might develop a "setting blitz" similar to the one described above as a prereading activity. With *The Big Wander,* for example, the teacher should select films and videos that feature the "four corners" region where Arizona, New Mexico, Colorado, and Utah are joined. Monument Valley, which is the setting for many Western television shows, is prominent in the novel, as are the Colorado River and its tributary, the San Juan River. Although it was actually filmed in British Columbia, the popular PG-13 movie *The River Wild,* starring Meryl Streep, Kevin Bacon, and David Strathairn, includes remarkable footage of a dangerous raft trip down a wild river. By showing carefully-selected excerpts from *The River Wild,* students can see the terrible power of the rivers that run through mountain regions.

Printed texts about the Monument Valley area could easily be obtained through the National Parks Service World Wide Web site or through a myriad of other travel-oriented sites. Sending letters requesting information may seem old-fashioned, but it is usually quite effective and rewarding for students if students do this early in the unit. Approximately two months before the reading of the novel, students could write to some of the National Parks in the four corners area requesting maps and brochures about flora, fauna, topography, and so on. Following are a few of the National Parks located in canyons and high places or plateaus in the area, and addresses to which inquiries by students and teachers may be sent.

Paria Canyon Primitive Area (Utah-Arizona)
    State Director, U.S. Bureau of Land Management,
    Federal Building, Phoenix, Arizona, 85025

Grand Gulch Primitive Area (Utah)
    District Manager, Bureau of Land Management,
    284 South First West, Box 1327, Monticello, Utah 48535

Monument Valley Tribal Park (Arizona)
    Chairman, Navajo Tribal Parks Commission,
    Window Rock, Arizona, 86515

Grand Canyon National Park (Arizona)
    Superintendent, Grand Canyon National Park,
    Grand Canyon, Arizona, 80623

Canyonlands National Park (Utah)
    Superintendent, Canyonlands National Park,
    446 South Main Street, Moab, Utah, 84532

Zion National Park (Utah),
    Superintendent, Zion National Park,
    Springdale, Utah, 84767

Capitol Reef National Park (Utah)
    Superintendent, Capitol Reef National Park,
    Torrey, Utah, 84775

Commercial bookstores and public libraries are also replete with books written for campers, hikers, and mountaineers about areas such as these.

An understanding of the geographical setting of *The Big Wander* will help students comprehend the magnitude of Clay's adventure. While reading, have students keep track of Clay's progress as he moves across the area. An over-sized map, similar to the map in the novel, can be created by the students or the teacher. Student volunteers can assume responsibility for marking Clay's progress at the end of each day of in-class or assigned homework reading, at the end of each chapter, or at other intervals as determined by readers and the teacher. Each point that denotes a place Clay visits should be numbered on the over-sized map. Encourage students to develop a legend that explains what happens to Clay at each numbered location and how he feels while there. This kind of plot and setting map will help students see the relationships of plot, setting, and characterization within this novel.

As a culminating activity to reinforce the series of lessons that focus on setting, students can be asked to imagine Clay not in the Southwest, but traveling through the

Yukon territory. What different kinds of obstacles would Clay face if he were wandering in the Yukon Territory? What would be his most important tools for survival? Ask students to imagine also that the temporal setting of *The Big Wander* shifts to the late 1800s and the Gold Rush. What would Clay's adventure entail if he found himself in a mining camp along the Klondike River? Students might want to write diary entries, letters home, short stories, or news articles all from Clay's perspective in these altered geographic and temporal settings.

## Literary Works that Focus on Point of View

Narrative poems that can be used to study point of view include excerpts from *The Canterbury Tales* by Geoffrey Chaucer, "The Death of the Hired Man" by Robert Frost, and "The Love Song of J. Alfred Prufrock" by T. S. Eliot. Annotations of recommended YA titles follow.

### *Shadow Boxer* by Chris Lynch (224 pp.)

George sees that his little brother, Monty, is becoming enchanted with the idea of being a boxer, but George knows an ugly truth. Boxing ruined, and finally killed, their father. George, as the man of the house, struggles to have a stronger influence over Monty than does the lure of the sport. (MS)

### *Crews* by Maria Hinojosa (192 pp.)

The author records interviews with members of youth gangs in New York City. The book's power is in its unadorned presentation of reality from the gang members' perspectives. (MS/HS)

### *Make Lemonade* by Virginia Euwer Wolff (208 pp.)

Using stream-of-consciousness narration that looks like free verse poetry, 14-year-old La Vaughn tells the story that begins when she accepts a job babysitting for the two fatherless children of 17-year-old Jolly, who is needy in many ways. (MS/HS)

### *Orfe* by Cynthia Voigt (120 pp.)

In this *Publishers' Weekly* Best Book of 1992, some call Orfe a "creature from outer space" (p. 6). Regardless, Enny befriends her and eventually becomes the manager of her attempt at a career as a singer-songwriter, an attempt that takes Orfe into a world of drugs and disappointments. Enny knows Orfe well enough to read the language of her eyes and knows when Orfe needs a friend. (HS)

### *Freedom's Children* by Ellen Levine (204 pp.)

This is a non-fiction collection of stories of young African Americans who were civil rights activists in the 1950s and 1960s. These adolescents tell of their struggle for desegregation and their basic human rights. (MS/HS)

*Freak the Mighty* by **Rodman Philbrick (176 pp.)**

This is a delightful and poignant book about Max, a kid whose body seems to never stop growing but whose intelligence is slow in developing, and Kevin, a kid whose body never grows but whose brain cannot be stopped. This odd pair, who together become "Freak the Mighty," are inseparable friends; they share in funny and dangerous adventures. In time, Kevin's physical condition grows critical and finally his body quits. He leaves Max, and others whose lives he touches, a legacy of strength, humor, and confidence. (MS/HS)

## Ideas for Teaching Point of View

Pairing "The Love Song of J. Alfred Prufrock" with *Freak the Mighty* is particularly effective for teaching point of view. Because of the difficulty of Eliot's poem, I recommend that the novel be read first. The novel establishes an entree through which students can consider the point of view in Eliot's poem. Many high school readers will be intrigued with Rodman Philbrick's portrayal of the odd pair who become friends. Max, the child of a convicted wife-murderer, is all brawn with little intelligence, whereas Kevin, whose external body does not grow quickly enough to allow for the expansion of his internal organs, uses his considerable intelligence to compensate for his disability. Either of the following activities should lay a foundation that will help students read and make some sense of "The Love Song of J. Alfred Prufrock."

### Activity #1

Small groups of students might stage, within each group, a "press conference" in which a class member poses as author Rodman Philbrick to answer questions from the press corps. The student press corps will ask questions that help them explore the issue of why Philbrick made the decision to have Max, not the ever-articulate Kevin, tell the friends' story. Each reporter will take notes, then write his or her own news story explaining the choice. The students who pose as Philbrick will write their own "diary entries" about what they realized about their use of point of view as a result of the press conference. If time allows, each group may select reporters to develop a newspaper feature, a radio broadcast, or a television news spot to showcase its findings.

### Activity #2

In small groups, students select one particular incident in *Freak the Mighty* and rewrite it from Kevin's perspective. After the rewriting is complete, have students share what they wrote and discuss the changes in the narrative that occur when the narrative voice is shifted. The class should address the effects of those changes on the quality of the literary experience that readers may have with this novel and others.

Active engagement in either of these simple activities has the potential to prepare students to approach "The Love Song of J. Alfred Prufrock" with an awareness of the impact of the speaker's perspective—his point of view in interpreting the setting, plot, and characters—on the "story" of the poem. A press conference similar to the one held for the author of *Freak the Mighty* might be held for T.S. Eliot. This second press conference allows student reporters the opportunity to ask questions about Eliot's perspective on Prufrock's story as well as to clarify for themselves parts of the story they don't understand. It is only when they learn to ask questions for themselves that students will grow as independent readers of literature.

Viewing excerpts from the R-rated movie *The Shawshank Redemption*, starring Tim Robbins and Morgan Freeman, might also promote awareness and understanding of point of view. In this movie, Freeman plays Red, a convicted murderer serving a life sentence in Shawshank prison. Robbins plays Andy, a presumedly innocent man convicted of murdering his wife. Red tells the story of Andy's 20 years in Shawshank and his escape from imprisonment to hope. The narrative point of view allows viewers an insider's understanding of the silent, innocent prisoner, and is likely to prompt much discussion about the effectiveness and the reliability of a first-person narrator who is also part of the story. This attention to point of view has the potential to increase students' awareness of the importance of the literary choices authors make.

## Literary Works that Focus on Tone and Style

Narrative poems that can be used to study tone and style include "The Walrus and the Carpenter" by Lewis Carroll, "Out, Out—" by Robert Frost, and "The Raven" by Edgar Allan Poe. Annotations of recommended YA titles follow.

### *Weetzie Bat* by Francesca Lia Block (88 pp.)

Weetzie not only looks odd, she also uses words in weird ways. She calls her boyfriend "My Secret Agent Lover Man" and names her Slinky Dog's puppies Pee Wee, Wee Wee, Teenine Wee, Tiki Wee, and Tee Pee. Weetzie, like her gay best friend, dances to the beat of a different saxophonist. Teens enjoy following Weetzie through her Bohemian days and nights. While reading, they become one of the group of her strange assortment of friends. (HS)

### *Sisters/Hermanas* by Gary Paulsen (144 pp.)

This novella, which takes no longer to read than a short story, revolves around the characters of Traci and Rosa. Beautiful Traci realizes that, despite her mother's supportive presence and plenty of money, she is "just the same" as Rosa, an illegal immigrant who must sell her body on Texas streets to survive and to send money home to her mother. The two protagonists' stories are told in alternating chapters and are joined in the final incident. (MS/HS)

### *Toning the Sweep* by Angela Johnson (103 pp.)

Emily and her mother go to bring Ola, Emily's sick grandmother, back to their home in Ohio. Ola is no usual grandmother. During her life, she has sent Emily pamphlets on world hunger, worn her hair in dreadlocks, hitchhiked across the country, and settled in the desert near Los Angeles. Ola teaches her daughter and granddaughter the value of holding onto some of their African-American traditions as well as learning to let go of some family things. This very short novel, winner of the 1994 Coretta Scott

King Award, a *School Library Journal* Best Book of 1993, and a 1993 *Booklist* Editor's Choice, reads almost like a long first-person narrative poem.

### *Athletic Shorts: Six Short Stories* by Chris Crutcher (154 pp.).

In this collection of six short stories, each involving a character from one of Crutcher's novels, readers can identify with characters who are either like themselves or like their own high school friends. Some characters miscommunicate with parents, some are socially inept and feel like failures, and others suffer tragedies and feel pain that is exacerbated by confusion and anger. All seek justice, friendship, understanding, and laughter. Crutcher, a family psychologist, knows the issues concerning teens and shares them with his readers through realistic characters and in a style that is as direct and unadorned as teens' emotions. (HS)

## Ideas for Teaching Tone and Style

The narrative classic "The Raven" can be effectively paired with Gary Paulsen's *Sisters/Hermanas* to help students explore tone and style. Tone is defined as "the author's attitude toward his or her subject and readers" (Lukens & Cline, p. 200). An author's style is defined as "the manner in which writers express their ideas" (Brown & Stephens, p. 175). These two elements, which are the most abstract of the literary concepts discussed here, are combined into a single category because the two are so closely linked. The tone of any particular piece of literature determines, at least in part, the style the author chooses to use in that piece.

In *Sisters/Hermanas*, students are introduced to two adolescent girls by a third-person omniscient narrator. Readers uncover each girl's story in alternating chapters. Fourteen-year-old Rosa is Catholic, loves her mother who still lives in Mexico, dreams of becoming a fashion model, and is a prostitute. Traci, also 14, has been raised to believe that "nothing was ever bad, nothing was ever impossible, nothing was ever ugly, nothing was ever, truly, wrong" (p. 21).

Through the use of figurative language, contrasting settings, and a narrator's comments on each character's actions and thoughts, Paulsen is able to develop in his readers different kinds of feelings for each girl. Rosa deserves sympathy, yet she also garners respect because of her strength. Traci evokes disgust because of her selfishness. On the other hand, Traci also arouses admiration, because she is able to see hints of the truth that there is pain and poverty and hurt around her despite the protective barrier that her mother builds for her.

*Sisters/Hermanas* reads very quickly. It is a useful vehicle for exploring, as a whole class or in small groups, how Paulsen is able to make us think differently about each of these 14-year-old girls. Following are some suggestions for focusing attention on tone and style as they relate to Paulsen's novel.

1. Ask students to rewrite an episode of the novel using the style and tone of any other author they have recently read in class. For example, how might Edgar Allan Poe depict Rosa and Traci? If Emily Dickinson were Traci, what might she write

as an epigrammatic poem? What might a humorist like Dave Barry find to write about in the story of Rosa or Traci?

2. Ask students to compile lines from popular poems, songs, and the novel itself to write a "found poem" that would be meaningful for Rosa; ask them to do the same for Traci. Students could then compare and contrast their choices of lines, discussing in small groups what their choices say about their perceptions of each character and about the way that Paulsen presents Rosa, Traci, and their individual situations.

3. A simple activity that begins with students' initial reactions to *Sisters/Hermanas* requires them to write a journal entry or a "letter" that would be appropriate to send to each of the protagonists. Having students offer advice, encouragement, praise, or condemnation and then discuss why they chose the comments they did may help them think about how the author's tone and style affect them as readers.

4. The teacher might begin a discussion of tone and style with questions that lead students to consider how the characters are portrayed in relation to the novella's themes: Which girl do you feel yourself pulling for and why? Who has the best chances of a happy and fulfilling life? How does Paulsen move his readers to respond to each girl differently? Encourage students to create their own questions and suggest answers concerning the author's style and tone.

After an exploration of the means by which Paulsen shapes or directs readers' attentions and attitudes toward his subject, students should be prepared to approach Poe's "The Raven" with an understanding of the importance of tone and style in creating the disturbing essence of the narrative poem. The journal writing and small group discussion ideas suggested for study of *Sisters/Hermanas* are also appropriate for use in developing an awareness of Poe's tone and style, as is the activity in which students impose another author's tone and style on the story of "The Raven" to work toward effects different from those Poe creates.

# Conclusion

This discussion is not meant to suggest that the study of any poem and novel should be restricted to focus on one isolated literary element. For example, I would not recommend that a teacher pair "The Highwayman" and *April and the Dragon Lady* for a concentration on plot structure if all other literary elements and personal responses were ignored. I would not suggest that a teacher concentrate on characterization in the pairing of "Ex-Basketball Player" and *I Hadn't Meant to Tell You This*, or on setting in the pairing of "The Cremation of Sam McGee" with *The Big Wander*, if such concentrations force attention away from the reader's personal engagement with the themes of any of the texts. No particular literary focus, especially one pre-determined by the teacher, should prevent readers from following their natural curiosity and interest into examining the other literary, social, and cultural issues within texts.

Pairing narrative poems and YA literature through the activities discussed above can help enhance students' appreciation of and interest in both genres. It may also help students learn to look for and recognize thematic and literary similarities in different kinds of writing. These activities, however, merely suggest focal points for teachers to incorporate when they decide that attention to the development of particular themes or literary elements is necessary, desirable, or serves as a means to greater enjoyment of the story within the poem or novel. Enjoyment is, after all, the main reason for reading literature. The adolescents who are in our classes will eventually become adults who will choose to read or not in the future. Teachers can make literature attractive to them, entice them to engage in pleasurable reading when they are young, and reinforce their decisions to read as they grow older and other activities compete for their time and attention.

# References

Beals, M. P. (1995). *Warriors don't cry: A searing memoir of the battle to integrate Little Rock's Central High.* New York: Pocket Books.

Block, F. L. (1991). *Weetzie bat.* New York: Harper Keypoint.

Bridgers, S. E. (1993). *Keeping Christina.* New York: HarperCollins.

Carroll, L. (1994). The walrus and the carpenter. In A. N. Applebee, A. B. Bermudez, S. Hynds, J. Langer, J. Marshall, & D. E. Norton's (Senior Consultants), *Literature and language.* Gold Level, 6. Evanston, IL: McDougal, Littell, pp. 92–95.

Chaucer, G. (1994). *The Canterbury tales.* Translated by N. Coghill. In A. N. Applebee, A. B. Bermudez, J. Langer, & J. Marshall's (Senior Consultants), *Literature and language.* Purple Level, 12. Evanston, IL: McDougal, Littell, pp. 117–125.

Cooney, C. B. (1991). *The party's over.* New York: Scholastic.

Crutcher, C. (1991). *Athletic shorts: Six short stories.* New York: Greenwillow Books.

Eliot, T. S. (1994). The love song of J. Alfred Prufrock. In A. N. Applebee, A. B. Bermudez, J. Langer, & J. Marshall's (Senior Consultants), *Literature and language.* Yellow Level, 11. Evanston, IL: McDougal, Littell, pp. 506–510.

Frost, R. (1994). The death of the hired man. In A. N. Applebee, A. B. Bermudez, J. Langer, & J. Marshall's (Senior Consultants), *Literature and language.* Yellow Level, 11. Evanston, IL: McDougal, Littell, pp. 541–545.

Frost, R. (1989). Out, out—. In R. Anderson, J. M. Brinnin, J. Leggett, J. Burroway, & D. A. Leeming's (Consultants), *Elements of literature.* Third Course. Austin, TX: Holt Rinehart Winston, p. 328.

Frost, R. (1994). The road not taken. In A. N. Applebee, A. B. Bermudez, J. Langer, & J. Marshall's (Senior Consultants), *Literature and language.* Yellow Level, 11. Evanston, IL: McDougal, Littell, pp. 541–545.

Garland, S. (1995). *Indio.* San Diego: Harcourt Brace.

Hinojosa, M. (1995). *Crews.* San Diego: Harcourt Brace.

Hobbs, W. (1992). *The big wander.* New York: Atheneum.

Hyppolite, J. (1995). *Seth and Samona.* New York: Delacorte Press.

Irwin, H. (1990). *So long at the fair.* New York: Avon Flare.

Johnson, A. (1993). *Toning the sweep*. New York: Scholastic.

Lasky, K. (1993). *A voice in the wind*. San Diego: Harcourt Brace.

Levine, E. (1993). *Freedom's children*. New York: Avon Flare.

Longfellow, H. W. (1994). Paul Revere's ride. In A.N. Applebee, A.B. Bermudez, S. Hynds, J. Langer, J. Marshall, & D. E. Norton's (Senior Consultants), *Literature and language*. Green Level, 8. Evanston, IL: McDougal, Littell, pp. 92–96.

Lord Tennyson, A. (1994). The charge of the light brigade. In A. N. Applebee, A. B. Bermudez, S. Hynds, J. Langer, J. Marshall, & D. E. Norton's (Senior Consultants), *Literature and language*. Red Level, 7. Evanston, IL: McDougal, Littell, pp. 87–88.

Lynch, C. (1993). *Shadow boxer*. New York: HarperTrophy.

McPhee, J. (1994). Survival in the Forty-Ninth. In A. N. Applebee, A. B. Bermudez, J. Langer, & J. Marshall's (Senior Consultants), *Literature and language*. Blue Level, 10. Evaston, IL: McDougal, Littell, pp. 269–274.

Meyer, C. (1993). *White lilacs*. New York: Gulliver Books.

Myers, W. D. (1988). *Fallen angels*. New York: Scholastic.

Namioka, L. (1994). *April and the dragon lady*. New York: Browndeer Press.

Nilsen, A. P. & Donelson, K. L. (1994). *Literature for today's young adults*. 4th Edition. Glenview, IL: Scott, Foresman.

Noyes, A. (1994). The highwayman. In A.N. Applebee, A.B. Bermudez, S. Hynds, J. Langer, J. Marshall, & D. E. Norton's (Senior Consultants), *Literature and language*. Red Level, 7. Evanston, IL: McDougal, Littell, pp. 409–413.

Paulsen, G. (1990). *Canyons*. New York: Delacorte Press.

Paulsen, G. (1988). *Hatchet*. New York: Trumpet Club.

Paulsen, G. (1993). *Sisters/Hermanas*. San Diego: Harcourt Brace.

Philbrick, R. (1993). *Freak the mighty*. New York: Scholastic.

Poe, E. A. (1994). The raven. In A.N. Applebee, A. B. Bermudez, J. Langer, & J. Marshall's (Senior Consultants), *Literature and language*. Yellow Level, 11. Evanston, IL: McDougal, Littell, pp. 236–239.

Raffel, B. (Trans.). (1994). *Beowulf*. In A. N. Applebee, A. B. Bermudez, J. Langer, & J. Marshall's (Senior Consultants), *Literature and language*. Purple Level, 12. Evanston, IL: McDougal, Littell, pp. 22–30.

Sanders, D. (1990). *Clover*. New York: Fawcett Columbine.

Scieszka, J. (1993). *Your mother was a Neanderthal*. New York: Puffin Books.

Service, R. (1994). The cremation of Sam McGee. In A. N. Applebee, A. B. Bermudez, S. Hynds, J. Langer, J. Marshall, & D. E. Norton's (Senior Consultants), *Literature and language*. Gold Level, 6. Evanston, IL: McDougal, Littell, pp. 132–137.

Spinelli, J. (1990). *Maniac Magee*. Boston: Little Brown Company.

Stafford, W. (1989). Fifteen. In R. Anderson, J. M. Brinnin, J. Leggett, J. Burroway, & D.A. Leeming's (Consultants), *Elements of literature*. Third Course. Austin, TX: Holt Rinehart Winston, p. 281.

Updike, J. (1994). Ex-basketball player. In A. N. Applebee, A. B. Bermudez, J. Langer, & J. Marshall's (Senior Consultants), *Literature and language*. Blue Level, 10. Evanston, IL: McDougal, Littell, p. 328

Voigt, C. (1992). *Orfe*. New York: Atheneum.

Wolff, V. E. (1993). *Make lemonade*. New York: Scholastic.

Woodson, J. (1994). *I hadn't meant to tell you this*. New York: Bantam.

Yep, L. (1989). *The rainbow people*. New York: Harper & Row.

Yolen, J. (1990). *The dragon's boy*. New York: Harper & Row.

Yolen, J. (1991). *Wizard's hall*. San Diego: Harcourt Brace.

Zindel, P. (1990). *A begonia for Miss Applebaum*. New York: Bantam Starfire.

## Films Cited (Each Available on Home Video)

Hansen, C. (Producer). (1994). *The river wild*. Universal City, CA: MCA Universal.

Marvin, N. (Producer). (1994). *The Shawshank redemption*. Castle Rock Entertainment: Columbia Tristar Home Video.

Marx, F., James, S., & Gilbert, P. (Producers). (1995). *Hoop dreams*. Turner Home Entertainment: New Line Home Video.

Steel, D. (Producer). (1993). *Cool runnings*. Burbank, CA: Walt Disney Home Video.

Watts, R. & Kennedy, K. (Producers). (1992). *Alive*. Burbank, CA: Touchstone Home Video.

# 5

# Intertextualities: *The Tempest* in *Morning Girl*, *Lizard*, and *In Summer Light*

*John Noell Moore*

## Introduction

The story of Shakespeare's *The Tempest* is actually inside, either explicitly or implicitly, Michael Dorris's *Morning Girl*, Dennis Covington's *Lizard*, and Zibby Oneal's *In Summer Light*. The interconnectedness of these texts, their intertextuality, is the basis on which I offer interpretive possibilities and suggestions about how the classic play and the young adult (YA) novels complement each other. English teachers of advanced juniors and seniors will, I believe, discover the benefits of opening up the relationship between the classical secondary canon and YA literature with their students. This approach will not consider *The Tempest* as the superior work and the YA novels as lesser lights which in some way illuminate the great classic text. Rather, all of these texts shed light on each other and enrich the experiences of reading, discussing, and writing about them.

The chapter begins with a reading of and some teaching suggestions for Michael Dorris's *Morning Girl*. Dorris writes about a precolonial Native American world on the eve of its discovery by Christopher Columbus. This story connects to *The Tempest*'s portrayal of Caliban and what he says about the effects of Prospero's colonization of the island left to him by his mother Sycorax. Dennis Covington's *Lizard*, a novel with Shakespeare's *The Tempest* right in the middle of it, is the most complex of the three YA novels in its intertextuality, both in structure and idea. Understanding it means knowing how to trace the weave of *The Tempest* through it. Next, Zibby Oneal's *In Summer Light*, a novel about interpreting literature, provides another explicit intertext for *The Tempest* because Kate, the young female protagonist, is writing a paper on the play. Kate is trying to decide how to interpret Prospero while also trying to understand her relationship to her father, a famous visual artist, and his effect on her identity and her own artistic life. In watching Kate wrestle with multiple interpretations of Prospero, students might reflect on how they interpret characters in the texts they read. Finally, the chapter concludes with other YA novels that teachers and students can explore using the ideas this chapter offers.

## Definitions of Text and Intertext

In formalism, a traditional reading strategy practiced in many secondary schools, a piece of literature is considered a finished work of art. Recent views of the term *text*, however, see literature as incomplete, open, a construction, woven of words, as its etymology declares: [text: ME. fr. MF *texte*, fr. ML *textus*, fr. L. texture, context, from *texere*, to weave]. Traditionally, interpretation meant analyzing a work of art to discover its unity and completeness, but recent attitudes toward reading describe interpretation as the act of tracing the weave of a text in all its complicated strands, including the reader's response to it (Marshall, p. 166). Intertextuality describes this interweaving of texts.

The purpose of this chapter is to explore the ways in which *The Tempest* is woven into the text of three YA novels. Specifically, this interweaving might include direct citations of one text in another, allusions, and structural likenesses to other specific texts. More generally, it might include familiar literary and linguistic conventions by which texts are constituted or made. In this sense, then, an intertext is "the site of numberless other texts, including those that will be written in the future" (Abrams, p. 284).

## The Classroom Environment

The kind of work described in this chapter can best take place in classrooms that reflect a particular attitude about what reading is and about how we teach students to interpret texts:

> Not a class that pushes for a single or best reading of a text but a class that pushes for multiple and various readings of a text and that devotes some time to reflecting on how one got to these readings. This is a call for teaching with less closure and less criticizing of bad or wrong readings and more affirmation of differences among readings.

> (Elbow, p. 39)

The intertextual relationships between *The Tempest, Morning Girl, Lizard,* and *In Summer Light* help us read these texts differently than we might otherwise. The reflective practice to which Elbow refers is a way of encouraging students to take a hard look at how they read, not just what they read, and to understand how different readers achieve different interpretations. Reflective practice that involves intertextuality helps students understand the rich heritage of literary traditions that are embedded in YA texts.

## *Morning Girl* by Michael Dorris (78 pp.)

### Introducing the Novel

Dorris's poetic novel consists of a series of alternating monologues by Morning Girl and her brother Star Boy, young Taino [pronounced Tie-no] Indians living on a Bahamian island in 1492. Introduce *Morning Girl* by reading the first two chapters aloud, opening it up to students before they read it alone or develop any preconceived notions about it. The goal is to engage students in the text, specifically in its highly figurative language. Have students focus on the language and what it tells us about the world of the Taino Indians.

### Chapter One: "Morning Girl"

Morning Girl introduces herself, explaining that her name derives from her practice of rising early "always with something on my mind" (p. 1). Awaking, she "sifts the ideas" that have come to her in the night. As she moves out into the world, she tries "to step gently on the path so that the sounds I make will blend into the rustle of the world." She introduces her brother, Star Boy, who, in contrast to her, "likes the darkness best" (p. 2). In the reflection of their island in a pond, Star Boy believes that the world is inverted, that humans are "like birds floating above that sky island" (p. 3).

At this point, stop reading and ask students to discuss the kind of world they are experiencing in the text. Most students will notice that these Taino Indians are very connected to the land and are full of wonder about nature. Ask them to talk about the images that Morning Girl and Star Boy use to describe their world, and ask them if this language fits their image of early Native Americans. Many students may never have thought about Native Americans in this way. At this point, you might ask them to talk about colonialism and the New World; this will give them an opportunity to mention other intertexts from world history and American history. Finally, plant the seed of *The Tempest* intertext by emphasizing that the novel takes place on an island, that it seems enchanted, and that a young girl is the first focus of our attention.

### Chapter Two: "Star Boy"

This chapter deserves equal attention because it provides a picture of Morning Gilrs's brother and his use of language to describe the world he sees. In contrast to Morning Girl, who opens her eyes wide to take in the dawn, Star Boy tells us with a simile what he sees when he closes his eyes during the day: "It's like deep water, a pond that's draped with shade. I don't know what makes it happen—the fins of tiny fish, or their eyes, the sparkle of agates—but there are lights moving down there, something to watch" (pp. 7-8). Have students examine his poetic language.

The agate is a perfect image for Star Boy's perception of the fishes' eyes. Here you may want to introduce another intertext. In antiquity, the agate was a prized gem symbolically associated with the moon or with the planet Mercury. It was believed to possess the magical power to ward off storms and keep rivers from overflowing their banks (Biedermann, p. 5). This information links one of the most important intertextual elements of our study—the role of tempests in all four texts: the storm that threatens Star Boy's life, the storm that opens *The Tempest,* and the literal and psychological storms that swirl about the worlds of *Lizard* and *In Summer Light.*

## Student Work with *Morning Girl*

After modeling this intertextual approach to the novel with the students, ask them to continue the work by preparing themselves to lead the next discussions of the novel.

Put the class in small groups and assign each group the responsibility of preparing a discussion for one of the remaining sections, including the Epilogue. Ask them to skim the rest of the novel, possibly in one sitting, so that they have a sense of the whole book. Then, tell them to note the passages that "speak to them" from their chapters and copy them at the top of a journal page. After each copied passage, students make their own connections with what they have read and make notes about other ideas that come to them.

Many passages (See Figure 5.1) continue the lines of thought that have already been established in the first discussion. Students will find many others as they follow the story of Morning Girl, Star Boy, their mother She Wins the Race, and their father Speaks to Birds in the three principal developments of the novel: (1) the storm (tempest) in which Star Boy is nearly drowned; (2) She Wins the Race's miscarriage; and (3) the arrival of Christopher Columbus to the island.

---

**Figure 5.1**

**Chapter Three: "Morning Girl" (Harmony in the World)**

. . . the world fits together so tightly, the pieces like pebbles and shells sunk into the sand after the tide has gone out, before anyone has walked on the beach and left footprints. (p. 14)

**Chapter Four: "Star Boy" (Connection to Nature)**

There are things I noticed as a rock that I never realized as a boy. I could feel the movement of a shadow on my body as the sun slid across the sky. . . . I could smell the skin of my arm, warm and sweet, like nothing in the world. . . . I got to know myself better as a rock even better than I had known myself as a person, one part at a time. (p. 27)

**Chapter Nine: "Morning Girl" (On First Seeing Columbus)**

Finally one of them spoke to me, but I couldn't understand anything he said. Maybe he was talking Carib or some other impossible language. But I was sure that we would find ways to get along together. . . . [B]y midday I was certain we would all be seated in a circle, eating steamed fish and giving each other presents. It would be a special day, a memorable day, a day full and new. (p. 71)

**Epilogue: "Christopher Columbus"**

They should be good and intelligent servants, for I see that they say very quickly everything that is said to them; and I believe that they would become Christians very easily, for it seems that they have no religion. Our Lord pleasing, at the time of my departure I will take six of them from here to Your Highness in order that they may learn to speak. (p. 74)

## Concluding the Reading

The final sections of the novel deserve careful reading with attention to the sharp contrast between Morning Girl's sense of wonder and expectation and Columbus's recording of the inferiority of the Taino. His words offer an excellent opportunity for the study of irony. Having listened to the two young narrators, students will be aware of how skillfully and beautifully they speak, and they will clearly see how Columbus misreads the Taino.

One of the most crucial things to note about *Morning Girl* is how it opens up the issue of language at the end of the novel. Morning Girl imagines a circle of conversation, inclusion, and unity with the newcomers to her island. In contrast, Columbus immediately conceives of a master-servant relationship in which he will own his "discovery" without thought for their past or their freedom.

### *Morning Girl:* Historical Context

*Morning Girl* is a novel with two tempests: the literal storm that nearly claims the life of Star Boy, and the historical tempest that emerges as a consequence of New World colonization. Another intertext—one that bridges the tempests of Dorris's novel, of colonial history, and of Shakespeare's play—is Dorris's commentary on his YA novel (See Figure 5.2). Distribute Dorris's comments for students to discuss in small reading groups. Ask them to talk about whether Dorris helps them see the novel differently after their own discussions about each chapter and the Epilogue. Have each group report its key ideas to the whole class.

---

**Figure 5.2**

**"Rewriting History" by Michael Dorris**

I admit, my first impulse in writing my young-adult novel, *Morning Girl,* had to do with justice. When Louise [his wife] and I were researching *The Crown of Columbus,* one of our frustrations was the virtual anonymity of the Taino. 'They should make good and intelligent servants,' was Columbus's initial and overriding impression. Among the first people he says he met was 'one very young girl,' and I wondered who she was, or rather, who she was prior to the encounter.

In fact the Taino didn't make any kind of servants. Susceptible to the diseases whose germs Columbus and his crew were carrying along with glass beads and red caps, they were virtually wiped out within a generation or two, and have been treated—in textbooks and in popular imagination—as a minor footnote. . . . The Taino's experience was, in the extreme case, a precursor of what happened to native peoples throughout the Western Hemisphere over the past five hundred years.

Too often, when we reflect on the sweep of history, we fail to see the individual tree for the forest. . . . All distinctions, for convenience, are swept aside in favor of the lump category: learning disabled, good servants, homeless, primitive. Invisible. Without a past. Without a future.

(*Paper Trail*, pp. 141–144)

---

Dorris raises the issues of the loss of identity, the loss of personal history, and the loss of a homeland when the colonizer subdues. Dorris's commentary provides an excellent transition into the text of *The Tempest* and a study of Caliban, the character who could be a Taino figure in the Shakespearean drama.

## *The Tempest* by William Shakespeare

### Reading #1: A Structural Analysis

When I teach a large scale piece of literature such as *The Tempest,* I ask my students to read it twice: first, to familiarize themselves with the characters and ideas, and second, to explore the text in depth. During the initial reading, I ask students to write a one page response to each act of the play. Then students are able to lead the first discussions by sharing ideas from their journals. I often use the overhead to record their ideas, writing the name of the student and the idea so that we can develop as a community of readers as we share our responses to the text. From these discussions emerge the basic knowledge with which we will begin our second reading.

One helpful activity after the first reading is to collaborate with students to create a structural analysis of the play. Such an analysis helps students see how Shakespeare weaves together the stories of the four principal groups of characters in the play. Figure 5.3 illustrates one possible analysis of Acts One and Two.

Exploring what happens with each of these groups gives readers different angles from which to interpret the play. Readers can explore the issues of colonialism in the story of Prospero's usurpation of Caliban's island; political intrigue in the story of Sebastian's usurpation of Prospero's dukedom in Milan, and Prospero's subsequent restoration to political power; romance and love in the story of the young adults Ferdinand and Miranda; and the comic subplot's combination of these three stories.

---

**Figure 5.3**

**A Sample Structural Analysis of *The Tempest***

1.1   Courtiers: Aboard ship during the tempest that Prospero conjures to bring his enemies to the island

1.2   Islanders: Four episodes

　　#1  Prospero and Miranda: family and personal history

　　#2  Prospero's long reminder to Ariel; Ariel's story about the tempest (as if it were a fairy tale)

　　#3  Prospero and Caliban: Issues of power and service

　　#4  Young Adults: Ferdinand and Miranda's love at first sight; Prospero's intervention

2.1   Courtiers:   Amazement at their survival; Ferdinand feared drowned; Sebastian and Antonio plot against Alonso

2.2   Comic Servants:   Stephano and Trinculo get Caliban drunk

---

# Reading #2: The Critical Perspective

The second reading specifically investigates the major ideas which will link *The Tempest* and the YA novels: 1) the issue of colonialism, the role of Caliban, and the intertextuality of *The Tempest* and *Morning Girl*; 2) the issue of physical deformity and difference in Caliban and Lucius Sims, and the role of theater as art in *Lizard*; and 3) the father-daughter relationship and the nature of artistic identity in *The Tempest* and *In Summer Light*.

## Linking *Morning Girl* and *The Tempest*

The link between Dorris's novel and the play may be explored with a series of questions. Discuss the possible structure of Caliban's life on the island before the arrival of Prospero. Could Caliban have been a version of Morning Girl and Star Boy? What evidence from *The Tempest* do you have to support your ideas? The goal of posing these questions is to set up a close reading of the specific passages in *The Tempest* which address the issue of colonialism and the effect of the colonizer on the colonized. Recall Dorris's commentary on the fate of the Taino after the arrival of Columbus.

## Responding to Critical Commentary on Caliban

The next work with *The Tempest* now focuses specifically on Caliban: his character, his language, and his difference from other figures in the play. Students have had an opportunity to offer their perceptions and interpretations of the play during the initial discussions. Now, introduce a critical perspective which helps them see how modern critics interpret the play in terms of cultural history.

Distribute the critical passage and put students in small groups to discuss it (See Figure 5.4). Have students make notes and prepare to share their discussion findings with the whole class. I do not comment on the passage until students develop their own responses. Observe what angles they bring to the language of this critical passage. Do they stay within the critical text, or do they begin to make connections between *Morning Girl* and *The Tempest* right away? Listen to the students' responses and then help them synthesize their ideas. Make connections between group responses and ask questions to help groups more fully develop and clearly articulate their stances. Again, using the overhead projector to record the developing ideas helps students see what they say.

In the discussion, emphasize that the colonial metaphor rests on the issue of difference—in culture, language, physical appearance—an issue that will provide an intertextual connection between Shakespeare's play and Covington's novel.

## Interpreting Caliban in the Play

To help students trace the weave of Caliban in the play, assign a dialectic notebook, a more complicated version of the response journal. I prefer this format for close readings of texts because I want each student to have the experience of dealing with specific textual language. Also, writing about a text in advance of group discussions

---

**Figure 5.4**

**A Critical Perspective on Caliban**

[I]n the 20th century Caliban is, for many interpreters, Shakespeare's prototype of the New World native—a 'noble savage' or, oppositely, Stuart England's dim view of 'natural man.' Other recent critics, for quite different reasons, see Caliban from starkly altered perspectives: Within the last few decades these have included Caliban as Caribbean, Caliban as South American, Caliban as African, even Caliban as Quebecois [a native of Quebec]. In short, Shakespeare's orphaned slave has been adopted by a remarkable assortment of foster parents, who have embraced him for their own intellectual, social, and political reasons. Although to some literary critics he is still a monster or benevolent wild man, he now most frequently symbolizes the exploited native—of whatever continent and whatever color—who struggles for freedom, dignity, and self-determination from European and American Prosperos.

(Vaughan & Vaughan, xxii-xxiii)

---

often gives reluctant group participants enough courage to add their ideas within the small group framework.

### The Dialectic Notebook

Distribute general instructions for keeping dialectic notebooks (See Figure 5.5). In *The Making of Meaning,* Ann Berthoff suggests that literary criticism "is knowing what you're doing and thereby how to do it. Criticism is method" (p. 41). She describes reading and writing as ways of making meaning with a text.

When we read critically, we are reading for meaning—and that is not the same as reading for 'message.' Meanings are not things, and finding them is not like going on an Easter egg hunt. Meanings are relationships; they are unstable, shifting, dynamic; they do not stay still nor can we prove the authenticity or validity of one or another meaning that we find.

(p. 42)

Dialectic notebooks can help us, she suggests, make "a careful case to support our interpretations" (p. 43).

### Shakespeare as Performance

As part of the discussion of the scenes for close analysis, have students practice and present portions of the scenes under discussion either before or after they share the insights of their dialectic journals. Another option is to show film clips of various scenes after discussion. Remind them that filmed versions such as John Gorrie's 1980 production of *The Tempest* represent only one interpretation of the text.

**Figure 5.5**

**Keeping a Dialectic Notebook**

Reading and writing are ways of making meaning with a text. I want you to dialogue with the text we are reading through the use of a double entry or dialectic notebook in which the acts of reading and writing complement each other. Here's the procedure:

1. Get a spiral-bound notebook, 8.5 X 11. One with 70 pages is not too small, not too bulky.

2. The notebook functions in two page units. Here's how: As you prepare to read an assignment, write the date, the name of the selection, and the name of the author at the top of the left side (the back of a page). As you read the assignment, make notes or lists, copy quotations, or do whatever you want to do that suggests how the text is engaging you. You might even draw a diagram or sketch an image.

3. When you have finished the reading and notations, on the facing page write about the perceptions and observations you have made. You might write summaries or paraphrases of complex material, try to decide what a symbol represents, write about how the imagery affects you, or agree or disagree with the author's perspective. You might write several short responses or one longer one. In this way the two pages are in dialogue with each other, and you are reflecting on the practice of reading, that is, you are thinking about your thinking.

4. Sometimes I may specifically assign the kind of conversation I'd like you to create; for example, I may ask you to copy a direct quotation from a novel, poem, play, or essay on the left side of the notebook and give a reading or an interpretation of it on the right. Or I may ask you to respond to elements of the text that intrigue or provoke you. No matter how we work with the notebook, I want you to understand the connection between writing and reading and to practice writing as a way of discovery, of learning.

## Working with *The Tempest* as Text

Assign each small group one of the following passages for analysis, reminding them to keep the Vaughan and Vaughan commentary on Caliban in mind (See Figure 5.6).

During class discussions of the scenes, you might use some of the questions to move the conversations forward, to complicate them, or to stimulate discussion of ideas that students do not introduce. Following the discussions of these passages, students are ready to move into Covington's *Lizard*. It is not necessary to conclude or tie up the discussions of *The Tempest*, since subsequent work with the next two YA novels will bring students back to specific passages in the play.

**Figure 5.6**
**Passages for Small Group Analysis**

**1.2. 308–373: Prospero, Miranda, Caliban**

1.   In what sense does the concept of slavery emerge in this scene?
2.   What is Caliban's history?
3.   What do Prospero and Sycorax have in common?
4.   What might be another explanation for Caliban's attempted rape of Miranda other than his bestial nature?
5.   What is Miranda's attitude toward Caliban's language and her own?
6.   Caliban curses Miranda for teaching him language. Why?

**2.2: Caliban, Stephano, and Trinculo**

1.   How do elements of this scene mirror other action in the play?
2.   In terms of the colonialist perspective, how might we interpret Trinculo's description of Caliban in lines 18-35?
3.   What does Stephano's line "Open your mouth—here is that which will give language to you, cat" (78–80) imply about his attitude toward Caliban?
4.   What is the effect of the repetition of "monster" and its many uses in 138–160?
5.   Even though the courtier's servants get Caliban drunk in this scene, what do we learn about Caliban's intelligence and his knowledge about how to live on the island?
6.   How do you interpret the final use of the word "monster" in the scene in Stephano's "O brave monster! Lead the way!" (182)?

**3.2: Caliban, Stephano, Trinculo**

1.   What do you make of all the opening references to Caliban as a "monster"? (Note how this repeats the earlier references in 2.2. Are these references different? If so, why?)
2.   How do all these images of Caliban as monster relate to the poetry of his "Be not afeard, the isle is full of noises" (133–141)?
3.   In terms of Caliban as a colonial metaphor, how do you interpret the line ". . . when I awaked / I cried to dream again" (141)?
     [Note: In anticipation of reading *Lizard*, during this discussion you might want to mention that this line is the epigraph to Covington's novel.]

**4.1. 171–262: The Comics: Caliban, Prospero, Ariel**

1.   Compare the lyricism of Caliban's poetry at the end of 3.2 with Ariel's description of the scene. What does Ariel's language suggest about his attitude (and Prospero's) toward the comic figures?
2.   Prospero writes off Caliban as one of his failures. Do you agree with this appraisal of Caliban?
3.   Caliban is resolute in carrying through the conspiracy plot. How do you read his sense of urgency? What might it mean in terms of the colonial metaphor?

**5.1. 251–297: Resolution of the Comic Plot**

1.   How are we to interpret Prospero's "this thing of darkness I / Acknowledge mine" (275)?
2.   What do you make of Caliban's final words in the play (294–297)?

# *Lizard* by Dennis Covington (198 pp.)

## *Lizard*: An Overview

Lucius Sims, an orphan, tells the story and interprets the events of May to October of his 13th year. He has physical deformities—eyes that "look in different directions," a nose that "lays down on its side," humped shoulders, and a limp (p. 3). As the narrative opens in De Ridder, Louisiana, Lucius is placed in the Leesville State School for Retarded Boys by Miss Cooley, a woman who has cared for him since the disappearance of his mother and the death of his father. There, another student nicknames him Lizard because of his looks. He escapes the school with the help of a pair of traveling actors—Callahan, who pretends to be his father, and Callahan's girlfriend, Sallie—who have put on a production of *Treasure Island* (another intertext) for the students. The actors are headed to Birmingham, Alabama, to be in a production of *The Tempest*. Because of his deformities, they want Lizard to play Caliban to Callahan's Prospero and Sallie's Ariel.

Before they leave Louisiana, however, Lizard meets another pair of characters—the orphans Sammy and his sister Rain, who are part Cherokee Indian and part African American. They live alone in a pump house near Newllano, a few miles from De Ridder, and they are harassed by Reverend Ephraim Smith, a black man who has raped Rain.

Lizard makes the journey to Birmingham, where he rehearses and performs the role of Caliban in a production of *The Tempest* directed by another pair of characters, Waldo and Maureen. During this experience Lizard comes to understand more about himself, his place in the world, and the power of language. As his story develops, he is increasingly concerned with his search for knowledge of his parents, the archetypal quest for the father and, here in Covington's expansion of *The Tempest*, for the mother.

The journey keeps him linked to Rain and Sammy, who have hidden a silver bowl in his belongings. Their instructions concerning the bowl lead him to a Birmingham museum where he meets another pair of characters—Mr. Howell, the curator and a benevolent Prospero figure, and the black man William Tyson, an Ariel who finds his freedom in sculpture and painting. Lizard's experiences with the theater and the museum echo the theme of the nature of art in *The Tempest*.

Following the journey, the trio of actors returns to Newllano, where Lizard learns the history of Rain and Sammy, a history that provides a Native American and a slave narrative intertext. Their story is resolved as Ephraim Smith is arrested for the murder of their mother and as their Aunt Eunice comes to take care of them. Finally, returning to De Ridder, Lizard learns that Miss Cooley is his mother and that she does not know who his father is. Callahan and Sallie part ways; the Ariel of the Birmingham *Tempest*, Sallie has found her freedom from Callahan.

Callahan leaves Lizard living with his mother in a room above the L & N Cafe. In the final scene of the novel, Lizard reports the resolution of the theater and museum stories. He reflects finally on Callahan and brings his search for a father to its conclusion: "It's true he was not my real father, but he might as well have been" (p. 197). In the final imagery of the novel, Lizard sees the world opened up before him.

## Linking *The Tempest* and *Lizard*

Covington makes *The Tempest* an intertext in his YA novel in a number of ways. The first and most obvious intertextual connection is the production of the play which takes place in Chapter 12 of *Lizard*, reminding us of the vanishing banquet and the wedding masque, the plays with the play, that Shakespeare inserts in *The Tempest*.

In a second and more complicated way, Covington's story of young Lucius Sims is *The Tempest* told from the perspective of Caliban. At this level, the novel centers on the familiar young adult theme of coming-of-age. Readers see what happens to Lizard as Caliban after the play ends.

On a third and more intricate level, Covington constructs his novel with subplots that mirror his main plot and that echo important ideas in *The Tempest*. Covington expands areas not developed in Shakespeare's play, most notably in his inclusion of important women characters—Miss Cooley in the main plot and Aunt Eunice in the subplot. These women play key roles in the novel, rescuing the orphaned children of the novel and providing them with the safety and security of home.

## Teaching Intertextualities: *Lizard, The Tempest*, and *Morning Girl*

### Introducing *Lizard*

The most obvious link between *The Tempest* and *Lizard* is the quotation which Covington uses as his epigraph for the novel: ". . . when I waked / I cried to dream again," from Caliban's vision of reality and illusion (3.2. 133-141). Readers often ignore the epigraphs with which novelists open their stories, and this provides a good opportunity to teach students to pay attention to these kinds of details.

A close reading of the passage from *The Tempest* 3.2. makes an excellent introduction to the novel and suggests a guiding question for the reading of *Lizard*: How does this epigraph function in terms of the characters and ideas of the novel? In the scene, Caliban tells Stephano and Trinculo not to fear the noises they hear on the island, the "Sounds and sweet airs, that give delight and hurt not." He reports that although he is sometimes jarred by "a thousand twanging instruments" humming about his ears, at other times he hears voices that, if he awakens from sleep, make him sleep again. When he dreams, he says, he thinks that the clouds might open up and shower him with riches. In reality he is, of course, a servant to Prospero, and his life is wretched, his island usurped. This contrast between reality and dream prompts him to say the words of Covington's epigraph.

Prospero's most famous lines in the play, his description of the wedding masque as illusion in 4.1. 148–158, link directly to Caliban's dream image and become a metaphor for art and artistic creation, a central theme in *Lizard*. Pairing this passage with Caliban's speech completes the introduction to the novel. Lead students through this close reading as Prospero says that the actors in the masque "were all spirits and / Are melted into air, into thin air." The final words of Prospero's speech recall Caliban's vision of dreams and reality: "We are such stuff / As dreams are made on, and our little life / Is rounded with a sleep" (4.1. 148-158). For Caliban, the illusion of dreams sustains him in the reality of Prospero's dominance. Prospero's last image makes the sleep and dream metaphoric, encompassing the sleep before birth and the sleep after death. Another guiding question for the novel might be this: How is the theme of illusion and reality woven into *Lizard?*

## Focusing the Intertextualities

As with *The Tempest,* I prefer a first quick reading, in this case without notes or writing, just to give students a more solid ground on which to base their close reading of the text. In preparation for the second reading of the novel, assign small groups or pairs of students one of the ideas (See Figure 5.7) that link *Lizard* to *The Tempest,* and in some cases, to *Morning Girl.* Instruct them to make reading notes on the connections they discover.

---

### Figure 5.7
### Linking *Lizard* to *The Tempest* (and *Morning Girl*)

**Tempests**

Tempests are real and metaphorical, physical and psychological storms. When do they occur in the novel, and what do they represent?

**Illusion and Reality**

Note the frequent references to dreams, and how they influence Lizard's thinking about the world. For example, "Even then, my sleeping was just one dream after another, each one flat and full of heat. I dreamed I was looking at myself in a mirror, and my reflection turned and walked away from me" (p. 163). Nightmares deserve attention, too, especially Lizard's description in Chapter 11.

**Coming-of-Age Theme**

Note the images of rocks and hard places that link Lizard to Caliban's imagery: "For I am all the subjects that you have, / Which first was mine own king, and here you sty [lodge] me / In this hard rock, whiles you do keep from me / The rest of the island" (1.2. 342-344). Covington internalizes the rock image. His Lizard as Caliban is not hidden in a cave; instead, as his identity and independence emerge, he says, "At the center of me there was a hard spot that hadn't been there before" (p. 123). Later, he is more specific: "And though I hadn't reasoned this out at the time, the hard part of me, the part that grew out of my not trusting Callahan—that part lay right under the surface like a rock" (p. 162). This rock image is an inversion of the image in *The Tempest.* In one sense, Caliban's revolt in the play may be interpreted as his emergence from the hard place in which Prospero locks him. Star Boy's description of himself as a rock in Chapter 4 of *Morning Girl* provides an intertext for this imagery.

**The Outsider/Sexual Abuse Parallel**

Examine the link between Miranda and Caliban and the story of Rain and Ephraim Smith.

Figure 5.7 continued on next page

Figure 5.7 continued

### Theater as Art

Think about Prospero's speech in 4.1. 148–158, especially in relation to the meanings and ramifications of Waldo's statement, "Let's not forget, this is not the play. This is only the physical space where it takes place. The real play is in the mind, the imagination" (p. 97). Pay close attention to Lizard's understanding of the Shakespearean text, to the way he explains what the text means to him, and to how he interprets it during the performance in Chapter Twelve.

### Callahan's Role in the Novel and Play

The similarity in the names Callahan and Caliban invites discussion about Callahan as Prospero and as Caliban. Is Covington suggesting that every Prospero is also a Caliban? In his portrayal of Lizard's goodness, is Covington also suggesting that physical deformities may lead to a misreading of a person? If a person possesses a kind of magic, is there a Prospero within?

### Racial and Cultural Difference

Is there a link between Tyson and the freedom of Rain's great-great grandmother and her slave narrative? Tyson's sculpture "Waking on the Other Side" reinforces the dream motif and introduces an historical and poetic intertext: the racially motivated bombing of a Birmingham, Alabama, church in 1963 which killed four black little girls (pp. 128–130). Dudley Randall's "Ballad of Birmingham" provides a poetic intertext for this moment in the novel. The poem retells the story from the perspective of one of the four girls and her conversation with her mother before the bombing. The child wants to participate in a Freedom March, but her mother, fearful for her safety, insists that she go to church instead. After the explosion the mother finds all that is left of her daughter—one small shoe.

### The Romance Theme

Examine the link between the young adults Lizard and Rain and Shakespeare's Ferdinand and Miranda. Also, pay particular attention to the stories of Ruth, Aunt Eunice, Napoleon, and the silver bowl.

### Language

Copy examples of Lizard's use of poetic language, particularly the imagery of nature that links him to Caliban, Morning Girl, and Star Boy. [Teachers: Good examples occur on pages 1, 64, 158, and 198 of the novel.]

### The Role of Magic and Charms

The key symbols in *Lizard* are the silver bowl (in the Rain and Sammy story) and the necklace with the wooden amulet that Tyson gives Lizard. Explore the different roles magic and charms play in the novel as compared to *The Tempest*.

Devote some time to Covington's text alone, so that it exists for the students on its own terms. Then spend time helping students make intertextual connections, seeing the novel in the context of the play it transforms and expands. The groups or partners might prepare a running list of the connections they see, perhaps duplicating these at the end of the discussions and distributing them to their classmates. This practice emphasizes the collaborative nature of class discussion.

### Writing Ideas

Any of these ideas that connect the novel and the play could lead to a series of short papers or to an extended project. Students might write about the connections, or they may choose to write about either the novel or the play. They already will have a good deal of material in their dialectic notebooks from which to create a writing project. Another possibility is a reflective paper in which students trace the development of their thinking about one idea as they have read and studied the text.

## *In Summer Light* by Zibby Oneal (149 pp.)

*Lizard* ends in summer light as Lucius Sims contemplates the world anew: "I'd forgotten how wide the sky was above the place where we lived, and how long during the summer it stayed light" (p. 198). In Oneal's novel, the summer light shines on Kate Brewer as she acquires new knowledge and rediscovers herself as a visual artist. Kate's relationship to her famous artist father Marcus Brewer is illuminated while Kate is writing an essay on *The Tempest* and enjoying a summer romance. Actual storms occur in Oneal's novel, but the real tempest brews in Kate's mind as she struggles with her father's power, a struggle that leads her to see him as a Prospero figure. As she interprets Prospero for her essay, she also interprets her father and how he has shaped her identity. From a critical reading and writing perspective, the novel provides students with an excellent opportunity to think metacritically about how they read characters, trace them through a text, and write about them. *In Summer Light* becomes, in this sense, a metaphor for the act of reading and interpreting literature, an act that is conditioned by who we are and the knowledge and experiences we bring to a text.

### *In Summer Light*: An Overview

The novel takes place in June on an island off the coast of Massachusetts; it opens in a violent rain that has lasted three days. Kate, a 17-year-old student, is home for the summer. At the end of the term she contracted mononucleosis, and as a result, she has not finished an English paper on *The Tempest*. One of her summer goals is to complete the paper. The essay and her ideas about the play are woven throughout the novel and inform the changes that occur in her thinking before she returns to school with an emerging adult identity. During the summer Ian Jackson, a young graduate student who is cataloguing Kate's father's work for a retrospective show, comes to the island and provides the novel's romance. Leah, a friend from school, also pays a visit. As the novel progresses, Kate's mother emerges from her place in the background of her husband's artistic life to become a quiet but important influence in Kate's transformation.

## Reading *In Summer Light*

As a variation on the dialectic notebook approach, students keep dialogic reading logs (See Figure 5.8). The purpose of these logs is to create a dialogue between students about the text they are reading. These written conversations, focusing now on the intertextual relationships between *The Tempest* and *In Summer Light*, will provide plenty of material for class discussions. They may also help students "to see the text, themselves, and one another more clearly" (Probst, pp. 11–12).

---

**Figure 5.8**

**Dialogic Reading Logs**

Using two adjacent pages of a notebook, divide the facing pages into two columns for four entries.

Entry #1:   The owner of the notebook (Writer #1) makes notes about the reading, copies out direct quotations, asks questions.

Entry #2:   Writer #1 responds to these notes in the second column.

Entry #3    Writer #2, perhaps a partner, comments on the first and second entries, perhaps adding another point of view, agreeing, disagreeing, suggesting other ways to think about the original notes.

Entry #4:   Writer #1 replies to the commentary of Writer #2.

---

# Intertextualities: Oneal and Shakespeare

The intertextual relationship between *The Tempest* and *In Summer Light* exists on a number of obvious levels. The novel takes place on an island paradise where Marcus Brewer (Prospero) is free to pursue his art. Visitors to the island call him an enchanter and describe his art as magic. The narrative opens with a storm, an echo of the three hour duration of *The Tempest*. Shortly afterward, Ian Jackson (Ferdinand) appears "wet as the survivor of a shipwreck" (p. 9). Ian plays an important role in Kate's (Miranda's) struggle to understand her father's art and its relationship to her identity. Oneal concentrates on the father-daughter relationship; consequently, other elements of *The Tempest* do not appear in the novel. There are no courtiers, no Caliban, no comic subplot, and no postcolonial theme. On a more complex level, intertextualities exist as a function of at least five concerns of the novel.

## The Father-Daughter Relationship

Kate casts Marcus Brewer as a version of Prospero to her Miranda, but Brewer makes no effort to match Kate up with Ian, and for most of the novel he is unaware of her concerns and her efforts to understand him and his world.

## Romance

Oneal's Kate is more psychologically complicated than Shakespeare's Miranda. Both are full of wonder at their handsome companions, but Kate's dilemma is not easily solved by the wonder of romance and the magic of marriage.

## The Nature of Art

The play focuses on Prospero's magical art as well as on the art of the theater, on illusion and reality. In the novel, Marcus Brewer's power as an artist is compared to the magic of creation, and the relationship between illusion and reality informs the entire book. The visual art of Oneal's novel serves as a metaphor for all art that informs and shapes the human imagination and world view.

## The Mother-Daughter Relationship

One of Miranda's questions to her father when he tells her the family history in *The Tempest* (1.2. 46-47) is "Where are all the women?" (Gilligan, p. 111). While Prospero essentially ignores Miranda's question, Oneal provides a different version: Kate's mother has been there all along, and Kate finally discovers both her mother's quiet power and her unspoken artistry.

## The Power of Language to Construct the World

As in *Morning Girl* and *Lizard*, metaphoric language links Oneal and Shakespeare, especially the language that describes the natural world.

All the YA novels share the five intertextual themes with *The Tempest*, although the theme of romance in *Morning Girl* applies to the parents and not to the young adult characters as it does in the other texts. I will not work out each of these interconnections in detail, but, by way of example, I will demonstrate how the father-daughter intertext connects them all.

# The Father-Daughter Relationship as Intertext

## The Father as Blocking Figure

The key to this connection between *The Tempest* and *In Summer Light* is the passage in the play in which Prospero, having arranged the meeting of Miranda and Ferdinand, decides that this is altogether too easy for Ferdinand and intervenes. Accusing Ferdinand of being a spy, he makes the prince his servant. Having gone to all the trouble to conjure up the tempest and get Ferdinand on the island, why does Prospero create this obstacle? In some of the early comedies and late romances, the father-daughter relationship is the "salient character 'structure'" that Shakespeare uses. The playwright "selects narratives in which the father is, for want of a better term, a blocking figure, the force threatening to prevent the marriage" (Wilson, p. 39). This structure is clear in *The Tempest* 1.2. 451-453. Oneal uses Marcus Brewer as a different kind of blocking figure. His fame, his power, and his inability to communicate combine to block Kate in her development as an artist.

Early in the novel Kate affirms that she dislikes *The Tempest* "because of Prospero. He reminds me of Father." As an artist, her father seems insulated; his studio seems "to float" in the island's center, "aloof on swells of green." As he paints, he and the canvas make "an island together on this larger island" (pp. 7–8). In discussing drama, we often speak of the play as a microcosm of the larger world (macrocosm). Kate's imagery suggests such a relationship between the studio and the island, between art and the world.

Kate thinks of her father in terms of Prospero's magic. Marcus's hands describe "circles in the air" as he makes "a magnetic field of the space around him" (p. 12). After he moved to the island, she remembers, he lost touch with the real world which slowly "disappeared from his canvases, replaced by shape and color alone. Self-portraits . . . . paintings of the contents of his mind" (p. 22). Oneal's novel is a self-portrait of Kate's mind, too, and appropriately, Kate's language to describe the effect of the summer mirrors that: "She felt as if she were losing focus, melting in the summer heat, dissolving into a shape without contours" (p. 31). This metaphor aptly suggests the loss of identity that Kate feels on the island, a dissolution that is the result of an earlier experience with her father. Her childhood desire was to become a painter like her father and to please him, but she lost her passion for painting when her father dismissed her award-winning work as "a nice little picture" (p. 67). Subsequently she describes her father in painterly terms as a person who "has to have the foreground all to himself. He has to be the center of attention" (p. 68).

## The Father as Magician

Ian tells Kate that "light defines everything" (p. 42), an indication of the power of Oneal's symbolism and its transformation of physical light into metaphor. As in the enchanted world of *The Tempest*, Kate begins to feel "a sense of time suspended" (p. 47) in a world where her friend Leah describes Marcus as "magic" and "unreal" (p. 52), where the island is "Prospero's island" (p. 57), and where Kate imagines that the rest of the island's inhabitants are "onlookers, observing some scene spun out by an enchanter" (p. 58). As she struggles with her Shakespeare essay, she links literature and life, wondering what the playwright meant Prospero to represent: "thinking of her classmates who interpreted Prospero as the artist, creating illusion from reality"; or those who felt that "the whole play was political"; or Leah who thought Prospero a "sweet, white-haired old magician" (pp. 83–84).

## The Artistic Self

At the turning point of the novel in Chapter 11, Kate rediscovers both her ability to paint and her passion for it. This follows a discussion she has with Ian about Keat's sonnet "On First Looking Into Chapman's Homer", which also makes an intertext for Oneal's novel. Keats describes his literary journeys to "goodly states and kingdoms" (Keats, p. 796) in contrast to his metaphoric journey into Chapman's translation of Homer. Like Cortez, silenced by his first glimpse of the Pacific Ocean, Keats is equally silenced by Chapman's new vision of Homer's world.

The Cortez scene in the sonnet prefigures Kate's own new vision of herself as an artist in an experience she has with Ian at the beach. She paints with clay, using the rock outcroppings as her canvas, finally climbing high up the rock surfaces, where she feels so triumphant that she wants "to keep climbing, to keep painting, to go on painting her way into the layers of blue above her" (p. 91). Finally, so sure of her artistic power that she wants to fly, she leaps off the rocks, "her body like an extension of the curves she had painted" (p. 92). Her identification with her own "magical" powers is complete, and the rest of the novel works out the consequences of her discovery.

## Journeys: Outward/Inward

Later, Kate's ability to see literally and metaphorically helps her to articulate her own inward journey. After falling in love with Ian, she asks him to take her with him on a trip to Boston. Her request, she senses, is "like a journey undertaken" with "wide spaces between the words, gaps big enough to fall through." When he rejects her request because "it wouldn't be fair to your father," she realizes that the "sentence had been the journey . . . . All the journey that there was going to be" (pp. 123–124). The journey in the novel is not literal but psychological, and Ian's refusal forces Kate as an articulate Miranda to confront her father as a blocking figure: "everything she had ever cared about belonged to her father—his to give and his to take away" (p. 125).

Ian makes the journey to Boston and returns. Before he leaves for his home in California, we have what I think of as "the Miranda moment," the point in the novel at which Kate identifies with her Shakespearean counterpart:

> . . . [S]he rested against him and felt his hand curve over the curve of her skull, and down along the nape of her neck, and over the hair on her shoulders. And she thought of Miranda, gazing for the first time on all the shipwrecked men, the first besides her father that she had ever seen.
>
> (p. 130)

## Reconciliation

With Ian gone, the novel moves beyond *The Tempest* to a resolution quite different from the happily anticipated wedding of Shakespeare's young adults. Kate visits her father's studio to discover that he has been frustrated for some time by his inability to create and to finish a painting. He considers the forthcoming retrospective exhibit an indication that everyone considers him beyond his prime. For the first time, Kate sees that her father has aged. After she returns from the studio, she reads her interpretation of Prospero, finished earlier, in which she accuses Prospero of being guilty of using others "for his own purposes with no concern for the cost to them," an action she finds "unforgivable." Her new vision of her aging father, however, leads her to write more, and what she writes reinterprets both Prospero and Marcus Brewer. In Shakespeare's Epilogue, she notes, Prospero is an old man who, his magical powers waning, asks the audience to "set him free. I think Shakespeare means for us to forgive him. I think he means that if we refuse, we will be trapped like Prospero was, on his island" (p. 143).

This is an excellent place to debate the validity of her interpretation. Has she allowed her experience with her father to push the reading too far? A close reading of the Shakespearean passage (5.1. 319–338) makes a fine conclusion for the intertextual study of the play and the novel, perhaps highlighting the relationship between the artist and the world that receives the artistic production. After the curtain comes down, after the last page of the novel, what matters?

## Other Links: *In Summer Light, Morning Girl,* and *Lizard*

The clearest link between *In Summer Light* and *Morning Girl* occurs when Kate remembers her teacher Mr. Kincaid's suggestion that Prospero might be interpreted as "a type of imperialist" who "stole the island from the natives" and "made them slaves" (p. 95). She rejects, of course, this kind of political reading of the play. Having finished reading all the texts, students might debate the various interpretations of Prospero, offering support for the readings they prefer or perhaps, even better, offering other readings.

Connections to *Lizard* exist in the search for the father motif and the subsequent reconciliation, the discovery of self through artistic creation, the role of mothers, the journey motif, and the gift of language in constructing the seen world and interpreting the unseen world.

If all four texts are studied together, a good way to wrap up the complications of the intertextualities is to divide students into groups to create charts or diagrams in which they articulate the crucial intertextual links and present them to the whole class. This will provide a final opportunity to synthesize their work. As a last critical move, teachers might ask students to choose the YA novel that provides what they believe to be the best intertext for *The Tempest* and to support their choice. In this way, students will have practiced the highest levels of critical thinking—analysis, synthesis, and evaluation. In the process they will have spent some time thinking about the acts of reading and writing as well as how texts that span centuries can be in conversation with each other.

## Related Young Adult Fiction

The following novels also provide connections with the four texts studied here. They could be paired with the YA texts, with *The Tempest*, or combined in other ways.

### Postcolonialism

*Chain of Fire* by Beverly Naidoo (242 pp.)
*Middle Passage* by Charles Johnson (209 pp.)
*The Slave Dancer* by Paula Fox (127 pp.)
*When the Legends Die* by Hal Borland (216 pp.)

## Father–Daughter Relationships, Mothers, and the Nature of Art

*Midnight Hour Encores* by Bruce Brooks (263 pp.)
*The Monument* by Gary Paulsen (151 pp.)
*Notes for Another Life* by Sue Ellen Bridgers (208 pp.)

## Conclusion

My approaches to the texts in this chapter do not aim for closure, but rather aim to open up texts, to delight in them, and to pursue the possibilities they present. Such teaching enables students to "come into their own powers of textualization" by helping them "see that every poem, play, and story is a text related to others, with verbal pre-texts and social subtexts, and all manner of post-texts, including their own responses, whether in speech, writing or action" (Scholes, p. 20). As students and teachers read classic texts and YA texts together, they produce texts, weaving their words together, creating strands of ideas, and threading themselves into each others' texts and into the intertexts of the world.

## References

Abrams, M. H. (1993). Text and writing (*ecriture*). *A glossary of literary terms*. Sixth Edition. Fort Worth, TX: Holt, Rinehart, & Winston.

Berthoff, A. E. (1981). A curious triangle and the double-entry notebook: Or how theory can help us teach reading and writing. *The making of meaning: Metaphors, models, and maxims for writing teachers*. Portsmouth, NH: Boynton Cook, pp. 41–47.

Biedermann, H. (1992). Agate. In J. Hulbert's (Trans.), *A dictionary of symbolism*. New York: Facts on File.

Borland, H. (1985). *When the legends die*. New York: Bantam.

Bridgers, S. E. (1981). *Notes for another life*. New York: Alfred A. Knopf.

Brooks, B. (1986). *Midnight hour encores*. New York: HarperCollins.

Covington, D. (1992). *Lizard*. New York: Delacorte Press.

Dorris, M. (1992). *Morning girl*. New York: Hyperion Books for Children.

Dorris, M. (1994). Rewriting history. *Paper trail: Essays*. New York: HarperCollins, pp. 133–144.

Elbow, P. (1990). Democracy through language. *What is English?* New York: Modern Language Association, pp. 31–43.

Fox, P. (1991). *The slave dancer*. New York: Dell.

Gilligan, C. (1992). Continuing the conversation: Gender and literature. In N. McCracken & B. Appleby's (Eds.), *Gender issues in the teaching of English*. Portsmouth, NH: Heinemann, p. 111.

Johnson, C. (1991). *Middle passage*. New York: Plume.

Keats, J. (1986). On first looking into Chapman's Homer. In M. H. Abrams's (Ed.), *The Norton anthology of English literature*. Fifth Edition. Volume Two. New York: Norton, p. 796.

Marshall, D. G. (1992). Literary interpretation. In J. Gibaldi's (Ed.), *Introduction to scholarship in modern language and literature*. New York: Modern Language Association, pp. 159–182.

Naidoo, B. (1989). *Chain of fire*. New York: HarperTrophy.

Oneal, Z. (1986). *In summer light*. New York: Bantam.

Paulsen, G. (1991). *The monument*. New York: Delacorte Press.

Probst, R. E. (1990). *Five kinds of literary knowing*. Albany, NY: Center for the Learning and Teaching of Literature.

Randall, D. (1983). Ballad of Birmingham. In X. J. Kennedy's (Ed.), *Literature: An introduction to fiction, poetry, and drama*. Third Edition. Boston: Little, Brown, & Company, pp. 750–751.

Scholes, R. E. (1985). The text in the class. *Textual power: Literary theory and the teaching of English*. New Haven: Yale University Press, pp. 18–36.

Shakespeare, W. (1987). *The tempest*. S. Orgel (Ed.). Oxford: Oxford University Press.

Vaughan, A. T. & Vaughan, V.M. (1991). *Shakespeare's Caliban: A cultural history*. Cambridge: Cambridge University Press, pp. ix–xxiii.

Wilson, R. F., Jr. (1992). Enframing style and the father/daughter theme in early Shakespearean comedy and late romance. In M. Hunt's (Ed.), *Approaches to teaching Shakespeare's the tempest and other late romances*. New York: Modern Language Association, pp. 38–48.

## Film Cited

Gorrie, J. (Director). (1980). *The tempest*. Video Production: BBC-TV/Time-Life, Inc.

# 6

# Race, Racism, and Racial Harmony: Using Classic and Young Adult Literature to Teach *Othello, The Moor of Venice*

*Leila Christenbury*

## Introduction

A number of plays by Shakespeare are staples in the English language arts curriculum. In almost every school in the country you can find in any year the teaching and learning of *Romeo and Juliet* (See *Adolescent Literature as a Complement to the Classics*, Volume One, Chapter 6), *The Tragedy of Julius Caesar* (See *Adolescent Literature as a Complement to the Classics*, Volume Two, Chapter 7), *Macbeth*, and *Hamlet*. Recently *A Midsummer Night's Dream* has become popular in middle and high school curricula, as has *The Tempest* (See Chapter 5 of this text). Less frequently taught but included in many school curricula is *King Lear*, a choice which may not be widely popular because it features an elderly main character as well as issues of age and aging. *Othello, The Moor of Venice*, is another of Shakespeare's plays found in only some school curricula, and it probably is not frequently taught because it raises the often uncomfortable specter of race and racism.

Yet no matter where we live and teach, the issue of race is most likely a compelling one in our community. Further, few communities have escaped the scourge of racism. Few schools, few cities, and few neighborhoods can boast of real racial harmony and equity. Most of us consider the maintenance of positive racial relations as an ongoing, continuing effort. In *Othello* Shakespeare asks us to consider race, racism, and specifically, interracial romance. While it is a play about many themes—some of which include deceit and trust, the civilian life versus the military life, and jealousy and nobility—*Othello* is primarily concerned with what happens to race relations when a black man marries into white society. The play is personal and surprisingly pertinent today. As James Baldwin (1993) notes in his essay, "Stranger in the Village": "The black man insists, by whatever means he finds at his disposal, that the white man cease to regard him as an exotic rarity and recognize him as a human being" (p. 72). Othello the man is not an "exotic rarity," as Baldwin observes, but indeed a "human being," who is betrayed less by one evil character than by an entire social situation.

In Shakespeare's *Othello*, the title character, a powerful and well-respected black man, falls in love with and marries Desdemona, a well-born white woman. For many reasons, not the least of which is his race, Othello becomes the object of hatred. Othello and Desdemona, while initially greatly in love, experience serious pressure both from family members and from professional colleagues. In particular, one close associate plots to destroy both Othello's marriage and his career. Sadly, the marriage ends when Othello, in a jealous rage, strangles Desdemona.

If we choose to teach *Othello*, there are a number of excellent parallel pieces of literature—both classic and young adult (YA), fiction and nonfiction—which can help students and teachers discuss the play and extend understanding. Teachers should let students explore, argue, and debate not just the themes of Othello's tragic flaw, of his trust in the evil Iago, or of his failure to recognize Desdemona's innocence and Cassio's friendship but, inescapably, also the theme of race and the topic of racism.

For teachers and students reading *Othello*, the question of race can be an uneasy one. It is not certain that any two classes, even in the same school community, will come to identical conclusions about *Othello*. Regardless of differing interpretations, however, it is simply not acceptable to read and discuss *Othello* and sidestep the issue of race and racism. While not every line of the play hammers home the point that Othello is black—and every other character in the play is white—there is quite sufficient comment and remark within the dialogue as well as underlying the plot to make the race of the characters a significant, *if not the most significant*, factor in this tragic masterpiece. To ignore the race matter is, simply put, not an acceptable teaching stance. Adding discussion of race and racism, on the other hand, does justice to the work and provides a consideration of a vital aspect of the play. Using other literature can also help teachers and students deal with the volatile aspects of this most important work and see *Othello* through a wider lens than just that of the Moor of Venice and his immediate situation.

## *Othello, The Moor of Venice:* **Background and Summary**

*Othello* was a work of William Shakespeare's maturity, written, it is believed, between *Hamlet* and *King Lear.* Completed in early 1604 and performed at Court on November 1st of that year, it is drawn from a mid-16th century tale in the *Hecatommithi* by Giraldi Cinthio. The original Italian story is, as scholars note, "crude" (Neilson & Hill, p. 1093). In essence, Shakespeare took an essentially melodramatic and shallow tale and made it into "a tragic drama of terrifying plausibility" (Neilson & Hill, p. 1094).

The Elizabethan attitude toward blacks was complicated and cannot be easily addressed in a piece of this length. Nevertheless, a few observations can be made. Certainly the ending of the original Italian tale upon which Shakespeare based *Othello* reveals a racial bias when the heroine says, "Italian ladies may learn from me not to marry a man whom nature, heaven, and manner of life have separated from us" (Neilson & Hill, p. 1094). Shakespearean critic M. C. Bradbrook reminds us that the image of black sin and white virtue is present in much literature, *Othello* included. Additionally, the black, non-Christian infidel is an archetype of the Elizabethan stage (Bradbrook, p. 135). Yet, Bradbrook also notes that the image of the noble black warrior is also part of the Elizabethan view, and Africa and black-skinned people were also positively associated with wealth and love. (Thus we might well remember that Romeo praises Juliet: "It seems she hangs upon the cheek of night / As a rich jewel in an Ethiop's ear," I, v, 47–48.)

While there is no conclusive evidence, Shakespeare may have seen black-skinned people in England. Certainly, in both 1596 and 1600, Queen Elizabeth announced that Negroes were competing with native Englishmen for scarce jobs and suggested that they be shipped out of the country (Mizener, p. 186). In 1601, a Lubeck merchant was ordered to return "Negars and Blackamoors" who had been in England for some time— "since the troubles between her Highness and the King of Spain" (Bradbrook, p. 141).

Turning to the plot, Othello, also known as the Moor of Venice—the subtitle of the play and a phrase which recurs repeatedly throughout the five acts—is a renowned general from foreign parts who is in service to the city of Venice. The war business is currently slow, however, and Othello has found himself in town with time on his hands. In the company of one of his lieutenants, the faithful and kind Michael Cassio, he has wooed and won the affection of the beautiful and shy Desdemona.

At the onset of the play, Desdemona and Othello have eloped in an interracial marriage. This scandalous fact is reported that night to Desdemona's unwitting father, Brabantio, one of the town luminaries. Brabantio, woken from sleep to hear his only daughter has taken off with the "sooty" Moor (I, ii, 70), is horrified. The news of the couple's elopement comes from two principal characters: one of Desdemona's disappointed suitors, Roderigo; and, more importantly, from one of Othello's ostensibly faithful ensigns, Iago. The two gather in the street under Brabantio's bedroom window and shout the details, which include bawdy speculations regarding the couple's nocturnal embraces. It is not a decorous scene, and Brabantio, shocked and alarmed, rushes to the Duke of Venice to force the eloped pair to return and nullify their union.

Othello, greatly in love with Desdemona and confident that "my parts, my title, and my perfect soul / Shall manifest me rightly" (I, ii, 31–32), appears calmly before the Duke with his bride. Both detail their courtship and declare their love and harmony. While Brabantio is bitterly disappointed in his daughter's choice of husband, the Duke allows the couple to continue their union in peace.

But peace is not to be had. Iago, Othello's ensign, is for varying reasons (all of which he offers at differing times in the play and none of which are wholly convincing) determined to bring the great general down. Now that Othello is married to Desdemona, Iago sets cunning trap after trap and, expertly playing on Othello's explosive nature, he makes the general believe that the young bride Desdemona is unfaithful and treacherous. Along the way, Iago schemes against the gullible Cassio, getting him drunk and causing Othello to suspect him. Further, Iago funds some of his plans using the money of the yearning suitor Roderigo, who pays Iago a small fortune in the vain hope that he will be able to bribe Desdemona's affections away from Othello. Iago also gets his unsuspecting wife, Emilia, Desdemona's maid, to cooperate in his plans. Finally, Desdemona, truly unschooled in the treachery of the world, walks blindly into compromising scene after compromising scene and, unwittingly, perfectly cooperates in the deceit and the resulting tragedy.

At the tragedy's end, Cassio is wounded, Bianca is under suspicion for plotting murder, Roderigo and Emilia are dead, and Othello has strangled Desdemona. When Othello finally sees the web in which he has been trapped, he—in a horrific scene of comprehension and bottomless remorse—commits suicide and falls upon the body of his dead bride. For his part, Iago is arrested and taken away for punishment. In one of Shakespeare's great strokes of genius, Iago refuses to detail his true motivation for the carnage and treachery. Iago exits the stage in silence, forever leaving us to puzzle over the real source of his evil animus.

## Critical Assessment of *Othello*

*Othello, The Moor of Venice* is a play of dignified beauty and distilled concentration with a "unitary, relentlessly progressing plot" (Mizener, p. 183). Despite its bloody conclusion, there is a deliberate stateliness to the action. The language is elevated, serious, and direct; the emotions described are of epic proportion. The poetic sections border on heart-breaking. While there is little foreshadowing and relatively few repeated images (reputation being the exception), the speeches are convincing and clear.

*Othello* moves very directly through its five acts. There is virtually no comic relief (See III, i, 1–31 and III, iv, 1–22 for two exceptions), no sub-plots (with the possible exception of the use of the prostitute, housewife Bianca), and a remarkably small cast of believable and fully drawn characters.

The "inhuman dog" (V, i, 63) Iago is the unifying force of the play; he figures in every major scene. Iago's interaction with Roderigo, Emilia, Cassio, and, most importantly, Othello, reveals a master manipulator at work. "I am not what I am" (I, i, 65) Iago tells all of us in the first scene of the first act. It is truer than anyone within the play—or even those viewing it—can at first comprehend, and it fuels the tragedy.

Othello, a mature and respected man at the apex of his powers, may be of noble descent (I, ii, 21–22). He is a "valiant" (I, iii, 47) man and "great of heart" (V, ii, 361), one of whom even Iago remarks, "another of his fathom they [Venice] have none!" (I, i, 153). Othello is caught in a web of betrayal, overmastered by concentrated cunning and deceit. Clearly talented in battle, Othello is helpless at the subtleties of social deceit and is indeed, in civilian society, the "dolt" (V, ii, 164) Emilia calls him. A great general who has taken time to pursue a personal life, Othello is somewhat like John Le Carre's spy who came in from the cold. Once he has let down his guard in love and marriage, he is vulnerable to the most insidious of betrayals.

Critics have argued the degree of Othello's moral culpability. In particular, T.S. Eliot has scorned Othello's dying speech as self justification. Regardless, there is a certain sense that, despite his bloody acts, Othello is as he describes himself on his deathbed—"one that lov'd not wisely but too well"(V, ii, 344).

## Challenges to Teaching *Othello, The Moor of Venice*

The above outlines the degree to which the issue of race is vital to the play itself and to the teaching of *Othello*. Certainly high school students are ready to tackle this important and often difficult subject. For many of them, its outlines are familiar in their own lives. Despite what some would like to contend, Shakespeare does not make Othello's race incidental or unimportant; thus, when we teach the play we must teach it fully and essentially honestly. Once again we return to James Baldwin's words, cited at the opening of this piece. Othello is a human being. He is also, however, a black human being operating in a white society, and that inescapable fact shapes him, shapes the play, and must shape our reading and reaction to *Othello, The Moor of Venice.*

# Before and During the Reading of *Othello, The Moor of Venice*

Some questions which students might want to consider before and during reading *Othello* follow. While final answers are more than likely unattainable, considering the issue to which race matters in *Othello, The Moor of Venice* will more authentically serve a reading of this great play. Students may want to consider the questions in discussion or journal entries. These topics may help students prepare for the issues of race, racism, and racial harmony and also put their reading of *Othello* in perspective. In addition, the use of fiction, nonfiction, classic, and YA literature can make discussion fuller and more reflective.

## The Concept of Race

We often refer to a person's "race." What is "race" and how is it defined in the dictionary? By you and your peers? How descriptive is "race" in today's society? Does it mean the same in your school as in, for example, a school in Miami or New York City or San Francisco or Seattle? What does "race" mean in *Othello?* In any of these settings, how does "race" function? What are its limits? Advantages? Disadvantages?

## The Influences of Race

Thinking of what you know and have experienced, how do you think "race" specifically influences a person and his or her attitudes? Values? Perceptions? To what degree can we separate Othello's "core" or inherent personality from his experience as a black man? Can you speculate on how differently Othello might have reacted to certain events if he were not black?

## Interracial Relationships

In Cornel West's (1993) *Race Matters*, the black scholar has a chapter entitled "Black Sexuality" in which he observes that "White fear of black sexuality is a basic ingredient of white racism. Social scientists have long acknowledged that interracial sex and marriage is the most *perceived* source of white fear of black people" (p. 86). To what extent do you agree with West's assessment? What in your opinion are the limitations (if any) of interracial friendships? Interracial romantic relationships? Interracial marriage? Integrated work places? Integrated churches? Integrated schools? How willing do you judge your school community to tolerate interracial institutions and couples?

## Changing Race Roles

Imagine Othello is white and the setting is no longer white Venice but black Dakar. To what extent would Othello's professional standing be altered? His relationship with his men? His marriage to Desdemona? His feelings?

# "Race" in Classic Literature: Baldwin, King, and Lee

Race is a perennial subject in literature. The following three works, nonfiction and fiction, may help students approach the reading of *Othello* with more interest and confidence.

### "Stranger in the Village" by James Baldwin

This essay is about Baldwin, a black American writer, living in the Caucasian Swiss Alps and his meditation on black and white relations in the United States. Have students consider, in particular, the following passage:

> The cathedral at Chartres . . . says something to the people of this village which it cannot say to me; but it is important to understand that this cathedral says something to me which it cannot say to them. Perhaps they are struck by the power of the spires, the glory of the windows; but they have known God, after all, longer than I have known him, and in a different way, and I am terrified by the slippery bottomless well to be found in the crypt, down which heretics were hurled to death, and by the obscene, inescapable gargoyles jutting out of the stone and seeming to say that God and the devil can never be divorced. I doubt that the villagers think of the devil when they face a cathedral because they have never been identified with the devil. But I must accept the status which myth, if nothing else, gives me in the West before I can hope to change the myth.
>
> (p. 76)

### Questions

What is Baldwin's point about cultural differences? About the myth of black people being identified with the devil? How might his point relate to today? To the issues and perceptions of those issues raised in *Othello*?

### "I Have a Dream" by Dr. Martin Luther King, Jr.

In his "I Have A Dream" speech, made during the historic March on Washington in 1963, Martin Luther King spoke for many African Americans when he said that he hoped his four children would one day "live in a nation where they will not be judged by the color of their skin, but the content of their character."

### Questions

In the historical context of King's landmark speech, what did he mean? Today, many years later, to what extent has this "dream" altered or stayed the same? How does King's hope relate to *Othello*?

## *To Kill A Mockingbird* by Harper Lee (281 pp.)

This novel was very important to the Civil Rights movement in the United States in the 1960s. This well-written, mainstream piece of literature made a point about social justice that many were finally ready to hear. *To Kill A Mockingbird* helped broaden the perception of many whites of the plight of blacks in the American South and of the injustice of many court systems. For a comprehensive discussion on this classic novel, see Bonnie Ericson's Chapter 7 in *Adolescent Literature as a Complement to the Classics*, Volume One.

### Questions

To what extent is the situation of Tom Robinson, the innocent black man charged with the rape of a white woman, like that of Othello? How is it different? How are the two men comparable? If Othello had had a friend or defender such as Atticus Finch, do you think he would have had the same relationship with Iago? With Cassio? Tom Robinson, unlike Othello, lives in a biracial society, yet he essentially cannot live his life safely. Why is this so?

## Interracial Relationships in Young Adult Fiction

## *Othello: A Novel* by Julius Lester (160 pp.)

Lester has turned Shakespeare's play into a novel, setting it in 16th-century England. In his interpretation, which he calls a "reconceptualization," Lester adds two characters: the King and Desdemona's mother. Additionally, he makes both Iago and Emilia Africans and more clearly highlights the issue of race and racism.

### Questions

Read Julius Lester's *Othello: A Novel* and consider how it is different from Shakespeare's play. To what extent do you agree with Lester's reconceptualization? Does it deepen your understanding of the original work? Does it change it? If you were William Shakespeare, would you approve of what Lester has done or would you object to it? Why?

## *A White Romance* by Virginia Hamilton (200 pp.)

Black track star Talley Barbour is a "good" girl who spends her time training and studying. When Talley's high school becomes a magnet school and white students are bused in, she makes friends with a white girl, Didi. Talley and Didi share a great deal and overcome their racial differences. When Didi falls in love with a fellow white student and drug dealer, Roady, Talley watches the relationship with interest and some envy. Then Talley is pursued by and falls in love with Roady's drug partner and friend, David, and her life changes dramatically. The interracial love is real, intense, and mutual, but it disintegrates under the pressure of David's erratic behavior and illegal trade. As a subtext, it is undeniable that race of and by itself is a great attraction between the two teens. Indeed, Hamilton leaves some doubt that the pair would be as interested in each other if they were not of different races.

### Questions

To what extent do you think this same aspect of attraction—the lure of the different—is also true of Othello and Desdemona? In general, what does the love between Talley and David in *A White Romance* tell us that *Othello* does not? Further, Talley is "rescued" by a black male friend, Victor. Could Cassio have similarly "saved" Desdemona? What is the same? What is different?

## *I Hadn't Meant to Tell You This* by Jacqueline Woodson (115 pp.)

In this Coretta Scott King Honor Book, Marie—who is black—is the product of a happy and financially secure home. By contrast, Lena—who is white—is poor and also sexually abused by her father. Despite their differences, the two become friends and eventually share their secrets. When Lena moves away, Marie mourns the loss of her friend and worries about her welfare and future.

### Questions

What can we learn about the strengths and the limits of interracial friendship in *I Hadn't Meant to Tell You This*? How is this different from *Othello*? How is this the same? What do Lena and Marie have in their friendship that Othello and Cassio lack? To what extent do you think Lena and Marie would have been friends if they were of the same race?

## *The Moves Make the Man* by Bruce Brooks (280 pp.)

In this story of interracial friendship, the black half of the pair is also the better adjusted and more stable of the two. Bix, who is a white baseball player, is a troubled young person who befriends Jerome. Bix learns much, not only about sports, but also about life, from his black friend. While there is tension in Jerome's life—he is the first black to integrate an all-white school and is resented—he has a happy and loving home life, unlike Bix. The two meet and try to help each other, especially in their interpretations of reality and in their ability to get along with their families and school friends.

### Questions

As with *I Hadn't Meant to Tell You This*, what can we learn about the strengths and limitations of interracial friendship from *The Moves Make the Man*? How is this different from *Othello*? How is this the same? What do Bix and Jerome have that Othello and Cassio lack? To what extent do you think Bix and Jerome would have been friends if they were of the same race?

### *The Cay* and *Timothy of the Cay* by Theodore Taylor (160 pp. & 145 pp.)

In the two award-winning Taylor novels, Phillip, a 15-year-old white boy, is shipwrecked on a Caribbean island with Timothy, an elderly and wise black man. Through Timothy's instruction, the blinded Phillip learns from and lives through the ordeal. In *The Cay*, Timothy dies during a subsequent hurricane. Phillip survives and in *Timothy of the Cay* returns to the island to visit Timothy's grave.

#### Questions

What are the positive aspects of this interracial relationship? The limitations? What would have happened to Timothy had he, not Phillip, been the one who was blind?

### *White Lilacs* by Carolyn Meyer (237 pp.)

In this ALA Best Book for Young Adults, an entire black community in the 1920s is dislodged from its location because the neighboring white community wishes to expand. The protagonist, Rose Lee, sees a great deal of unkindness from her white neighbors but also witnesses the good deeds of Miss Firth and Catherine Jane. Based on a true event, *White Lilacs* is a historical novel which comments seriously on interracial relations and their economic and social dimensions.

#### Questions

What makes Miss Firth and Catherine Jane different from the other white neighbors? Why have they chosen to behave differently towards Rose Lee? As a friend of Rose Lee's, what would you advise her to do?

## Interracial Relationships in Young Adult Nonfiction

A number of excellent nonfiction resources also provide background on race and racism. Susan Kuklin's *Speaking Out: Teenagers Take on Race, Sex, and Identity*, an ALA Quick Picks for Young Adults and a Booklist Editors' Choice, contains student discussions about racial prejudice and being different.

Other resources include John Langone's *Spreading Poison: A Book about Racism and Prejudice*, which gives in detail the origins of racism and prejudice. Linda Mizell's *Think about Racism* offers historical accounts of racism up until the present time. Michael Kronenwetter's *United They Hate: White Supremacist Groups in America* gives a history and background of the various groups which have championed the white race in America since the 19th century.

# Conclusion

Responsible teachers will teach *Othello* fully, and that means encouraging students to consider the play's central theme of race and the topic of racism. Certainly the past few years, in particular through the widely discussed and avidly watched O.J. Simpson trial, have shown us that American society is nowhere near finished discussing and reacting to the subject of race. Especially when we add the possibility of interracial romance, the topic can be volatile. Through the reading of *Othello* and related works—both classic and young adult, fiction and nonfiction—students and their teachers can seriously consider these issues and, perhaps, come closer to some sort of mutual understanding.

I live in the South, in Richmond, Virginia, which has been since its founding in the 18th century a biracial city. Caucasians and African Americans have lived and worked side-by-side for generations. Richmond was also the Capital of the Confederacy due to its pivotal importance during the American Civil War, 1861–1865.

One very late spring afternoon in Richmond, I drove by the famous and increasingly controversial statue of General Robert E. Lee, the legendary Confederate leader who is honored by a huge and park-like landscaped monument. Not every Richmond citizen enjoys passing by the historic statue. For black citizens in particular, Lee does not represent a defense of states' rights in the Civil War but a defense of the institution of slavery. Yet the statue remains—a huge representation of a uniformed and mounted General Lee, set in the middle of a traffic circle on a grassy plot and towering above the neighboring buildings. And this particular late afternoon, it was host not only to joggers and Frisbee throwers but also to a couple clearly in love. As I rode by in my car, the pair were at the statue's white marble base, sitting very close and kissing. In the late spring light, the scene of the lovers was magical and touching, and I thought even the stern general might approve of their public tenderness as they sat in his statue's shadow. And driving by, in the dying twilight, here in the Capital of the Confederacy, here in the shadow of Robert E. Lee, I saw the young man's deep brown arms entwined around the woman's white shoulders—a new Othello, a new Desdemona.

# References

Baldwin, J. (1993). Stranger in the village. In C. Klaus, C. Anderson, & R. Faery's (Eds.), *In depth: Essayists for our time*. Second Edition. San Diego: Harcourt Brace.

Bradbrook, M. C. (1984). *Muriel Bradbrook on Shakespeare*. Sussex, England: The Harvester Press.

Brooks, B. (1984). *The moves make the man*. New York: Harper & Row.

Daniel, P. L. (1995). Relationships and identity: Young adult literature and the *Tragedy of Julius Caesar*. In J. F. Kaywell's (Ed.), *Adolescent literature as a complement to the classics*. Volume Two. Norwood, MA: Christopher-Gordon Publishers, Inc., pp. 145–161.

Ericson, B. O. (1993). Introducing *To kill a mockingbird* with collaborative group reading of related young adult novels. In J.F. Kaywell's (Ed.), *Adolescent literature as a complement to the classics*. Volume One. Norwood, MA: Christopher-Gordon Publishers, Inc., pp. 1–12.

Hamilton, V. (1987). *A white romance*. New York: Philomel.

King, M. L. (1992). I have a dream. In James Melvin Washington's (Ed.), *I have a dream: Writings and speeches that changed the world*. San Francisco: Harper.

Kronenwetter, M. (1992). *United they hate: White supremacist groups in America*. New York: Walker.

Kuklin, S. (1993). *Speaking out: Teenagers take on race, sex, and identity*. New York: G.P. Putnam's Sons.

Langone, J. (1993). *Spreading poison: A book about racism and prejudice*. Boston: Little, Brown, & Company.

Le Carre, J. (1992). *The spy who came in from the cold*. New York: Ballantine.

Lee, H. (1960). *To kill a mockingbird*. New York: Warner Books.

Lester, J. (1995). *Othello: A novel*. New York: Scholastic.

Meyer, C. (1993). *White lilacs*. San Diego: Harcourt Brace.

Mizell, L. (1992). *Think about racism*. New York: Walker.

Mizener, A. (Ed.). (1969). *Teaching Shakespeare*. New York: New American Library.

Reed, A. J. S. (1993). Using young adult literature to modernize the teaching of *Romeo and Juliet*. In J. F. Kaywell's (Ed.), *Adolescent literature as a complement to the classics*. Volume One. Norwood, MA: Christopher-Gordon Publishers, Inc., pp. 93–115.

Shakespeare, W. (1942). *Othello, the moor of Venice. Romeo and Juliet*. In W. A. Neilson & C. J. Hill's (Eds.), *The complete plays and poems of William Shakespeare*. New York: Houghton Mifflin.

Taylor, T. (1977). *The cay*. New York: Avon Books.

Taylor, T. (1993). *Timothy of the cay*. New York: Avon Books.

West, C. (1993). *Race matters*. Boston: Beacon Press.

Woodson, J. (1994). *I hadn't meant to tell you this*. New York: Bantam.

# The Journey Towards Home: Connecting *White Lilacs* and *A Raisin in the Sun*

*Janet Allen*

> *"If you would have a lovely garden,*
> *you will have a lovely life."*

Shaker poem

## Introduction

Linehan (cited in Kaywell, 1993, p. 148) estimates that on any given night there are between 68 thousand and half a million children in America who are homeless. Finding home, both in the literal and the figurative senses of the word, must seem elusive to those children. Unfortunately, the problems that accompany such poverty are the reality for many: lack of proper nutrition, poor health, lack of medical treatment, violence, crime, dysfunctional and separated families, and despair. Surrounding all of that pain is the knowledge that there is absolutely no place for them, no bedroom, no shared space, nothing that is one's own—no home. Kozol reminds readers that "The loss of childhood is irreversible. You never get to be a child twice" (Goodwillie, 1993, p. xiv).

On the surface, it might seem that only those who are homeless in the purest sense of the word could understand the depths of that despair. One cannot ignore, however, the many people who struggle all of their lives in search of a place where they can live in peace and acceptance. For some, that place may be a state of mind, but for many people in our country, that place is physical. For the African-American members of the community in Carolyn Meyer's young adult (YA) book *White Lilacs* and the Younger family in Lorraine Hansberry's play *A Raisin in the Sun*, the physical place and the state of mind are inextricably connected. The characters fight voices from within and without that try to keep them from making their journeys home.

## *White Lilacs* by Carolyn Meyer (237 pp.)

*White Lilacs* is a fictional account of an historic event which occurred in Denton, Texas, in the early 1920s. Whites force the African-American community of Quakertown to relocate in order to make room for a park. In Meyer's historical notes, she takes these words from the bronze plaque that commemorates this community:

> In its heyday, Quakertown contained fiftyeight [sic] families, stores, restaurants, a doctor's office, a mortuary and three churches.

> In April of 1921, a bond election was held to raise $75,000, to create a city park on the 27 acre Quakertown site. In spite of opposition from the residents, this proposal passed 367 to 240. By 1923, the residents of Quakertown were required to move.
>
> (p. 240)

This historical background provides the backdrop, but it's through Meyer's fictional characters that readers vicariously experience the emotional and physical struggles that these families experience as they are forced to abandon their homes and the community of Freedomtown in Dillon, Texas.

The story is told from the perspective of Rose Lee, a young black girl who begins working in Mrs. Bell's home. Rose Lee's father, a barber, is a respected member of the black community of Freedomtown. The opening chapter foreshadows the conflict that lies ahead. Rose Lee's grandfather, Jim Williams, spends all of his spare time tending his beautiful garden of wild and colorful trees and flowers. His garden is a source of pride for all of the members of the black community, and Rose Lee describes the colors of the garden jumbled together in such a way that it looks like "the first Garden of Eden" (p. 4). Mr. Williams also tends Mrs. Bell's garden, but her garden lacks variety and color. Mrs. Bell has Jim literally remove yellow, orange, and orangy-red flowers because Mrs. Bell has "never been fond of those colors" (p. 4).

While strolling through Mrs. Bell's garden, the women of the Dillon Garden Club converse about a plan to relocate the members of Freedomtown. Rose Lee overhears one of the ladies saying, " 'We'll simply move them to a more appropriate area. But they're like children. They may have to be persuaded that it's for everyone's good' " (p. 10). Rose Lee shares what she's heard, and conflicts arise immediately. The members of Freedomtown are resolute about staying in the physical and spiritual community they have created.

From a 1990s perspective, it is shocking to be reminded of the lack of legal support available to African Americans in the 1920s. In spite of the fact that many African Americans owned their own land, Dillon officials could simply take their property and give them a pittance of its value. Few options are available for those members of Freedomtown who want to live someplace other than the open-sewer area that is designated as the new site of their community. The community's unity is divided as families and friends move away. Because some African Americans refuse to move from Freedomtown, the conflict becomes more violent; schools are burned and lives are threatened.

Rose Lee's family is at the center of the conflict because the barbershop is the established meeting place for "business." Those meetings make her family a target not only of people like the Bells but also for the Ku Klux Klan. Henry, Rose Lee's brother, is tarred and feathered and has to flee from town for trying to get his family and friends to join with Marcus Garvey and the United Negro Improvement Association. When Henry is criticized for his political actions, Rose Lee's father replies, "Henry's not about to accept some white man's idea of what his place is" (p. 21).

Rose Lee finally comes to terms with the loss of Freedomtown when Miss Firth, a Northern art teacher, encourages her to document the homes, the gardens, the business community, and the people of the community by sketching them. As Rose Lee looks beyond the pain and confusion, she sees the futility of believing that the community of Freedomtown would ever be the same even if the people managed to stay together. Rose Lee mourns the loss of her community and her innocence: "I used to be like that, young and carefree, having only to mind my momma and not worry about a thing except when I was going to have a chance to play with my friends. But today I felt about a hundred years old" (p. 22). Through her sketches, however, she finds a way to salvage the memory of her community. She gives them to her brother as Henry leaves Freedomtown before several Dillon residents make good on their threat to kill him. In an unusual twist, Mrs. Bell's daughter, Catherine Jane, saves Henry by driving him out of town and away from the vigilantes. Henry and Rose Lee must now try to make new homes for themselves, away from their beloved Freedomtown.

## *A Raisin in the Sun* by Lorraine Hansberry (151 pp.)

Lorraine Hansberry's play *A Raisin in the Sun* was written in 1958 and first produced in 1959. Historically, this is a significant play for a number of reasons. In his introduction to the play, Robert Nemiroff synthesizes the significance of "bringing to Broadway the first play by a black (young and unknown) woman, to be directed, moreover, by another unknown black 'first,' in a theater where black audiences virtually did not exist—and where, in the entire history of the American stage, there had never been a serious commercially successful black drama" (p. x).

Apart from the historical significance, if indeed that can be separated, this play has literary significance. *A Raisin in the Sun* has the complex issues and characters that embody good literature. Although this play was not written specifically for young adults, it has numerous issues that are central to adolescence: intergenerational conflicts, tension between new and old ways, oppression, dreams, and the struggle for recognition and approval.

The play centers around the Youngers, a multigenerational family who live together in a small apartment on the south side of Chicago. Lena Younger (Mama) is a widowed day worker; her daughter, Beneatha, is a student at the university; her son, Walter Lee, is a chauffeur; his wife, Ruth, is a maid; and Travis is Ruth and Walter Lee's son. On the surface, this family seems to struggle with the daily grind of making a living and surviving. Underneath that struggle is the constant sense that this family has not found a place, a home that is their own.

In spite of the long hours of tedious work, there is little hope that the family will ever break the cycle of just making ends meet. Their only hope rests in an anticipated check which the Youngers are expecting from Lena's husband's life insurance policy; Big Walter had struggled to keep it paid until his death. The Youngers not only experience typical family struggles between husband and wife, brother and sister, and children and parents, but they also struggle against oppression and racism and for dreams and a decent home. These latter struggles can get right through to the hearts of victims everywhere. Petty squabbles in the Younger family quickly explode into arguments over independence and aspirations.

When Mama takes the insurance check to make a down payment on a little house in the suburbs, her family has mixed emotions about her surprise purchase. Walter Lee is appalled that Mama thinks she can buy them peace by trying to acquire a home in a white neighborhood. Mama tells him, "I just tried to find the nicest place for the least amount of money for my family" (p. 93). Travis shares his grandmother's childlike joy at being able to make a move. Ruth and Beneatha are also excited about moving from their tenement to a house but acknowledge the lack of acceptance or shared community they can anticipate from this move.

It takes an emotional outburst from Walter Lee for Mama to realize the importance of bringing him into the decision she has made. In an attempt to reunite her family, Mama gives Walter Lee the remaining money for a business investment. Walter Lee takes not only the money she gives him to invest, but also his sister's $3000 college fund. He, then, gives it all to a man who turns out to be a con artist. With the loss of this money, the family's hopes for a different future evaporate.

As the family attempts to rebuild their lives after this deceit and failure, Karl Lindner arrives. He claims to represent the Clybourne Park Improvement Association, a euphemism for the group of white families who don't want the Youngers living in their neighborhood. Walter Lee's initial reaction is to take the money offered for their new house. Later, when he has to accept the offer in front of his son, Walter Lee realizes that there isn't enough money in the world to allow people to have "a way of telling us we wasn't fit to walk the earth" (p. 143). The play ends with the Youngers moving to their new house in Clybourne Park but knowing that their struggle to find *home* may be just beginning.

## Prereading Focus for the Young Adult Novel and the Play

Activating prior knowledge is an essential support for readers both prior to and during the reading of any work of literature. For some students, these two texts will be an easy read. For others, the historical information in *White Lilacs* and the play format in *A Raisin in the Sun* might present some reading challenges. One way to help students overcome these challenges is through the use of prereading activities that guide students into the focus and underlying ideas in the reading. The prereading focus for this connection begins with students' definitions of *home*, what it means to struggle for both a physical and a mental *home*, and what it means to be part of a community. Kirby and Liner (1988) suggest using "Here and Nows" as a way to give students the opportunity to think and write about the day's reading, writing, and discussion. The prompts and ideas listed can be used for that purpose throughout the unit as well as for the two activities suggested here.

## Here & Now Prompts

### "The Lightwell" by Laurence Yep

In the following excerpt, Yep describes his grandmother's tiny studio apartment in Chinatown, where there is no direct sunlight, but where she is connected to the others in the building through the noises she hears from her stairwell:

> Side by side, top and below, each of us lives in our own separate time and space.
> And yet we all belong to the same building, our lives touching however briefly and
> faintly.
>
> (p. 11)

Ask students how their memories of *home* connect them to others and/or keep them separated in the time and space that they call *home*.

### *Fly Away Home* by Eve Bunting

After reading this picture book aloud to your students, give them time to write about the things they value in their homes. What would be lost if someone forced them to leave their homes?

### "Another Day in Paradise" by Phil Collins

Play Collins's song at least twice, allowing students to freewrite both during and after the song. Their responses can form the basis for many discussions of what *home* means to them and their responsibility in helping others find or keep their homes.

### *Of Mice and Men* by John Steinbeck

Read aloud the dream dialogue between George and Lennie (See Chapter 3 of this text):

> 'Someday—we're gonna get the jack together and we're gonna have a little house
> and a couple of acres an' a cow and some pigs and—'
> 'An' live off the fatta the lan',' Lennie shouted. 'An' have rabbits. Go on, George!'
>
> (pp. 14–15)

Ask students to discuss the importance of having a place or home to call their own.

### "The Way It Is" by Bruce Hornsby

After listening to this song, ask students to write about things in life that people believe to be "just the way it is." How would they go about changing those things?

### "Skin Deep" by Angela Shelf Medearis

After reading this poem aloud, ask students to think-write about what they would like people to see inside of them if their skins came with a zipper. In other words, what is on their outsides that keeps people from seeing their real selves on the inside?

## Uncommon Commonalities

In a Kagan cooperative learning workshop, I was introduced to an activity entitled "Uncommon Commonalities." This activity is designed to get members of a group to find out information about each other individually and then as a group. This activity can be adapted by following the steps listed in Figure 7.1.

---

**Figure 7.1**

**Adapting "Uncommon Commonalities" to Examine Home**

1.  Close your eyes and think about home. Now try to lock a picture or image of this home in your mind.
2.  Now freewrite for five to ten minutes about home.
3.  Stop writing and complete the "Images of Home" graphic organizer. You may draw pictures if necessary.

**Images of Home**

What do you see? _____

_____

_____

What do you hear? _____

_____

_____

What do you touch? _____

_____

_____

What do you smell? _____

_____

_____

What do you taste? _____

_____

_____

4.  After completing the "Images of Home" graphic organizer individually, get into groups of four or five and complete the "Memories of Home" comparison organizer as a group. Transfer your data onto a transparency to share with the class.

Figure 7.1 continued on next page

---

---

Figure 7.1 continued

### Memories of Home

In the first column, list all of the images of *home* your group members have in common. In the second column, list those qualities of *home* that are unique to each person. Discuss what makes a house a *home*. In your discussion, attempt to define the American dream in regards to *home*.

| **Common Commonalities: Shared Images of Home** | **Uncommon Commonalities: What Makes a House a Home?** |
|---|---|
| _____ | _____ |
| _____ | _____ |
| _____ | _____ |
| _____ | _____ |
| _____ | _____ |
| _____ | _____ |
| _____ | _____ |
| _____ | _____ |
| _____ | _____ |

5. Elect a spokesperson from your group and share your findings with the class, using the overhead projector.

---

## The Questions Game

Chambers' (1996) "'Tell Me' Games" has some strategies for helping students get to deeper meanings in a text. In one of the activities, students do multiple readings of a piece as a way to question and rethink their responses to a poem, short story, or essay. Students read a selection and write three questions they have from that reading. Then individuals exchange the three questions with a partner. Each person attempts to answer her or his partner's questions. Following that discussion, each partnered pair then develops three new questions based on the reading and their discussion. These three questions are then exchanged with another pair of students who tries to answer these questions. The two pairs then combine, discuss the questions and answers, and together make up one new question that they bring to the whole class discussion.

By this time, everyone in the class has participated in the discussion, formulated questions, and done multiple readings of the selection. While there are probably hundreds of poems, short stories, and essays related to finding and returning *home,* the following four poems seem to work well with middle and high school students: "I Am Asking You to Come Back Home" by Jo Carson, "Stopping by Home" by David Huddle, "Return" by Mark Vinz, and "A Letter from Home" by Mary Oliver. Each of these poems has enough complexity to require a second glance, yet each speaks to adolescents about the journeys individuals take in life.

# Reading the Core Works of Literature

## Reading *White Lilacs*

*White Lilacs* makes an excellent read aloud either for students who are reluctant to read or for those who enjoy reading a novel together. The dialogue is realistic, the characters are interesting, and there is a fair amount of action. This novel is also one which could be easily read independently by most students. There are several interesting points for discussion as well as connections to other historical events and time periods that might come up during the reading of the novel. Quotations, questions, and "I wonders" that I highlight during the reading are listed in Figure 7.2.

---

**Figure 7.2**
**Exploring and Extending *White Lilacs***

1. The title of Chapter One is "Garden of Eden." In what ways is Mrs. Bell's garden unlike the biblical Garden of Eden and how does Mr. Williams's garden differ from hers?

2. Momma says that Henry doesn't "know his place" (p. 20). How is knowing your place different from finding your place?

3. What does the following statement tell you about the power structure of Dillon/ Freedomtown in the 1920s: "You can say all you like, but if they decide to knock down our homes to make their park, then you can bet there will be a park right where we're standing" (p. 27)? In what ways has that power structure changed for African Americans?

4. When Miss Firth tells Rose Lee that she is talented, Rose Lee responds by saying, "I just do what I like to do" (p. 35). In what ways does doing what you like to do impact your ability to do a job?

5. Henry joins the United Negro Improvement Association led by Marcus Garvey, but his father and friends prefer the ideas of Booker T. Washington. In what ways are their causes and ideas the same, and in what ways do these men and their ideas differ?

6. Henry says that Garvey favors African Americans returning to Africa in order to be free. His father responds, "Insisting on our right to stay here where we belong is where we got to take our stand" (p. 40). What point is Mr. Jefferson making with this statement?

7. When Dr. Thompson is talking with the men of Dillon about the most appropriate way to handle the relocation, he says, "If the, uh, present inhabitants were permitted to remain where they are, then I think sensitive, astute parents like yourselves certainly have some justifiable concerns" (p. 62). How is language used here to inflame this situation? How is Dr. Thompson manipulating the men of Dillon?

Figure 7.2 continued on next page

Figure 7.2 continued

8. Rose Lee says the men talk about Freedomtown as if she is invisible. How does the idea that the men of Dillon see the people of Freedomtown as invisible help them not feel guilty?

9. As a punishment for speaking out, Henry is "tarred and feathered" (p. 142). In addition to the physical anguish this process causes, what emotional damage might the victim suffer? Is Henry the only one victimized, or are the other townspeople affected by this act?

10. The members of Freedomtown who decide to move to Buttermilk Hill are left the message, ". . . if you don't want trouble, go where you been told to go" (p. 168). In what ways does this kind of intimidation keep the community members "in line" and unable to take control of their lives and community?

11. Mr. Taylor tells Mr. Jefferson that he "won't stay in a place that doesn't want me as much as Dillon doesn't want me" (p. 188). Why would some people want to move because of this, and why would some want to stay in spite of this situation? Would you be a mover or a stayer?

12. Each of the members in the Jefferson family deals with his or her grief in different ways and to some extent each finds a way to keep his or her memories alive. How do their memories help sustain them?

13. When Rose Lee's grandfather is dying, he asks her to "take care of it [the white lilac] for me" (p. 236). In what ways does Rose Lee do that?

14. The people of Dillon just wanted the land in Freedomtown, but the people of Freedomtown lost much more than land. Are there ways that these losses could now be repaid to the children of Freedomtown?

15. In what ways could this relocation compare to that of the Japanese Americans in World War II? What other examples of forced relocation can be compared to the events that happened in Dillon, Texas?

## Reading *A Raisin in the Sun*

*White Lilacs* certainly stands on its own as a historical novel of merit, but the events in the novel also serve as excellent comparisons to the events and conflicts experienced by the Younger family in *A Raisin in the Sun*. Since this is a play and the language is easily read, *A Raisin in the Sun* can be read aloud by students. With different members of the class taking the parts of the characters, the play can be brought to life in a more realistic way than through silent reading. There are also excellent audio and visual productions of this play which can be used to supplement the in-class reading. Discussion highlights for this play are noted in Figure 7.3.

## Figure 7.3

### Exploring and Extending *A Raisin in the Sun*

1. As the play begins, readers see what appears to be a typical day in the Younger family. In what ways does the playwright give us clues about the family dynamics?

2. Although we quickly see the conflict between Beneatha and Walter Lee, in what ways are their goals the same?

3. Walter Lee tells Ruth, "You tired, ain't you? Tired of everything. Me, the boy, the way we live—this beat-up hole—everything" (p. 32). How does tiredness permeate this play?

4. Walter Lee tells Beneatha, "Who the hell told you you had to be a doctor? If you so crazy 'bout messing 'round with sick people—then go be a nurse like other women—or just get married and be quiet" (p. 38). Why might Walter Lee resent his sister's dreams?

5. If everything in life is a tradeoff, what has Walter Lee traded and what has he managed to get in the trade?

6. Ruth confides to Mama that Walter Lee needs something that she can't give him. What kind of pain is Walter Lee suffering that only he can cure?

7. This play is about dreams. In what ways do the characters' dreams differ from each other? How do their dreams change throughout the play?

8. What qualities does George Murchison have that Walter Lee admires and that Beneatha dislikes?

9. What is the significance of Asagai giving Beneatha a new name? How does her name fit the person she is or the person she wants to be? If you were choosing a new name for yourself that fits who you are or want to be, what would it be?

10. Some families appear to be stronger because of their intergenerational connections. Would you say the Youngers are stronger because of the three generations living together? What strengths come from this living situation and what difficulties does the situation cause?

11. Mama asks Beneatha, "What is it you want to express?" and Beneatha replies, "Me!" (p. 48). Why would Beneatha's belief that it is important to find ways to express herself seem ridiculous to Walter Lee, Ruth, and Mama?

12. When Asagai comes to visit Beneatha, he brings her a gift. During their conversation (pp. 60–63), Asagai makes some stereotypical remarks about women. How are your reactions to those remarks similar to or different from Beneatha's? What has or hasn't changed in our culture that would make those remarks more or less accurate?

Figure 7.3 continued on next page

Figure 7.3 continued

13. How do the roles of women in Nigeria impact Asagai's beliefs about women?

14. In a confrontational dialogue between George Murchison and Beneatha, Beneatha explains her definition of assimilationism (pp. 80–81). Brainstorm examples of assimilationism evident in the United States in the 1990s. Do you think it is easier or harder to find examples today than it was in the late 1950s, when this play was written? To what do you attribute the change?

15. On pages 108–109, Walter Lee tells us his vision of the American dream. Do you think this American dream is still the predominant dream of Americans in the 1990s? What has caused changes in the dream?

16. When Mr. Lindner comes to offer the Youngers money not to move into Clybourne Park, Beneatha says, "Thirty pieces and not a coin less!" (p. 118). What is the literary allusion in this line, and how does knowing the biblical allusion increase the impact of the line?

17. On page 141, Walter Lee gives us his philosophy of life. In one hundred words or less, write your philosophy of life. How does it compare to Walter Lee's? What experiences in life have an impact on our philosophies?

18. Mama says, "He finally come into his manhood today" (p. 151). While Walter Lee is somewhat older than a man usually is when he goes through a rite of passage, in what ways has this experience been a rite of passage for Walter Lee? What conditions have to be in place for a person to move from childhood into adulthood? What are some of the rites of passage in our society today? How have those rites changed over time? How do our rites of passage compare with those in other cultures?

19. The ending of *A Raisin in the Sun* seems to be optimistic. With your knowledge of the time period of the play and the family's encounters with Mr. Lindner, what are your predictions about their future at Clybourne Park?

20. What, if anything, do you think Mr. Lindner might have learned from his encounter with the Youngers?

## Connecting the Core Literature

*White Lilacs* and *A Raisin in the Sun* make excellent pieces for comparison in several areas: historical connections of segregation; personal exploration and writing connections related to home and family; symbolism related to flowers, gardens, and new life; and the examination of the source of strength some family members have and manage to pass along to others. After both the play and the novel have been read, the extensions and explorations which follow could be added to those the students might suggest (See Figure 7.4).

---

**Figure 7.4**

**Exploring and Connecting the Core Reading**

1. Read Langston Hughes poems, "Mother to Son," "I, Too," "Dreams," and "A Dream Deferred," and examine the role that struggle has in making our dreams reality. Develop your own American Dream plans, listing the steps you will have to take in order to make your dreams reality.

2. Explore the concept of "the group" in power. Look for examples in videos, comic strips, newspapers, and magazines which illustrate the ways that people gain and keep power. From this, examine the abuse of power as seen in both *White Lilacs* and *A Raisin in the Sun*.

3. When Walter Lee realizes that his money has been stolen, he says, "That money is made out of my father's flesh" (p. 128). In what ways was Freedomtown made out of the Jeffersons' and Mr. Williams's flesh? Explore the paths that have been forged for us by our ancestors. Look at ways in which some negative paths may have been chosen for us.

4. When the members of Freedomtown left, they scattered to different parts of Texas as well as the rest of the United States. In what way is "community" part of our definition of *home*? What would your ideal community look like? How do closed communities or clubs fit with the notion of integration? Where would the Williams, the Jeffersons, and the Youngers stand on the subject of closed communities or clubs?

5. If Mr. Williams from *White Lilacs* could talk with Walter Lee Younger from *A Raisin in the Sun*, what advice would he give him about his move to Clybourne Park?

6. In what ways do Mama's plant and Mr. Williams's garden represent the best of what people can be? Create a visual of the thing or things that would represent those qualities in your life.

7. Create a timeline of the laws that have been passed since the 1920s which have impacted a community's ability to exclude people of color. Use this timeline to create a prediction line for the amount of time and the kinds of laws which will have to be passed before everyone enjoys equality.

---

# Finding *Home* in Young Adult Literature

Teachers wishing to expand the unit might suggest the following picture book and YA titles for students to read either during or after the unit. Bringing in multiple selections based on the same theme not only adds breadth and depth to an instructional unit but also encourages independent, life-long reading.

## Children's Picture Book

### *Fly Away Home* by Eve Bunting (32 pp.)

A young boy and his father live in an airport. Andrew's father only has weekend janitorial work, which isn't enough to afford them an apartment. Andrew is discouraged with their homelessness until he sees a bird that is trapped inside the airport escape. Andrew begins to believe that he, too, may escape. As for the trapped bird, "It took a while, but a door opened" (p. 32).

## Young Adult Fiction

### *Street Child* by Berlie Doherty (154 pp.)

This descriptive novel tells the story of Jim Jarvis, a coal lighter who escapes from a workhouse and forced labor in 1860s London. His freedom from slave labor only pushes him into a life of poverty and homelessness as he finds himself starving and living in the streets. This is a fictional account of the real boy who inspired Thomas John Barnardo to create homes for poor children.

### *Nightfather* by Carl Friedman (136 pp.)

When Carl Friedman's father is asked by his children to tell a story, he tells his story of being in camp. Readers soon discover that the camp is a concentration camp, which sadly was home for him and thousands of others.

### *Jemmy* by Jon Hassler (149 pp.)

When Jemmy's mother dies, she is left with an alcoholic father and a younger brother and sister. Jemmy's father decides that Jemmy must quit school to care for the children, and Jemmy is relieved because school is painful for her. Half white and half Indian, she constantly finds herself searching for her identity. When Jemmy is emotionally and physically taken in by the Chapman family, she is able to begin to see how she might be able to make a home for her siblings and herself.

### *The Frozen Waterfall* by Gaye Hicyilmaz (325 pp.)

Selda leaves "her culture and her brains back in Turkey" when her family immigrates to Switzerland. Her language and culture left behind, Selda begins a friendship with the daughter of a rich family. When this friendship puts her in danger, Selda is able to regain some of the confidence she lost when she emigrated to a foreign country.

### *Letters From the Inside* by John Marsden (146 pp.)

When Mandy responds to a newspaper ad requesting a penpal, she assumes that she has found a friend with an ideal life. A surprising story unravels as Mandy catches Tracy in the first of many lies. This Australian novel is told through a series of letters and leaves the reader saying, "What happened?"

### *Darnell Rock Reporting* by Walter Dean Myers (135 pp.)

When 13-year-old Darnell Rock joins the school newspaper, it is one of the first times that he has shown any interest toward school. His research into the problems of a homeless man helps him to see the value of *home* and school.

### *Shakedown Street* by Jonathan Nasaw (197 pp.)

Caro and her mother are good people who find themselves homeless and living on the streets. While trying to survive, they find *home* and family with a variety of street people. Through this process, they come to realize the importance of creating *home* wherever one lands.

### *Almost a Hero* by John Neufeld (147 pp.)

When Ben's middle school teacher assigns his class a community service project during their vacation, Ben and his classmates are not pleased. Ben's assignment at a day-care center for the children of the homeless, however, leads Ben into learning about *home* and family in ways that he could never have imagined.

### *Out of Nowhere* by Ouida Sebestyen (183 pp.)

When Harley's mother leaves him in the middle of the Arizona desert to go with yet another boyfriend, he realizes that he and his mother are never going to be a family. Armed with only $40.00, Harley is determined to find a family and a home that represent what he imagines *home* could be. Fortunately, he meets a newly abandoned 69-year-old woman named May and a dog named Ish, who help him learn what it means to be part of a family.

### *Jesse* by Gary Soto (166 pp.)

Jesse and Abel leave home in order to escape a stepfather and the stress that he has caused in their family. While doing field work in order to make ends meet and attending college in the hopes of making a new and better life for themselves, they realize that their definition of *home* and family has changed.

## Young Adult Nonfiction and Poetry

### *Latino Voices* edited by Frances R. Arparicio (144 pp.)

This is a powerful collection of poems, essays, and novel-excerpts by Latino writers reflecting many of the experiences and struggles of Latino teenagers. The book also offers brief descriptions of Latino culture which provide background for readers.

### *Stories I Ain't Told Nobody Yet* by Jo Carson (96 pp.)

This collection of numbered poems contains poetry that reaches into the heart of *home* and family. The power is in how the poetry addresses the feelings of those who lose their families.

### *Voices From the Future: Our Children Tell Us About Violence in America* edited by Susan Goodwillie (257 pp.)

This is an honest, uncensored compilation of the words of children and teenagers in America. Introduced by Jonathan Kozol, these words reflect the children's hope and hopelessness, their rage and their pain. These are children without homes, families, and support, but they are children who are still willing to believe that perhaps their words can make a difference.

### *Farewell to Manzanar* by Jeanne Wakatsuki Houston and James D. Houston (145 pp.)

This poignant story of life in an internment camp gives readers a glimpse of the pain of being torn away from the only home one has known and forced to move into a camp. Jeanne Wakatsuki describes her life with 10,000 other Japanese Americans who were forced to leave home and live in Manzanar during World War II.

### *Going Over to Your Place: Poems for Each Other* edited by Paul B. Janeczko (159 pp.)

This collection of American poetry reflects the rich emotions of *home*, family, and life. Many of the poems are reflective of those first experiences that stay in our memories for a lifetime.

### *Strings: A Gathering of Family Poems* edited by Paul B. Janeczko (161 pp.)

This is another multi-author collection of 125 poems reflecting family and home life. The poems are all based on the experiences of the poets with their families and the lives they shared with them.

### *Home: A Collaboration of Thirty Distinguished Authors and Illustrators of Children's Books to Aid the Homeless* edited by Michael J. Rosen (32 pp.)

On each page of this collection of memories, an author or illustrator has captured the space and the place that says *home* for him or her. In his introduction, Rosen says that "Home is what you take away each time you leave the house" (p. 1). The words and pictures of home have a lasting impact: The profits from the book go to support Share Our Strength, which provides funds for food and aid to the homeless.

### *A Summer Life* by Gary Soto (150 pp.)

This collection of essays is Soto's depiction of *home*, community, and family as he grew up in Fresno, California. The essays remind readers of the impact that children's things have on their abilities to vividly remember *home*.

### *I Never Saw Another Butterfly* edited by Hana Volavkova (106 pp.)

This amazing collection of poetry, illustrations, and short narrative pieces chronicles the lives of children whose *home* was the Terezin Concentration Camp. The emotionally-charged pieces remind readers of children's amazing capacity to turn the most gruesome conditions into hope.

### *My Brother, My Sister, and I* by Yoko Kawashima Watkins (233 pp.)

When Yoko and her older brother and sister find themselves alone in post-war Japan in 1947, they learn that they must make a home together. As they struggle to find their missing father, they make a home in a warehouse where they suffer a fire, injuries, and false charges of arson, theft, and murder.

### *American Dragons: Twenty-five Asian American Voices* edited by Laurence Yep (237 pp.)

Yep has collected poetry, short stories, and excerpts from longer works for this collection. Each of the pieces vividly illustrates the sense of home, family, and culture that these Asian Americans have experienced growing up in this country.

## Conclusion

The dream we all share of finding and being able to choose the place that we call home is a critical goal in our lives. Many would agree that home is a basic need; certainly, the physical aspect of shelter is. Georgia Heard (1995) describes home for us:

> Home is what can be recalled without effort. . . . Memories are the blueprints of home. A memoir is a home built from those blueprints. If we carry that home with us all the time, we'll be able to take more risks. We can leave on wild excursions, knowing we'll return.

(p. 2)

By giving students the opportunity to examine home, not only from multiple literary perspectives but also from the perspectives of their community and family lives, we encourage them to define *home* for themselves. Through reading *White Lilacs* and *A Raisin in the Sun*, most students have to move out of their personal experiences with home to times, places, and situations that control where *home* is located for many people. Through reading, writing, and discussion, they may come to realize the historical implications of segregation and the personal implications of choice. Hopefully, they will also come to understand their responsibility in helping to create a world where everyone has a home—a place of shelter in a world that has become unsafe for too many.

## References

Arparicio, F. R. (Ed.). (1994). *Latino voices*. New York: The Millbrook Press, Inc.

Bunting, E. (1991). *Fly away home*. New York: Clarion.

Carson, J. (1989). I am asking you to come back home. In *Stories I ain't told nobody yet*. New York: Theater Communications Group, Inc., p. 93.

Carson, J. (1989). *Stories I ain't told nobody yet*. New York: Theater Communications Group, Inc.

Chambers, A. (1996). *Tell me: Children reading and talk*. York, ME: Stenhouse Publishers.

Doherty, B. (1994). *Street child*. New York: Orchard Books.

Friedman, C. (1991). *Nightfather*. New York: Persea Books.

Goodwillie, S. (Ed.). (1993). *Voices from the future: Our children tell us about violence in America*. New York: Crown Publishers, Inc.

Hansberry, L. (1958). *A raisin in the sun*. New York: New American Library.

Hassler, J. (1980). *Jemmy*. New York: Ballantine Books.

Heard, G. (1995). *Writing toward home: Tales and lessons to find your way*. Portsmouth, NH: Heinemann.

Hicyilmaz, G. (1994). *The frozen waterfall*. New York: Farrar, Straus, & Giroux.

Houston, J. W. & Houston, J. D. (1973). *Farewell to Manzanar*. New York: Bantam.

Huddle, D. (1987). Stopping by home. In P. B. Janeczko's (Ed.), *Going over to your place: Poems for each other*. New York: Bradbury Press, pp. 51–56.

Hughes, L. (1958). A dream deferred. In L. Hansberry's, *A raisin in the sun*. New York: New American Library, p. 5.

Hughes, L. (1984). Dreams. In G. Kearns's (General Adviser), *Understanding literature*. New York: Macmillan Publishing Company, p. 203.

Hughes, L. (1993). I, Too. In R. Anderson, J. M. Brinnin, J. Leggett, G. Q. Arpin, and S. A. Toth's, *Elements of literature*. Fifth Course. Orlando, FL: Holt, Rinehart, & Winston, p. 690.

Hughes, Langston. (1993). Mother to son. In R. Anderson, J. M. Brinnin, J. Leggett, J. Burroway, V. Hamilton, and D. A. Leeming's, *Elements of literature*. Fourth Course. Orlando, FL: Holt, Rinehart, & Winston, p. 232.

Janeczko, P. B. (Ed.). (1987). *Going over to your place: Poems for each other*. New York: Bradbury Press.

Janeczko, P. B. (Ed.). (1984). *Strings: A gathering of family poems*. New York: Bradbury Press.

Kaywell, J. F. (1993). *Adolescents at risk: A guide to fiction and nonfiction for young adults, parents, and professionals*. Westport, CN: Greenwood Press.

Kirby, D. & Liner, T. (1988). *Inside out: Developmental strategies for teaching writing*. Portsmouth, NH: Boynton Cook.

Marsden, J. (1991). *Letters from the inside*. New York: Bantam.

Medearis, A. S. (1995). Skin deep. In *Skin deep and other teenage reflections*. New York: Macmillan, p. 9.

Meyer, C. (1993). *White lilacs*. San Diego: Harcourt Brace.

Myers, W. D. (1994). *Darnell Rock reporting*. New York: Delacorte Press.

Nasaw, J. (1993). *Shakedown street*. New York: Bantam.

Neufeld, J. (1995). *Almost a hero*. New York: Atheneum.

Oliver, M. (1984). A letter from home. In P. B. Janeczko's (Ed.), *Strings: A gathering of family poems*. New York: Bradbury Press, p. 58.

Rosen, M. J. (Ed.). (1992). *Home: A collaboration of thirty distinguished authors and illustrators of children's books to aid the homeless*. New York: HarperCollins.

Sebestyen, O. (1994). *Out of nowhere*. New York: Penguin.

Soto, G. (1994). *Jesse*. San Diego: Harcourt Brace.

Soto, G. (1990). *A summer life*. New York: Dell.

Steinbeck, J. (1993). *Of mice and men.* New York: Viking.

Vinz, M. (1987). Return. In P. B. Janeczko's (Ed.), *Going over to your place: Poems for each other.* New York: Bradbury Press, p. 114.

Volavkova, H. (Ed.). (1993). *I never saw another butterfly.* New York: Schocken Books.

Watkins, Y. K. (1996). *My brother, my sister, and I.* New York: Simon & Schuster.

Yep, L. (Ed.). (1993). *American dragons: Twenty-five Asian American voices.* New York: HarperTrophy.

Yep, L. (1992). The lightwell. In M. J. Rosen's (Ed.), *Home: A collaboration of thirty distinguished authors and illustrators of children's books to aid the homeless.* New York: HarperCollins, p. 12.

## Songs Cited

Collins, P. (1989). Another day in paradise. In *But seriously.* New York: Atlantic Recording Corporation.

Hornsby, B. (1986). The way it is. In *The way it is.* New York: RCA Records.

# The Theme of Belonging in *Jane Eyre* and Young Adult Literature

*Pam B. Cole*

## Introduction

Each of us has a strong need to belong, to feel accepted in the world in which we live. At no period of life is this need stronger than during adolescence. Though Charlotte Bronte's *Jane Eyre* contains numerous themes—feminism, mental illness, domestic violence, abuse, orphans and orphanages, independence, and love—the one theme with which all adolescents will readily identify is that of belonging, of feeling a part of the society or world in which they live.

Unfortunately *Jane Eyre*, which was first published in 1847, is not a readily accessible novel for many high school students. The complexity of the novel alienates many students and leaves them questioning the relevancy of the work to their own lives. For this reason, high school students often do not see the connections between Jane's desire to belong and their own. A preponderance of young adult (YA) literature exists, however, that carries this theme. When YA literature is connected with the reading of *Jane Eyre*, students make real connections with the classic and their own lives.

Numerous YA novels deal with young adults finding their place in the world, but I believe the following titles pair especially well with *Jane Eyre*: *The Midwife's Apprentice*, *Nobody's Daughter*, *Walking Up a Rainbow*, *Keeping the Good Light*, *The Ruby in the Smoke*, and *The Witch of Blackbird Pond*. For the most part, I have chosen to use YA novels that have heroines because of the feminist issues present in *Jane Eyre*. James Bennett's *Dakota Dream*, however, has a male protagonist who also addresses his sense of belonging.

The unit begins with pre-reading activities, moves into selecting and reading YA novels which carry the theme of belonging, and ends with reading and responding to *Jane Eyre*. Using this classic in connection with adolescent literature can bring an otherwise "dead" work to life for adolescents, enabling them to make connections with their own personal experiences and possibly develop an appreciation for an otherwise dreaded piece of literature.

## Building Background Information Through Pre-reading Activities

Before students actually begin reading any of the novels, provide pre-reading activities which will tap their prior knowledge and encourage them to begin thinking about the theme of belonging. Listed below are a number of pre-reading activities that will work well with this unit.

### Questions for Thought

Any of the following questions will be good lead questions for this unit. You may have students discuss them with partners, in small groups, or as a whole class. If choosing whole class discussion, I suggest having all students freewrite about the question(s) prior to discussion to ensure that all students participate and have given thought to the issues.

1. Think of a time when you felt either out of place or alone or felt a strong need to belong. Describe the situation(s) and tell how you felt.
2. What does homelessness mean to you?
3. What do you know about orphans and orphanages?
4. What does being independent mean to you? Do you consider yourself independent? Why or why not?

### Making Connections Through Music and Videos

An effective pre-reading strategy that I have employed in my classroom capitalizes on students' natural interests. Music, MTV, and videos are central to the lives of today's adolescents. Ask students to bring in examples of music and videos that carry the theme of belonging. I generally give students the theme a week or two in advance of the unit to allow them time to make their selections. Remind them that their selections must be appropriate for the classroom. I recommend that the teacher preview and make final selections from the students' suggestions. Once the final selections have been made, I play several of the pieces to the class. While listening, students freewrite and talk about their thoughts regarding the music and the theme of belonging.

### Making Connections Through Children's Literature

Reading children's literature that carries the theme of belonging is another excellent way of introducing the unit. Two books that address this topic particularly well are *All the Places to Love* and *The Little Match Girl*. While the former story illustrates a happy child who has a loving home, the latter one paints a rather stark picture of a child in need.

#### *All the Places to Love* by Patricia MacLachlan (32 pp.)

A young boy, Eli, describes the special places he shares with his family on their farm. The meadow, the hayfields, and the river all carry special meanings for him. Though Eli is not an orphan or an abused child like Jane Eyre, the theme of belonging is very apparent in this book. This story can help students reflect on the importance of having family, of belonging somewhere in life.

### *The Little Match Girl* by Hans Christian Anderson (32 pp.)

While *All the Places to Love* paints a picture of a happy child, *The Little Match Girl* draws a contrasting scene. Fearing for her life, a little girl endures the cold of New Year's Eve to sell matches for her abusive father. Hungry, scared, and cold, the scantily clad child finds a corner that shelters her somewhat from the wind. In this place she lights the matches and imagines food, a warm fire, and the embrace of her loving grandmother. In the bitter cold, she dies a tragic death. This children's story makes a wonderful introduction to the unit because the central character has much in common with Jane Eyre and the heroines of the YA novels. Though not an orphan, she is abused and she lacks food, shelter, and a loving home.

I suggest reading both stories and having students make connections between the two. First, have students read *All the Places to Love* and freewrite about their reactions to the reading. What are their thoughts about the story? How does the ending make them feel and why? Allow students time for discussion of their feelings. Move then to the reading of *The Little Match Girl*, which will provide a stark contrast to the first story. Give students time to freewrite and discuss their feelings regarding this second story and then compare their feelings with those evoked by the first.

## Selecting and Reading the Young Adult Novels

### Six Young Adult Novel Annotations

#### *The Midwife's Apprentice* by Karen Cushman (122 pp.)

An ill-tempered town midwife discovers a homeless young girl sleeping in a dung heap. Jane, the midwife, needs help in her midwifery practice and takes on the girl, known only by the names Brat and Beetle, as an apprentice. Though Brat a.k.a. Beetle sleeps on the raw cottage floor, receives scant food for gathering herbs and doing domestic chores, and is both physically and mentally abused by the midwife and the village boys, she is initially content, for this life is better than any she has known. She becomes discontented when she begins questioning her identity and her future. She discards the names Brat and Beetle, adopts the name Alyce, and yearns to belong.

Alyce proceeds to learn the midwifery profession, and one day is actually called to attend a mother in labor. Flattered by the request, Alyce goes by herself but discovers that she cannot help the mother through a complicated birth. The midwife delivers the baby, leaving Alyce feeling helpless, stupid, and defeated. Alyce flees the town and takes a position in a nearby town as a waitress. One day, the midwife happens to be passing through the town and stops at the inn where Alyce works. Alyce overhears the midwife talking about how Alyce ran away because she gave up. After reflecting on the midwife's words, Alyce decides to return to her home village, where she is once again taken in by the midwife.

Set in medieval England, this 1996 Newbery Award-winning novel has themes similar to those of *Jane Eyre*. Like Jane, Alyce is an orphan looking for a place to belong. She is also abused both verbally and physically by those around her. Despite the abuse, she grows to be self-assured, independent, and strong, like Jane.

### *Nobody's Daughter* by Susan Beth Pfeffer (160 pp.)

When 11-year-old Emily Hasbrouck's great aunt dies, Emily is sent to the Austen Home, a girls' orphanage. Though the girls are treated well at the home, they live a very rigid, disciplined life. Emily makes friends with Gracie and Mary Kate, two other girls in the orphanage. Together they dream about finding happiness, security, and a place to belong. Mary Kate dreams about running away, making it big on the stage, and receiving expensive gifts from men; Gracie longs for the day her mother will return and take her away; and Emily yearns to find her sister and become part of the family that adopted her.

Emily, Gracie, and Mary Kate attend the town school in Oakbridge. One morning, they are accosted both verbally and physically by Isabella, Florrie, and Harriet, three daughters of well-to-do townspeople who resent their attending the public school. The three girls retaliate, only to be accused of starting the incident by Miss Upshaw, the schoolteacher. Because the orphanage is dependent upon donations from the townspeople, Mrs. Browne, the supervisor of the orphanage, forces the girls to make an apology and tells them to turn the other cheek. The three town girls continue to harass the orphans, but Emily seeks comfort in the friendship of Miss Alice Webber, the local librarian, who happens to know the truth.

Emily's friendship with Miss Alice grows. Emily often eats dinner at Miss Alice's house, where she meets Miss Alice's mother. Emily discovers that both Miss Alice and her mother, Aunt Bessie, are strong, independent women. After Emily acquires a job at the library, she shares her dream about finding her younger sister with both of them. Miss Alice and Aunt Bessie help Emily discover the couple, an attorney and his wife, who adopted her sister.

One day Gracie and Emily are accosted by the town girls, but this time Gracie refuses to move from the sidewalk. Upon her refusal, Harriet and Isabella shove her into the street, where she falls and hits her head sharply on a rock; Gracie is killed. Despite Emily's protests, the townspeople claim the event was an accident. Emily, devastated by Gracie's death and the townspeople's refusal to accept the truth, buys a train ticket to Longview, the nearby town where her younger sister lives. There Emily seeks out Ralph Smiley, the attorney who adopted her sister, confident he will take her in and accept her as his own.

Emily is shocked by her encounter with Ralph. He is cold toward her and warns her to stay away from his daughter or else he will have to impose serious discipline on his own child. Emily, out of love for her sister and fear for her sister's happiness, agrees to leave. In the meantime, Miss Alice tracks Emily down and takes her back to Oakbridge. Together they confront the town about Gracie's death.

Set in the early 1900s, this novel depicts a number of strong, independent female characters: Miss Alice, who is not afraid of confronting the wealthy citizens in the community; Aunt Bessie, who refuses to wed again for convenience and security; and Gracie, who refuses to walk in the streets for the benefit of the wealthy town girls. Emily, too, gains strength and courage through the aid of Miss Alice and the memory of Gracie. Emily, an orphan like Jane Eyre, yearns to belong and be loved.

### *Walking Up a Rainbow* by Theodore Taylor (276 pp.)

After 14-year-old Susan Carlisle's parents are killed in a buggy accident, Susan inherits her father's medical practice, the family house in Iowa, and her father's $15,000 debt. G.B. Minzter, owner of a local house of ill repute, holds a lien against Susan's property. In an effort to save her house and land, Susan writes to Brett Pettit, a sheep drover. Susan forges this letter in her father's name, requesting that Mr. Pettit drive her sheep to California, where they can be sold for a handsome profit.

Against Pettit's wishes, Susan and her court-appointed guardian, Indian Myrt, accompany Pettit and his workers on the long and perilous expedition. On the journey, Susan falls in love with one of the hired hands, Clay Carmer. Along with the drover and the herders, Susan and Indian endure heat, physical exhaustion, and Rocky Mountain spotted fever. They also survive attacks from the hired guns of G.B. Minzter, who is determined that Susan will fail on her journey. Susan reveals her strength of character and heroism on several occasions. She amputates a sheep worker's hand and nurses most of the train, including Clay Carmer, through the Rocky Mountain spotted fever.

Upon reaching their San Francisco destination, the party learns that the price of sheep has fallen drastically. Though Susan sells the sheep's wool prior to selling the sheep, she does not collect enough money to cover her father's debt. In desperation, Susan gives the money to Pettit and asks that he take a chance at gambling. Pettit bets the money on a bear and bull fight. He wins, and Susan heads back to Iowa with her money, only to discover that she is too late. The judge, having not heard from Susan, has awarded all of her property to Mintzer. Susan is at first heartbroken, but she turns her attention to her love for Clay Carmer and leaves Kanesville to find him.

In the character of Susan Carlisle, Taylor has crafted an independent, intelligent, and spirited young woman. Like Jane Eyre, Susan is an orphan who must search for her place in the world. Though she initially believes her life's mission is to remain in Kanesville, Iowa, and do everything in her power to hold onto her family home, she learns toward the end of her journey that she has outgrown Kanesville and must move on. Like Jane Eyre, Susan is mature beyond her years and knows what she wants in life.

### *Keeping the Good Light* by Kathryn Kirkpatrick (192 pp.)

Sixteen-year-old Eliza Brown, the daughter of a lighthouse keeper, lives a lonely and melancholy life on Long Island Sound. She lives there with her parents and two older brothers, both of whom she adores. While Eliza's father is a reserved and uncommunicative man, her mother is vocal and critical of Eliza's every move. Eliza's only escape from the island is the schooling she receives on the mainland.

Eliza is particularly fond of her older brother Peter, a lover of boats and the sea. Peter acquires a job working for the owner of the *Reliance,* an America's Cup racing yacht; however, he drowns while trying to save a capsized ship. Stricken by the death of their son and realizing Eliza's loss, Eliza's parents decide to send Eliza to live with her sister, Amanda Jane, and Amanda Jane's husband, Lawrence, on the mainland.

When Eliza arrives on the mainland, Peter's former girlfriend, Sophie, arranges with the school principal to have Eliza fill in as a substitute teacher. Unaccustomed to such freedom and searching for an escape from her present life, Eliza finds herself falling in love with Ralph, a shiftless dreamer. Fearing that Ralph has left town without telling her goodbye, Eliza begins searching the town for him. In a disreputable saloon, a saloon girl reveals Ralph's dishonesty to Eliza. Deeply affected by the revelation, Eliza accepts a marriage proposal from Charles Boxley, a well-to-do young man who is smitten with Eliza. Eliza breaks the engagement, however, upon receiving an offer to become an itinerant schoolteacher of lighthouse children.

Kirkpatrick has created a spirited and rebellious character in Eliza Brown. Though independent and self-determined in many ways, Eliza yearns to belong, to find her space in the world. Like Jane Eyre, Eliza Brown is a strong, independent female character. In addition, she has interests similar to those of Jane: She enjoys drawing, learning, and teaching school. Both young women feel alone and search their inner souls for happiness. Though both are offered convenient marriages, marriages that will ensure they are taken care of, both refuse and choose alternate directions for their lives.

### *The Ruby in the Smoke* by **Philip Pullman (208 pp.)**

Orphaned at 16, Sally Lockhart lives an unhappy life with Mrs. Rees, a cruel distant relative who resents having to take care of the girl. After receiving a crumbled note posted from Singapore telling her to beware of the Seven Blessings, Sally sets out to ask questions, knowing the answers in some way relate to her father's death in the South China Sea. The note sets up a series of unpredictable events in which Sally quickly learns she has an enemy, the wicked Mrs. Holland, who will stop short of nothing but murder to get her hands on a prized ruby. Apparently, Mrs. Holland believes that Sally knows the whereabouts of this ruby.

After Sally becomes aware that her life is in danger, she finds safety in the home of Fredrick and Rosa Garland, a brother and sister who run a photography business. With their aid and that of Jim Taylor, an employee of her father's law firm, Sally begins unraveling the mystery surrounding her father's death. Death, mayhem, danger, a missing ruby, and opium combine to make a story of compelling intrigue.

This novel parallels beautifully with *Jane Eyre.* Like Bronte, Pullman chooses mid-19th century England for his setting. He frequently employs Gothic elements to create a foreboding sense of doom, horror, and mystery. Also, the central characters, both of whom are orphans, find themselves under the guardianship of unwilling and resentful trustees. Mrs. Rees, Sally's guardian, is both cruel and verbally abusive to Sally, just as Mrs. Reed is abusive to Jane. In addition, Sally is a feminist far ahead of her time, much like Jane Eyre. Though she is "unaccomplished" in many traditional female skills, Sally is educated and excels in manly activities: shooting a hand gun, playing the stock market, and keeping financial records for her friends' business.

### *The Witch of Blackbird Pond* by Elizabeth George Speare (256 pp.)

Never having known her parents, Kit Tyler travels to America to live with her aunt's family after the death of her grandfather. Upon arriving, Kit learns that her refined elegance, her lavish wardrobe, and her unique breeding are out of place in her aunt's Puritan household. Kit makes awkward attempts at domestic chores but fails to fit into the harsh Puritan family. She finds an escape through visits to the nearby meadow by Blackbird Pond, where she encounters three significant friends: Hannah, an eccentric elderly woman considered by the colonists to be a witch; Nat Eaton, the Captain's son, with whom she falls in love; and Prudence, the small child whom she teaches to read.

Set in Connecticut during the 17th century, this novel depicts another strong female character. Though on one level the novel is a love story, on another level it can be viewed as a strong representation of feminist literature. Like Jane Eyre, Kit Tyler is an orphan looking for a place to belong. Kit is high-spirited and yearns for a better life; she grows in independence, responsibility, initiative, and in understanding the world around her.

## Introducing the Young Adult Novels

Introduce the six novels to the class without giving away the ending of the books. You may choose an interesting passage to read or perhaps pose a "What If? " question. For example, for *The Midwife's Apprentice,* you might pose the question, "If given a choice, would you rather live with an abusive caretaker or live alone on the streets sleeping in dung heaps to stay warm?" To introduce *Walking Up a Rainbow*, ask students, "What would you do if you inherited a lot of money after your parents' tragic deaths, only to learn that someone was trying to take away your home? Would you move on or would you fight to keep your property?" *Nobody's Daughter* might be introduced by asking students, "What would you do if you were abused daily by other students at school?" Interest in *Keeping the Good Light* may be aroused by asking students, "What would you do if you lived a lonely life on a lighthouse island? Would you consider marrying someone you didn't love as a means of escape?" Or, to introduce *The Ruby in the Smoke* you might ask the students, "What would you do if you learned who was responsible for your father's death?" You might draw students to *The Witch of Blackbird Pond* by asking, "What would you do if you were an orphan living with relatives whose values, beliefs, and customs were very different from your own?" When you have presented all six of the novels, students should choose one to read.

## Concurrent Activities While Reading the Young Adult Novels

One major obstacle adolescents confront when reading a classic, particularly one such as *Jane Eyre,* is making connections with the time period of the novel. Today's adolescents are far removed from the social events, customs, and beliefs of earlier time periods and often either do not care or cannot see similarities and relationships with their own lives. To help students overcome this obstacle, have them maintain a simulated journal—that is, a journal in which the reader takes on the role of a central character in the story. In this simulated role, students are to reflect on their situations as characters in the stories.

This activity works particularly well with these YA novels because all six are set in the past—in medieval or Victorian England, during the Industrial Revolution, in colonial America, or during the American Gold Rush. Thus, having students write about five to ten events that occur in the story, why they do what they do, how they feel about the situations they find themselves in, et cetera, will aid them in thinking about the central character's reactions to events in her life and in comprehending the central character's viewpoints (Tompkins, 1994). Students' reflections and understanding can be deepened by having students meet in small groups two to three times to share thoughts from their simulated journals.

## Post-reading of the Young Adult Novels

After students have read their chosen YA novels, encourage students to work in some book groups to create a visual representation of their novels. This activity works well if you give each group a flipchart and markers. If flipcharts are not available, consider taping large pieces of bulletin board paper on the chalkboard or wall. The idea is to represent the novel through pictures and symbols and only a few key words. After students have completed their visuals, allow them to explain their visual representations. Listen carefully for key elements that will relate to *Jane Eyre* (e.g., belonging, independence, mental illness, and abuse) and capitalize on these in the discussion. To conclude the activity, inform students that they will find many of these ideas in *Jane Eyre*.

## Other Young Adult Novels Worth Considering

### Feminism (Strong Female Characters Who Take Initiative)

*Anne of Green Gables* by Lucy M. Montgomery (429 pp.)

*Catherine, Called Birdy* by Karen Cushman (224 pp.)

*Caught in the Act* by Joan Lowery Nixon (160 pp.)

*A Dangerous Promise* by Joan Lowery Nixon (160 pp.)

*A Family Apart* by Joan Lowery Nixon (162 pp.)

*Finishing Becca* by Ann Rinaldi (304 pp.)

*In the Face of Danger* by Joan Lowery Nixon (176 pp.)

*Keeping Secrets* by Joan Lowery Nixon (163 pp.)

*The Last Silk Dress* by Ann Rinaldi (368 pp.)

*Leona: A Love Story* by Elizabeth Borton de Trevino (151 pp.)

*A Place to Belong* by Joan Lowery Nixon (160 pp.)

*A Ride into Morning: The Story of Tempe Wick* by Ann Rinaldi (368 pp.)

*Winter of Fire* by Sherry Jordan (336 pp.)

**Orphans**

*Anne of Green Gables* by Lucy M. Montgomery (429 pp.)

*The Castle in the Sea* by Scott O'Dell (192 pp.)

*Caught in the Act* by Joan Lowery Nixon (160 pp.)

*Dakota Dream* by James Bennett (182 pp.)

*A Dangerous Promise* by Joan Lowery Nixon (160 pp.)

*A Family Apart* by Joan Lowery Nixon (162 pp.)

*Homecoming* by Cynthia Voigt (312 pp.)

*Indio* by Sherry Garland (304 pp.)

*In the Face of Danger* by Joan Lowery Nixon (176 pp.)

*Keeping Secrets* by Joan Lowery Nixon (163 pp.)

*A Place to Belong* by Joan Lowery Nixon (160 pp.)

*Plainsong for Caitlin* by Elizabeth M. Rees (176 pp.)

*River Rats* by Caroline Stevermer (214 pp.)

*Shadow in the North* by Philip Pullman (320 pp.)

*Tiger in the Well* by Philip Pullman (320 pp.)

*The Tin Princess* by Philip Pullman (304 pp.)

# Reading and Responding to *Jane Eyre*

## *Jane Eyre* by Charlotte Bronte (433 pp.)

Having lost both of her parents as an infant, the young Jane Eyre is reluctantly raised by Mrs. Sarah Reed, her cruel aunt. While in her household, Jane is abused by Mrs. Reed's three children: John, Georgiana, and Eliza. Tired of Jane's presence, Mrs. Reed sends Jane to Lowood Boarding School, an abominable, neglected institute where Jane suffers eight years of hunger, cold, and mental abuse. While there, Jane becomes a model pupil, excelling in her academic studies, particularly art. Jane grows into an independent, mature young woman despite her surroundings and gains her freedom by applying for a governess job and being accepted for employment by the housekeeper of Thornfield Estate.

Though she thinks her surroundings at Thornfield Estate are boring and depressing, Jane finds contentment in teaching the master's foster child, Adele Varens. Edward Rochester, the master of the estate, is a stern, unattractive gentleman, but Jane is fascinated by his personality and charm and falls in love with him. Jane's days at Thornfield take on vitality and life; however, she is haunted by piercing screams and fiendish laughter coming from the attic. One night Jane is awakened by these sounds and goes to investigate. While walking down the hallway, Jane discovers that Mr. Rochester's bed—with him in it—is on fire. She douses the flames with water, saving his life. Mr. Rochester blames the fire on Grace Poole, one of the servants, and convinces Jane to keep the incident a secret.

Jane's love for Mr. Rochester grows. When Mr. Rochester begins dating a local beauty named Blanche Ingram, Jane is devastated. Though Jane sees that Blanche's beauty and wealth surpass her own, she is not bewitched by her charms. Jane sees Blanche for what she is—a very haughty, shallow, and inconsiderate individual. Meanwhile, Mr. Richard Mason arrives at the estate and is physically assaulted by Grace Poole in the middle of the night. Mr. Rochester asks Jane to attend to Mr. Mason's wounds and she complies.

Jane temporarily leaves Thornfield Estate to visit her former caretaker, Sarah Reed, who is ill. On her deathbed, Mrs. Reed informs Jane that Jane has a wealthy uncle living in the West Indies who has been trying unsuccessfully to locate her. Mrs. Reed dies, and Jane returns to Thornfield Estate, where she finds that Mr. Rochester has ended his relationship with Blanche Ingram. He unexpectedly proposes to Jane, she accepts, and wedding plans are made.

Jane's happiness is shattered on her wedding day when Mr. Briggs, a stranger to the community, announces that Mr. Rochester is already married to Mr. Mason's sister. Knowing he has no other recourse, Mr. Rochester escorts the wedding party to the attic of the estate. There they find Grace Poole attending a raging, animalistic lunatic. She is Bertha Rochester, Mr. Rochester's wife. Bertha is the one responsible for setting Mr. Rochester's bed on fire and for injuring her brother. Devastated, Jane flees the estate in the middle of the night.

After traveling on foot for several days and suffering from cold and hunger, Jane collapses at the door of Manor House, where she is taken in by the occupants. Jane recuperates physically while being tended by the owners of the house: St. John and his two sisters, Diana and Mary. Jane settles into her new life after accepting a teaching position in a village school and inheriting her uncle's wealth. She shares her newfound wealth with St. John, Diana, and Mary, who turn out to be distant relatives. When St. John asks her to marry him, she declines, recognizing her continued love for Mr. Rochester.

One night Jane hears a distant voice calling to her; the voice can only belong to Mr. Rochester. She hires a carriage to take her back to Thornfield Estate, where she discovers the estate a charred ruin. As it turns out, Mrs. Rochester destroyed the estate with a fire, killing herself in the process. In an effort to save the lives of everyone in the house, Mr. Rochester loses his sight and a hand. Jane goes to Mr. Rochester's aid, and they finally marry.

## Reading *Jane Eyre*

### Simulated Journals

Because of this novel's difficulty, you may wish to divide the reading of the novel into several parts—perhaps five. While students read the novel, have them maintain a simulated journal similar to the one they kept while reading the YA novels. Decide on a minimum number of responses for this journal. For example, you may decide 12 responses equal an A; nine responses equal a B; six responses equal a C; three a D, and so forth.

Let students meet in collaborative groups of three or four to periodically share their thoughts and feelings about their reading. In these groups, have students identify one major viewpoint to discuss with the rest of the class. Once all groups have identified a major point, have a whole class discussion. Though students should come up with their own questions for discussion, listed below are a few key questions which may facilitate their reading.

1. What feeling does any one of the central characters evoke in you? Why?
2. To what situations or events can you relate?
3. What do you see as major issues in the novel?
4. What character do you most enjoy? Least enjoy? Why?
5. Does anyone in the story remind you of someone you know? Explain.
6. Do you share any of the feelings expressed in this novel? Explain.

### Paired Reading

An additional activity that will facilitate the reading of this complex novel is paired reading. Assign a section of the novel and then pair students. One student is to summarize and paraphrase the reading assignment, while the other student takes on the role of listener. At the end of the summary and paraphrase, the listener must fill in gaps in his or her partner's summary of the story. If there is an odd number of students, assign two students the listener's role. Because adolescents are social beings, this activity works particularly well and encourages students to be active readers.

## Postreading of *Jane Eyre*

Postreading activities for *Jane Eyre* should help students make connections between *Jane Eyre* and the YA novels the students read. I suggest having students create questions and answers that connect major points in the YA novel they read with those in the classic. These questions and answers may take the form of discussions and/or writing. Though students will make some surprising comparisons and contrasts on their own, listed below are some key ideas you may use to facilitate this activity.

1. Compare the setting of your YA novel with that of *Jane Eyre*. What effects do they have on the stories?
2. Compare and contrast the heroines of each novel. In what ways are they alike? Different?
3. Discuss the theme of belonging as it applies to each heroine. Does one heroine struggle more than the other? How so?
4. Compare and contrast the independence of each heroine. Which heroine is more independent? Why? Least independent? Why?
5. How is each heroine affected by her past life as an orphan?
6. Define feminism. In what way is each heroine a feminist?

# Culminating the Unit with Group and/or Individual Projects

Because *Jane Eyre* is so rich in theme and substance, ideas for group and/or individual projects abound. Though I have listed several ideas below, the most meaningful projects are those designed and created by the students themselves. Thus, students should be given every chance to create their own responses to the reading. Students may work on these projects individually, in pairs, or in small groups.

### Movie Review

Have students watch and write a review of either Goetz's *Jane Eyre*, starring Orson Welles and Joan Fontaine, or the newly released version by Franco Zeffirelli. Ask students to think about the ways in which the movie is unlike the novel and speculate or rationalize why certain differences exist. Their responses may take any form, oral or written.

### Here and Now

Have students gather information on current happenings that are similar to those found in one or more of their novels. Have students place this information in folders, and reserve a day for a class share where students talk about what they found and why they included it in their folders.

### Life Map

Feigning the identity of either Jane Eyre or Edward Rochester, students may wish to create a life map of either character. Students draw significant events in the lives of the two central characters using illustrations, a limited number of key words, or symbols. After completing their maps, students explain their work to the class. The simulated journals may serve as a springboard for this activity.

### I-Search Project

Students may choose to complete an I-search paper (Macrorie, 1988) on a topic related to the reading of the novels. For example, students may be drawn to such issues as homelessness, mental illness, abuse, domestic violence, feminism, or the changing roles of women in today's society.

### Media Response Project

Computer wizards will love the opportunity to create a computer presentation. There are numerous programs, such as Hyperstudio and PowerPoint, that would work well for this type of activity. Even if the technology is limited in your school, remember that a growing number of students have access to such powerful programs as Microsoft Office at home and may relish in sharing their "expertise" with the class.

### World Wide Web Search

Students may be interested in surfing the web for information on *Jane Eyre*, Charlotte Bronte, the literary time period in which she wrote, any of the YA novels or their authors, or any of the themes that arose during the reading of the novels. This search can also take the form of an I-search paper. Also, if a number of students choose this activity, you may wish to create a log sheet on which students write down the site addresses, along with the name of the organization and the information they found at each site. You can use this information to help track the time they put into the project, and students can trade site addresses to facilitate their own research.

### Community Resources

Have students think about guest speakers who could share their expertise on any of the topics discussed in class. Together, consider inviting a worker, administrator, or former resident of a local children's home to talk to the class about the experiences of orphans or homeless children. Other possibilities include acquiring a speaker from a women's shelter or a mental institution.

### Social Action Project

Obviously, the most meaningful responses will be those in which students make personal connections with the novels. Students may wish to move beyond the context of the novel into looking at such issues as homelessness or child abuse in their own communities. For instance, students may wish to volunteer time in a homeless shelter or visit a children's home and a women's shelter. They may also write a paper or give a presentation to the class based on their experiences.

### Mentoring Relationship

As a college instructor, I have had my college students go into middle school classrooms and act as research facilitators for middle school students researching such issues as domestic violence and abuse. A mentoring relationship often evolves between my students and the middle schoolers. Many upper elementary and lower middle school teachers welcome the opportunity of having older students come into their classes and talk about serious issues with their students.

Some students may be interested in sharing newfound knowledge about children growing up without parents with younger students. This idea may take two directions: (1) You may have your students conduct research about orphans and deliver this presentation to younger students; or (2) you may arrange with the classroom teacher ahead of time to have the younger students read a novel in the *Boxcar Children* series—an upper elementary, lower middle series dealing with a group of orphans. Your students read the novel as well and attend the middle schoolers' classes one day to facilitate a class discussion on the novel. Mentoring possibilities are endless.

## Conclusion

With the increase in the number of children living in nontraditional homes, the issue of belonging—of having family—is a major concern for today's adolescents. Because such books as *The Midwife's Apprentice, Nobody's Daughter, Walking Up a Rainbow, Keeping the Good Light, The Ruby in the Smoke,* and *The Witch of Blackbird*

*Pond* are briefer and more accessible to students, high school students can more readily make connections with the central characters in these works. Once they are able to do so, they can more readily understand and appreciate the complexity of *Jane Eyre*.

# References

Anderson, H. C. (1987). *The little match girl*. New York: Sandcastle Books.

Bennett, J. (1994). *Dakota dream*. New York: Scholastic.

Bronte, C. (1986). *Jane Eyre*. New York: Bantam.

Cushman, K. (1994). *Catherine, called Birdy*. New York: Clarion.

Cushman, K. (1995). *The midwife's apprentice*. New York: Clarion.

de Trevino, E. B. (1994). *Leona: A love story*. New York: Farrar, Straus, & Giroux.

Garland, S. (1995). *Indio*. San Diego: Harcourt Brace.

Jordan, S. (1992). *Winter of fire*. New York: Scholastic.

Kirkpatrick, K. (1995). *Keeping the good light*. New York: Delacorte Press.

MacLachlan, P. (1994). *All the places to love*. New York: HarperCollins.

Macrorie, K. (1988). *The I-search paper*. Portsmouth, NH: Boynton Cook.

Montgomery, L. M. (1908). *Anne of Green Gables*. Boston: L.C. Page & Company.

Nixon, J. L. (1988). *Caught in the act*. New York: Bantam.

Nixon, J. L. (1994). *A dangerous promise*. New York: Bantam.

Nixon, J. L. (1987). *A family apart*. New York: Bantam.

Nixon, J. L. (1988). *In the face of danger*. New York: Bantam.

Nixon, J. L. (1995). *Keeping secrets*. New York: Delacorte Press.

Nixon, J. L. (1990). *A place to belong*. New York: Bantam.

O'Dell, S. (1983). *The castle in the sea*. Boston: Houghton Mifflin.

Pfeffer, S. B. (1995). *Nobody's daughter*. New York: Delacorte Press.

Pullman, P. (1987). *The ruby in the smoke*. New York: Alfred A. Knopf.

Pullman, P. (1988). *Shadow in the north*. New York: Alfred A. Knopf.

Pullman, P. (1990). *Tiger in the well*. New York: Alfred A. Knopf.

Pullman, P. (1996). *The tin princess*. New York: Random House.

Rees, E. M. (1996). *Plainsong for Caitlin*. New York: Avon Books.

Rinaldi, A. (1994). *Finishing Becca*. San Diego: Harcourt Brace.

Rinaldi, A. (1988). *The last silk dress*. New York: Holiday House.

Rinaldi, A. (1991). *A ride into morning: The story of Tempe Wick*. San Diego: Harcourt Brace.

Speare, E. G. (1958). *The witch of Blackbird Pond*. New York: Dell.

Stevermer, C. (1992). *River rats*. New York: Harcourt Brace Jovanovich.

Taylor, T. (1994). *Walking up a rainbow*. San Diego: Harcourt Brace.

Tompkins, G. E. (1994). *Teaching writing: Balancing process and product*. 2nd edition. Englewood Cliffs, NJ: Merrill.

Voigt, C. (1981). *Homecoming*. New York: Atheneum.

Warner, G. C. (1993). *The boxcar children*. New Hyde Park, NY: Learning Links.

## Films Cited (Each Available on Home Video)

Goetz, W. (Producer). (1944/1972). *Jane Eyre*. Beverly Hills, CA: 20th Century Fox.

Zeffirelli, F. (1996). *Jane Eyre*. Miramax Films.

# Is the Dream Still Impossible?: Using Young Adult Literature from Diverse Hispanic Cultures to Illuminate Themes in *Don Quixote*

**9**

*Connie S. Zitlow & Lois T. Stover*

## Introduction

Increasingly, English teachers are finding that they are being asked to teach world literature. The National Council of Teachers of English (NCTE) *Guidelines for the Preparation of Teachers of English Language Arts* (1986) recommends that English teachers have knowledge of titles from cultures around the world reflecting many rich and varied literary heritages (See Note at chapter's end.). From the Spanish-speaking world, the one "classic" text most English teachers are familiar with is *The Adventures of Don Quixote* by Miguel de Cervantes Saavedra, the story of an idealistic man who transforms himself into a knight and sets out to do battle with the giants and ogres of his day. At times Don Quixote finds he is tilting his lance at windmills, but at other times he accomplishes something of substance.

Margaret Hodges introduces her adaptation, titled *Don Quixote and Sancho Panza*, by referring to a statement from the Mexican author Carlos Fuentes: "When Don Quixote mounted his horse and rode away from his village, the modern world began" (Hodges, p. 1). According to Hodges, many writers believe *Don Quixote* is not only the world's first modern novel but also might be the world's greatest novel. Written in the 17th century by a Spanish author, *Don Quixote* is not reflective of contemporary culture within Spain, nor can it be viewed as representative of the widely diverse contemporary Hispanic life around the globe. The themes embodied in *Don Quixote*, however,—of idealism, friendship, and responsibility—are timeless and universal. They echo through texts from very different countries in which Spanish is spoken and through various Hispanic/Latin-American cultures. The premise of this chapter is that when *Don Quixote* is paired with Young Adult (YA) titles about adolescents of diverse Hispanic origins, today's youth will gain a deeper understanding of the classic tale and will learn more about their peers from modern Spain, South and Central America, Mexico, and from Chicano and Latino-American cultures. Three young adult protagonists who are representative of these contemporary peers are Laetitia "Lacey" Johnson (*For the Life of Laetitia* by Merle Hodge), Isabel Pacay Choy (*Imagining Isabel* by Omar S. Castañeda), and Juanita Chavez (*Juanita Fights the School Board* by Gloria Velásquez).

137

Laetitia "Lacey" Johnson is the first in her extended family to qualify for secondary school. She is thrilled, but to attend the school, she must leave her grandmother and her happy Caribbean village home. She is not sure her dream of graduating is possible. It means she must live with her strange, distant father and oppressed stepmother and learn to deal with many difficulties at school, including prejudiced teachers. The dreams of Lacey's new school friend, Anjanee, seem even more impossible. Anjanee is very poor and struggles with helping her mother care for her large family while also pursuing an education in hopes of having a life less burdened than her mother's.

In Guatemala, 16-year-old Isabel Pacay Choy also struggles to fulfill her dream. To accept the government's invitation to attend a teacher-training program, she must leave her new husband and her recently widowed father. Isabel knows she is expected to stay home and lead a traditional life in her Mayan village. Even though she does manage her studies while still caring for her young sister, she is haunted by mysterious events, strange political turmoil, and frightening people. Isabel often wonders what or who is really in control of her life. Like Lacey and Anjanee, Isabel must battle poverty and prejudice.

To keep from being expelled from her high school, Juanita Chávez, a poor Mexican American, must battle the whole school board and others in her California town. Juanita, like Anjanee and Isabel, takes over adult responsibilities in caring for the little ones in her family and wants to succeed in school. After she is forced into a fight with a fellow student who spreads rumors about her family, it seems Juanita has shattered the dream she and her family have of her becoming the first one to graduate from high school.

Lacey, Isabel, and Juanita each inhabit difficult, conflicting worlds: the real world of a home life filled with hardship and a world represented by school and dreams of a different future. With self-determination, persistence, and pride, they try to bridge the two worlds. They hope to re-create themselves and succeed regardless of threatening prejudice and resistance from others. Are their dreams impossible?

Like the legendary Don Quixote, these young protagonists are driven by idealism and an imagination that keeps the self alive. Their dreams are constantly threatened by earthbound common sense and forces much larger than themselves. Is it foolhardy for them to be optimistic? Are they "mad" to live in dreams amidst grim reality? Are their journeys worth the struggles? How are they different from the ones who do not try to fight the "knights" or the monstrous giants of poverty and prejudice? As exemplified by the brief summaries, there are overlapping themes in these novels that deserve discussion.

In this chapter, we will show how the following selected themes from the classic work *The Adventures of Don Quixote* are also themes in contemporary YA literature: Battling Windmills or the Monstrous Giants of Poverty and Prejudice; Pride and Persistence; Re-Creating Self; Companions in Battle; Reality and Fantasy; and Living in Dreams Amidst Grim Reality with an Imagination that Keeps the Self Alive.

Following a brief discussion about *Don Quixote*, the first part of each section will examine how the timeless themes from Cervantes' novel are woven through the stories of Lacey, Isabel, and Juanita. These stories, reflective of the wide cultural diversity of the people who speak Spanish, are examples of YA literature with thematic connections to *Don Quixote*. The issues and situations in these novels are faced by contemporary protagonists whose stories are dominated by universal questions about seemingly impossible dreams. The second part of each section is an annotated list of numerous Hispanic-American and Latin-American works related to the themes. All the YA novels included can be used as bridges into the world of the classic knight whose story is as relevant today as it was in the 17th century.

## Don Quixote, the Man of La Mancha

The story of literature's best-known dreamer is the basis for the musical *Man of La Mancha* and the well-known song "To Dream the Impossible Dream." The first part of the book about an old Spanish gentleman who believes he is a knight appeared in 1604. Walter Starkie in his introduction to a 1957 edition wrote, "Don Quixote, a lanky scarecrow of a man with his withered face and lantern jaw, dons his rusty armor and mounts his ramshackle steed Rozinante. With lance couched he still rides through our lives followed by his pot-bellied squire Sancho Panza" (p. ix).

Although knights had not ridden in Spain for hundreds of years, Don Quixote transforms himself into a knight. He sees perilous adventures where others see humdrum realities. His imagination transforms everything he encounters as he travels on Rozinante through the countryside with his faithful but dubious companion, Sancho. They ride from one adventure to another in search of ogres, giants, and evil knights. In one famous episode, Quixote charges straight into the flailing arms of a windmill, which he sees as a monstrous giant. Through many grueling, life-threatening situations, Don Quixote's imagination keeps him alive. To him, an inn becomes a castle where he is cared for by prostitutes whom he sees as ladies in waiting; sheep become armies to conquer; and a farm girl, Aldonza Lorenzo, becomes his "Lady Dulcinea del Toboso." His friends think he is mad. His fantasy is in vivid contrast to the reality Sancho and others see. Why does he continue when threatened by the grim realities of hunger, poverty, and numerous batterings from people and objects?

In spite of the ridicule, Don Quixote remains quixotic, an idealist who urges Sancho on: "Learn, Sancho, that one man is not more than another unless he achieves more than another. All those storms that fall upon us are signs that soon the weather will be fair, and things will go smoothly, for it is not possible for evil or good to last for ever" (p. 78). Don Quixote gradually convinces Sancho to be more idealistic. At the end of the novel, Sancho urges his master to live, ". . . take my advice and live on for many a year; sure 'tis the maddest trick a man can play in his life, to yield up the ghost without more ado, . . . Who knows but we may find Lady Dulcinea behind a hedge and disenchanted and as fresh as a daisy" (p. 431).

### Three Contemporary Young Dreamers

While the story of *Don Quixote* with all its comic scenes is a satire of the extravagances of chivalry as well as one of the best adventure stories of world literature, it is more. It is a romance about knighthood, one placed in a real world. Its serious and universal themes transcend time and place and are found in numerous contemporary stories as represented by these three young dreamers: the protagonists Laetitia ("Lacey"), Isabel, and Juanita, who dream of better lives and futures in the midst of grim realities.

### *For the Life of Laetitia* by Merle Hodge (213 pp.)

**Laetitia.**    "Lacey" tells her own story as she is headed to the biggest and most modern thing in La Puerta, the secondary school where she has earned a place. Her whole extended family has celebrated, especially her Ma (grandmother) and Uncle Leroy. Her mother, who is working in New York, has agreed that even though Lacey barely knows her father, she will have to stay at his house in La Puerta. Lacey thinks she can adjust to living with him, his wife Miss Velma, and her difficult little stepbrother Michael as long as she can go home every weekend to her beloved Sooklal Trace. At school, Lacey has a wonderful English teacher who tells the class that the *Tales of the Greek Heroes* are old-time folktales like the Anansi stories of Lacey's own heritage. But how can she learn from the strange Spanish teacher who does not even look at his students; or from Mrs. Lopez, the math teacher, who is dressed like a "circus-horse;" or from the social studies teacher who teaches that children who do not live in a house with their own birth mothers and fathers are "unhappy children" living in "broken homes" (p. 50)?

Things get tougher when Lacey's father refuses to give her weekend bus fare. Lacey's challenges are nothing, however, compared to those of Anjanee. Anjanee cannot buy books, gets up at four o'clock to help her mother clean, cook, and care for the little ones, and then walks many miles to school. Her father and brothers, who do not want her to go to school, refuse to give her money for a taxi ride to the bus stop. Anjanee is always tired, often misses school, is ridiculed by the math teacher, and has trouble passing until Lacey tutors her. Even more than the challenges Lacey faces, Anjanee's situation is a vivid example of tension between a seemingly impossible goal and the reality of her life.

Even though Lacey's father warns her about befriending a "coolie" and Mrs. Lopez tells her that "when you play with dogs, you get fleas" (p. 198), Lacey will not abandon Anjanee. In spite of getting in trouble at school, being threatened by her father, becoming very sick, and confronting Anjanee's grim realities, Lacey persists. Her stepmother Miss Velma and Anjanee's mother represent the monstrous giants of poverty and male domination of women that she fights. Her pride and determination, like Don Quixote's, cause her pain and difficulty but also keep her from thinking her dream is impossible.

### *Imagining Isabel* by Omar S. Castañeda (192 pp.)

**Isabel.**    As for Lacey and Anjanee, it would be easier for Isabel if she did not pursue an education. She lives in the Central American country of Guatemala. Even though she is surrounded by poverty and political unrest, Isabel is proud of her traditional Mayan background. Like Lacey, Isabel is a loving, intelligent female whose dreams have difficulty surviving in the context of her life's hardships and expectations. As the oldest female in her family, she knows it is her duty to care for her little sister Marcelina, her brothers, and her father.

Soon after marrying her beloved Lucas, she receives an official letter saying she has been recommended for a training program designed to educate rural students and place them back into their villages as teachers:

> The letter should have been a flash of light in her life, but instead it reminded her of all her ambivalence. . . . [It] is one thing to have unlikely dreams stored in the pockets of one's being so that even that little weight made one bend forward and take steps . . . in the direction of the dreams. It was a very different thing to have unlikely dreams with no weight at all, or to chop them up with fear or with the safe certainty that the dreams would never happen.
>
> (pp. 12–13)

If she remains at home to care for her family, she has no chance of fulfilling her dream of being a teacher. Would it be foolish for her to leave her new husband, Lucas, and accept the government's invitation to attend school? Not only does Lucas seem to understand Isabel's dream, but because the program includes a stipend and they need the money, Lucas urges Isabel to accept. Isabel does accept, but she must take her little sister, Marcelina, with her.

Isabel's goal is threatened by many realities: caring for Marcelina, adjusting to the teachers and other students, studying to succeed at school, and dealing with strange political events and mysterious people. She has many questions: Who is the person who leads her to the body of a dead man? Is it too much of a fantasy for her to pretend she did not see the body? Are some of the other students spies for the guerrilla resistance? Who has control of the culture? Is it the Ladinos created by the Spanish conquerors, the Mayans, the American government, or the males? At one point in the story, Isabel imagines herself fleshed out and strong because of her certainty and ability to defend herself. She blushes at her own idealism when she declares to Lucas, "I see now what I have been thinking all along. That maybe in one of those children I teach there will be—could be—just one or two who are stronger than I am, one who will be able to go out for all of us" (p. 175). When faced with frightening situations, Isabel finds out how strong and courageous she is.

Isabel's story begins as her dying mother gives her a sacred bundle of tokens passed down through 11 generations of women. Isabel knows it is a unique legacy of "utterly common" objects imbued with something far more powerful than what it seems on the surface. For her it symbolizes not what someone else imagines for her, but her dream of a transformation of herself. Like the legendary Don Quixote, she wants to live her own dream regardless of the realities that surround her.

### *Juanita Fights the School Board* by Gloria Velásquez (149 pp.)

**Juanita.**   Like Lacey and Isabel, Juanita has her own story to tell. Her counselor, Dr. Sandra Martínez, also narrates some chapters in the story. Juanita, one of six children of Mexican immigrants, lives in a town where there are only a small number of Mexicans and blacks. She wants to graduate from Roosevelt High School and eventually become a Spanish teacher. Unfortunately, Juanita is expelled from school for fighting with Sheena, a girl who spreads lies about the Chávez family. While she is out of school, Juanita works at home caring for her little siblings and meets regularly with Dr. Martínez. As she lives with the very difficult repercussions of events caused by her own actions, Juanita knows she will have to learn to control her temper.

Sometimes at night when everyone is asleep, Juanita cries because she misses school so much. She also finds it difficult to obey her strict father, who will not let her go to dances even though she is sixteen. Juanita's dream of returning to school and graduating does not seem very likely given the prejudices expressed by the school administrators and the realization that the school board seems to have made a decision before the scheduled hearing. Juanita's family is treated with rudeness and disrespect. They need an attorney to help, but they have no money. Dr. Martínez elicits the help of Sam, a white lawyer, who donates his time to help Juanita battle the school board.

# Selected Universal Themes in Related Young Adult Literature

The themes from the classic *Don Quixote* and the three YA novels from different settings are also clearly echoed in the poetic voices of Lori M. Carlson's edited collection *Cool Salsa: Bilingual Poems on Growing Up Latino in the United States,* selected portions of which will introduce each theme in the following discussion.

To show the universality of the struggles and powerful dreams of Lacey, Isabel, and Juanita, an annotated bibliography of contemporary YA works organized by their thematic connections with *Don Quixote* is also included. It is striking to note the connections with both the YA protagonists featured and the poetic voices in Carlson's *Cool Salsa.* The annotated list features examples of YA books from Hispanic, Chicano, and various Latino cultures. These books would be particularly useful for individual and small group reading as adolescents expand their understanding of the universal themes in classic and contemporary literary works.

## Battling Windmills or the Monstrous Giants of Poverty and Prejudice

The following is an excerpt from "The Secret" by Pablo Medina (Carlson, p. 51).

> When I made it to school
> they thought I didn't
> have a mind in English and if
> you don't have a mind in English
> you have a mind in nothing.

Lacey, Isabel, and Juanita have many encounters with monstrous giants that threaten their dreams. They would understand the hunger and discrimination Don Quixote and Sancho face. The young women all live with the reality that their families have very little money, not even enough to pay for bus fare associated with their schooling. They are expected to help their families obtain food and clothing, not use the money for other things. Besides being part of poor families, all three face teachers, peers, and, in some cases, whole communities who see them as members of an inferior race and class of people. They are ridiculed for the way they talk and dress, and their families are scorned.

### *Heart of Aztlan* by **Rudolfo A. Anaya (209 pp.)**

Anaya uses the myth of Aztlan, the mythological place of the Aztecs, as the basis for this novel. Chavez, a former ranch hand now living in the impoverished barrio of Albuquerque, faces chronic unemployment, prejudice, and discrimination that tear away at his hopes and self-esteem. Yet with the help of Crispin, a man known within the barrio as a sage, Chavez comes to understand the sources of the poverty and inequities he and his people face. In the process of challenging the inequities, he also becomes a leader. (Chicano, high school)

### *Voices from the Fields: Children of Migrant Farmworkers Tell Their Stories* by **Beth S. Atkin (96 pp.)**

Atkin has collected poetry, photographs, and personal narratives from the children of migrant workers living in the Salinas Valley of California. The pages of this work convey the difficulties of living in poverty, of working the fields, of battling against stereotypes, and of surviving the pressures of gangs and families. (Chicano, middle school)

### *Fear the Condor* by **David Nelson Blair (160 pp.)**

Bartolina, an Amarya Indian of Bolivia, battles against the monsters of poverty which chain her family to a farm. Bartolina also confronts the superstitions of her grandmother, which create fear in her heart. Eventually, Bartolina runs away from the life she has known rather than continue to live as a slave to traditions and conflict. (Latino (Bolivia), high school)

### *Journey of the Sparrows* by **Fran Leeper Buss with Daisy Cubias (155 pp.)**

In this 1992 Jane Addams Award-winner, Buss describes in detail and with empathy the plight of the illegal alien. After Maria's father and brother-in-law are murdered, the rest of the family flees from war-torn El Salvador and goes into hiding in Mexico. Then, in a daring move, Maria and her younger brother and pregnant sister ride into the United States inside of a nailed crate on the bed of a truck. They make their way to Chicago, where they live in poverty and in fear of the immigration officials who search for illegal aliens. Not only do they struggle to survive in the city, but they must also figure out a way to get the rest of their family out of Mexico. (Latino (El Salvador), high school)

### *El Salvador: Country in Crisis* by **Glenn Alan Cheney (127 pp.)**

Although peace accords have now been signed in El Salvador, the tension lingers as a result of the country's protracted civil war. Cheney's text explores the issues of poverty, class, and injustice that contributed to that war as well as to the current political climate in El Salvador. Cheney also reveals how land reform efforts and the ideological differences among various parties, including the guerrilla FMLN and a militaristic government, affect the lives of the people living there. (Latino (El Salvador), middle or high school)

### *An Island Like You: Stories of the Barrio* by **Judith Ortez Cofer (165 pp.)**

Drawing on her memories of how it feels to be caught between two cultures, Cofer gives the reader 12 loosely interconnected stories about the joys and difficulties inherent in coming of age in El Barrio in New Jersey. Sandi, in "Beauty Lessons," unfavorably compares her own looks to the conventional Latino ideal of female beauty; Arturo, of "Arturo's Flight," fantasizes about leaving the Barrio, where he is an outsider because he does not conform to Latino notions of manhood. In "Home to El Building," Anita, too, dreams of breaking free of the poverty and prejudice that keep her and her peers trapped where they are. (Chicano, high school)

### *Inside Nicaragua: Young People's Dreams and Fears* by **Rita Golden Gelman (189 pp.)**

Through hundreds of interviews with Nicaraguans from diverse backgrounds, Gelman exposes the human side of the history of revolution and conflict that has colored life in Nicaragua for so long. Readers meet 12-year-olds who join the army, guerrillas, haters of the Contras, Sandinista opponents, teachers, and government workers. All express their disapproval of the U.S. government's financial support of the Contras, and Gelman makes her own position clearly known as well. In this text, published before the Sandinistas were defeated in the national election, Gelman provides great insight into the reasons for that defeat and introduces American readers to a point of view—that of the Nicaraguans themselves—seldom expressed in U.S. coverage of events. (Latino (Nicaragua), middle or high school)

### *Schoolland* by **Max Martinez (250 pp.)**

Set in the 1950s and based on his own experiences as an adolescent, Martinez's novel describes the coming of age of a Mexican-American teenager who has to cope with the hardships caused by a Texas drought. Intense racism and prejudice abound. (Chicano, high school)

### *El Bronx Remembered: A Novella and Stories* by **Nicholasa Mohr (179 pp.)**

In all of her stories, Mohr provides readers with insights into the complexities of immigrant life. In "A Special Pet," for example, the reader experiences the despair born of poverty. When Mrs. Fernandez has to sacrifice her children's pet hen, named for Joan Crawford, in order to make chicken soup for her sick husband, her children react with anger.

In "Shoes for Hector," the protagonist hates a particular pair of shoes he has been forced to wear for his graduation. Because of economic reality, Hector must borrow these ugly, long and pointed orange shoes from his uncle if he wants to have something to wear on his feet for this special occasion. When Hector receives monetary gifts in celebration of the event, there is no doubt that he has to purchase a pair of shoes rather than do something perhaps more practical with the money.

In another story, a group of girls are so absorbed in their game of bouncing a ball that they momentarily forget their whereabouts and the very real dangers of life in the ghetto. The girls are, therefore, nonplussed when they stumble across a corpse, a victim of the violence that is so commonplace in their lives. (Chicano, middle or high school)

### Sisters/Hermanas by Gary Paulsen (230 pp.)

In this bilingual text, Paulsen contrasts the worlds of two very different young women, Traci and Rosa. Traci is born into a well-to-do family who has expectations for her that do not mesh with her own definition of "success." Then there is Rosa, a Mexican girl, who is trying to break the chains of poverty designed to keep her in her place within the materialistic U.S. society. In spite of their differences, these two young women are "sisters" in their need to cope with the prejudices that can make it difficult to be oneself. (Chicano, middle school)

### The Migrant Earth by Tomas Rivera (160 pp.)

In poetic language, Rivera weaves a series of 14 vignettes to create a moving novel about the miseries experienced by Mexican-American migrant workers. Rivera's characters search for their identities while battling the injustices of American con men, an educational system that does not value their culture, and the difficulties inherent in a life of manual labor in the fields. (Chicano, high school)

### North of the Rio Grande: The Mexican-American Experience in Short Fiction edited by Edward Simmen (448 pp.)

These stories explore the issues of discrimination as experienced by Mexican Americans in the United States. Both Chicano and Anglo authors as varied in style and insight as Sandra Cisneros, Willa Cather, Stephen Crane, and Carlos Flores are included. (Chicano, high school)

### Baseball in April: And Other Stories by Gary Soto (125 pp.)

With this collection of short stories, Soto captures the feelings of adolescents everywhere. Soto battles the windmills of prejudice and stereotyping by describing the joys, sadness, humor, and emotional tensions of his Chicano characters. There is Manuel, who tries to impersonate Richie Valens at a school talent contest. There is Lupe, a "brain," who uses her head to become the marble champion of her street so that she can fit in with her peers. And there's Yollie, who is angry at her mother and with being poor. But when a special boy asks Yollie to the movies, her mother understands and uses the money from her cigar-box savings to buy an outfit from Macy's that Yollie can wear with pride. (Chicano, middle school)

### *Benito Juarez* by Dennis Wepman (112 pp.)

In exciting narrative fashion, Wepman tells about Benito Juarez's quest to obtain a better life for his people. Juarez, a Zapotec Indian and an ardent admirer of Lincoln, knew early in life that he needed to leave Oaxaca in order to pursue his dreams. After earning a law degree, Juarez works within the legal system to support the poor. As a legislator, Juarez helps create a constitution for Mexico modeled after the U.S. Constitution in an attempt to abolish the peonage system and to separate the powers of church and state in Mexico. While learning about Mexican history, readers see events in U.S. history from a different perspective. (Hispanic/Mexico, middle or high school)

## Pride and Persistence

The following is an excerpt from "Why Am I So Brown?" by Trinidad Sánchez, Jr. (Carlson, p. 110).

> God wants you to understand . . . brown
> is not a color . . . it is:
> a state of being a very human texture
> alive and full of song, celebrating—
> dancing to the new world
> which is for everyone . . .

Don Quixote is so proud of his role as a knight and persists in his journey regardless of his many hardships and mishaps. Lacey, Isabel, and Juanita, too, regardless of their situations and the many difficulties they face, exhibit unique pride about who they are and who they hope to become. While some of their cultural and social roots cause them to wonder where they fit in, they are proud of their families and their heritage. Their persistence and courage are most noticeably exemplified by their determination to successfully complete more education, although there are many obstacles in the way.

### *Where Angels Glide at Dawn: Stories from Latin America* edited by Lori M. Carlson and Cynthia L. Ventura (114 pp.)

Carlson and Ventura have selected ten stories specifically for young adults, representing diverse Hispanic cultures such as those of Argentina, El Salvador, Mexico, Chile, Peru, Panama, Puerto Rico, and the barrios of New York. The stories address the politics of these diverse societies and convey the pride individuals from these cultures feel in their origins. Some of the stories are humorous in tone; others are ironic. Almost all of them introduce young readers to the magical realism prevalent in Hispanic cultures that authors often use as a vehicle to comment upon personal and political events. (Latino, middle or high school)

### *And Also Teach Them to Read* by Sheryl Hirshon and Judy Butler (240 pp.)

In this autobiographical account, Hirshon describes how she, a former middle school English teacher, took part in the massive literacy campaign undertaken by Nicaragua the year after the revolutionary government finally succeeded in winning power. Hirshon led a group of Managuan boys into the countryside of war-torn Nicaragua. Hirshorn's sympathies lie with the Sandinistas, but her story and insights are less important than the stories of her young men and their fight against illiteracy. As they struggle to adjust to rural life, sometimes antagonizing the older peasants they have been sent to educate, these young men gain pride in themselves and in their country. (Latino (Nicaragua), high school)

### *Rio Grande Stories* by Carolyn Meyer (224 pp.)

Rio Grande Middle School in Albuquerque is a magnet school for talented adolescents. When the 7th graders at this school are asked to implement a project that will fit the curricular demands and help raise money for the school, they decide to research their own heritages and create a book about the various ways of life along the Rio Grande. Meyer alternates between the students' contributions and the stories of how individuals came to write what they did in a collection that celebrates the diversity and pride of those who live in New Mexico along the river's banks. (Chicano, middle or high school)

### *Latinos: A Biography of the People* by Earl Shorris (520 pp.)

Using individual stories interspersed with journalistic commentary, Shorris presents an historic overview and contemporary analysis of the ways in which Latinos attempt to preserve their pride in their culture while dealing with issues such as bilingualism and the need to assimilate into mainstream culture in order to achieve economic security. (Latino, high school)

### *Jesse* by Gary Soto (176 pp.)

Jesse, a son of migrant workers, is a talented artist who has done fairly well in school. When his brother is drafted and goes off to fight for the United States in Vietnam, Jesse has to make difficult decisions about his own politics and level of involvement in efforts to improve the lot of his people. (Chicano, high school)

### *Living Up the Street: Narrative Recollections* by Gary Soto (159 pp.)

The teenagers in Soto's stories resemble adolescents everywhere. They are mischievous, rambunctious, loyal to each other, sometimes courageous, and sometimes deceitful. Based on his own adolescence in Fresno, Soto's characters show the reader the determination and humor it takes to come of age in the barrio. (Chicano, middle or high school)

**Pieces of the Heart: New Chicano Fiction edited by Gary Soto (179 pp.)**

Sixteen stories by various Americans of Mexican descent are included. Although the stories are diverse in plot, tone, and mood, each one demonstrates the Chicano pride in heritage and courage of the heart that breaks the stereotype many readers have of Mexican Americans. (Chicano, middle or high school)

## Re-Creating Self

The following is an excerpt from "Love Poem for My People" by Pedro Pietri (Carlson, p. 121).

> . . . if you want
> to feel very rich
> look at your hands
> that is where
> the definition of magic
> is located at

Among the "giants" or obstacles the young women in these novels must battle are century-old expectations of their roles as females. Isabel knows what her father, brothers, and even her husband expect of her, regardless of her desire to become a teacher. Lacey's friend Anjanee knows her father does not want her to go school and will not help her. He says that she knows all a woman needs to know. Anjanee tells Lacey that her father and brothers do not even see the work her mother does: "And she working day and night for *them*—she don't get to do one thing for herself" (p. 65). Lacey is told what is expected of a woman when Miss Velma warns her, "Your father, you mustn't go against him. It don't pay to get them vex . . . you have to please them. That is a woman's lot" (p. 86). Miss Velma's warning sounds like the orders of the mother in the poem "The Changeling" by Judith Ortíz Cofer. Dressing in her brother's clothes and telling "tales of battles and brotherhood" in an attempt to impress her father, the young girl is told by her mother to "return invisible, as myself, to the real world of her kitchen" (Carlson, pp. 37–38). Juanita, who also wants the attention and privileges given by her father to her brothers, would understand the longing expressed in the poem.

These young women want to be something different from what others expect. They do not always know why they are so determined, but their dreams to transform themselves, which cause them great hardships, also move them forward. They would understand what Luis J. Rodríguez says in his poem "The Calling" about what he is called to become and to achieve. (Carlson, pp. 123–124). Is their idealism as foolish as Don Quixote's seems to be at first or can they, too, eventually convince others to believe in their dreams?

**How the Garcia Girls Lost Their Accents by Julia Alvarez (308 pp.)**

In a series of 15 interconnected stories, Alvarez describes the relationships among the Garcia girls as they move from the Dominican Republic to the United States. These four daughters of a Dominican doctor must try to recreate themselves as American women. (Hispanic (Dominican Republic), high school)

### *Among the Volcanoes* by Omar S. Castañeda (183 pp.)

Castañeda explores the clash of both old and new cultures as well as Guatemalan and western ones. Isabel, the eldest daughter of a Mayan family, wants to become educated and have a career as a teacher. Her family, however, expects her to care for her sickly mother. Some episodes, such as those involving the Guatemalan military, seem to be included more to make a point than to further the story, but the author's prose evokes the beauty of Isabel's homeland and the intensity of her struggles to determine a life and identity of her own. The story is continued in *Imagining Isabel*. (Latino (Guatemala), middle or high school)

### *Celebrating the Hero* by Lyll Becerra de Jenkins (160 pp.)

After Camilla's mother's death, Camilla decides to remember her by attending a ceremony honoring her grandfather in her mother's hometown in Columbia. While in the country of her origins, Camilla learns a great deal about her family's cultural heritage, including information about political repression, religious traditions, and oral storytelling. She then begins to incorporate these insights into her evolving sense of self. (Hispanic (Columbia), high school)

### *The Honorable Prison* by Lyll Bercerra de Jenkins (199 pp.)

Because Marta's father, a journalist, opposes the government of an unnamed South American country and takes a firm stand in favor of human rights, Marta and her family must serve internal exile in a cold, damp corner of that country. The climate is devastating for her father, who has weak lungs; food is scarce and money is even more so. Marta's isolation, her boredom, her brushes with despair, and her conflicting feelings toward her father are conveyed in almost poetic prose. As Marta learns to depend on her own resources and struggles to understand her father's position, she comes to a new sense of who she is and who she wants to be. (Latino, middle or high school)

### *Nilda* by Nicholasa Mohr (292 pp.)

Nilda, a young woman from Puerto Rico who is living in New York, is struggling with identity issues. Nilda has to determine who she is and wants to be within the context of the Hispanic culture and its values and established roles for women. She also has to cope with bad feelings when she is shunned by a young woman from Spain who believes Nilda's dialect reflects a lack of breeding and social status. Caught between her father's communism and her mother's Catholicism, Nilda struggles to define her own set of beliefs as she tries to answer for herself the typical adolescent question, "Who am I?" (Latino, high school)

### *My Friend, the Painter* by Lygia Bojunga Nunes (85 pp.)

After his painter friend is found dead, Claudio seeks to learn whether or not the man committed suicide. As he investigates the background of his friend, whom he loved for teaching about colors and textures including the "color of longing," Claudio discovers that the painter had spent several years in prison for his political involvement. Claudio is a much more philosophical young man than most American adolescents, but his efforts to deal with death, to learn about himself, and to gain appreciation for his own life in the process are issues that all young adults need to address. (Latino, middle school)

### *Days of Obligation: An Argument with My Father* by Richard Rodríguez (240 pp.)

These autobiographical essays explore Rodríguez's sense that he is caught between two cultures, the tragic vision represented by Mexico and the more optimistic viewpoint of contemporary California. As an academic and native of California, the author struggles to determine what it means to be a dark-skinned young man who views himself as American but who also knows the meaning of his roots as the child of Mexican immigrants. (Chicano, high school)

### *Chileno!* by Antonio Skarmeta (92 pp.)

Lucho moves to Berlin when his family is forced to flee their native Chile in the aftermath of the military coup of 1973. As the first member of the family to learn German, Lucho has to deal with both increased responsibilities and increased tensions with his father. His initial failure to understand the German way of doing things leads him into a physical conflict that helps him begin to establish a bicultural identity. As Lucho experiences the loneliness and sense of exclusion political exiles often feel, his sense of humor helps him survive. This well-crafted novel shows a young man struggling to create a sense of self under difficult circumstances. (Latino (Chile), middle or high school)

### *El Yanqui* by Douglas Unger (300 pp.)

James becomes Diego when he is taken into the home of an upper-class Argentine family as part of the International Student Exchange Program. Diego welcomes the chance to escape his lower-class, tension-filled American family. Although he is able to give up the drugs that characterized his life on Long Island, he still gets into trouble. Diego enjoys adventure and the company of young women too much for his own good. Diego is eventually arrested and beaten by the police. Meanwhile, his new family is getting involved with terrorist activities. Because they are attached to their American friend, they do everything they can to try to help Diego recreate himself within the context of their world. (Latino (Argentina), high school)

## Companions in Battles

The following is an excerpt from "Brown Girl, Blonde Okie" by Gary Soto (Carlson, p. 94).

> Jackie and I cross-legged
> In the yard, plucking at
> Grass, cupping flies . . .
> Talking not dogs or baseball
> But whom will we love, . . .

Certainly the role of a companion is a key part of *Don Quixote*. To be a knight, one must have a squire to support him in battle. Sancho not only stands by Don Quixote, he believes his companion's promise that he will become a governor. Their dialogue, their mutual dependencies, their different reactions to the same adventures, and the change in their relationship to each other all exemplify what is essential to the process of learning about and reacting to life.

Lacey, Isabel, and Juanita have companions who support them and whom they support as they battle to reach their dreams. Without Lacey's friendship and support, Anjanee has no chance to succeed; Lacey finds it very difficult to continue in school without Anjanee there. Isabel has the support of Lucas, the affection of her loving little sister, and eventually, even the help of strange Nina. At times, however, each of her companions adds to Isabel's burden in one way or another. Juanita also has a variety of companions who each serve a different purpose: her younger sister, Celia, who helps her care for the little ones; Dr. Martínez, who counsels her; and Sam, who serves as her attorney at the school board hearing.

### *Intaglio: A Novel in Six Stories* by Roberta Fernandez (160 pp.)

Nenita is the 13-year-old narrator who weaves together the threads of the lives of many women who help shape her in various ways. Readers meet several of Nenita's friends: Esmerelda, a beautiful young woman who sells tickets at a movie theater; Amanda, who sews by day and concocts herbal cures by night; Andrea, a ballerina who seems to have escaped Nenita's life and who sends pictures back to her friend from all the cities where she performs; Filomena, from Mexico, who never intended to spend her life in Texas; and Zulema, who makes the Mexican revolution come alive for Nenita. (Chicano, high school)

### *The Sabbath Garden* by Patricia Baird Greene (192 pp.)

Opie is a 14-year-old basketball star. Choncita is a beautiful Puerto Rican girl. Mr. Leshko is the only remaining Jew in the tenement in which they all live. Together, they create a garden in the midst of their otherwise bleak landscape, providing the community with a reason to come together and to work toward a common goal. (Latino, middle or high school)

### *Luisa's American Dream* by Claudia Mills (160 pp.)

Fourteen-year-old Luisa Ruiz has a dream: Blond, blue-eyed Travis, the object of her crush, will fall in love with her. Unfortunately, Travis is neither from the Eastside nor Cuban-American like Luisa. She is afraid Travis will reject her if he learns the truth about her family and her origins. Luisa's best friend, Beth, and her brother, Tom, help her in her quest to feel good about herself while coping with the everyday problems of being a teenager in love. Luisa's feelings of shame are portrayed realistically, providing readers with a great deal of insight into the nature of the Cuban exile's experience in the United States. (Latino (Cuba), middle or high school)

### *The Forty-Third War* by Louise Moeri (200 pp.)

Through the adventure story of three young boys, Moeri explores the issues of civil war and its effects on children. After Uno, Lolo, and Nacio are kidnapped by the army of their unnamed Central American country, they are given eight days of minimal training and are expected to fight in a battle. Not only are the forces clearly unprepared, but the boys do not understand the causes of the battle. After meeting and getting to know the commander of the revolutionary forces, the boys develop a sense of loyalty to his cause and a respect for him as an individual. (Latino, middle school)

### *Pacific Crossing* by Gary Soto (144 pp.)

Lincoln, a Mexican-American youth, and his friend Tony are participants in a student exchange program that sends them to study martial arts in Japan for six weeks. The Japanese hosts and their son, Mitsuo, are eager to learn about Lincoln's culture, and Lincoln comes to appreciate theirs. There are some humorous incidents when the two cultures collide. (Chicano, middle or high school)

### *I, Juan de Pareja* by Elizabeth Borton de Trevino (192 pp.)

Juan de Pareja begins life as the slave of a merchant but then is sold to Velázquez, the court painter of 17th-century Spain. In secret, Juan learns to read, write, and even paint. He becomes a friend to his master, earning the respect of the great man for his loyalty and dedication to his art. Ultimately, the painter frees de Pareja, who then pursues his own career as an artist. Although de Trevino admits in the afterword that she took some liberties in writing about these two historical figures, she also states that their mutual affection and respect is a documented fact. (Hispanic (Spain), middle school)

## Reality and Fantasy

The following is an excerpt from "'Race' Politics" by Luis J. Rodríguez (Carlson, p. 69).

> When they had enough, they threw us back,
> dirty and lacerated,
> back to Watts, its towers shiny
> across the orange-red sky.

What is true and just? In *Don Quixote*, poor Andrew is beaten by his master who says Andrew is careless with the sheep. Andrew, however, says his master just looks for an excuse to get out of paying him. Whose truth should Don Quixote and Sancho believe? With this episode and others in the classic novel, Cervantes explores the complexities of reality and fantasy, justice and injustice, truth and lies.

Lacey, Isabel, and Juanita also experience the complexities of wondering about truth and must battle injustice if their dreams are to become realities. Lacey wonders about the reality of what her teacher says about happy families. Her wonderful extended family is not like the broken one the teacher described, nor is Anjanee's family what Lacey would think of as a happy one. Isabel eventually asks Nina about the real purpose of the school and wonders who imagined her in the role of one who would help the cause of the guerrilla fighters. Juanita's truth about the fight with Sheena in school is very different from the "truth" the school board would like to believe.

### *Bless Me, Ultima* by Rudolfo A. Anaya (249 pp.)

Ultima is the local faith healer. Aged and alone with no family of her own, Ultima is brought to live with 17-year-old Antonio Marez and his family. Antonio adores her and is in awe of this older woman's powers, which she uses only for the good of the community. When Ultima becomes the object of the wrath of a local sorcerer, a practitioner of black magic, Antonio finds himself in the middle of intense conflict. He tries to comprehend the struggle going on in his community, and, at the same time, to determine his own sense of self in relationship to both his family and the community. Through dream sequences in which Antonio attempts to understand the ways in which Ultima has affected his life, Anaya explores the multifaceted nature of human experience. (Chicano, high school)

### *The Enchanted Raisin* by Jacqueline Balcells (104 pp.)

Balcells combines a whimsical tone with the devices of the traditional folklore of her native Chile in these seven stories that, nevertheless, demonstrate her modern outlook. Her use of hyperbole and metaphor (in one story, a mother tells her sons that their misbehavior is causing her to turn wrinkled and old before her time—she does, eventually, shrivel up and turn into a raisin), her references to the land and its potential violent impact through earthquakes and volcanoes, and her descriptions of traditional family life combine to provide the reader with a strong feeling for Chile and its people. (Latino (Chile), middle school)

### *The Mythology of Mexico and Central America* by John Bierhorst (256 pp.)

This work includes a brief history of the peoples of various regions, an overview of basic myths, and an analysis of the basic myths within the historical context out of which they arose. With this knowledge, readers can begin to recognize the nature of the common belief structure that helps define a culture. (Hispanic/Latino, high school)

### *The Mythology of South America* by John Bierhorst (256 pp.)

The creation myths, trickster myths, and myths about the relationships between men and women of seven distinctive regions of South America are presented here within the context of Bierhorst's analysis of the nature of myth and of its origins. Bierhorst also evaluates the political uses and significance of myths within South America's tumultuous political climate. The text is supplemented with photographs of artifacts—masks, pottery, and other crafts—associated with the transmission of myths from one generation to the next. (Hispanic/Latino, high school)

### *Woman Hollering Creek and Other Stories* by Sandra Cisneros (165 pp.)

In the 22 stories that make up this anthology, Cisneros displays a wide range of mood and emotion, from the intensity of the rage in "Never Marry a Mexican," to the humor of "Barbie-Q," about two young girls playing with their Barbie dolls. In "Eyes of Zapata," the author introduces a note of magical realism to make her point, tying her soundly to the literary traditions of Isabelle Allende and Gabriel García Márquez. (Chicano, high school)

### *One Day in the Tropical Rain Forest* by Jean Craighead George (56 pp.)

Weaving fact and fiction in a story of adventure, George entertains and educates readers about the plight of the Latin American rain forest. Tepi, the protagonist of this story, works with scientists in an effort to protect the rain forest. On his way back to the lab, Tepi sees an approaching caravan of bulldozers and trucks, sent to tear down the trees. Thus, Tepi knows that he and his adult colleagues have only one day left to find a currently unknown butterfly; if they can do so, a wealthy man will buy the land and preserve it in exchange for being able to name the butterfly for his daughter. Tepi is successful and the rain forest of George's story is saved, but she points out that others are not so fortunate. (Latin America, middle school)

### *Sor Juana Ines de la Cruz* by Kathleen Thompson (32 pp.)

Juana Ines de la Cruz is considered one of Mexico's finest mystic poets. Blessed with remarkable intelligence, she learned to read at a very young age and became a well-educated young woman in spite of the odds against her. At the time, her society was under the influence of a powerful archbishop who believed that women had no right to study, pursue artistic endeavors, or debate religion and politics. Juana, however, disagreed and did whatever it took to get educated, even if that meant dressing as a boy in order to attend college. As a result of her experiences, Juana made a commitment to battle the prejudices against well-educated females existing within her society. The bilingual text is highlighted with full-color illustrations. (Hispanic (Mexico), high school)

## Living in Dreams Amidst Grim Reality with an Imagination that Keeps the Self Alive

The following is an excerpt from "We Would Like You to Know" by Ana Castillo (Carlson, p. 113).

We would like you to know
we are not all docile
nor revolutionaries
but we are all survivors.

Like the legendary Don Quixote, if Lacey, Isabel, and Juanita did not imagine themselves as transformed, they would have no dreams. The overwhelming burdens of poverty, prejudice, and cultural expectations are grim realities that could easily defeat
them. Fortunately, in their imaginations they are something more than a poor girl from
the English-speaking Caribbean, or a young wife from Guatemala, or a hot-tempered
Mexican-American girl from Roosevelt High School. It is because of the relentless
existence they know so well that they are afraid not to dream.

### *Children of the Maya: A Guatemalan Indian Odyssey* by Brent Ashabranner (96 pp.)

Based on interviews with Mayan Indians who have fled from the repression and
war of their native land to one Florida community, Ashabranner describes the forced
relocations, compulsory military service, and other hardships that led to their desire to
emigrate to America. Ashabranner also focuses on their efforts to preserve their heritage within a very different context, allowing them to tell their stories in their own
words so that readers understand the dreams and the realities that make it sometimes
difficult to preserve a sense of idealism. (Hispanic (Guatemala), middle school)

### *The Most Beautiful Place in the World* by Ann Cameron (64 pp.)

After his mother abandons him, 7-year-old Juan struggles to keep his dreams—of
going to school, learning to read and write, and creating a better life for himself—
alive. Juan has to live with his grandmother, who sells arroz con leche at the market
where she expects him to shine shoes, contributing his earnings to the family. Although Juan, at seven, may seem young, his desire to know whether or not his grandmother truly loves him, and his efforts to make something more of himself than society
would have him be, make him an appealing character to older readers as well as to
younger ones. (Hispanic (Guatemala), middle school)

### *The House on Mango Street* by Sandra Cisneros (134 pp.)

In highly poetic style, Cisneros presents vignettes drawn from her own childhood
experiences, scarred by poverty and oppression in the barrios of Chicago. Esperanza,
the young woman narrator, dreams of a home of her own, a place of space and light.
Esperanza is a victim of the deprivations associated with class prejudice as well as the
boundaries she experiences as a result of being a female in a male-dominated culture.
(Chicano, middle or high school)

### *Sandino's Daughters: Testimonies of Nicaraguan Women in Struggle* by Margaret Randall (224 pp.)

Women made up a large portion of the revolutionary Sandinista forces that acted to overthrow the Somoza dictatorship of Nicaragua in 1979. Randall, a photographer and writer, spent two years in the country just after the coup interviewing many women about their reasons for participating in the revolution. The women represent a wide cross-section of the population. Readers meet teenagers, high-ranking military officials, members of the upper-class, young mothers, and older women all desperate for change and willing to risk their lives to accomplish it. (Latino (Nicaragua), high school)

### *Burning Patience* by Antonio Skarmeta (118 pp.)

Mario, at eighteen, delivers mail on La Isla Negra, where Chilean poet Pablo Neruda lives. When he falls in love with Beatriz, daughter of the local innkeeper, Mario enlists the aid of his poet friend in his quest for her hand. Then, Neruda leaves the island to serve as ambassador to France for the newly elected socialist president Salvador Allende. Neruda returns two years later, dying of cancer. The country, in which socialism seems to be at death's door, is in the wake of the bloody coup of 1973. Mario scrambles against various obstacles to say goodbye to his hero but is taken away by soldiers of the new government. References to Neruda's poetry, sexual references, and a sophisticated brand of humor make this poetically written novel best suited for older readers, who can gain valuable insight into Chile and its people from this book. (Latino (Chile), high school)

### *We Live in Mexico* by Carlos Somonte (60 pp.)

Men and women from various Mexican villages and cities, representing several generations, tell about who they are and what they do. Each interviewee's first-person narrative is accompanied by several color photographs that highlight the distinctive aspects of their lives. The author provides a section outlining basic facts about Mexico and a glossary of Spanish terms. (Hispanic/Mexico, middle school)

## Conclusion

The determination to look ahead and be something as characterized by the many young protagonists in the literature annotated in this chapter is reflected in Ana Castillo's words, "We are going forward. There is no going back" (Carlson, p. 103), and in the poem "Return" as translated from the Spanish by Lori M. Carlson, "Better that today shine on tomorrow that will lead us to the future" (p. 106). The ability to look forward and to dream, themes explored in *Don Quixote,* are certainly part of literature from all over the world, including works especially written for young adults.

**Note:** See Kaywell's Chapter 6 in *Adolescent Literature as a Complement to the Classics*, Volume Two, for a comprehensive discussion on "Using Young Adult Literature to Develop a Comprehensive World Literature Course Around Several Classics."

# References

Alvarez, J. (1991). *How the Garcia girls lost their accents*. Chapel Hill, NC: Algonguin.

Anaya, R. A. (1972). *Bless me, Ultima*. Berkeley, CA: Tonatiuh-Quinto Sol International Publications.

Anaya, R. A. (1976). *Heart of Aztlan*. Berkeley, CA: Editorial Justa.

Ashabranner, B. (1986). *Children of the Maya: A Guatemalan Indian odyssey*. New York: Putnam.

Atkin, B.S. (1993). *Voices from the fields: Children of migrant farm workers tell their stories*. Boston: Little, Brown, & Company.

Balcells, J. (1989). *The enchanted raisin*. Swissdale, PA: Latin American Literary Review Press.

Bierhorst, J. (1990). *The mythology of Mexico and Central America*. New York: William Morrow.

Bierhorst, J. (1988). *The mythology of South America*. New York: William Morrow.

Blair, D. N. (1992). *Fear the condor*. New York: Lodestar Books.

Buss, F. L. & Cubias, D. (1991). *Journey of the sparrows*. New York: Lodestar Books.

Cameron, A. (1988). *The most beautiful place in the world*. New York: Alfred A. Knopf.

Carlson, L. M. (Ed.). (1994). *Cool salsa: Bilingual poems on growing up Latin in the United States*. New York: Henry Holt.

Carlson, L. M. & Ventura, C.L. (Eds.). (1990). *Where angels glide at dawn: Stories from Latin America*. New York: HarperCollins.

Castañeda, O. S. (1991). *Among the volcanoes*. New York: Lodestar Books.

Castañeda, O. S. (1994). *Imagining Isabel*. New York: Lodestar Books.

Cervantes, S. M. (1957). *Don Quixote*. Translated by Walter Starkie. New York: Mentor (Penguin).

Cheney, G. A. (1990). *El Salvador: Country in crisis*. New York: Franklin Watts.

Cisneros, S. (1991). *The house on Mango Street*. New York: Random House.

Cisneros, S. (1991). *Woman hollering creek and other stories*. New York: Random House.

Cofer, J. O. (1995). *An island like you: Stories of the barrio*. New York: Orchard Books.

de Jenkins, L. B. (1993). *Celebrating the hero*. New York: Lodestar Books.

de Jenkins, L. B. (1989). *The honorable prison*. New York: Puffin Books.

de Trevino, E.B. (1987). *I, Juan de Pareja*. New York: Farrar,. Straus, & Giroux.

Fernandez, R. (1990). *Intaglio: A novel in six stories*. Houston, TX: Arte Publico Press.

Gelman, R. G. (1988). *Inside Nicaragua: Young people's dreams and fears*. New York: Franklin Watts.

George, J. C. (1990). *One day in the tropical rain forest*. New York: HarperCollins.

Greene, P.B. (1993). *The Sabbath garden*. New York: Lodestar Books.

Hirshon, S. & Butler, J. (1984). *And also teach them to read*. Westport, CT: Lawrence Hill.

Hodge, M. (1993). *For the life of Laetitia*. New York: Farrar, Straus, & Giroux.

Hodges, M. (1992). *Don Quixote and Sancho Panza*. Illustrated by Stephen Marchesi. New York: Charles Scribner's Sons.

Kaywell, J. F. (1995). Using young adult literature to develop a comprehensive world literature course around several classics. In J.F. Kaywell's (Ed.), *Adolescent literature as a complement to the classics*. Volume Two. Norwood, MA: Christopher-Gordon Publishers, Inc., pp. 111–143.

Martinez, M. (1988). *Schoolland*. Houston, TX: Arte Publico Press.

Meyer, C. (1994). *Rio Grande stories*. San Diego: Harcourt Brace.

Mills, C. (1981). *Luisa's American dream*. New York: Four Winds Press.

Moeri, L. (1989). *The forty-third war*. Boston: Houghton Mifflin.

Mohr, N. (1975). *El Bronx remembered: A novella and stories*. New York: Harper & Row.

Mohr, N. (1973). *Nilda*. New York: Harper & Row.

National Council of Teachers of English. (1986). *Guidelines for the preparation of teachers of English language arts*. Urbana, IL: National Council of Teachers of English.

Nunes, L. B. (1991). *My friend, the painter*. New York: Harcourt Brace Jovanovich.

Paulsen, G. (1993). *Sisters/Hermanas*. San Diego: Harcourt Brace.

Randall, M. (1995). *Sandino's daughters: Testimonies of Nicaraguan women in struggle*. New Brunswick, NJ: Rutgers University Press.

Rivera, T. (1986). *The migrant earth*. Houston, TX: Arte Publico Press.

Rodríguez, R. (1993). *Days of obligation: An argument with my father*. New York: Penguin.

Shorris, E. (1994). *Latinos: A biography of the people*. New York: Avon Books.

Simmen, E. (Ed.). (1992). *North of the Rio Grande: The Mexican-American experience in short fiction*. New York: Mentor (Penguin).

Skarmeta, A. (1987). *Burning patience*. New York: Pantheon.

Skarmeta, A. (1979). *Chileno!* New York: William Morrow.

Somonte, C. (1985). *We live in Mexico*. Living Here Series. New York: Franklin Watts.

Soto, G. (1990). *Baseball in April: And other stories*. New York: Harcourt Brace Jovanovich.

Soto, G. (1994). *Jesse*. San Diego: Harcourt Brace.

Soto, G. (1985). *Living up the street: Narrative recollections*. San Francisco: Strawberry Hill Press.

Soto, G. (1992). *Pacific crossing*. New York: Harcourt Brace Jovanovich.

Soto, G. (Ed.). (1993). *Pieces of the heart: New Chicano fiction*. San Francisco: Chronicle Books.

Thompson, K. (1990). *Sor Juana Ines de la Cruz*. Milwaukee, WI: Raintree.

Unger, D. (1988). *El Yanqui*. New York: Harper & Row.

Velásquez, G. (1994). *Juanita fights the school board*. Houston, TX: Arte Publico Press.

Wepman, D. (1987). *Benito Juarez*. World Leaders Past and Present Series. New Haven, CT: Chelsea House.

## Song Cited

Kapp, M. (1973). To dream the impossible dream. In *Man of La Mancha*. Universal City, CA: MCA Records.

# 10

# Love & Sacrifice:
## *Staying Fat for Sarah Byrnes,*
## Seven Young Adult Novels, and
## *A Tale of Two Cities*

*Patricia L. Daniel*

## Introduction

Most young adults will have experienced, at some level, both the pleasure and the pain of being in love. Focusing on the theme of love and sacrifice in *A Tale of Two Cities*, several young adult (YA) novels will be presented that will help prepare students to embrace Dickens's tale. I personally want students to be moved every time they hear the words, "It was the best of times, it was the worst of times. . . ." (p. 9) and for them mentally, if not verbally, to finish the sentence. I want students to have connected with Sydney Carton and his willingness to sacrifice himself because of his strong love when they read and later hear, "It is a far, far better thing that I do, than I have ever done. It is a far, far better rest that I go to, than I have ever known" (p. 351).

## *A Tale of Two Cities* by Charles Dickens (352 pp.)

First published in 1859, this classic tale is Dickens's portrayal of the horrors of the French Revolution. The revolution occurred because the aristocracy exploited the poor and forced such class-hatred that the poor had nothing to lose by revolting against the aristocracy. As Dickens tells his story, he focuses on the people both in England and in France. Dickens makes his characters' personal pain, determination, patience, cunning, love, and sacrifice driving forces because he does not want England to endure a similar revolution.

Dickens's characters embody the good and the evil of two cities. For example, Madame Defarge embodies the hatred of the working-class that overthrew the Bastille and killed many government officials, impaling their heads on sticks. She is patient in her revenge, and she cunningly manages people. Her patience is misinterpreted by many because she appears to be unobservant; however, she knits the names of her intended victims in garments. Her hatred is complete and her willingness to sacrifice her own life is evident in the all-consuming nature of her thoughts. She is also willing to sacrifice anyone else for her cause, and no one is bigger than the cause.

Sydney Carton, on the other hand, embodies what is noble of character. He is a frustrated, intelligent man who has finally surrendered to his low level of living. Carton proclaims his love for Lucie Manette and his willingness to sacrifice himself for her or anyone she loves. Years later he has the opportunity to rescue Charles Darnay, Lucie's husband, and take his place at the guillotine; Carton's love for Lucie is complete and sacrificial.

## Beginning the Unit

Begin this unit by reading a YA novel aloud to the class. Students will benefit from hearing an experienced reader reading fluently; they will benefit from hearing how others interpret passages differently through the spontaneous discussions that occur; and they will benefit from writing (and then owning) their thoughts, feelings, and predictions in a reading log. I advocate using a reader response approach derived from Louise Rosenblatt's (1938) transactional theory of reading. By emphasizing the aesthetic stance, teachers encourage students to develop a life-long love for reading. When readers or listeners adopt an aesthetic stance, they focus on what they are feeling or thinking during the actual reading event rather than looking for the "right answer." According to Rosenblatt, reading is the transaction between readers and texts. Students bring to a text their past life histories, attitudes, and previous reading experiences, which affect their engagement with the text; thus, students are making or constructing meaning as they read.

When readers have been truly impressed by a book, Iser (1972) explains, they want to discuss it with others in an effort to understand the experience better. Rosenblatt (1989) also encourages group discussions about texts in order to stimulate thought and promote reading skills. When students realize others interpret a text differently, they are simultaneously made aware of the availability of different interpretations and their own habits of making meaning. By reading one book together at the beginning, everyone shares the same reference point with which to make comparisons. I suggest using Chris Crutcher's *Staying Fat for Sarah Byrnes* because the characters are believable and memorable, and the problems presented make discussion necessary.

### *Staying Fat for Sarah Byrnes* by Chris Crutcher (216 pp.)

This unusual love story makes a nice parallel for Sydney Carton's love of Lucie in *A Tale of Two Cities*. Eric Calhoune's best friend of eight years is Sarah Byrnes. They find each other as misfits often do. Eric is fat, and Sarah's face is scarred severely from burns. Eric is soft on the inside as well as on the outside, but Sarah is tough—inside and out. When Eric starts to slim down after joining the swim team, Sarah tells him that he will probably stop being her friend when he is no longer overweight. To reassure her, Eric eats voraciously and stays fat for Sarah Byrnes for a year to prove his undying love for her. He will do anything for her, but Sarah often verbally abuses him.

Sarah has reason to be tough, because her father, Virgil Byrnes, is meaner than Madame Defarge is patient. Madame Defarge is out for revenge against the Evremonde family, whereas Byrnes' meanness is directed toward his family—his possession. Sarah has lived alone with her dad since she was three-and-a-half years old. It was then that Sarah's father tried to kill her mother. When Sarah tried to intervene, her face got burned on the wood stove. Her mother deserted the family, leaving Sarah to fend for herself. Sarah's father has threatened to burn the rest of her body if she ever tells anyone the truth, so she submits by telling everybody that she accidentally pulled a pot of spaghetti off of the stove onto herself.

One day in social studies class, Sarah just zones out. She won't get up, she won't talk, and an ambulance takes her away to the psychiatric ward of the hospital. The therapists tell Eric to talk to her as normally as possible, so he conducts an incessant monologue about their past, their Contemporary American Thought (CAT) class, and his swimming. Eric is deeply moved by Sarah's being in the psychiatric unit, especially because she is characteristically so tough. If the strong Sarah Byrnes could have a breakdown, then he knows he is vulnerable.

Sarah finally breaks her silence and tells Eric that she is really okay, explaining that this is her only way of getting somewhere safe so she can think of a plan to get away from her dad. Sarah is more afraid of Virgil than usual due to his increased drinking. She eventually tells Eric how she was really burned and makes him swear not to tell anyone. Eric is torn:

> All I really want to do is the right thing. But how do you ever know what that is? I mean, I know some people who could help me with Sarah Byrnes's dilemma—Lemry [the CAT teacher] for one, my mother for another—but I promised not to tell. So is it right to go for help when I've promised I wouldn't, or is it the right thing to keep my promise? The stakes are high. You don't have to look into Virgil Byrnes's eyes more than a second to know that.
>
> (p. 122)

Sarah writes an incriminating letter to Eric and threatens him to keep the secret to himself. Eric reasons,

> It boiled down to this: Somebody a whole lot smarter than me and Sarah Byrnes needs to help keep her old man off her and get a start on the life she got a glimpse of writing that letter. If I didn't do *something*, Sarah Byrnes would either get dragged back home by her dad, or she'd run away and be alone. The letter was clear: shaky as I was, I was her only friend. I'd rather have her hate my guts and be safe than love me and be alone.
>
> (p. 131)

Eric does show Sarah's letter to Ms. Lemry, the CAT teacher and swimming coach. When she gets involved, the drama continues.

In this extraordinary love story, there is much more that takes place—such as an open discussion about abortion—as is typical of a Chris Crutcher novel. The novel obviously illustrates love and sacrifice, but the believable characters also embody goodness and evil. Eric is similar to Sydney Carton in his sacrificial love for Sarah, and Virgil Byrnes epitomizes oppression. Students will be able to make strong comparisons between them and the characters in their other YA novels as well as the characters in *A Tale of Two Cities*.

# Introducing Other Young Adult Novels for Small Groups

The theme of love and sacrifice can be found in many different contexts. The YA novels presented in this chapter fall into two primary thematic categories: (1) family members demonstrating love and sacrifice, and (2) people sacrificed by the system. In many ways, these categories overlap. As a way of introducing the YA titles to a class, give a brief booktalk for each book. Then have students participate in a book pass where students read portions of each book for five minutes in order to choose which book they want to read (Tchudi & Mitchell, pp. 139–140). Group students according to their choices, with no more than five in a group.

## Family Members Demonstrating Love and Sacrifice

Novels in this category address the unpleasant reality of children being abandoned by their parents. These YA novels describe the heroic characters of older siblings who instinctively take the responsibility of caring for younger siblings or parents and grandparents who take over when others abdicate their parental responsibilities. Students reading novels in this category may make connections with *A Tale of Two Cities* as they recognize that loving someone makes you want the best for that person, but does not provide the means to or the insights into how to provide what is best.

### *Changes in Latitudes* by Will Hobbs (162 pps.).

Travis, the oldest of three siblings, is psyched to vacation in Mexico, even if it is with his mom, sister, and little brother. This egocentric narrator has fantasies of meeting beautiful women on the beaches and having the time of his life. Travis's fantasies help him ignore his mother's anger at his father's unwillingness to vacation with them. Although his mother is physically present, she is emotionally checked out.

Travis is up front about being first in his life. When he discovers that his mother is having an affair, however, his life gets off center. To escape the realization, he invites his little brother Teddy to watch endangered sea turtles nesting on a nearby beach. Unbeknownst to Travis, Teddy has been sneaking out at night to watch these turtles and has befriended Casey, a marine biologist. Casey invites the boys out on his boat to swim with the sea turtles.

Later Travis and Teddy discover that men at a laboratory are butchering the female sea turtles and digging up the eggs. Casey is responsible for counting them, bearing witness to the slaughter of an entire species. Casey explains that he is optimistic that the laws will be enforced more rigorously before all of the sea turtles are killed, but Teddy cannot see that far ahead. On their last night in Mexico, Teddy decides to go by himself to let out all of the hatchlings from the laboratory. Unfortunately, the adult sea turtles in the pen are way too heavy for him. The physical exertion bursts an undetected aneurysm and Teddy dies.

Students may see some parallels between Teddy's selfless actions and those of Sydney Carton's. Teddy's willingness to sacrifice his life to save the sea turtles is in direct contrast to his family members' indulgent self-interests. When a society operates like this family, anarchy can result. Parallels can be drawn to the French Revolution in *A Tale of Two Cities*. Teddy's sacrifice, however, may have saved more than the sea turtles; he may have saved his family from destruction. Travis and his mother grieve over Teddy's death but also embrace their future as a family. "All those years we spent maneuvering for position were gone. We needed each other now. I guess we always had, but now we knew it. It was Teddy who brought us to terms" (p. 161). Sydney Carton also sacrificed his life for love of another, and through the sacrifice, he saw a better world. Both this book and the classic end with hope for the future.

### *No Kidding* by Bruce Brooks (207 pps.).

In this futuristic novel about 21st century life, alcohol abuse is rampant. Sam and Ollie's mother is an alcoholic. As the older brother, 13-year-old Sam decides to commit their mother to an alcohol rehabilitation center so Ollie won't be exposed to her alcoholism and can grow up in a stable home. Sam finds a foster home and is willing to sacrifice his mother and his own desire to live with Ollie for what he thinks are in his little brother's best interests. There is no question that Sam loves his family, but he can only respond on an intellectual level in regards to Ollie. Never once does he consider anyone else's feelings when making his decisions. Because Sam has not experienced being loved, he is also at a disadvantage in demonstrating his love. Sam has always lived his life through his head, insulating himself from his emotions.

A year later Sam has their mother released. He has made all of the preparations he can think of to ensure her continued sobriety but must now decide whether Ollie will be better off living with his foster parents or with his mother. Ollie first learns of his mother's alcoholism by seeing her in a drunken state, and his response is bizarre. He plays his saxophone at her and then preaches at her, using words from sermons he has listened to regarding alcohol. The borrowed words are on an intellectual level which cannot touch, much less relieve, his pain. His saxophone playing is mostly an emotional response, but it does not give him the relief he craves. Ollie does not know how to appropriately vent his pain and anger because Sam has always protected him from the truth.

Ollie's response is similar to Dr. Manette's cobbling and Madame Defarge's knitting. Each character resorts to a pleasurable activity in an attempt to release tension and stress. Sam, however, is in direct contrast to Sydney Carton, because Sam tries to be what he thinks others want him to be. Carton has a strong sense of self and accepts his station in life. He professes his love for Lucie even though he knows she will not choose him to be her husband. In contrast, it is extremely difficult for Sam to accept his limitations in controlling his own life and the lives of those he loves.

### *The Great Gilly Hopkins* by Katherine Paterson (156 pp.)

Galadriel "Gilly" Hopkins loves her biological mother and tenaciously holds on to her absent mother's love. After all, she does have a signed picture from her mother that reads, "For my beautiful Galadriel, I will always love you." Gilly has lived with several foster parents but thwarts any gestures they make that might undermine her goal to live with her "real" mother again. Her social worker is neither cruel or compassionate, but her concern is not for what is best for Gilly; she just doesn't want any trouble.

Gilly almost loses herself in her fight against a system that is only trying to help. The system would have completely failed Gilly except for the unlikely character of Mamie Trotter. Trotter loves her way into Gilly's heart, but it's too late. By working the system, Gilly's grandmother has already received guardianship of Gilly and reveals the truth about Gilly's irresponsible mother. Gilly phones Trotter in desperation and asks her to take her back to her home, but Trotter's love gives Gilly the strength to make her new home with her grandmother.

Gilly was willing to sacrifice herself and many chances at having a loving family for her belief in her mother's love. Trotter willingly sacrifices everything for her foster children; she truly wants the best for them even when the best is painful. Trotter is able to see the big picture and does not give in to the temptation of immediate gratification for herself or for Gilly. Trotter is similar to Sydney Carton in that both choose to endure pain so that those they love can live more fully.

### *Midnight Hour Encores* by Bruce Brooks (263 pp.)

Taxi loves his daughter, but they have an atypical father-daughter relationship. When his wife chooses freedom over motherhood, Taxi willingly agrees to raise Sibilance alone. When Sib turns 16, she asks Taxi to take her to California so she can audition at the Phrygian Institute as a cellist and visit her mother. During the long journey to California, Taxi goes to great lengths to favorably portray Connie—the woman he had once known and loved—to his daughter. He wants Sib to understand how life and attitudes were in the 1960s because he does not want Sib to judge and condemn her mother. On the way, Taxi tells Sib about their lives before her birth. As he tells the story, Sib puts the story to music with her cello, calling it "The Peace and Love Shuffle."

After Sib meets her mother, she decides she wants to try living with her for awhile, and Taxi loves her enough to let her. At her cello audition, Sib plays sensationally, then plays "The Peace and Love Shuffle" as an encore to publicly acknowledge her love for Taxi. Sib forgives her mother for abandoning her, but in the end she chooses to continue living with Taxi. He is the person who willingly sacrifices everything for her. Strong connections can be made between the ending of this book and the ending of *A Tale of Two Cities*.

### *Mama, Let's Dance* by Patricia Hermes (168 pps.)

Ariel and Mary Belle inherit the responsibility of caring for their little sister, Callie, when their Mama deserts them. They had suffered neglect even when Mama was physically present, so her leaving doesn't change things much for this family. Because the siblings remember how they had been separated and placed in foster homes when their Papa left them, they do not tell anyone that they are alone. The trio go to great lengths to look neat and clean and have their homework done so no one will suspect that both of their parents are gone. Ariel takes it upon himself to work after school to earn money for food, and Mary Belle cooks and keeps the household running.

Eventually a neighbor, Amarius, learns of their abandonment and promises to only tell his niece, Miss Dearly. Together they try to get the children adequate food, but the years of malnourishment have taken their toll. Callie becomes sick and is unable to get well. After Callie's death, the whole town finds out that their Mama left them. Mary Belle and Ariel go to live with Amarius and Miss Dearly, and for the first time, experience life with responsible and caring adults.

Although Mary Belle and Ariel loved Callie completely and unselfishly, they were not equipped to properly care for her when she became sick. By comparing Ariel and Mary Belle to Madame Defarge, students might see how sacrificing one's life for someone else, or for a cause, does not necessarily make the sacrifice good or the cause right. They simply did not trust the system that was supposed to help them. Readers are left wondering if they should have risked the consequences and requested medical attention for Callie sooner. Because their love was encapsulated in fear, they lost what they loved most dearly—their little sister. One can wonder whether the French Revolution, with its similar systemic distrust, was worth the deaths that occurred, or whether there were other ways to achieve the same end.

## People Sacrificed by the System

The YA novels in this category illustrate how people can be hurt, even sacrificed, by the very system that is designed to protect them. The working class people were victimized by the greed of the aristocracy, which led to the French Revolution. Madame Defarge's hatred of the people who benefited from the system was complete, but she did not see how the uncontrollable revenge that she promoted was equally evil. Madame Defarge particularly directs her hatred at the Evremonde family after witnessing the Marquis St. Evremonde's cold response to accidentally running over and killing a child in a crowd; he throws two gold coins at the father as compensation.

Charles Darnay, the Marquis' nephew, refuses his uncle's inheritance, not wanting to participate in the unbalanced French system. Madame Defarge does not take into account that Darnay did not benefit monetarily from his uncle's death, and she dismisses the fact that he had assumed an English name, not wanting to bear the family name. Madame Defarge is unable to see and evaluate the system from an objective vantage point. She sees it only from her own perspective, lumping everyone rich into one despicable category.

### *Nothing But the Truth* by Avi (212 pp.)

Phillip Malloy attends Harrison High School, where every morning a tape of the National Anthem is played. Phillip softly sings the words, and Miss Narwin, his English teacher, asks him to stop. When he doesn't stop singing, she sends him to the assistant principal's office. The assistant principal does not view this as a major infraction, citing some of the other problems he has to deal with. Phillip wants to be transferred to another homeroom because he thinks Miss Narwin picks on him. He is granted the transfer, but he is also suspended for two days for breaking the rule that requires students to be silent and respectful during the National Anthem.

Phillip's father tells a candidate running for the school board, Ted Griffen, that Phillip was suspended for singing the National Anthem. Mr. Griffen invites Phillip to tell the story to a reporter for the local newspaper. The reporter checks out the story with the superintendent, who denies that the school has a rule that keeps students from singing the anthem. The reporter calls the principal, assistant principal, and the teacher. When the story is picked up by the wire service, the issue becomes a topic of discussion on talk radio shows. Telegrams from all over the nation are sent to Phillip and to the school personnel. Miss Narwin receives numerous letters condemning her. Phillip wants to do some extra work in Miss Narwin's class so he can improve his grade in English and make the track team. Miss Narwin informs him that he is no longer in her class. Phillip talks to the coach, and the coach unsympathetically tells him that he should have followed the rules. Phillip has suddenly become the "bad guy" at school. The consequences of his small rebellion in Miss Narwin's class have spiraled out of control.

Even though Miss Narwin's request to take a summer class had been denied due to lack of school funds, she is suddenly asked to take a leave with full pay because of all the negative publicity. Phillip doesn't want to go to school anymore because he feels that the kids hate him. He doesn't like all the attention and transfers to another school.

Students who read this book might make connections between Madame Defarge and the unbridled bloodthirstiness of the mob. When Charles Darnay is accused of treason the second time and sentenced to the guillotine, the mockery of justice is obvious. Similarly, everyone uses the National Anthem incident for their own selfish purposes; the well-being of both Phillip Malloy and Miss Narwin is forgotten. The protagonists are victimized when the other characters get caught up in the details and lose sight of the big picture. The characters use the system to promote and protect their own interests and are not concerned with the truth.

### *The Giver* by Lois Lowry (180 pp.)

In this dystopian society, everything is the same for everyone. There is no conflict, poverty, unemployment, or divorce. Neither is there memory, color, music, change of seasons, or emotions. Jonas is preparing to receive his Assignment during the Ceremony of Twelve, where the Committee of Elders assigns each 12-year-old his or her adult title or station. Jonas is selected to be the next Receiver of Memory, because the community only has one and he is getting old.

The current Receiver of Memory becomes the Giver of Memory to Jonas. The Giver explains to Jonas that he will receive all the memories of the whole world. Jonas has no concept of anything but the present, so this is difficult for him to understand. Once the Giver transmits a memory to Jonas, the Giver no longer has it. The first memory he transmits is one of riding a sled in the snow. Jonas enjoys receiving that memory and asks the Giver, " 'What happened to those things? Snow, and the rest of it?' " The Giver explains, " 'Climate Control. Snow made growing food difficult. . . . And unpredictable weather made transportation almost impossible at times. It wasn't a practical thing, so it became obsolete when we went to Sameness' " (pp. 83–84). Later

Jonas understands the concept of the color red and asks the Giver why everyone can't see it. The Giver replies, " 'We relinquished color when we relinquished sunshine and did away with differences. . . . We gained control of many things. But we had to let go of others' " (pp. 95–96).

Soon Jonas realizes that the people in his society have never felt pain, but he will be hurt by many of the Giver's memories. He suggests that everyone should share the memories; that would be easier on him and the Giver. The Giver agrees but says, " '. . . then everyone would be burdened and pained. They don't want that. And that's the real reason The Receiver is so vital to them, and so honored. They selected me— and you—to lift that burden from themselves' " (p. 113).

Jonas's father's assignment is Nurturer. This job requires him to look after children until they are ready for Naming and Placement. He has been given permission to temporarily bring home a third child (families are generally only allowed two children) until the decision is made whether to "release" Gabriel or give him to a family. Jonas questions the concept of being released, and the Giver allows him to watch his father "release" an identical twin. The one weighing two ounces more goes to the Nurturing Center, while the other is injected with a liquid, placed in a box, and dropped into a chute similar to one that used for trash at school.

Jonas, horrified by this new knowledge, cannot return to his family unit and stays the night with the Giver. The Giver shares his plan for changing the society. Jonas must escape to Elsewhere after releasing all of the memories into the community. The Giver must stay to help the people understand the memories and cope with their emotions. Jonas wants the Giver to go with him, arguing that they don't need to care about the others. "The Giver looked at him with a questioning smile. Jonas hung his head. Of course they needed to care. It was the meaning of everything" (p. 157).

Jonas's determination to experience life beyond Sameness is a testimony to the human spirit and the wisdom of valuing differences. Jonas is willing to sacrifice life as he knows it for a chance to fully live. Jonas is like Sydney Carton, who willingly goes to the guillotine to leave his present life. Both envision a better future and quality of life for their societies. Students will be able to compare the last scene of this novel with Sydney Carton's vision.

> I see a beautiful city and a brilliant people rising from this abyss, and, in their struggles to be truly free, in their triumphs and defeats, through long long years to come, I see the evil of this time and of the previous time of which this is the natural birth, gradually making expiation for itself and wearing out.
>
> (p. 350)

(See *Adolescent Literature as a Complement to the Classics,* Volume Two, Chapter 11 for additional information on pairing this YA novel with Huxley's classic, *Brave New World.*)

## Sharing the Young Adult Novels

Students independently read their chosen books and keep double-entry reading logs (See Figure 10.1). I recommend reading and responding to their reading logs once a week.

**Figure 10.1**
**Double-entry Reading Logs**

Directions: Divide your paper vertically in half. Label the left side "Reading Notes" and the right side "Discussion Notes." Record ideas, questions, predictions, or memorable excerpts from your reading on the left side of the paper. Be sure to include the page number(s) that prompted your notations. At the end of each chapter or two, discuss your reading with the other students reading the same book. Record or log any new insights gleaned from your discussion on the right side of the paper. The following is an unfinished example from *Changes in Latitudes* by Will Hobbs:

| Reading Notes | Discussion Notes |
|---|---|
| I was so moved by the passage on pages 64–65. The language propelled me into swimming with Teddy and Travis and the sea turtle. It made me realize once again that life is short, and I will not be on this earth forever. Whatever I am going to do, I have to do it now and not put it off for someone else to do. I think a metaphor for the passage, "I felt like we were of the moment and they [sea turtles] were of the ages" (p. 64) would be we are a blink of the eye and they are a long stare. | Lisa had a better metaphor than I did for that beautiful passage. She said we are a drop of water, and they are the ocean. Bart added that if we are a drop of water, we are important to their quality of life even if they do live much longer than we do. Our short existence can impact them for a very long time. Wow! I can see how our actions have a ripple effect on others who we might not ever meet. We never know how others are influenced by what we say and do. |

After students have finished reading, discussing, and writing about their books, each group decides how to present the novel to the class. Encourage students to reread their notes and reflect on what they wrote and how they think and feel now that they have completed their reading. These notes can serve as a guide to the development of their own ideas for presenting their novels to their peers, emphasizing the love and sacrifice theme demonstrated in their novel. I offer the following only as suggestions: Students might want to prepare and present a readers' theater script, make and explain a collage, use a talk show format to introduce the characters to the rest of the class, write letters to the different characters addressing their situations as a friend, or write letters from the characters explaining how the situations affected them.

# Conclusion

At this point in the unit, each student has had a thorough experience with two novels and has knowledge of six other novels, all of which help to prepare students to relate to *A Tale of Two Cities*. As Rosenblatt (1978) explains, no one can aesthetically read for someone else. Students must make their own connections with each novel. As teachers, we can set up the learning experience and invest class time in our students' reading and discussing YA novels in preparation for Dickens's novel. I recommend that students participate in small discussion groups as they read *A Tale of Two Cities*. Again, students will benefit from the rich discussion that will take place as they draw upon their recent literary experiences, making comparisons to characters, situations, and the theme of love and sacrifice. Students are more likely to have a positive and memorable experience with *A Tale of Two Cities* through this approach, actually learning to appreciate Dickens's work.

# References

Allen, J. S. (1995). Exploring the individual's responsibility in society in *The giver* and *Brave new world*. In J. F. Kaywell's (Ed.), *Adolescent literature as a complement to the classics*. Volume Two. Norwood, MA: Christopher-Gordon Publishers, Inc., pp. 199–212.

Avi. (1993). *Nothing but the truth*. New York: Avon Books.

Brooks, B. (1986). *Midnight hour encores*. New York: HarperCollins.

Brooks, B. (1989). *No kidding*. New York: HarperKeypoint.

Crutcher, C. (1993). *Staying fat for Sarah Byrnes*. New York: Bantam.

Dickens, C. (1983). *A tale of two cities*. New York: Bantam.

Hermes, P. (1991). *Mama, let's dance*. Boston: Little, Brown, & Company.

Hobbs, W. (1988). *Changes in latitudes*. New York: Atheneum.

Iser, W. (1972). The reading process: A phenomenological approach. *New Literary History*, 3, pp. 279–300.

Lowry, L. (1993). *The giver*. Boston: Houghton Mifflin.

Paterson, K. (1987). *The great Gilly Hopkins*. New York: Avon Books.

Rosenblatt, L. M. (1938). *Literature as exploration*. New York: D. Appleton-Century.

Rosenblatt, L. M. (1978). *The reader, the text, the poem: The transactional theory of the literary work*. Carbondale, IL: Southern Illinois University Press.

Rosenblatt, L. M. (1989). Writing and reading: The transactional theory. In J. M. Mason's (Ed.), *Reading and writing connections*. Boston: Allyn & Bacon, pp. 153–176.

Tchudi, S. & Mitchell, D. (1989). *Explorations in the teaching of English*. New York: Harper & Row.

# War! What Is It Good For? *A Farewell to Arms* and Young Adult War Novels

*Teri S. Lesesne*

## Introduction

During the Gulf War several years ago, my husband and I joined millions of other anxious viewers and watched scud missiles exploding in the night sky. We followed the briefings of Norman Schwarzkopf and the reports on the evening news. Here was a war being played out in prime time for all to see, and my students were riveted by the coverage. These were a rather bloodthirsty lot, asking why the United States just didn't drop a big bomb (preferably nuclear) and end the war immediately. "Kick butt and take names" was their anthem.

My husband and I had a slightly different take on the situation, since our 25-year-old son was in the Air Force and was flying in those scud-laden skies. Of course, we feared for his safety and for the safety of all of those involved. I found myself wanting to provide a different perspective on war for these adolescents. I turned, as I frequently do when faced with a challenge, to the world of literature. *A Farewell to Arms* by Ernest Hemingway is the American classic that most students are required to read. This became the core novel of a thematic unit designed to provide adolescent readers with a chance to explore some different perspectives of war.

By pulling together several different reading selections on a similar theme, teachers can better cater to the various abilities of their students. The thematic unit that follows includes some children's books, young adult (YA) novels, a play, and a poem. The works cover wars, both real and imagined. It has been my experience that most students rarely get beyond the study of World War II in their history classes. This approach not only introduces students to more recent wars, but more importantly, it assists students in their understanding of the complexities and ramifications of war.

What follows is a description of a six week unit on war divided into three phases: prereading materials and activities, activities during the reading of *A Farewell to Arms*, and postreading materials and activities. Annotations of several YA novels dealing with the Vietnam War, political unrest overseas, and nuclear war are also included.

# Prereading Materials and Activities

Preparing students for the reading of *A Farewell to Arms* is an essential piece of this thematic unit. Hemingway's narrative is deceptively simple. Some of the symbolism may escape readers' attention unless they understand something about his style. Likewise, readers need to know how Hemingway's involvement in Word War I may have colored his perceptions of the war. Rather than simply lecturing about these and other elements of literary analysis, teachers can guide students toward a better understanding by having them read poems and picture books such as "Song Vu Chine," *Hiroshima No Pika*, and *Faithful Elephants*. Each offers readers a slightly different perspective on wars than what students may have encountered in their United States' history books.

## Read-Alouds

In *Hirosima No Pika* the author admits that the atomic bomb stopped the war, but Maruki questions whether it was worth the price. In the afterword, Maruki states, "It is very difficult to tell young people about something very bad that happened in the hope that their knowing will help keep this from happening again." The simple texts and haunting illustrations make the following award-winning picture books and poem deserving of older readers.

### *Hiroshima No Pika* by Toshi Maruki (48 pp.)

This picture book presents the devastation of Hiroshima after the atomic bomb on August 6, 1945; the title translates as "the flash of Hiroshima." At 8:15 that dreadful morning, 7-year-old Mii and her parents are happily eating breakfast. Then, the atomic bomb falls and devastates Mii's world in a single bright flash. As Mii and her parents flee toward the river, they pass heaps of dead and crowds of wounded and frightened people. Maruki graphically shows piles of dead bodies, the injured with no available medical treatment, destroyed buildings, and the mass confusion and fear. Mii and her mother somehow manage to survive, though not without some lasting effects from the radiation. The book ends with Mii and her mother celebrating Peace Day, the anniversary of that fateful day in August.

### *Faithful Elephants* by Yukio Tsuchiya (28 pp.)

Set during the latter part of World War II, this tale focuses on a decision that was made because of daily air bombings in Tokyo. Subtitled "A Little Story of Animals, People, and War," *Faithful Elephants* is the story about the systematic killing of Japanese zoo animals. The army commanded that all zoo animals should be put to death to forestall the possibility that a bomb might destroy their confinements, freeing the animals and causing further destruction. Three performing elephants, John, Wanly, and Tonky—the Faithful Elephants—are to die. They are starved to death, a process which takes several weeks. A tomb on the zoo grounds contains the bodies of the three elephants and is continuously decorated by thousands of paper cranes. Each year the story of John, Wanly, and Tonky is read aloud on Japanese radio to mark the anniversary of Japan's surrender during World War II.

### "Song Vu Chine" in *Class Dismissed* by Mel Glenn (96 pp.)

This poem, told from the point of view of a Vietnamese refugee, tells of the horror of war unknown to most American teens. Read this poem aloud to students, asking them to note how the point of view of the speaker affects the narrative.

## Discussing Point of View

These works can lead naturally to a discussion of point of view. How does one's involvement in a war change one's point of view about war? Hemingway explores various points of view in *A Farewell to Arms*, and Hemingway's own experiences as an ambulance driver during World War I may have affected his point of view as well. Reading the poem and two picture books to students before beginning a study of the core novel will provide them with some background on the essential role of the point of view of the author.

## Reading Logs

Before proceeding with the reading of the core novel, students can engage in additional activities to prepare them for a meaningful reading of *A Farewell to Arms*. First, have students establish a reading log, a journal of sorts in which they record their responses to the readings, any questions the readings might raise, and any other notations they might make. The reading log could be divided into three sections to mirror the format of the thematic unit. In the prereading section of their logs, ask students to record answers to the following:

1. What does the title *A Farewell to Arms* tell you about the book? What do you think is the title's significance?

2. The story you are about to read is set during World War I. What do you know about this period of history? What do you expect you will learn about this time from reading the novel?

3. Hemingway served as an ambulance driver during Word War I. Based upon your reading of "Song Vu Chine," *Faithful Elephants*, and *Hiroshima No Pika*, how might this experience have affected Hemingway's perspective on the war?

Because Hemingway's chapters tend to be rather brief, two-to-four pages on average, suggest that students pause to record and respond to several chapters at a time or after each division in the book. If students divide their paper into five columns, one for each of the books in the novel, they can do a side-by-side comparison of the similarities and differences among the five sections. Another page or section of the log could be devoted to notes about the characters in the novel. For example, what do students learn about Catherine and Henry in each of the five books? If students are comfortable with the use of reading logs, they might be asked to record and respond as they deem necessary.

Ask students to make careful notations of Hemingway's references to the war. Asking students to note any references to light, dark, rain, and sleeping will provide them with a sense of how symbolism is developed. Teachers might also ask students to respond to excerpts such as the following:

1. "This is the picturesque front" (p. 20).
2. "There is no finish to a war" (p. 50).

## Activities During Reading of the Core Novel

Because of the varying abilities of students within the class, teachers might wish to consider how best to begin the reading of the core novel. Certainly reading the first chapter or two aloud will provide a model for students unfamiliar with the rhythms and cadences of Hemingway's style. Teachers might also consider using a recorded version of the novel. Unabridged audiotapes will assist less able readers in their efforts. They can follow along while listening to an expert reader. Audiotapes also take into account the fact that some students are auditory learners. Utilizing readers' theater techniques or pairing less able readers with better readers are other alternative means of presenting the book to students.

### A Synopsis of *A Farewell to Arms*

#### Book One

In Book One (Chapters 1–12), readers encounter an anonymous narrator, a priest, and a doctor. Later, we learn the narrator's name is Frederic Henry. Henry is an American who has volunteered his services to the Italian Army and is serving as an ambulance driver. Soon Frederic Henry meets Catherine Barkley, a British nurse who is also a volunteer. While Henry vows not to become romantically entangled, he finds himself drawn to Catherine, and a romance develops. Henry's descriptions of the war in this section suggest that the war has been rather gentlemanly, a civil affair. All of this is about to change suddenly and irrevocably for both Frederic and Catherine. Henry is badly wounded and sent to the American hospital in Milan to recuperate.

#### Book Two

Though Book One introduces the major characters, themes, and symbols of the entire work, Book Two (Chapters 13–24) develops them more fully. All of the action in this section takes place in the American hospital during Henry's recuperation. Frederic and Catherine are reunited at the hospital. The two make plans to marry but part when Henry must return to the war.

The symbolism of rain is highly evident in this section of the novel. Catherine sees herself dead in the rain and thus is fearful of the rain at all times. As students note their responses in their reading logs, ask them to make special note of Hemingway's allusions to light and dark. Students might also respond to the passage in which Catherine and Henry have a fight and then attempt to reconcile their differences. How is this passage indicative of Hemingway's take on the nature of war?

> "But people do. They love each other and they misunderstand on purpose and they fight and then suddenly they aren't the same. . . ." (p. 139)

### Book Three

It is in Book Three (Chapters 25–32) that Hemingway removes all veneer of civility from the war. The war has dragged on much too long, and the soldiers cannot muster much enthusiasm for battle. One of Henry's drivers attempts to desert and is shot and killed by one of his own countrymen. Shortly after, Henry also attempts to escape from all of the confusion of the war. He comes face-to-face with the military police, manages to escape, and flees. In addition to noting responses to the reading, direct students to comment specifically on the murder of the ambulance driver and Henry's confrontation with the military police. Henry knows that he must withdraw even further in order to make his escape from war complete.

### Book Four

In Book Four (Chapters 33–37), Henry and Catherine seek safety in Switzerland. Henry believes that the two of them will be happy once they have fled the war and are together. In Switzerland, Catherine announces that she is pregnant. Again students should be looking for references to rain, a symbol which is omnipresent in this section of the novel. Have students revisit the question posed in the prereading: What is the significance of the title? What arms are being bid farewell? By whom? Why?

### Book Five

Book Five (Chapters 38–41), though it begins on a happy note, contains many foreshadowings of what is to come for the ill-fated lovers. At first, life in Switzerland is idyllic, but then Catherine and the baby die. Henry is left alone with the realization that he cannot fight all foes and win. There are some battles one is destined to lose. Again, students should comment upon the meaning of the title. How has it changed from Book Four to Book Five? How does Henry say farewell to arms?

## Postreading Materials and Activities

While *A Farewell to Arms* serves as the core novel for this unit, students should be encouraged to read other selections with similar themes. Suggestions for further readings about war and its effect on the participants follows. Teachers might wish to assign certain works to students or allow for some self selection. Group students according to their reading choices. While this list contains mostly novels, other genres might be included.

## A Young Adult Play

### "War of the Words" by Robin Brancato (26 pp.)

In this short play, two rival gangs known as the Notes and the Grunts are about to rumble. The weapons? Words, words, words. This is a one-act play easily performed in the classroom as readers' theater. It can also serve as a model for creating a readers' theater script for *A Farewell to Arms*. Students may be placed in five groups, one for each book in the novel. Each group selects the key scene from its book and creates a presentation for the class using a minimum of props and costuming.

## Young Adult Novels About the Vietnam War

### *Charlie Pippin* by Candy Dawson Boyd (192 pp.)

When Charlie's father returns from the Vietnam War, he is a different person. He is bitter, and Charlie finds it increasingly difficult to understand him. Charlie decides to research the Vietnam War and learns that African Americans contributed more than their fair share. Students may want to research the role of African Americans during World War I and II.

### *Young Man in Vietnam* by Charles Coe (115 pp.)

The author writes about his experiences as a young Marine lieutenant leading a company of men during the Vietnam War. Coe retells his experiences with war: the first time he went into combat, the first patrol he went on, the death of one of his friends, and his own injury. Using an interview format, students could have Coe ask Henry about his reflections on being wounded or his thoughts regarding the death of the ambulance driver.

### *Dear America: Letters Home from Vietnam* edited by Bernard Edelman (316 pp.)

This American Library Association Best of the Best Books for Young Adults is a collection of letters from soldiers to their families at home. These letters reveal the soldiers' pain, frustration, confusion, and anger towards the Vietnam War. Students could pick several characters from *A Farewell to Arms* and write the letters they would have sent home.

### *Letters from 'Nam* edited by Bradshaw Frey (125 pp.)

Brad Frey published a collection of letters written by his brother, Bill, to his family about his experiences in the Vietnam War. Bill, a 20-year-old army specialist, arrived in Vietnam eager to start his duty. He had had good training and had a fiancée waiting for him upon the completion of his tour of duty. Before long, his letters reflect a change of heart about the war, and he is disciplined for going Absent Without Leave (AWOL). The letters are painfully honest and trace the span of Bill's service all the way up to his death, just 33 days before the end of his required service. Like Bill, Henry went AWOL. Have students write Henry's letter right before he leaves for Switzerland.

### *Homecoming: When the Soldiers Returned from Vietnam* by Bob Greene (256 pp.)

Troubled by reports of soldiers saying they were treated disrespectfully upon their return from Vietnam, Greene asked readers of his syndicated column if they would be willing to share their accounts with him. This book is Greene's collection of soldiers' replies to his request. Students can research how World War I or World War II veterans were treated after the war.

### *December Stillness* by Mary Dowing Hahn (192 pp.)

Thirteen-year-old Kelly McAlister is bored with school, life, and just about everything until she befriends Mr. Weems. Mr. Weems is a homeless Vietnam veteran, and Kelly's friends and family discourage her from helping him. Students might cast Henry 50 years into the future and create a dialogue between Henry and a young teenager about his experience in the war.

### *Pocket Change* by Kathryn Jensen (171 pp.)

Josie's dad is becoming increasingly strange. He makes unusual demands, leaves the house for extended periods, says weird things, does not work like he used to, and is violent. Marsha, Josie's stepmother, denies there is a problem, but Josie is not convinced. She senses that his behavior is related to his service in Vietnam 15 years ago and calls a professional for help. The problem finally comes to a head when her father almost kills Josie's half brother. Students can research post traumatic stress syndrome, and how it affects soldiers and their families.

### *Long Time Passing* by Adrienne Jones (256 pp.)

When Jonas was 17 years old, he had a lot to deal with: the death of his mother, adjusting to living with an aunt in California, and his father's serving in Vietnam. When Jonas gets old enough, he joins the Marines in order to look for his missing-in-action (MIA) father. The novel fluctuates from present to past, using first person narration for the present and third person for the past. Following this narrative format, students can create a sibling for Henry whose mission is to find his lost brother.

### *In Country* by Bobbie Ann Mason (247 pp.)

In this American Library Association Best of the Best Books for Young Adults, Samantha "Sam" Hughes is a recent high school graduate who is rightfully confused. Her father died in the Vietnam War before she was born, and her Uncle Emmett suffers from post war shock. Sam struggles to make sense of a war that is still affecting her life years later. Assume Frederic Henry has grandchildren, and have students describe the possible effects his participation in the war might have on them.

### *What Should We Tell Our Children about Vietnam?* by Bill McCloud (176 pp.)

As a junior high school social studies teacher and a Vietnam veteran, McCloud wondered what he should tell his students about the war. He posed the question to several people involved in various aspects of the war—from politicians to protesters—

and captured their responses in a readable form. Students can develop a picture book, modeled after *Hiroshima No Pika* and based on *A Farewell to Arms,* that they would want to share with elementary students.

### *Fallen Angels* by Walter Dean Myers (309 pp.)

Richie Perry, a 17-year-old boy from Harlem, tells of his coming-of-age through his experiences in the Vietnam War. This tough war novel shows the price five black soldiers pay for their tour of duty in Vietnam. These young men have but one goal: get out alive! Frederic Henry is an American serving as a volunteer in the Italian Army. In many ways, he is isolated from the others in his unit. How is his experience similar to those of the main characters in Myers's work?

### *The Things They Carried* by Tim O'Brien (273 pp.)

For mature readers, this is a powerful collection of stories set during the Vietnam War. Each story focuses on some possession a soldier has carried into battle, a talisman of sorts. Were there any similar talismans carried into battle by the characters in *A Farewell to Arms?* If not, what object would be appropriate for Frederic? For Catherine? For Rinaldi? Why?

### *The Monument* by Gary Paulsen (151 pp.)

A town wishes to have its war dead commemorated and commissions an artist to design a fitting tribute to those who gave their lives for their country. The artist, assisted by a young girl from their town, believes he must first know the town and its people before he can create a monument. What kind of a monument would be appropriate for Catherine? Students might wish to design an epitaph or a marker for her burial plot.

### *My Name is San Ho* by Jayne Pettit (149 pp.)

San Ho grew up in Vietnam during the Vietnam War but escaped to America to live with his Vietnamese mother and American stepfather when he was twelve. Now he has another type of growing up to do: He must learn how to be accepted by others at his school. San Ho struggles with English and the need for friends but makes some progress through his athletic capabilities. Have students imagine that Lieutenant Rinaldi has a little brother who escapes to America during the war. What would life be like for this Italian immigrant?

### *Hometown* by Marsha Qualey (192 pp.)

What happens when someone refuses to fight in a war? Qualey explores the consequences affecting a Vietnam draft dodger and his adolescent son some 20 years after the end of the war. The pairing of this novel with the core novel allows students to explore what they think happens to Henry after the conclusion of *A Farewell to Arms.* Writing scenarios for Henry's life 5, 10, or 20 years later is one possible activity.

### *A Blue-Eyed Daisy* by Cynthia Rylant (112 pp.)

When 11-year-old Ellie Farley's uncle comes to visit, things change for the entire family. Uncle Joe has just returned from the Vietnam War, but neither he or Ellie's family are willing to talk about it. What would it be like for Henry to return to the United States after the war? What would he say about his experiences to an 11-year-old?

### *Caribou* by Meg Wolitzer (176 pp.)

Threatened by the draft, Stevie flees to Canada to escape the Vietnam War, leaving his family, his girlfriend, and his band. His 12-year-old sister, Becca, tells the story of her confusion about his decision. Have students relate Henry's escape to Switzerland as told by a mock 12-year-old little sister.

## Young Adult Novels About Political Unrest Overseas

Students can research other, more recent wars and share their findings with their peers. By having readers see war from another's point of view, authors raise some interesting points of comparison. How might Henry have viewed his involvement in World War I differently if he, like some of these characters, experienced the war from another perspective?

### *Waiting for the Rain: A Novel of South Africa* by Sheila Gordon (224 pp.)

In this American Library Association Best Book for Young Adults, Tengo is black and Frikkie is a white Afrikaaner. As children, they are great friends, but apartheid changes things as both boys participate in the struggle. The boys' experiences are set against the backdrop of the ongoing tragedy of South Africa.

### *Winnie Mandela: Life of Struggle* by Jim Haskins (173 pp.)

The life of the wife of Nelson Mandela and her joint suffering with her husband is presented. The biography begins in 1936 and traces the events of her life through their efforts to abolish apartheid in South Africa.

### *The Clay Marble* by Min Fong Ho (163 pp.)

During the Cambodian conflict in 1980, 12-year-old Dara and her family flee to a refugee camp on the Thailand border. While they struggle to make a life for themselves, Dara finds a new friend, Jantu, who teaches her how to make toys from clay. Dara finds magic in a clay marble, a thing that keeps her dream of returning home alive. Eventually, Dara discovers that the real magic of life exists in the belief in oneself.

### *Kiss the Dust* by Elizabeth Laird (281 pp.)

Tara and her Kurdish family must flee Iraq and travel over the mountains into Iran. There they are treated as refugees, and Tara must wear the "chador" while in the camp. Things are still unsettled, and the family makes a harrowing escape from Iran.

### *Whole of a Morning Sky* by Grace Nichols (156 pp.)

Twelve-year-old Gem shares what it is like growing up in the political unrest of Guyana, then British Guiana.

### *Andi's War* by Billi Rosen (136 pp.)

Antigone, better known as Andi, and her younger brother have lived with their grandparents since their parents enlisted in the Greek Civil War, which lasted from May 1946 to October 1949. This novel portrays how children are affected by the atrocities of war.

### *Gulf* by Robert Westall (96 pp.)

As the Persian Gulf conflict escalates to the brink of war, Tom's younger brother Andy begins to have nightmares about an Iraqi soldier named Latin.

## Young Adult Novels About Nuclear War

During the Gulf War, my students were hoping that the United States would "nuke 'em" and get the war over with. As adults, we know that we are still living with the aftermath of Hiroshima's radiation and Vietnam's agent orange. With these novels, students are asked to consider what will happen if there is a nuclear war.

### *Fiskadoro* by Denis Johnson (221 pp.)

Fiskadoro is a teenager who has survived an atomic war which killed practically everybody else. He is living in the Florida Keys, the last saved area of the United States, with his music teacher, Anthony Cheung. His parents are dead, and Mr. Cheung is preoccupied with solving the mysteries of the former period. Cheung's grandmother, in dreamlike ramblings, reveals reasons why the world was destroyed.

### *After the Bomb* by Gloria D. Miklowitz (165 pp.)

Phillip Singer, a 16-year-old, has never had to use his wits the way he has done since the Russians accidentally dropped the bomb on Los Angeles. Somehow, he manages to get his radiation-sick mother to a hospital and finds a way to get water there.

### *Z for Zachariah* by Robert C. O'Brien (256 pp.)

After "the war," Ann Burden thinks she is the only survivor in the valley until she meets Loomis. His appearance is ominous; he is wearing a "safe-suit" to protect himself against the effects of radiation. Ann quickly learns that his appearance is a direct reflection of his personality, one that tries to enslave and dominate. Readers can sympathize with Ann, who has survived the war only to find that she must outsmart Loomis in order to survive. This novel is an ALA Notable Children's Book, an ALA Best Book for Young Adults, on the Horn Book Fanfare List, and a Children's Book of the Year.

### *Brother in the Land* by Robert Swindells (151 pp.)

Danny Lodge has survived the initial devastation of the nuclear holocaust, but he wonders if he can handle the aftermath. Thankfully, both his father and younger brother, Ben, survived, though not without harm. In the midst of chaos, Danny finds he is drawn to Kim, and they support each other through some horrible times. The macrocosmic devastation is brought to microcosmic reality when Ben dies of radiation sickness and Danny must bury him.

### *The Bomb* by Theodore Taylor (208 pp.)

The setting is the Bimini Atoll in 1946. The U.S. begins to move natives from their island paradise so they can further examine the power of the atomic bomb which devastated Hiroshima and Nagasaki. Sorry, a young native, decides he must protest what is to happen. Taylor prefaces each chapter with excerpts from government documents, news reports, and scientific research of the era.

### *Pride of the Peacock* by Stephanie S. Tolan (168 pp.)

This easy-to-read novel deals with the scary subject of nuclear war in a down-to-earth manner. After reading Jonathan Schell's *The Fate of the Earth*, Whitney Whitehurst becomes obsessed with fear of a nuclear war. She allows her fear to interfere with her school, friends, and family. She becomes friends with Theodora Bourke, a famous sculptor and new owner of the "Old Place," a childhood play area in her neighborhood. Theodora owns a peacock which serves as a catalyst in making Whitney place her fears in perspective. Whitney ultimately realizes that she must exchange her fear for faith in people and their actions.

## Culminating Activities

Postreading activities might also include comparisons of *A Farewell to Arms* with one of the preceding selections. Students might be placed into groups and asked to share the different books they read with the rest of the group. When students share books in this manner, others are frequently motivated to read the works recommended by their peers. Lining classroom walls with butcher paper and asking students to create murals based upon their books is another possible activity. Charting the symbols from the various works might also create an interesting display.

### *A Farewell to Arms*: The Movie

A natural tie-in for this unit is viewing the classic black-and-white movie based upon the novel. This movie, starring Gary Cooper and Helen Hayes, may be shown either before or after reading. Research with secondary students suggests that showing the movie beforehand is motivational for reading the book. Plotting the similarities and differences between the two media is a natural outgrowth of this activity. During the viewing of the movie, ask students to be aware of the role of music as a backdrop to the story. In addition, students might comment upon the casting of the film. How might the casting be different if the movie were to be remade today? Who would they assign for the various roles and why? Should the movie be shot in color or in black and white? Students could create a movie poster based upon their remake ideas.

## Conclusion

Though this thematic unit centers around a core novel, teachers should feel free to modify the unit to suit their needs. Students do not have to read *A Farewell to Arms*. One of the other selections might easily function as the core novel. Teachers should consider allowing students some choice within the unit in terms of reading material and activities. As a person who shops in the "women's department" and other euphemistically labeled places, I know the fallacy of "one size fits all." There are few, if any, novels which are suitable for all of the students in our classrooms. Using thematic units, pairing classics to YA texts, and offering audiotape versions of a text are just a handful of ways in which we might better meet the diverse needs of our students.

## References

Boyd, C. D. (1987). *Charlie Pippin*. New York: Puffin Books.

Brancato, R. F. (1990). War of the words. In D.R. Gallo's (Ed.), *Center stage*. New York: HarperCollins, pp. 335–361.

Coe, C. (1990). *Young man in Vietnam*. New York: Scholastic.

Edelman, B. (Ed.). (1985). *Dear America: Letters home from Vietnam*. New York: Norton.

Frey, B. (Ed.). (1992). *Letters from 'Nam*. New York: Warner Books.

Glenn, M. (1982). *Class dismissed: High school poems*. New York: Clarion.

Gordon, S. (1990). *Waiting for the rain: A novel of South Africa*. New York: Bantam.

Greene, B. (1989). *Homecoming: When the soldiers returned from Vietnam*. New York: G. P. Putnam's Sons.

Hahn, M. D. (1988). *December stillness*. New York: Clarion.

Haskins, J. (1988). *Winnie Mandela: Life of struggle*. New York: G.P. Putnam's Sons.

Ho, M. (1991). *The clay marble*. New York: Farrar, Straus, & Giroux.

Jensen, K. (1989). *Pocket change*. New York: Macmillan.

Johnson, D. (1985). *Fiskadoro*. New York: Alfred A. Knopf.

Jones, A. (1990). *Long time passing*. New York: Harper & Row.

Laird, E. (1991). *Kiss the dust*. New York: E.P. Dutton.

Maruki, T. (1980). *Hiroshima no Pika*. New York: Lothrop, Lee, & Shepard.

Mason, B. A. (1985). *In country*. New York: Harper & Row.

McCloud, B. (1992). *What should we tell our children about Vietnam?* New York: Berkley Publishing Group.

Miklowitz, G. D. (1985). *After the bomb*. New York: Scholastic.

Myers, W. D. (1988). *Fallen angels*. New York: Scholastic.

Nichols, G. (1986). *Whole of a morning sky*. London: Virago.

O'Brien, R. C. (1975). *Z for Zachariah*. New York: Atheneum.

O'Brien, T. (1990). *The things they carried*. Boston: Houghton Mifflin.

Paulsen, G. (1991). *The monument*. New York: Delacorte Press.

Pettit, J. (1992). *My name is San Ho*. New York: Scholastic.

Qualey, M. (1995). *Hometown*. Boston: Houghton Mifflin.

Rosen, B. (1989). *Andi's war*. New York: E.P. Dutton.

Rylant, C. (1985). *A blue-eyed daisy*. New York: Bradbury Press.

Swindells, R. (1985). *Brother in the land*. New York: Holiday House.

Taylor, T. (1995). *The bomb*. San Diego: Harcourt Brace.

Tolan, S. S. (1987). *Pride of the peacock*. New York: Ballantine Books.

Tsuchiya, Y. (1988). *Faithful elephants*. Boston: Houghton Mifflin.

Westall, R. (1995). *Gulf*. New York: Scholastic.

Wolitzer, M. (1986). *Caribou*. New York: Bantam Starfire.

## Film Cited (Available on Home Video)

Borzage, F. (Producer). (1991). *A farewell to arms*. Cincinnati, OH: The Congress Video Group.

# The Return of the Vampire: *Dracula* and Young Adult Literature

*Rosemary Oliphant Ingham*

*But, on the instant, came the sweep and flash of Jonathan's great knife. I shrieked as I saw it shear through the throat; whilst at the same moment Mr. Morris' bowie knife plunged in the heart.*

*It was like a miracle; but before our very eyes, and almost in the drawing of a breath, the whole body crumbled into dust and passed from our sight.*

*I shall be glad as long as I live that even in that moment of final dissolution there was in the face a look of peace, such as I never could have imagined might have rested there.*

(Mina Harker's Journal, *Dracula*, p. 377.)

## Introduction

If Bram Stoker believed that Dr. Van Helsing, Mr. Morris, and Jonathan Harker destroyed Dracula on that fateful night over a century ago, he was sorely mistaken. Since the publication of *Dracula* in 1897, countless Draculesque vampires have appeared in literature and film. Novels, plays, films, and short stories for adults, adolescents, and children have driven readers to look warily at dark corners and approach suave strangers with caution, especially if those strangers are dressed in black.

Go to any bookstore and check the shelves for stories that deal with the occult; vampire books will be plentiful. Stephen King and Anne Rice are only two of the many adult authors who have made their reputations from books dealing with the "undead." People working with students of any age will readily recognize the names of R.L. Stine, Christopher Pike, Caroline Cooney, John Peel, et al. As the immense popularity of these writers indicates, horror fiction is "in". Therefore, *Dracula* is a natural for any high school literature class. With *Dracula*, you can provide your students with high-interest, quality literature that will stretch their reading, interpretive, and critical skills.

As a teacher of literature, my first goal is to produce life-long readers. Using Dracula along with the numerous young adult (YA) literature books with the vampire motif may be just the avenue needed to create these readers. R.L. Stine is presently the best-selling author of adolescent and children's books in America. If this is what students are reading, then let's take this interest and build on it. The references at the end of this chapter list several authors who write about vampires or the "undead," but there are dozens more. Add the many stories of ghosts, witches, Frankenstein, werewolves, and the Jason and Freddy Krueger spin-offs, and you have a library that will keep your students reading for a long, long time.

It is generally believed that students ought to have diverse reading experiences. Because I subscribe to that belief, I use vampire and related stories to bridge into other literature—specifically the classics. From R.L. Stine, we can move on to Christopher Pike or John Peel. From Pike and Peel we can move on to Cooney, Klause, and Rice, then *Dracula*. And from *Dracula* we can move on to, would you believe, Coleridge? Did you know that "Death in *The Rime of the Ancient Mariner* hints of vampirism" or that Byron's "'Christabel' suggests a vampire lesbian relationship" (Sullivan, p. 437)? Do you have students who would gladly read these poems just to see if this is true?

No matter what reason students have for reading a certain book, the bottom line is that they are reading. And that is my purpose—to create readers! The following goals and activities can be adapted in any way that is appropriate for your classes. Add to them, delete the ones that you don't like, expand on others, but let your students have fun with the literature.

## Historical View of Vampires

The origin of the Dracula story, like Dracula himself, cannot be traced with any definite accuracy. *The Penguin Encyclopedia of Horror and the Supernatural* offers one of the best concise histories of vampires. The first recorded story comes from Palestine, where Lilith, the first wife of Adam, was said to be "a Canaanite Hecate who attacked newborn infants and sucked the blood of men in their sleep. The ravages of Lilith were continued by the Lilim (children of Lilith), and her powers were so feared that the Jews used magical means to protect themselves from her murderous prowlings as late as the Middle Ages" (Sullivan, p. 436). *Next Year in Jerusalem: 3000 Years of Jewish Stories* chronicles the exploits of another early vampire in the story "The Vampire Demon," which takes place during the time of King Solomon. This casts doubt on the idea that Dracula was the original vampire. Stoker was no doubt influenced by previous vampire stories and, according to Sullivan, grim Irish folklore told to him by his mother.

From ancient Greece to Anne Rice, the "profound ambiguity of vampires—their simultaneous repulsiveness and glamour—. . . makes them a fascinating subject for poetry and pathology" (Sullivan, p. 435). The ancient Greeks saw vampires as demonic blood-sucking females. During the Medieval era, the Catholic Church passed censorious laws that would excommunicate vampires from the Church. In many Christian cultures, vampires were outcasts who died in a state of sin. The Romanian *nosferatu* is "a blood-crazed living corpse that turns its victims into new vampires and can be combated with an odd, elaborate mixture of pagan and Christian remedies, including garlic, holy water, decapitation, a cross, a wooden stake driven through the heart, and (one of the more amusing and less exploited methods) tying the vampire up in his coffin with complicated knots" (Sullivan, p. 436). Included in Chinese folklore is *Kian-si*. This nocturnal demon sports long fingernails. The American Indian version has a trumpet-shaped mouth for sucking out the sleeping victim's brains through his ears, while the Hindu version has a fetish for drunk or insane women. In India there's a myth about *Kali,* the Dark Mother. Her bloodlust is so insatiable that she might slash her own throat and catch the rush of blood in her mouth if there's not another victim handy.

Real people also helped to create the vampire myth. The Marquis de Sade, Countess Elizabeth Bathory, and Gilles de Rais were noted for their macabre cruelty. Probably the best known of these historical figures, as far as the vampire legend goes, is Vlad IV. A Transylvanian ruler during the 15th century, Vlad IV was the original Count Dracula. It is said that he enjoyed "impaling his victims on stakes and torturing them to death as he dined with his court" (Sullivan, p. 436). It is Vlad IV's castle in Romania that Stoker used as the model for *Dracula.* According to Sullivan, "It was Stoker's stroke of genius to fuse the historical brutality of Vlad IV, described in his British Museum sources as 'a bloodthirsty monster', with the Transylvanian legend of the *nosferatu,* creating a novel that interweaves history with fantasy" (pp. 436–437).

*Dracula* is by far the most popular book about vampires, but it was not the first. Goethe wrote *Die Braut von Korinth*, or *The Bride of Korinth*, in 1798; an anonymous Victorian potboiler wrote *Varney the Vampire*, or *The Feast of Blood,* in 1847; and Sheridan Le Fanu wrote *Carmilla* in 1870. The first vampire tale in English fiction, *The Vampyre* by John Polidori, was published in London's *New Monthly Magazine* in April 1819. *The Vampyre* "was popular primarily because its author was originally believed, incorrectly, to be the famous poet, Lord Byron" (Cohen, p. 2). Sullivan explains where this belief originated: "On a legendary evening in June 1816 Lord Byron read 'Christabel' aloud to Mary Shelley; her husband Percy Shelley; and Byron's physician, John Polidori, inspiring not only Shelley's *Frankenstein* but Polidori's *The Vampyre. . .*" (p. 437).

## Bram Stoker

Abraham (Bram) Stoker was born in November 1847 in Dublin, Ireland. He was educated at Dublin's Trinity College, where he received honors in science. Stoker began his career as an Irish civil servant. During this time, he also was an unpaid drama critic for Dublin's *Evening Mail.* For a short period, he was a barrister of the Inner Temple, but his longest tenure was serving as business manager for the actor Henry Irving. At the end of his career, he served on the literary staff of the London *Telegraph.* He died in London in 1912. Although writing fiction was never his primary occupation, Stoker consistently published works from 1881 until 1911. *Dracula* is the only one of his more than a dozen publications that has survived in print, and it has become a touchstone for horror stories.

Some critics argue that Stoker was not a particularly great writer, while others praise his research and writing skills. A.N. Wilson in the introduction to the Oxford University Press edition of *Dracula* (1983) states, "It is not a great work of literature. The writing is of a powerful, workday sensationalist kind. No one in their right mind would think of Stoker as a 'great writer'" (p. xiv). Sullivan, on the other hand, says that *Dracula* contains ". . . magnificent descriptive passages" and "even the *Christian World* called it 'one of the most enthralling and unique romances ever written'" (p. 405).

## *Dracula* by Bram Stoker (432 pp.)

Jonathan Harker's mission is a seemingly simple task. A Count Dracula has purchased property in England, and Jonathan is delivering the necessary papers to the castle in Transylvania. What was to be a short business trip turns into a nightmare when Jonathan becomes a prisoner of the Count. It soon becomes apparent to Jonathan that he will be killed by vampires if he does not escape. He manages to escape, but Count Dracula has already succeeded in fleeing to England where he begins his reign of terror—sucking the lifeblood from unsuspecting victims.

Thinking his story is too unbelievable, Jonathan hides his diary, which contains his frightening ordeal, from everyone, including his fiancée Mina Murray. But when strange illnesses and murders begin to happen in England, Jonathan knows he must fight this monster who so frightens him. With the help of Professor Van Helsing, Dr. Seward, Lord Godalming, and Mr. Morris, Jonathan drafts a plan to destroy Count Dracula.

## Studying *Dracula*

There are several reasons why today's students can benefit from the study of the macabre, specifically *Dracula* in conjunction with several young adult (YA) novels of this genre. First and foremost, students can have an enjoyable experience reading a classic novel. Studying YA literature can help students understand and appreciate this classic text. Additionally, it is always fascinating to read several adaptations of the Dracula story and then read "the original" to see how the stories were modified. There are also several film versions that lend themselves to comparative study.

Begin this unit by holding up a striking photo of Dracula and having students do a free write on what they know about this character. Most students will have read books or stories, seen movies or TV shows, or will in some way have knowledge about vampires. Having them do an initial journal piece on the origins of vampires, how one can become a vampire, and how vampires can be destroyed will give students an opportunity to display knowledge that has previously been "useless" in school. Activating students' prior knowledge—even though it may not be academic or school knowledge—is a very effective teaching strategy.

Reader response journals, an effective teaching tool first described by Louise Rosenblatt in 1938, can either be fun or a drag, depending on the way the teacher structures the class. One successful way to deal with journals is to give the students open-ended questions like these to respond to: "What did you think about . . .?" or "How did you feel when you read about 'this and such'?" or "Do you think Lucy from

*Dracula* (or plug in any one of numerous names from the YA books) was weak because she let Dracula seduce her? Why or why not?" Reader response journals should help students connect with the literature and allow them to explore their reactions freely. Using journals as a way of testing to see if the assigned reading has been done is not using reader response journals in the most productive and creative way.

## Dracula in Young Adult Literature

Depending on the cultural climate of your school, all of the YA books listed in the bibliography may not be appropriate; therefore, I strongly urge you to read any book before using it in class or suggesting it to your students. Brief descriptions of the books—some individual, some grouped—follow.

### *The Band* by Carmen Adams (133 pp.)

Megan has just moved from Colorado to southern California. Wanting to be popular at her new school, she becomes involved with a group whose members turn out to be "revenant"—victims of violent deaths who cannot find a resting place for their souls.

### *Vampire's Kiss* by Nicholas Adams (211 pp.), *Nightmare Hall: The Vampire's Kiss* by Diane Hoh (145 pp.), *Tombstones: The Last Drop* by John Peel (150 pp.), and *Goodnight Kiss* by R.L. Stine (224 pp.)

Susan (*Vampire's Kiss*), Janie (*Nightmare Hall*), Lindsey (*Tombstones*), and Matt (*Goodnight Kiss*) must each deal with a vampire in order to solve a murder. The mysteries aren't hard to solve, but convincing others to believe their improbable stories becomes their greatest obstacle.

### *The Cheerleader* (192 pp.) and *The Return of the Vampire* by Caroline Cooney (176 pp.)

Althea is plain, passive, and unpopular at her school. She dreams of becoming one of the in-crowd by making the cheerleading squad and is willing to "sell her soul" to get what she wants. Being a cheerleader would solve all of her problems, but is it worth draining the lives of her new, supposed friends?

Like Althea in *The Cheerleader*, Devnee just wants to be popular at her school and is willing to sell out to a vampire to reach this goal.

### *The Silver Kiss* by Annette Curtis Klause (198 pp.)

Zoe's hospitalized mother is dying of cancer, and her father only seems to be interested in keeping her as far away from the tragedy as possible. Zoe feels deserted and finds comfort in getting to know Simon, a vampire seeking revenge for the tragic death of his own mother centuries before.

### *Night Wings* by John Peel (144 pp.)

The Duke of Petronseni recruits Rob to be a vampire hunter in Romania. Rob's artificial neck—the result of a car accident—makes him perfect for the job.

### *The Last Vampire* series by Christopher Pike

Christopher Pike's *Last Vampire* series chronicles the life of Sita, a five thousand-year-old vampire. The four books have contemporary settings but give Sita's history in flashbacks. These books are by far the most risky ones listed because of the sex and graphic violence contained in them.

### *The Vampire Diaries* series by L.J. Smith

Elena has everything: poise, popularity, beauty, brains, and money. Every boy in school would gladly do her bidding—that is, all except Stefan. Eventually Elena and Stefan fall in love, but together they must fight the evil forces of the night.

### *Vampires* edited by Jane Yolen (240 pp.)

*Vampires* is a collection of original short stories about this creature of the night—or possibly the day, too. Could that "rad hunk" at the mall, the cousins left to take care of orphan Clarisse Delmonde, or that nice sweet piano teacher be vampires? Good vampires, bad vampires, being a vampire, or being afraid of vampires—there's a story in this collection for everyone.

## Activities

### I Promise. Nothing But the Truth . . .

Using journals, letters, and newspaper accounts to carry an unbelievable storyline is one way authors deal with the verisimilitude issue. In Mary Shelley's *Frankenstein*, for example, Robert Walton wrote letters to his sister detailing his interactions with Dr. Frankenstein (See *Adolescent Literature as a Complement to the Classics*, Volume Two, Chapter 10). Similarly, Stoker used journals, letters, and newspapers in his writing of *Dracula*.

Two YA novels that are told through the use of diary entries, letters, and newspaper accounts are *Strange Objects* by Gary Crew (224 pp.) and *Nothing but the Truth* by Avi (224 pp.). Although neither story has to do with vampires, students will get exposure to the purpose and effectiveness of this type of writing style before they begin reading *Dracula*.

**Diaries, Letters, and Newspaper Accounts.**   After reading any one of the aforementioned YA novels, have students retell the story using diaries, letters, and newspaper accounts. Remind students that their primary purpose is to convince someone that vampires are real. The Adams, Hoh, Peel, and Stine mysteries work especially well for this activity.

**Review *Dracula* in an Hour.**   Put students in groups of four or five. Have each group keep a running record of the use of journals, letters, and newspaper reports relating to Jonathan Harker, Mina Murray-Harker, Lucy Westenra, or Dr. Seward. Groups can report their information to the class like the characters do in *Dracula* when they meet in Dr. Seward's study. A good follow-up question to ask students is, "Could you figure out the mystery with only the information related to your character?"

### A Word Is an Utterance Is a Locution???

While students read *Dracula*, have them keep a personal log of any five words that are unfamiliar to them. Have students copy the pertinent passage, underline the troublesome word, and include the page number where it is located in the text. Have students look up the dictionary definitions of their words and translate them into "kid language" to be submitted for a class list. For example, a student might copy the following sentence from Dr. Seward's diary: "The Professor's actions were certainly odd, and not to be found in any *pharmacopoeia* that I ever heard of" (p. 131), and rewrite its dictionary definition (according to *Webster's*, an authoritative book containing a list and description of drugs and medicinal products together with the standards established under law for their production, dispensation, use, etc.) as *pharmacopoeia*—a medical reference book.

**Etymologies.**    Teachers take all of the students' submissions in order to compile a class list to be distributed to each class member. These entries can lead to wonderful class discussions on etymologies or word origins. Some students will take it upon themselves to do unassigned additional research because this activity involves words of their own choosing.

**Synonyms.**    Alternatively, have students research all the different names that can be applied to vampires. Then have students compile several examples from local newspapers in which a journalist tells about one team beating another, such as "Gators Chomp Seminoles" or "Seminoles Capture Gators." Noticing how writers use different ways to say the same thing may inspire students to try similar techniques in their own writing. This is particularly useful if students opt to make a newspaper account of their Dracula story.

### Who Does What? Where?

**Characterization.**    Although most of Stoker's characters are well-developed, some are still stereotypical. Mr. Morris is portrayed as the "rough around the edges" American, and specifically, Texan. Mina has to be a resourceful young lady because she has not had a privileged background like Lucy. Have students pay attention to any stereotyping used by their YA novelists and discuss the effectiveness or the lack thereof of that kind of characterization.

**Setting.**    Stoker has been credited with being a genius for using Victorian England and the area around the Carpathian Mountains as the setting for *Dracula*. Ask students to decide on a good place to set a 1990s version of a vampire story. If students prefer, have them critique their YA author's choice of setting.

### *Dracula* Revisited

As your students read novels or short stories about vampires, they can't help but realize that the variations of the central vampire story are numerous. Share with them different versions of well-known folktales. Let them discuss why these versions might exist or how they came about. Versions of a story such as *Cinderella*, for example, will often reflect the cultural origin of the story.

**Parodies.**   Jon Scieszka has become well known in children's literature for his humorous versions of folktales such as *The Stinky Cheese Man and Other Fairly Stupid Tales*, *The True Story of the 3 Little Pigs!* and *The Frog Prince Continued*. After reading one of his stories, ask students to write a parody of *Dracula*. Then have students view either Kaufman and Hamilton's G-rated *Love at First Bite*, starring George Hamilton, Susan Saint James, and Robert Kaufman, or Mel Brooks's recent PG-13 spoof *Dracula: Dead and Loving It*, starring Leslie Nielsen, Amy Yasbeck, and Steven Weber to see how professionals make light of a serious story. Paul Fleischman in *A Fate Totally Worse Than Death* (128 pp.) has taken all the horror motifs and put them together into one hilarious story. After having read several YA vampire books, students might enjoy doing a similar parody.

**Comparison and Contrast.**   After reading the novel and viewing Laemmle and Browning's 1931 classic black-and-white film version of *Dracula*, starring Bela Lugosi, or Hinds's *Horror of Dracula*, starring Christopher Lee, have your students do a comparison and contrast activity. Depending on your particular class, you may choose to view the film(s) either before or after reading *Dracula*. This activity could be done in their journals, as a formal paper, or in a class discussion.

**Movie Adaptations.**   Several students are apt to be familiar with more recent Dracula films, such as Francis Ford Coppola's R-rated version of Stoker's *Dracula*, starring Anthony Hopkins, Gary Oldman, and Winona Ryder; Woolley and Geffen's R-rated *Interview with the Vampire*, starring Tom Cruise, Brad Pitt, and Christian Slater; Murphy and Lipsky's R-rated *Vampire in Brooklyn*, starring Eddie Murphy and Angela Bassett; or the *Munsters* and *Dark Shadows* television series. After reading one of the YA novels about vampires, ask students to develop a plan to make their book into a film or a TV series. Remind students to think of who they would cast in the lead roles. Other things to consider would be whether or not they want to film their stories in black and white or color, where the best setting would be, and what parts were crucial to the storyline and what parts should be omitted.

# Conclusion

If we get our students reading willingly in class, we are more likely to produce students who will continue to read outside of school. To accomplish this worthwhile goal, teachers can enhance the prescribed curriculum with the use of YA and children's literature. Young adult literature might have a negative connotation for some English language arts teachers, and vampire books are sometimes not readily accepted as appropriate works to be studied. Nonetheless, if our bottom line is to create readers, we must work with our students' interests. At the end of this unit, students will know that Dracula sucks blood but won't think that "*Dracula* sucks!"

# References

Adams, C. (1994). *The band*. New York: Avon Books.

Adams, N. (1994). *Vampire's kiss*. New York: HarperCollins.

Avi. (1993). *Nothing but the truth*. New York: Avon Books.

Cohen, D. (1995). *Real vampires*. New York: E.P. Dutton.

Cooney, C. B. (1991). *The cheerleader*. New York: Scholastic.

Cooney, C. B. (1991). *The return of the vampire*. New York: Scholastic.

Crew, G. (1993). *Strange objects*. New York: Simon & Schuster.

Fleischman, P. (1995). *A fate totally worse than death*. Cambridge, MA: Candlewick Press.

Grimm, J. & Grimm, W. (1976). *The complete Grimm's fairy tales*. New York: Pantheon Books.

Hoh, D. (1995). *Nightmare hall: The vampire's kiss*. New York: Scholastic.

Klause, A. C. (1990). *The silver kiss*. New York: Bantam.

Lesesne, T. S. (1993). Exploring the horror within: Themes of duality of humanity in Mary Shelley's *Frankenstein* and ten related young adult novels. In J. F. Kaywell's (Ed.), *Adolescent literature as a complement to the classics*. Volume Two. Norwood, MA: Christopher-Gordon Publishers, Inc., pp. 187–197.

Peel, J. (1993). *Night wings*. New York: G.P. Putnam's Sons

Peel, J. (1995). *Tombstones: The last drop*. New York: Pocket Books.

Perrault, C. (1973). *Cinderella*. New York: Bradbury Press.

Pike, C. (1994). *The last vampire*. New York: Pocket Books.

Pike, C. (1994). *The last vampire 2: Black blood*. New York: Pocket Books.

Pike, C. (1995). *The last vampire 3: Red dice*. New York: Pocket Books.

Pike, C. (1996). *The last vampire 4: Phantom*. New York: Pocket Books.

Rosenblatt, L. M. (1995). *Literature as exploration*. New York: Modern Language Association.

San Souci, R. D. (1989). *The talking eggs*. New York: Dial Press.

Schwartz, H. (1996). *Next year in Jerusalem: 3000 years of Jewish stories*. New York: Viking.

Scieszka, J. & Johnson, S. (1991). *The frog prince continued*. New York: Viking.

Scieszka, J. & Smith, L. (1992). *The stinky cheese man and other fairly stupid tales*. New York: Viking.

Scieszka, J. & Smith, L. (1989). *The true story of the 3 little pigs!* New York: Viking.

Shelley, M. (1993). *Frankenstein*. New York: Random House.

Smith, L. J. (1991). *The vampire diaries: The awakening*. New York: HarperCollins.

Smith, L. J. (1992). *The vampire diaries: Dark reunion*. New York: HarperCollins.

Smith, L. J. (1991). *The vampire diaries: The fury*. New York: HarperCollins.

Smith, L. J. (1991). *The vampire diaries: The struggle*. New York: HarperCollins.

Stine, R. L. (1992). *Goodnight kiss*. New York: Pocket Books.

Stoker, B. (1983). *Dracula*. New York: Bantam.

Sullivan, J. (Ed.). (1986). *The Penguin encyclopedia of horror and the supernatural*. New York: Viking.

Yolen, J. (1991). *Vampires*. New York: HarperCollins.

## Films Cited (Each Available on Home Video)

Brooks, M. (Producer). (1995). *Dracula: Dead and loving it*. Castle Rock Entertainment: Columbia TriStar Home Video.

Coppola, F. F., Fuchs, F., & Mulvehill, C. (Producers). (1993). *Dracula*. Burbank, CA: Columbia Pictures.

Hinds, A. (Producer). (1985). *Horror of Dracula*. Burbank, CA: Warner Home Video.

Kaufman, R. & Hamilton, G. (Producers). (1979). *Love at first bite*. Melvin Simon Productions: Orion Home Video.

Laemmle, C., Jr. & Browning, T. (Producers). (1931). *Dracula*. Universal City, CA: MCA Home Video.

Murphy, E. & Lipsky, M. (Producers). (1996). *Vampire in Brooklyn*. Hollywood, CA: Paramount Pictures.

Woolley, S. & Geffen, D. (Producers). (1995). *Interview with the vampire: The vampire chronicles*. Geffen Pictures: Warner Home Video.

# 13

# From Survival to Success: Moving from *The Call of the Wild* to "I Have a Dream" Using Young Adult Literature

*Joan F. Kaywell*

## Introduction

According to Peter Lowe (1995), there are four levels of life: survival, security, success, and significance. A person at the survival level operates in a live-for-the-moment mentality and is often at risk. People with security are stable and have provided for emergencies as well as a few extras. Successful people are those who are way ahead, having much more [*fill-in-the-blank*] than needed. The highest level of life, significance, is not determined by how much a person has but how much a person gives.

Many people will recognize me as the author of a reference text called *Adolescents At Risk: A Guide to Fiction and Nonfiction for Young Adults, Parents, and Professionals*. My area of expertise is disadvantaged youth—those just barely surviving in schools—and the development of their literacy skills. This chapter is written in the hopes that at-risk adolescents can be guided from survival mentalities to ones of significance.

## Introducing the Concept of Survival

Begin the unit by having students participate in one or both of the following survival games: NASA Moon Survival Task (See Figure 13.1) and the Surviving a Plane Crash (See Figure 13.2).

Once students are given the instructions for Surviving a Plane Crash, it is important that the teacher no longer provide any leadership (remember, you did not survive the crash). It is interesting to note the initial silence followed by immediate chaos as students argue over what is most important for survival. By observing your students while they are engaged in this activity, you can discover the natural leaders of the class for subsequent cooperative learning groups.

**Figure 13.1**
**NASA Moon Survival Task**

Think of yourself as a member of a space crew whose mission is to rendezvous with a Mother Ship on the moon. Due to mechanical difficulties, your ship has crash landed some 200 miles from the rendezvous site. All equipment with the exception of 15 items was destroyed in the crash. Since survival depends upon reaching the Mother Ship, you and your fellow crew members must determine which among the 15 items of equipment left intact are the most crucial for survival.

The 15 items left intact after the crash are listed below. Rank these in order of their importance for ensuring survival. Place the number "1" in the space by the item you feel is the most critical, the number "2" by the second most important, and so on through number 15 for the least important item. After you have individually ranked the items, get with three or four other peers and rank the items according to group consensus.

_____ box of matches

_____ food concentrate

_____ 50 feet of nylon rope

_____ parachute silk

_____ portable heating unit

_____ two 45 caliber pistols

_____ one case dehydrated Pet milk

_____ two 100-pound tanks of oxygen

_____ stellar map

_____ life raft

_____ magnetic compass

_____ five gallons of water

_____ signal flares

_____ first aid kit containing injection needles

_____ solar-powered FM receiver-transmitter

– – – – – – – – – – – – – – – – – – – – – – – – – – – – – –

**Answers**

The following rankings are from the NASA Space Center in Florida: (1) two 100-pound tanks of oxygen, (2) five gallons of water, (3) stellar map, (4) food concentrate, (5) solar-powered FM receiver-transmitter, (6) 50 feet of nylon rope, (7) first aid kit containing injection needles, (8) parachute silk, (9) life raft, (10) signal flares, (11) two 45 caliber pistols, (12) one case dehydrated Pet milk, (13) portable heating unit, (14) magnetic compass, and (15) box of matches.

---

**Figure 13.2**
**Surviving a Plane Crash**

In a long distance flight across the ocean, your plane crash lands on an island. Your pilot (the teacher) has been killed in the crash, some of you are wounded, and others are dead. Half of the plane, including other passengers, the radio, and baggage, is no longer in sight. You and the other survivors (your classmates) must reach a consensus about the rank ordering of what-to-dos. You have 20 minutes to reach that consensus before you all die. Rank order the following, with one being the first thing to do and ten being the last thing to do. Good luck!

_____   look for the other half of the plane

_____   look for food

_____   establish rules for group behavior

_____   look for water

_____   make a signal for help

_____   bury the dead

_____   decide who holds the gun

_____   tend to the wounded

_____   look for shelter

_____   look for other survivors

---

# Survival Literature

There are many classic and young adult (YA) titles that address the theme of survival. Group classes into learning teams consisting of four or five students. Each learning team then decides which of the five classic options they will study as a group; Option #1 is the most difficult reading and Option #5 is the least difficult. Teachers might make suggestions to individual learning teams on how they might best proceed with their reading. For example, strong readers who choose Option #1 may feel comfortable reading the classic independently. Other groups reading Option #1 may prefer to divide the novel by chapters with each member reading the amount appropriate to his or her skill level and summarizing his or her reading for the group. Students reading Option #5 might want to read the narrative poem and short stories aloud to each other within their small group. The main goal is to ensure that the reading of the classics is not laborious.

Students are also expected to individually read a YA novel that accompanies their chosen classic so that all listed YA novels are included. Encourage students to keep reader response journals to record their significant insights as well as document their reading. Reader response journals should satisfy two criteria. First, students must prove that they have read the YA novel in its entirety. Second, students must prove that they have thought deeply about their reading, connecting it to their own lives in some way. (Refer to *Adolescent Literature as a Complement to the Classics*, Volume One, Chapter 3 (pp. 46–52) and Volume Two, Chapter 6 (pp. 134–137) for several individual and group project ideas for reporting on the survival literature.) For each option, movies are available to also complement students' study of survival.

## Classic Survival Literature Option #1

### *Robinson Crusoe* by Daniel Defoe (337 pp.)

Originally published in 1719, this classic has withstood the test of time for a number of reasons. At the surface level, the survival aspect of this novel is certainly entertaining. Robinson Crusoe, having been shipwrecked at sea, survives for most of his adult life on an island. His ingenuity at creating suitable habitats, growing and harvesting food, making tools, and raising livestock is nothing short of amazing. Not only is he able to "conquer" nature, but he finds himself lord over his kingdom:

> I had nothing to covet; for I had all that I was now capable of enjoying. I was lord of the whole manor; or if I pleased, I might call myself king, or emperor over the whole country which I had possession of.
>
> (p. 143)

At a deeper level, this novel addresses Robinson Crusoe's drive to be master over nature and other humans. On the island, Crusoe saves a man (whom he later names Friday) from cannibals. Crusoe, grateful for the companionship, teaches Friday how to speak English and "taught him to say 'Master,' and then let him know that was to be my name" (p. 227). Friday pledges his faithful allegiance and servitude; "never man had a more faithful, loving, sincere servant than Friday was to [Crusoe]" (p. 230). Later, he and Friday save a Spaniard and Friday's father from cannibals, and they, too, swear their devotion to Robinson Crusoe. Next, Crusoe is able to rescue a captain and his mates from a mutiny. The captain and several of his men are so grateful to Crusoe for saving them that the captain agrees to take Crusoe back to his homeland. Once there, Robinson Crusoe learns that he has acquired wealth and receives a handsome sum of money for the sale of his plantation. Years later, in a terribly sexist move, he sends seven women "besides other supplies" (p. 336) to *his* colony on *his* island.

Although readers will probably find Crusoe's patriarchal regard for others offensive, he is not totally despicable. Many insights may be gleaned when readers study Robinson Crusoe's relationship with God. In this third possible level of study, readers are introduced to everything from the pagan belief system of cannibals to Crusoe's dependence on God and his belief in Providence. While stranded on the island with more gold, silver, and money than he could have imagined, he muses over the folly of it all, recognizing that "discontented people . . . cannot enjoy comfortably what God has given them because they see and covet something that He has not given them. All our discontents about what we want appeared to me to spring from the want of thankfulness for what we have" (pp. 144–145).

## Young Adult Survival Literature Accompanying Option #1

### *Hatchet* (195 pp.), *The River* (132 pp.), and *Brian's Winter* (133 pp.) by Gary Paulsen

While en route to visit his father, Brian survives the crash landing of a plane after the pilot dies of a heart attack. Alone in the wilderness, Brian has only one survival tool—the hatchet his mother gave him as a going away present. In the sequel to *Hatchet*, *The River*, Brian is asked to return to the wilderness so that a psychologist can take notes on Brian's survival skills. The psychologist is struck by lightning, and Brian finds himself in another struggle for survival as he travels down a 100-mile river for help. In *Brian's Winter*, Paulsen refers back to *Hatchet* but instead answers the question frequently posed by his readers: "What would happen if Brian hadn't been rescued, if he had had to survive in the winter?" (p. 1) The novel continues Brian's struggle for survival in the Canadian wilderness.

### *Walker of Time* (205 pp.) and *Walker's Journey Home* by Helen Hughes Vick (182 pp.)

A 1994 ALA Best Book for Young Adults, *Walker of Time* is the story of a young Hopi Indian, Walker, and his struggle to lead the Sinaguas out of their dry and barren land to the better land of the Hopi. *Walker's Journey Home* continues the story of their adventures and their struggles to cross the Arizona desert and get to the Hopi mesas.

## Classic Survival Literature Option #2

### *Lord of the Flies* by William Golding (187 pp.)

Golding's novel, originally published in 1954, tells the story of psychological transformation of a group of English boys, ages five to twelve, from regular kids to murderous heathens. The boys, who are being evacuated from war-torn England, survive a plane crash and are marooned without adults on a tropical island. Ralph is elected leader because he is the one among the older ones who has the initiative to call a meeting to order. Readers will learn that he is the one of all of the boys who tries the hardest to maintain some semblance of order in their chaotic state. Jack, on the other hand, hungers for the power leadership brings. He and Ralph constantly struggle over authority, presenting two opposing viewpoints: Jack hunts, kills, and manipulates the "littluns" into servitude, but Ralph uses democratic ways to systematically ensure their survival.

As time passes, the contrasts between the boys become even more marked. They begin to speak of "a beast", a nameless dark being that inspires both fear and sick excitement. When the twins, Sam and Eric, see a monstrous being in the trees, the boys' fear has a real focus. There is a "real" beast to fear.

As the beast assumes symbolic proportions for the boys, they divide into two groups: the hunters—Jack, Roger, Bill, Robert, and some of the littluns—and the non-hunters—Ralph, Simon, Piggy, "Samneric", and the weaker littluns. Led by Jack, the hunters become increasingly more barbaric, engaging in games of "'Kill the pig! Cut his throat! Kill the pig! Bash him in!'" (p.106). They brutalize a wild pig and cover themselves in blood, painting their faces. Meanwhile, Ralph and Piggy long for the normalcy of civilized life, watching helplessly as their group breaks down.

It is the odd loner Simon who first recognizes the true nature of the beast. Faced with the "Lord of the Flies" (p. 128)—a dead pig's head that Jack has impaled and left in a clearing—Simon recognizes that the real beast is the savagery of the boys themselves. As he makes his way back to camp, he sees Samneric's beast—a dead parachutist hanging in the trees—and knows he must tell the others before the beast in themselves totally consumes them. But he is too late. When he returns to the group, they are engaged in a frenzied dance, and in their frenzy they mistake Simon for the beast and viciously murder him (p. 141).

Piggy, in a last desperate attempt to regain order, shouts, " 'Which is better—to be a pack of painted Indians like you are, or to be sensible like Ralph is? . . . Which is better—to have rules and agree, or to hunt and kill?' " (p. 166). The hunters are too far gone, though, and Piggy, too, is murdered after a futile attempt to sway the boys from their savage behavior. In a terrible race for his own safety from the murderous Jack and his followers, Ralph finally reaches the beach and miraculously looks up into the face of a naval officer who misinterprets the boys' antics as "fun and games" (p. 185). (See *Adolescent Literature as a Complement to the Classics*, Volume One, Chapter 12, for a complete unit centered around this classic.)

## Young Adult Survival Literature Accompanying Option #2

### *Downriver* by Will Hobbs (204 pp.)

After her father remarries, Jessie is sent to Discovery Unlimited for nine weeks. There she joins seven other troubled teenagers in an outdoor education program designed to teach them self-reliance, discipline, and survival skills. A counselor explains, "sometimes self-reliance is the key to survival, but other times cooperation is" (p. 5). The teens, bored by their adult guide, hijack the van and equipment and attempt to go white-water river rafting down the Colorado River by themselves. A handsome boy, Troy, is bent on controlling others and throws their map of the river away, leaving all of them to struggle for their lives. Surprisingly, it is the quiet boy, Freddy, who uses his ingenuity to save the others.

### *The Kraken* by Don C. Reed (217 pp.)

This novel, set in 1873, is the story of Mark and his family's struggle to survive off the coast of Newfoundland. Not only is the food scarce and the winters harsh, but Mark encounters the Kraken—a giant squid—on a fishing expedition. Surviving the perils of nature is one thing, but having to overcome obstacles created by fellow humans is quite another. Inevitably, Mark learns that simply because that's the way something is doesn't necessarily make it right; he vows to make the world a better place.

### The Cay (160 pp.) and Timothy of the Cay (161 pp.) by Theodore Taylor

In *The Cay,* Phillip, a prejudiced 11-year-old white boy, becomes blind after a shipwreck leaves him stranded on a Caribbean island. Ironically, an old black sailor named Timothy helps him survive. The prequel-sequel, *Timothy of the Cay,* juxtaposes Timothy's childhood on St. Thomas with Phillip's life after his rescue.

## Classic Survival and Young Adult Literature Option #3

### The Diary of a Young Girl by Anne Frank (241 pp.)

For a complete unit about this classic nonfiction work, teachers are asked to refer to *Adolescent Literature as a Complement to the Classics,* Volume One, Chapter 2, "Anne Frank's *The Diary of a Young Girl:* World War II and Young Adult Literature."

## Classic Survival Literature Option #4

### The Call of the Wild by Jack London (45 pp.)

Buck, the 140-pound son of a huge St. Bernard and a Scotch shepherd dog, rules for years in aristocratic style in the big house of Judge Miller. With the discovery of gold in 1896 in the Yukon territory of northwestern Canada, dogs become necessary travel companions. One of the Judge's opportunistic gardeners sells Buck to a despicable man. After several exchanges and brutal beatings, Buck is eventually sold to a couple of Canadian gold seekers named Perrault and Francois. Through the firm hand of Francois and the return of Buck's primordial instincts, Buck becomes the lead sled dog. Buck adjusts to this new lifestyle:

> Sometimes he thought of Judge Miller's big house . . . but oftener he remembered the man in the red sweater [who beat him], the great fight with Spitz [the previous lead sled dog], and the good things he had eaten or would like to eat. He was not homesick. . . . and such memories had no power over him. Far more potent were the memories of his heredity that gave things he had never seen before a seeming familiarity; the instincts (which were but the memories of his ancestors become habits) which had lapsed . . . quickened and became alive again.
>
> (p. 512)

Buck's life with Perrault and Francois ends when he is sold to a mail carrier, a Scotsman who nearly works Buck and the dogs to death. He sells Buck to three inexperienced fortune finders: Charles; his wife, Mercedes; and her brother, Hal. Partly out of ignorance and partly through desperation, they brutally beat their dogs to pull their overloaded sled. When Buck refuses to pull, a first for Buck, Hal exchanges his whip for a club, but Buck still does not budge. Another man, John Thornton, leaps upon Hal, shouting, " 'If you strike that dog again, I'll kill you' " (p. 521).

For the first time in his life, Buck experiences genuine love for his new master, and their relationship grows to legendary proportions. Indeed, one day John bets all of his life savings on Buck's ability to pull start an iced-sled loaded with 1000 pounds. When it is time to mush, Thornton whispers in Buck's ear, " 'As you love me, Buck. As you love me' " (p. 529). Buck earns sixteen hundred dollars in five minutes that day, a prize that enables John to pay off his debts and seek "a fabled lost mine" (p. 530). Life is good, but irresistible impulses sometimes seize Buck. The wild calls him, but he can never totally leave his master until Thornton is brutally murdered by the Yeehats. Buck cuts all ties with civilization and joins the wolves in singing "a song of the younger world, which is the song of the pack" (p. 539).

## Young Adult Survival Literature Accompanying Option #4

### *Dogsong* by Gary Paulsen (177 pp.)

This Newbery Honor Book is the story of a 14-year-old Inuit boy, Russel Suskitt, who's haunted by dreams of another long-ago self. In an effort to discover who he is, Russel attempts a personal journey across the frozen Alaskan tundra. Before leaving, however, he seeks guidance from Oogruk, an old, blind man who knows the old ways of survival. Snowmobiles and other modern conveniences have stripped people of their ability to survive in nature. Russel and his team of sled dogs must overcome hunger, deal with the threat of a polar bear, and save a pregnant girl from death.

### *Woodsong* by Gary Paulsen (132 pp.)

This is Paulsen's autobiographical rendering of his participation in Alaska's Iditarod. The Iditarod is a 1000-mile, man and sled dog team race across the frozen Arctic wasteland. Paulsen barely survives, but afterwards is able to share his experiences with his readers.

## Classic Survival Literature Option #5

### "The Cremation of Sam McGee" by Robert Service (5 pp.), "To Build a Fire" by Jack London (11 pp.) and "The Open Boat" by Stephen Crane (15 pp.)

These three works epitomize classic survival short tales. The first example is a narrative poem about a gold seeker, Sam McGee, who dies in the Yukon. Before his demise, he makes his traveling companion promise to cremate him rather than leave him frozen solid.

In "To Build a Fire," a man and his wolf-dog are pitted against a relentless Alaskan winter. An old-timer warns him about traveling alone in such weather, but the desire for gold makes this newcomer ignore the advice.

> The trouble with him was that he was without imagination. He was quick and alert in the things of life, but only in the things, and not in the significances. Fifty degrees below zero meant eighty-odd degrees of frost. Such fact impressed him as being cold and uncomfortable, and that was all. . . . He knew that at fifty below spittle crackled on the snow, but this spittle crackled in the air.
>
> (p. 342)

As the man makes a desperate and ultimately vain attempt to build a fire, he mumbles, "You were right, old hoss [old-timer]; you were right" (p. 351), then dies.

"The Open Boat" was written after Stephen Crane, a news correspondent aboard the *Commodore,* almost lost his life when the ship sank off the Florida coast. Crane and some crew members spent a worrisome day and night aboard a ten-foot dingy; one man drowned. Crane writes of four castaways alone in a small boat on the sea: a cook, the oiler, the correspondent, and the injured captain. Together, they struggle within sight of land but cannot get there, lamenting, "'If I am going to be drowned—if I am going to be drowned, why, in the name of the seven mad gods who rule the sea, was I allowed to come thus far and contemplate sand and trees'" (p. 470). The same lament is made (p. 472) after the men see people on the beach who simply wave at them, apparently unaware of their plight. And again, while spending the night among swirling sharks, they utter the same lament (p. 473).

The correspondent, while deliriously rowing, recalls a poem he once studied in school about "A soldier of the Legion . . . dying in Algiers" (p. 474). At the time he studied the poem, it meant "less to him than the breaking of a pencil's point" (p. 474). Now, facing his own mortality, the correspondent experiences true sorrow for the soldier who knew before his death that he would never see his native land again. Finally, three of the men are received warmly by the land, "but a still and dripping shape was carried slowly up the beach, and the land's welcome for it could only be the different and sinister hospitality of the grave" (p. 478).

## Young Adult Survival Literature Accompanying Option #5

### *The Shark Callers* by Eric Campbell (232 pp.)

A young boy, Kaleka, is training to become a shark caller for shark hunts. Meanwhile, the Thompsons are evacuating from Matupi, New Britain, which is facing an impending volcanic eruption. They successfully set sail, but their boat is swamped by a tidal wave, putting them in a struggle for survival.

### *Between a Rock and a Hard Place* by Alden R. Carter (213 pp.)

Family tradition and a "that's-just-the-way-it-is" mentality force an unwilling Mark to accompany his inexperienced cousin, Randy, on a canoe trip in Minnesota's Boundary Waters. The boys have to learn to survive first after a bear gets into their food and destroys Randy's insulin, and then when Mark gets their canoe smashed, leaving them stranded in the wilderness.

### *Where's Home?* by Jonathan London (89 pp.)

Life for 14-year-old Aaron and his father goes from bad to worse after they decide to leave West Virginia in pursuit of a San Franciscan dream. With no work, no food, and no money, they resort to surviving life in the streets among the homeless. Aaron's only comforts are his journal, "his million dollar imagination," and a friendship with Maria.

### *Mr. Tucket* by Gary Paulsen (166 pp.)

Francis Tucket, a 14-year-old adventurer, is traveling on a wagon train with his family. The family is headed for Oregon in the hopes of finding a better life. Along the way, Francis is captured by the Pawnee Indians. He is unsuccessful at escaping until he befriends Mr. Grimes, a trapper who sells gunpowder to the Pawnees. Through Mr. Grimes's guidance, Francis learns how to survive and becomes a person worthy of the name Mister Tucket.

## Survival Films Accompanying This Unit

### *Swiss Family Robinson* produced by Bill Anderson

Based on Wyss's 1949 classic novel, *The Swiss Family Robinson,* this G-rated movie chronicles the lives of the Robinson family after they are shipwrecked on a deserted island. The family does a decent job of making a home on the island, but pirates threaten their survival. (Best suited for Option #1)

### *Cliffhanger* produced by Gene Hines, James R. Zatolokin, and David Rotman

Teachers may wish to show excerpts or recommend this R-rated movie, starring Sylvester Stallone and John Lithgow, to students. Gabe Walker heads the Rocky Mountain Rescue team's mission to save five climbers trapped on an icy mountain. Unbeknownst to his team, the distress call is a vicious trap set by a merciless international terrorist. (Best suited for Option #2)

### *Schindler's List* produced by Steven Spielberg, Gerald R. Molen, and Branko Lustig

Most students will be familiar with this Academy Award-winning R-rated film, starring Liam Neeson and Ben Kingsley. Based on a true story, this movie recounts the survival stories of hundreds of Jews saved by Oskar Schindler during the Holocaust. (Best suited for Option #3)

### *Call of the Wild* produced by Alan Jacobs

Rick Schroder and Mia Sara star in this film based upon London's classic novella. The movie centers around John Thornton and his quest for gold in the 1897 Yukon Gold Rush. In his struggle for survival, it is his dog Buck who teaches him the true meaning of life. (Best suited for Option #4)

### *White Fang* produced by MaryKay Powell and *White Fang 2: Myth of the White Wolf* produced by Justis Greene and David Fallon

Jack, in an attempt to fulfill his dying father's dream of discovering gold, embarks on a test of survival in the frozen Yukon. There he meets and befriends White Fang, a half-dog and half-wolf. *White Fang 2,* starring Scott Bairstow and Geoffrey Lewis, is the continuing story of *White Fang.* In 1906, Jack and his companion White Fang try to protect peaceful Indians from the threat of encroaching gold miners in Alaska. Both movies are rated PG. (Best suited for Option #4)

### *Iron Will* produced by Patrick Palmer and Robert Schwartz

This PG-rated movie, starring Kevin Spacey and Brian Cox, is based on a true story. After the accidental death of Will Stoneman's father, 17-year-old Will decides to participate in a cross-country race through the frozen Alaskan wilderness to help relieve his mother's financial woes. This movie reflects "Iron Will's" determination to win the $10,000 purse with his team of sled dogs led by Gus, his father's prize dog. (Best suited for Options #4 and #5)

### *Alive* produced by Robert Watts and Kathleen Kennedy and *Alive 20 Years Later* produced by Jill Fullerton-Smith

*Alive* is an R-rated movie based on Read's nonfiction novel by the same name. On a Friday-the-13th in 1972, a rugby team's plane crashes in the Andes Mountains. Sixteen of 32 players are eventually rescued after a harrowing two-month struggle for survival. The non-rated film *Alive 20 Years Later* is just as its name implies, except this film contains actual footage of the survivors themselves. (Best suited for Option #5)

### *White Wolves: A Cry in the Wild II* produced by Julie Corman

This PG-rated movie, starring Amy O'Neill and Matt McCoy, is about five teenagers and an adult guide who embark on a two-week pleasure trek through the Cascade Mountains. Their adventure turns into a test of survival when their leader gets seriously injured. (Best suited for Option #5)

## Moving from Survival to Significance

From Patrick Henry in his famous "Speech to the Virginia Convention," where he proclaims, "give me liberty, or give me death!" (p. 90) to Martin Luther King in his well-known "I Have a Dream" speech, where he dreams that his "four little children will one day live in a nation where they will not be judged by the color of their skin but by the content of their character" (p. 298), there have been people who have been willing to live lives of utmost significance. Because of my involvement with at-risk adolescents, I wanted to see if I could teach a group of students what it feels like to give of themselves by participating in a "Project of Significance."

## A Project of Significance

During the 1995–1996 school year, I approached Peter Lowe, a famous motivational speaker, about doing this "Project of Significance" with my students. Mr. Lowe has conducted interviews with George and Barbara Bush, Debbie Fields, Colin Powell, Mary Lou Retton, Norman Schwartzkopf, and Zig Ziglar, among others; has written and produced a series of "Success Tapes" for adults about what it means to be successful; and has conducted Success Seminars all over the world.

I explained to Mr. Lowe that my students from Corpus Christi Catholic School in Tampa, Florida, were likely to become "successful" adults, by his definition. I wanted to teach my students what it would feel like to go beyond successful, to live lives of *significance*, by participating in a "Project of Significance." Mr. Lowe agreed to sponsor our project, which was simply this: Using his success tapes that were written for adults as models, my students interviewed "successful" teenagers to produce a success tape written by kids for kids about what it means to be a successful teenager in the 1990s.

Following Peter Lowe's cassette tape format, we interviewed a famous teenager—in our case, Joanna Garcia, the star of the Nickelodeon series "Are You Afraid of the Dark?"—about the secrets of her success. In order to find a "successful" teenager to interview, my students had to learn how to write persuasive letters. Then, for side two, my eighth graders synthesized the essential and useful tips or suggestions they gleaned from numerous interviews of successful teenagers from four predominant areas: 1) academic scholars; 2) athletic champions; 3) talented musicians, artists, and dancers; and 4) teenagers who have overcome negative situations in positive ways. By learning information about adolescents' success strategies and recording them for others, my students were able to share or "give back" to other young adults. (See Figure 13.3 for the results of our "Project of Significance.")

---

**Figure 13.3**

**Project of Significance Results: Eight Essential Tips or Suggestions for Teenagers Wishing to Improve Their Lives**

1. **Set Immediate and Distant Goals**

   Whether it's going to college, making straight A's, becoming a pediatrician, obtaining a scholarship, getting into Notre Dame, going to the Olympics, becoming captain of the swimming team, making a movie with Spielberg, or becoming an actor or opera singer, you need to have a major goal in life and develop a plan to make the goal a reality. It is important to make the plan as specific as possible so you're able to see some results.

   Goals may change in life, but it's important to always have an intended direction. Finding a goal can be difficult for some, but one teenager advises, "keep searching for something you're good at and stick with it." Goals have to come from within and cannot be forced upon you. Remember that each one of us has a special talent waiting to be developed, so what is it that you love?

   **Examples for Inspiration.**    View any of these contemporary movies: *Mr. Holland's Opus, Rudy, Sandlot,* or *Wild Hearts Can't be Broken.*

2. **Don't Give Up**

   Life is like a roller coaster—it has its ups and downs. When you're in a down time, it's important to remember that "life will go on" no matter what. The sun will rise, and tomorrow is a new day. All people experience bad days, but successful teenagers view the bad days as learning opportunities; they believe that "everything happens for a reason." Bad things happen to everybody; it's what a person does with it that determines the character of a person. It's important to just keep on going, don't take things for granted, and "when you don't succeed, try try again!"

   Figure 13.3 continued on next page

Figure 13.3 continued

Sometimes stepping back and looking at how much you have improved or how far you've come helps you to get past the rough times. Relax when necessary and have outlets to help you forget your problems for a little while. Develop a hobby or find something that you like to do that is completely unrelated to your goal.

**Examples for Inspiration.**    Read any one of the following young adult novels: *Alicia My Story* (433 pp.) by Alicia Appleman-Jurman (a Holocaust survivor's story); *Winning* (211 pp.) by Robin Brancato (a story about a star football player who is paralyzed from the shoulders down after a routine tackle); *Silver Rights* (258 pp.) by Constance Curry (the true story of the Carter children's desegregation of an all-white school system in the Mississippi Delta in 1965); *The Story of My Life* (213 pp.) by Helen Keller (overcoming deafness and blindness); *It Happened to Nancy* (241 pp.) edited by Dr. Beatrice Sparks (based on a true story about a girl with AIDS); or *Ryan White: My Own Story* (277 pp.) by Ryan White and Anne Marie Cunningham (a true story about a boy with AIDS).

3. **Have a Positive Outlook and Believe in Yourself**

Do whatever you can to develop a positive attitude, not only about life but about yourself. Tell yourself over and over again, "I can and will be successful because I want to succeed!" Associate with happy, positive people, keep an open mind, try to be happy, and smile as often as possible. There is humor in almost everything if you look hard enough. Don't get involved with the wrong crowd, and be proactive in pushing away negative thoughts.

**Examples for Inspiration.**    Read either of the following two young adult novels, and view these three contemporary movies: *The Outsiders* (156 pp.) by S.E. Hinton (two rival gangs, the Socs and the Greasers, discover that life is rough all over) and *Izzy, Willy-Nilly* (262 pp.) by Cynthia Voigt (a popular teenager loses a leg in a drunk driving accident), *Forrest Gump*, *Karate Kid*, and *Hoop It Up*.

4. **Develop a Support Group Who Expect the Best From You**

Whether it's their immediate family, a coach, a teacher, or other teens or adults, successful teenagers surround themselves with people who are supportive of their goals. Include your parents in your plans for the future. Most parents are willing to do all that they can in supporting positive goals. Those teenagers who do not have the support of their families develop relationships with other adults who offer them encouragement. Some teenagers find inspiration by reading about the success stories of others. Others make it a point to surround themselves with others who have similar dreams and goals. Find role models for yourself, and learn everything you can from them.

**Examples for Inspiration.**    View any of these contemporary movies: *Sister Act II*, *Stand and Deliver*, and *Dangerous Minds*.

Figure 13.3 continued on next page

Figure 13.3 continued

### 5.   The Three D's—Dedication, Discipline, and Determination

When you have your goal in place, you have to be dedicated enough to strive and work hard to attain it. In other words, you have to practice, practice, practice. You have to look for ways to improve and then go for it. If you have to do something that you don't want to do in order to achieve your goal, turn it around and make it positive. Sometimes practicing scales on the piano can be tedious, but it can also be fun if you make a game out of it. Remember, first things first. Sometimes you have to give up something fun in order to do something that will benefit you later.

Use your inner drive to get you through slumps. Don't be afraid to fail, because nothing ventured, nothing gained. We learn from our mistakes; the secret is to keep on going. Realize that if you keep trying and never give up, you will eventually get to where you are going.

**Examples for Inspiration.**   Read the following young adult novel, and view these contemporary movies: *Hatchet* (195 pp.) by Gary Paulsen(a boy struggles for survival alone in the Canadian wilderness); *Cool Runnings, The Mighty Ducks, The Air Up There, Wild Hearts Can't Be Broken, Cutting Edge, Sunset Park,* and *Braveheart.*

### 6.   Always Do Your Best—It's Your Choice

All you can do is your best; anything less and you'll never win. Exceptional teenagers would rather do their best and lose than win not doing their best, unless they could not see that they were making any progress. Some people think you can coast at the top, but actually you have to work twice as hard to challenge yourself. Be a risk taker with a go-for-it attitude! The bottom line is this: No matter what you decide you want to do, as long as you are doing the very best you can do, that's all there is. You are the only one who knows how hard you are pushing yourself! Your destiny is in your own hands. Do not cast blame!

**Examples for Inspiration.**   Read the following young adult novel, and view either of these contemporary movies: *Coming of Age in Mississippi* (384 pp.) by Anne Moody (the author relives her courage in challenging a racist society in the 1940s and 1950s), *Cool Runnings,* or *A League of Their Own.*

### 7.   Books Before the Ball

Successful teenagers believe that their studies will contribute to their being successful adults. All mentioned that they studied hard. In the words of one teen, "Don't fall asleep in school! No matter how tired you are, make yourself stay awake!" Passion develops when understanding develops. "Be thankful if your parents give you an education rather than a car—BELIEVE IT!!"

**Examples for Inspiration.** View any of these contemporary movies: *Stand and Deliver, The Principal, Lean on Me, Dead Poets Society,* and *The Corn Is Green.*

### 8.   Pray

Most of the successful teenagers interviewed commented on the value of prayer for giving them inner strength.

# Conclusion

There are many ways to participate in projects that move students from survival mentalities to significant ones. Students might wish to replicate the project that my eighth graders did; they might want to focus on one aspect of success by reading all of the books and seeing all of the movies in one particular section, such as "Have a Positive Outlook and Believe in Yourself;" or they might want to conduct comparative research on the attitudes of people barely surviving—dropouts, welfare recipients, the homeless—with the attitudes of people living lives of significance—missionaries, volunteers, charity workers. Of course, there is no conclusive evidence that engaging in "Projects of Significance" with your students will make them successful adults living significant lives. I do know that my eighth graders experienced pride upon completion of the project. As their teacher, I only hope that the result of my students' involvement not only helps them become successful, but also makes them want to give to others.

# References

Appleman-Jurman, A. (1988). *Alicia my story*. New York: Bantam.

Brancato, R. (1988). *Winning*. New York: Alfred A. Knopf.

Campbell, E. (1994). *The shark callers*. San Diego: Harcourt Brace.

Carter, A. R. (1995). *Between a rock and a hard place*. New York: Scholastic.

Crane, S. (1957). The open boat. In R. Anderson, J.M. Brinnin, J. Leggett, G. Q. Arpin, & S. A. Toth's (1993),   *Elements of literature*. Orlando, FL: Holt, Rinehart, & Winston, pp. 464–478.

Curry, C. (1995). *Silver rights*. Chapel Hill, NC: Algonquin Books.

Defoe, D. (1988). *Robinson Crusoe*. New York: Tom Doherty Associates.

Frank, A. (1995). *Anne Frank: The diary of a young girl*. New York: Doubleday.

Golding, W. (1954). *Lord of the flies*. New York: Paragon Books.

Henry, P. (1755). Speech to the Virginia convention. In R. Anderson, J. M. Brinnin, J. Leggett, G. Q. Arpin, & S. A. Toth's (1993), *Elements of literature*. Fifth Course. Orlando, FL: Holt, Rinehart & Winston, pp. 88–90.

Higgins, J. & Fowinkle, J. (1993). *The adventures of Huckleberry Finn*, prejudice, and adolescent literature. In J. F. Kaywell's (Ed.), *Adolescent literature as a complement to the classics*. Volume One. Norwood, MA: Christopher-Gordon Publishers, Inc., pp. 37–59.

Hinton, S. E. (1989). *The outsiders*. New York: Dell.

Hobbs, W. (1991). *Downriver*. New York: Atheneum.

Kaywell, J. F. (1993). *Adolescents at risk: A guide to fiction and nonfiction for young adults, parents, and professionals*. Westport, CN: Greenwood Press.

Kaywell, J. F. (1993). Anne Frank's *The diary of a young girl*: World War II and young adult literature. In J. F. Kaywell's (Ed.), *Adolescent literature as a complement to the classics*. Volume One. Norwood, MA: Christopher-Gordon Publishers, Inc., pp. 13–35.

Kaywell, J. F. (1995). Using young adult literature to develop a comprehensive world literature course around several classics. In J. F. Kaywell's (Ed.), *Adolescent literature as a complement to the classics*. Volume Two. Norwood, MA: Christopher-Gordon Publishers, Inc. pp., 111–143.

Keller, H. (1988). *The story of my life*. New York: New American Library.

King, M. L. (1963). I have a dream. In G. Kearns's (1984), *Appreciating literature*. New York: Macmillan, pp. 295–299.

London, J. (1903). *The call of the wild*. In G. Kearns's (1984), *Understanding literature*. New York: Macmillan, pp., 493–539.

London, J. (1903). To build a fire. In G. Kearns's (1984), *American literature*. New York: Macmillan, pp. 341–351.

London, J. (1995). *Where's home?* New York: Viking.

Lowe, P. (1995). *Success talk: Featuring Jimmy Johnson*. Tampa, FL: Peter Lowe International, Inc., Side B.

Moody, A. (1968). *Coming of age in Mississippi*. New York: Dell.

Paulsen, G. (1996). *Brian's winter*. New York: Delacorte Press.

Paulsen, G. (1985). *Dogsong*. New York: Scholastic.

Paulsen, G. (1988). *Hatchet*. New York: Puffin.

Paulsen, G. (1994). *Mr. Tucket*. New York: Delacorte Press.

Paulsen, G. (1991). *The river*. New York: Dell.

Paulsen, G. (1987). *Woodsong*. New York: Puffin.

Read, P. P. (1974). *Alive*. New York: Avon Books.

Reed, D. C. (1995). *The kraken*. Honesdale, PA: Boyds Mills Press.

Samuels, B. G. (1993). The beast within: Using and abusing power in *Lord of the flies*, *The chocolate war*, and other readings. In J. F. Kaywell's (Ed.), *Adolescent literature as a complement to the classics*. Volume One. Norwood, MA: Christopher-Gordon Publishers, Inc. pp. 195–214.

Service, R. (1994). The cremation of Sam McGee. In A.N. Applebee, A.B. Bermudez, S. Hynds, J. Langer, J. Marshall, & D.E. Norton's (Senior Consultants), *Literature and language*. Gold Level, 6. Evanston, IL: McDougal, Littell, pp. 132–137.

Sparks, B. (Ed.). (1994). *It happened to Nancy*. New York: Avon Books.

Taylor, T. (1977). *The cay*. New York: Avon Books.

Taylor, T. (1993). *Timothy of the cay*. New York: Avon Books.

Vick, H. H. (1994). *Walker of time*. Tucson, AZ: Harbinger House.

Vick, H. H. (1995). *Walker's journey home*. Tucson, AZ: Harbinger House.

Voigt, C. (1987). *Izzy, willy-nilly*. New York: Fawcett Juniper.

White, R. & Cunningham, A. M. (1991). *Ryan White: My own story*. New York: Dial Press.

Wyss, J. D. (1991). *The Swiss family Robinson*. New York: Bantam.

## Films Cited (Each Available on Home Video)

Anderson, B. (Producer). (1960). *Swiss family Robinson*. Burbank, CA: Walt Disney Home Video.

Corman, J. (Producer). (1993). *White wolves: A cry in the wild II*. New Horizons Home Video.

Fullerton-Smith, J. (Producer). (1992). *Alive 20 years later*. Burbank, CA: Touchstone Home Video.

Greene, J. & Fallon, D. (Producers). (1994). *White Fang 2: Myth of the white wolf*. Burbank, CA: Walt Disney Home Video.

Hines, G., Zatolokin, J.R., & Rotman, D. (Producers). (1993). *Cliffhanger*. TriStar: Columbia TriStar Home Video.

Jacobs, A. (Producer). (1993). *Call of the wild*. Cabin Fever Entertainment.

Palmer, P. & Schwartz, R. (Producers). (1993). *Iron Will*. Burbank, CA: Walt Disney Home Video.

Powell, M. (Producer). (1991). *White Fang*. Burbank, CA: Walt Disney Home Video.

Spielberg, S., Molen, G. R., & Lustig, B. (Producers). (1994). *Schindler's list*. Universal City, CA: MCA Universal Home Video.

Watts, R. & Kennedy, K. (Producers). (1992). *Alive*. Burbank, CA: Touchstone Home Video.

# 14

# Laughing With Thurber and Young Adult Literature

*Jeffrey S. Kaplan*

## Introduction

"This is funny?"

I looked up from my desk to see who was talking.

"This is funny? Is this supposed to be funny?"

It was a student in the first row.

"Well, er, yes," I said.

"It is?"

And he continued reading. "Well, I don't get it."

We were reading James Thurber, and in particular, "The Catbird Seat," a literary selection in our 11th grade anthology. As literary selections go, I sensed things were not running smoothly.

"What don't you get?" I asked, trying to head off the impasse.

"It's kind of slow, you know."

"Yeah, well, . . ."

"And I'm not sure. . . ."

"You're not sure what's going on?" I asked, expecting more of the same. "Maybe I can help. . . ."

At which point I tried to explain, as I had to the class earlier, what the story was all about.

"You see, class, this is a very funny story about a male office worker who is driven crazy by an overly efficient and critical female co-worker . . ."

Stares.

". . . and how their eventual sparring leads to a hilarious showdown, and. . . ."

More stares. Suddenly I realized I was getting nowhere, and the fault rested with me.

## The Problem

Although James Thurber is a gifted writer, his work is mainly for adults. His short stories, essays, and drawings have delighted readers since their appearance in the acclaimed literary magazine *New Yorker* in the early 1920s, but his art serves as a wry and satiric commentary on adult situations. Thurber's dominant theme is the war between modern man and an unfeeling universe, personified by women, animals, and machines. Harried husbands spar with overbearing wives. Beleaguered fathers war with rebellious children. Disillusioned boyfriends haggle with contentious girlfriends, and oversensitive, dissatisfied men struggle with the complications of the modern world. All these and more define James Thurber. He is the American master of portraying the frustrations and banalities of everyday life as seen through the eyes of middle-aged, world-weary men.

Thurber's work, however, is not "hah, hah, funny" and certainly not kid-oriented. Yes, his stories reflect universal themes—loneliness, frustration, and alienation—but his heroes are middle-aged adults, mostly male, who are wrestling with middle-aged problems. The characters in Thurber's many stories often are the victims of shrewish women, dreaded machines (such as kitchen appliances and automobiles), and of course, the pressures of their jobs. Often, they try to escape from their problems through alcohol or daydreams.

Thurber's most popular short story, "The Secret Life of Walter Mitty," for example, portrays a man who finds himself the tortured husband of a nagging wife. Seeking to escape her persistent and nagging ways, Walter Mitty daydreams incessantly about what it would like to be someone else. His fantasies include his becoming a valiant Navy pilot, a dashing swashbuckler, and a miracle-producing surgeon. Mitty's vivid imagination is his desperate escape from an untenable and stifling marriage. This is certainly a popular and often repeated premise throughout literature, particularly in selections intended to be comedic. The humor is unusually difficult to translate to adolescents, however, especially given that Thurber relies heavily on verbal wordplay and metaphor.

The same is true for Thurber's short story, "The Catbird Seat," an intricate and elaborately written tale about a veteran male office worker and a newly employed female office worker. The veteran quietly ponders "bumping her off" while she is bent on proving her efficiency. Adults can recognize and appreciate the cleverly-crafted, subtle humor and irony in the story. In contrast, it is hardly the stuff that most teenagers find fall-down funny. Indeed, the only thing most teenagers trip over are the words. The word play is often too abstract for them, and they just "don't get it." Although James Thurber is a gifted writer whose vision can often be cynical and amusing, his work is not for everyone. And my mistake was assuming that it was.

## James Thurber, The Man

Born in Columbus, Ohio, on December 8, 1894, James Thurber became a celebrated American humorist, famous for both his comic writing and his cartoon drawings. His writings reflect his native Columbus and the colorful characters of his youth. His humor grew out of his own personal insecurities and misfortunes.

When James Thurber was six years old, his older brother William accidentally shot him in the left eye during a game of William Tell. Following the advice of a local doctor, his parents failed to have the injured eye removed promptly, and disease set in in both eyes. Thurber's right eye was attacked by what was then known as *sympathetic ophthalmia*. Fortunately the disease arrested itself, allowing Thurber nearly 40 years of weakened sight. Thurber's vision started to weaken further in the late 1930s. Between 1940 and 1941, Thurber underwent five operations, after which he was legally blind.

As a child his eye injury made him feel inferior at sports, compelling him to be more of a spectator than a player. Frustrated by his growing inability to see clearly, he turned his energy toward literary pursuits. This at least was one area where he felt he had control.

Thurber was a tall, gangly, shy youngster who suffered a typical bout of teenage depression in high school. Eventually, he overcame his initial awkwardness and became the president of his Columbus High School senior class. Later, though, while attending Ohio State, Thurber again felt out-of-step, socially inept and awkward. Finally, after unofficially dropping out of college for a year, he returned to Ohio State and found his niche in life when he began to write for the campus newspaper. There, Thurber honed his literary and comedic skills, first as a campus journalist, then as the editor of the *Sundial*, Ohio State's humor and literary magazine.

When World War I broke out, Thurber left the university without a degree and became a code clerk for the United States Embassy in Paris. After returning to the United States, he wrote for the *Columbus Dispatch* but soon realized that his passion was for creative writing, not journalism. He found a creative outlet in writing features for the Sunday paper, and fancying himself "a real writer," he left the *Columbus Dispatch* in 1926 to write the "great American novel."

Thurber had no luck. After a brief writing stint in Europe, he was forced to return to the gritty world of real journalism. In the late 1920s, Thurber obtained a job as a reporter for the *New York Evening Post*, meanwhile doggedly continuing to write fiction in his spare time. He began sending pieces to the newly founded *New Yorker*, which accepted his writings for publication. Through hard work, determination, and luck, Thurber had finally found a wonderful and nurturing home for his wry and humorous short essays.

At the *New Yorker*, Thurber also found a career. There, he met E.B. White, the soon-to-be author of *Charlotte's Web* and *Stuart Little*. Through a long association with White and others, Thurber launched his literary life. Writing short, funny pieces eventually led to longer works and a long career as a writer, illustrator, and social satirist.

His first work was a collaboration with E.B. White, a timely satire entitled *Is Sex Necessary?* (1929). This work, an analysis of the "war between the sexes," brought out another one of Thurber's talents—his ability to create whimsical illustrations. *Is Sex Necessary?* became an immediate literary sensation, and Thurber, in his mid-30s, was acclaimed as both a visual and verbal artist.

From there, Thurber followed in rapid succession with a series of books, each of which added to his growing fame: *The Owl in the Attic and Other Perplexities* (1931), *The Seal in the Bedroom and Other Predicaments* (1932), *The Middle-Age Man on the Flying Trapeze* (1935), *Let Your Mind Alone!* (1937), *The Last Flower* and *Cream of Thurber* (1939), *Fables for Our Time and Famous Poems Illustrated* with *New Yorker* editor Eliot Nugent (1940), *My World—And Welcome to It* (1942), *Many Moons* (1943), *Men, Women and Dogs* (1943), *The Great Quillow* (1944), *The White Deer* (1945), *The Beast In Me and Other Animals* (1948), *The 13 Clocks* (1950), *The Thurber Album* (1952), *Thurber Country* (1953), *Thurber's Dogs* (1955), *Further Fables for Our Time* (1956), *Alarms and Diversions* and *The Wonderful O* (1957), and *The Years with Ross*—a historical and critical account of the *New Yorker* and its first editor (1959).

In 1960, New York audiences were treated to a dramatic revue of Thurber's work. His stories, drawings, captions, and fables were presented in a well-received play entitled *A Thurber Carnival*. Thurber himself appeared in the cast. This tall, gangly, anxiety-ridden and nearly blind individual, who had spent a lifetime bemoaning man's fate and the cruelties of human injustice and indifference, finally witnessed firsthand the accolades of an adoring and bemused public. It was to be one of his final public appearances. James Thurber died on November 2, 1961, in New York City.

## Themes in Thurber's Work

Thurber's work describes the anxieties of the average individual in modern society. He writes chiefly about middle-aged men who feel trapped by the banalities of modern existence and the frustrations of marriages plagued by domineering wives and rebellious children. Through stories, essays, and drawings, he captures frightened men, menacing women, wicked children, and sad dogs. His sketches, whether in words or cartoons, depict the dark side of the middle class, where distressed and reluctant men face women, children, and animals who are insensitive to their needs.

Thurber's stories portray the discord of contemporary life that has been brought on by the hazards of technology and the complex pressures of modern times. People—husbands and wives, fathers and teenagers, bosses and office workers—bicker over ordinary, everyday things because life is so complicated and demanding. Modern technologies and bureaucracies make man, representing all individuals, downtrodden, depressed, and at times, irrational. Hence, Thurber's characters seek refuge and escape from the daily pressures of everyday life.

> Thurber resembles many modern thinkers, for the psychological discovery of the unconscious, the nightmare of total war, the spread of dictatorship, the unnerving growth of technological and bureaucratic complexities, and the widespread loss of faith in religious and moral certainties have undermined the facile optimism that reason is sufficient to keep man from acting irrationally.
>
> (Morsberger, p. 603)

Throughout his long literary career, James Thurber reiterated his theme of the beleaguered husband coping with the modern world. His husbands are emblematic of all individuals seeking refuge from the storm, troubled by an incomprehensible universe and plagued by uncertainty and doubt. Thurber is not making fun of women, though, so much as using types—the domineering housewife, the frustrated spouse, the put-upon lover—to symbolize the impotence of both sexes to live in harmony and peaceful coexistence. Marriage becomes the last refuge for sane and rational discourse, but it is often reduced to petty arguments and banal frustrations because individual whims and fancies prevent real conversation.

Despite how it may appear in his work, Thurber wants both sexes to be liberated and objects to sexual stereotyping. He believes that women who keep saying, "Isn't that just like a man?" and men who keep echoing, "Oh, well, you know how women are," are more likely to grow farther apart through the years. If men and women could just see past their petty differences, their sexual frustrations, and their anxieties, Thurber rationalizes in the subtext of his many writings, then perhaps humankind could live peacefully and prosperously. So, one might ask, "Where's the humor?" Much of what Thurber writes is humor defined by literary allusions, introspective wordplay, and sophisticated adult situations beyond the grasp of most adolescents.

## Why and How Should Teachers Teach Thurber to Students?

Given the adult themes and sophisticated humor characteristic of Thurber's work, what are teachers to do? How should teachers approach the teaching of James Thurber to young adults when his literary pieces appear in their school anthologies? Moreover, how should teachers introduce young students to writing defined as "classic American funny" when the humor is over their heads? The answer lies, naturally, in knowing one's audience.

When I taught Thurber's "The Catbird Seat" to my 11th graders several years ago, I clearly did not know my audience. I assumed that they would find the literary and cerebral machinations of a man trying to kill his obnoxious and perfidious female office worker amusing.

Silly me.

They found the narrative tedious and the point belabored. This is not to say that Thurber's work is not amusing, or well-written, or insightful. Indeed, in the story "The Catbird Seat," Thurber cleverly illustrates how careers can be destroyed and dreams shattered, and how women were viewed in the early 20th century workplace. Teachers must see that his writing is not appealing to all, especially middle and high school students whose concerns are more immediate than office politics and whose humor is much broader than dazzling verbal wordplay and literary allusions.

To my 11th graders, Thurber wasn't funny at all. In fact, he was downright depressing to them. I suppose I should have been suspicious of Thurber's viability in the classroom when, years earlier, I had taught 7th grade language arts. As with most middle school English teachers, I found "The Secret Life of Walter Mitty" staring me in the face, waiting with bold print and colorful illustrations in my literary anthology to be read by my unsuspecting 7th graders. So I quickly thought, "This looks funny. I remember it was funny when I read it in college. They'll find it funny, too!"

Wrong!

The attempts of a middle-aged man trying to escape his nagging wife by imagining himself as a dashing hero in all sorts of glorious fantasies were slightly amusing to some, but for most the story was confusing and dull. The story's premise was all right, but it probably would have been more real to them if Thurber had been talking about someone their own age, with their interests, using their own language.

Imagine, let's say, a 12- or maybe 16-year-old who is being annoyed to death by nagging parents, teachers, or assorted other grown-ups, who secretly daydreams of escaping their constant carping by becoming a world famous rock-and-roll singer or maybe a professional sports star. Then imagine these same annoying grown-ups begging for an autograph or a chance to touch the world famous star, who politely does a "star turn" and says to the adoring fans, "You want what? Ha! Get a life!" And then walks away in triumphant victory! Something like that students can understand.

I turned to young adult (YA) literature because I wanted my then 7th grade language arts students to read novels written in a contemporary language that they could readily comprehend. I wanted my middle school students to laugh at recognizable characters in equally recognizable situations. I believe that so much of beginning reading is visiting the familiar set to print and that young readers should be consistently exposed to writing that reflects their everyday lives in a language and style that is both amusing and beguiling. These two attributes—humor and intrigue—make a winning combination for any reader, and when presented in a form palpable to young adults, promote real reading.

My mistake was not recognizing that my 11th grade English students needed such a form as well. Assuming that they were older, and perhaps, more mature readers, I rationalized that they would be ready for literate, introspective writing. I know now that young readers, like all readers, can appreciate Thurber for his delicate stylizations, but adolescents much prefer stories with a more contemporary "with-it" feel.

Seeking alternatives, I found YA literature, particularly YA literature that speaks of domesticity in a funny sense. Students' open recognition of human frailties and shared commonalties define for them what it means to be a living, breathing, and thinking individual. Above all, I want young adult readers to enjoy, and hopefully, laugh. I believe laughter is the "fruit of the gods" and that a merry heart is the sign of a sound mind. I knew my students were not finding Thurber merry. His writing, for them, proved to be more somber than jovial, so I was pleasantly stuck with finding alternatives. And there are plenty of alternatives to be had!

For me, the surest way to a person's heart is through humor. I have found that making someone laugh touches that person's soul in a way that mere pleasantries and niceties sometimes fail to do. A quick joke or a pithy verbal aside shared between knowing friends can often cement a relationship faster than almost anything. The two joke tellers, both the teller and the receiver, share an instant bond that defines their humanness and their morality. It is often said similar values and a shared sense of humor are the glue to good relationships. Laughter is the tie that binds, and the cement to lasting friendships. In essence, if more people could simply laugh at petty things and see more humor in their daily existences, the world would be a better place.

# What Kind of Young Adult Literature Complements Thurber?

Any literary unit that begins with a study of the life and times of James Thurber can be definitely enhanced by any one of many adolescent novels that depict very human and domestic situations in a funny light. When the language is straightforward and simple and the feel is realistic and modern, kids of all ages delight in reading about "family problems" that underline how amusing life can be when observed with a detached and wary eye. Domestic strife, as found in so much of Thurber's work, is the stuff of many YA novels, where the protagonists are often teenagers. The sophistication of the novels' tones vary from author to author, but there is something, to be sure, for everyone to read and enjoy.

When I look for YA novels that can serve as companions, or perhaps substitutes, to the works of James Thurber, I search for three types. First, I want humorous writing about domestic situations. Thurber is the master American humorist who underscores the pain of ordinary existence; he sees the funny in the everyday. He feels the pain and pleasure of living in a household of less than perfect people and conveys his knowing ways in a satirical and often sardonic light. Still, Thurber is an optimist at heart.

Second, I seek YA novels that reflects the world as my students know it. Yes, I believe it is important for young people to read works of historical context. Yes, I believe that young people should read literature that speaks of a world larger than theirs. And yes, I believe that students can find humor in far-removed time periods from their own. But I seek works that would most complement Thurber while reflecting, like he does, the "feel of the time." So much of humor is impeded by the fact that it soon becomes dated if it reflects only passing fads and follies. This is true of Thurber, and this will be true years from now of today's humorists, like Erma Bombeck and Dave Barry.

Third, I seek YA novels that tell stories of personal strife and success. Thurber does the same. As with most humorists, his arena is the mundane and how the human species is both horrible and wonderful. He is a not a political satirist, although he does have sharp political views. Thurber is primarily a wry commentator on the human condition, and his commentary rarely touches on anything but domestic discord. Thurber's intent is to give his readers the comfortable feeling that one's life is pretty peaceful and comfortable in comparison with the lives of his characters. I want my students to recognize the same, to see their lives in YA novels that speak of everyday heroes who overcome domestic strife in funny and amusing ways. Many YA authors probe the same comedic territory, producing funny gems of domestic bliss. They say what Thurber says—that life and relationships can be both confusing and amusing—in their own inimical style and language. Their references are contemporary; their language, common; and their characters, real.

What follows is a list of adolescent novels to complement the study of James Thurber's work. To be sure, this is not an exhaustive list of YA novels. Nonetheless, I can safely say that what follows is a representative list of some of the very best in funny YA fiction about modern family life.

Each book is briefly annotated with some reference to age level and classroom suitability (MS for middle school and HS for high school), though I do believe that high school students enjoy reading books primarily geared for middle school readers and vice versa. There is an attraction to the familiar regardless of one's age. I suppose that explains my personal affinity for YA literature as well my 10-year-old daughter's attraction to television sitcoms. My daughter watches reruns of *I Love Lucy, Bewitched,* and *Mary Tyler Moore* because she likes to see recognizable adults living in a familiar world. She sees them doing adults things and interacting with other adults—sometimes arguing, sometimes kidding, sometimes kissing—yet always triumphant. In the end, laughter, optimism, and sheer bliss win the day.

That sounds like Thurber to me.

## Funny Animal Stories

### *The Cat Who Came to Christmas* by Cleveland Amory (240 pp.)

Thurber uses animals in both his drawings and writings, and Cleveland Amory does the same. In this amusing nonfiction story Amory recounts what it is like to be owned by a cat. (HS)

### *All My Patients Are Under the Bed* by Louis J. Camuti with Marilyn Frankel and Haskel Frankel (222 pp.)

Dr. Louis J. Camuti, a veterinarian, tells amusing and touching vignettes about his life as a cat doctor. Have you ever heard of a cat having a bar mitzvah? You will if you read this book, which also serves as a good read aloud. (MS/HS)

### *James Herriot's Dog Stories* by James Herriot (427 pp.)

For the true animal lover, there is always acclaimed storyteller James Herriot, the English veterinarian who wrote *All Creatures Great and Small* and *All Creatures Bright and Beautiful.* Here are a collection of 50 stories bound to amuse readers who enjoy reading about animals who act like human beings. (HS)

## Funny Romances

### *The Things I Did For Love* by Ellen Conford (137 pp.)

Stephanie, a high school junior, writes a term paper entitled "Why Do Fools Fall in Love?" even though she has never been in love herself. Chaos ensues and domestic bliss is temporarily waylaid when she falls in love with a high school dropout who rides a motorcycle and sports an earring. (MS)

### *You Can Never Tell* by Ellen Conford (153 pp.)

Conford comically illustrates the pain of teenagers in love. In this "dream come true" story, 16-year-old Kate Bennett dates a daytime TV soap opera star who enrolls in her high school. The question: Is Kate in love with the real person or the TV personality? (MS)

### *The Love Letters of J. Timothy Owen* by Constance C. Greene (181 pp.)

Tim has no luck when it comes to love. In a desperate attempt to win the affection of Sophie, Tim sends her "borrowed" love letters from an old poetry book but uses his own name. His romance doesn't go as planned, and Tim ends up taking Sophie's younger sister to the school dance instead. Thurber would be amused by this one and so will lovestruck teenagers. (MS/HS)

### *Whoppers* by Nancy J. Hopper (150 pp.)

Allison, a high school junior, is painfully in love with Jerry. She keeps trying to impress him by telling him "whoppers" of lies. Finally he asks her out, but will he like her true self? (MS)

### *My First Love and Other Disasters* by Francine Pascal (173 pp.)

Fifteen-year-old Victoria is in love with someone who hardly knows she exists. In her manipulative adventures to gain his affections, she encounters one mishap after another, to her own as well as her friends' amusement and embarrassment. (MS)

### *Love and Betrayal and Hold the Mayo!* by Francine Pascal (210 pp.)

In this sequel to *My First Love and Other Disasters*, Victoria experiences "first love" at summer camp. Unfortunately, her new love happens to be her best friend's boyfriend. Teenagers suffering first time crushes will delight in recognizing common lovelorn dilemmas. (MS)

### *I Was a Fifteen-Year-Old Blimp* by Patti Stren (156 pp.)

Gabby Finkelstein, better known as "Flabby Gabby," decides to lose weight in order to enhance her self-esteem and her love life. Gabby tries many outlandish schemes to rid herself of fat, only to learn that true beauty is really skin deep. (MS)

### *The Amazing and Death-Defying Diary of Eugene Dingman* by Paul Zindel (208 pp.)

This *American Bookseller* Pick of the Lists is good for laughs while confronting harsh truths. Fifteen-year-old Eugene Dingman spends a summer as a waiter at a fancy Adirondack mountain resort. In diary form, he reveals the painful and jumbled emotions he feels as a teenager hopelessly in love with a waitress whose boyfriend despises him. (HS)

## Funny Family Relationships

### *Glass Slippers Give You Blisters* by Mary Jane Auch (109 pp.)

Kelly earns a production job in the Riverton Junior High production of *Cinderella*, but her overly critical mother disapproves of anything to do with the theater. Through several mishaps and some good timing, Kelly eventually enjoys *Cinderella*—and her mother. (MS)

### *Are You There God? It's Me, Margaret* by Judy Blume (149 pp.)

Eleven-year-old Margaret Simon is struggling to define herself, mainly because of her parents' different religious backgrounds: her father's Jewish and her mother's Catholic. This is a funny and touching account of one young girl's turbulent ride into adolescence and her own painful awareness of herself. (MS)

### *It's an Aardvark-Eat-Turtle World* by Paula Danziger (132 pp.)

Fourteen-year-old Rosie becomes part of a real family when her mother moves in with her best friend's father. Trouble ensues when Rosie's best friend does not make a terrific sister. Danziger finds humor in the most painful of human relationships. Other Danziger books that have a contemporary "sitcomish" feel include *The Cat Ate My Gymsuit, The Pistachio Prescription,* and *Make Like a Tree and Leave.* (MS)

### *This Place Has No Atmosphere* by Paula Danziger (156 pp.)

Through a whimsical take on the ordinary, Danziger tells the story of a young girl confronting life's problems in the 21st century. Aurora's parents decide to move to the moon for five years, and this 14-year-old finds herself having to deal with so many problems: Will she find a cute guy? Will her parents embarrass her? Will her hair wilt? This and more await readers eager to learn how life's problems never really change. (MS)

### *Alias Madame Doubtfire* by Anne Fine (160 pp.)

A divorced dad disguises himself as a female housekeeper for his ex-wife just so he can spend time with his kids; antics abound. Most students will be familiar with the highly popular and hilarious PG-13 movie *Mrs. Doubtfire,* starring Robin Williams and Sally Field. (MS/HS)

### *Credit-Card Carole* by Sheila Solomon Klass (137 pp.)

Carole is a 16-year-old shopping fanatic who's embarrassed by her parents. Her successful dentist father and businesswoman mother give up their financial security to live a Bohemian lifestyle. Carole and her friends cannot understand her parents, and she tries desperately to balance her materialism with her parents' blasé ideas about money. (MS/HS)

### *With a Name Like Lulu, Who Needs More Trouble?* by Tricia Springstubb (167 pp.)

Lulu, an overly shy middle schooler, suddenly finds herself thrust into the spotlight when, out of the blue, she catches a baby who falls from a three-story apartment window! Lulu becomes an instant celebrity, and laughs follow as Lulu overcomes her shyness and learns who she really is. (MS)

### *The Adrian Mole Diaries* by Sue Townsend (342 pp.)

Adrian Mole, a British teenager age 13 and three-quarters, chronicles in diary form his parents' divorce, his painful love-life, his running away from home, and his funny observations about his troubled life and times. Adrian Mole, the Holden Caulfield of his time, is a funny kid with much to say about being human. (HS)

### *The Farewell Kid* by Barbara Wersba (155 pp.)

Heidi Rosenbloom is a 17-year-old whose mission in life, much to her parents' dismay, is to save all the stray dogs in New York. She also wants to say good-bye to the "male species" and her own adolescence, which she likens to a long illness. Other books that chronicle her misadventures are *Just Be Gorgeous* and *Wonderful Me*. (MS/HS)

## Funny School Stories

### *Buffalo Brenda* by Jill Pinkwater (203 pp.)

Two girls cause quite a stir after they're expelled from the school newspaper staff. These freshmen start their own underground newspaper and adopt a bison from the federal government to serve as their mascot. (HS)

### *Dogs Don't Tell Jokes* by Louis Sachar (209 pp.)

"Goon" longs to be accepted by his peers, but his incessant joke-telling alienates all his classmates. The school talent show is his last chance to redeem himself and acquire his long sought-after fame. Goon plunges headfirst into show business, and the results are non-stop hilarity. Other humorous books written by Sachar include *Sixth Grade Blues, Wayside School Gets A Little Stranger, Sideways Arithmetic from Wayside School, More Sideways Arithmetic from Wayside School*, and *There's a Boy in the Girl's Bathroom!* (MS)

### *There's a Girl in My Hammerlock* by Jerry Spinelli (199 pp.)

An 8th grade girl, Maisie Brown, tries out for the school's wrestling team despite everyone thinking she is crazy. Maisie is not deterred and fights for her goal. With his light and amusing touch, Spinelli is perfect for readers who like books that pack a funny punch. Other good Spinelli books for young readers are *Fourth Grade Rats, Space Station Seventh Grade*, and *Who Put that Hair in My Toothbrush?* (MS)

## Teaching Ideas to Complement Funny Young Adult Literature

When I taught public school there would invariably come, in the middle of some lesson in which my students were having more fun than they were legally allowed, a loud knock on my classroom wall. The incessant pounding would be followed by the usual verbal plea from the teacher next door, "A little less noise please! Your laughing is making it hard for us to concentrate!" The unstated belief was simply, "If you're laughing, then obviously, real learning is not happening." Of course, nothing is further from the truth. Real laughter is a sign of real learning. When students are laughing, they are signaling that they are listening, enjoying, and what's more, recognizing "what is so funny." Their verbal responses—loud or soft, uproarious or quiet, howling or chuckling—are all indications that they are really paying attention, and they are thinking on many levels. They not only "get it," but they also see how the ordinary can become extraordinary with a simple verbal twist or exaggeration. It is quite an accomplishment when students can recognize everything from puns to gross distortions in a matter of seconds.

Humor is what makes learning pleasurable. Comic relief was as relevant to the Greeks and Shakespeare as it is today, and young children (as well as big kids and their teachers) need to laugh as much as their ancient forbears. Learning cannot occur without mutual recognition, warmth, and shared goodness. Adolescents will never care what their teachers know if they do not recognize how much they care about them. Laughter is a surefire way to their heart.

Laughter is also the thinking person's mental exercise. Sheer fun—everything from the comic pratfall to the most cerebral verbal wordplay—requires the observer, the listener, and the reader to actively engage their thinking about a given circumstance. Many questions can pop up when people share laughter. Why is this funny? What makes this funny? Would it be just as funny if it were true? Does the fact that it isn't true make it even more funny? What makes one person funny and not another? Can I be funny if I do this? Can I find humor in something similar? Will other people find me funny? Teachers who want to share humorous YA literature with their students might try many of the creative and critical thinking activities listed below.

## A Funny Thing Happened on the Way to ...

Students can brainstorm events in their lives that made them laugh, and share their memories with their classmates either in writing or through oral storytelling.

### Preview Prompts

Jog students' memories by asking them to think about a time when they were embarrassed or amused to the point where they could not stop laughing. Teachers might say, "You've heard people say, 'I laughed so hard it hurt,' or 'I laughed till I cried!' Think about a time when you or someone you know did this. What was so funny?"

### Storytelling Activity

After students have spent time recalling funny moments in their lives, ask them to write their stories in a way that illustrates the humor in the situation. Alternatively, students might get together in small groups and tell each other their stories. Then each group could choose the funniest story and write it out. Compile stories into a humorous class book.

# Want a Good Laugh? Read . . .

What makes a book funny to a reader? One students might find a particular book hilarious, while another might not "get" the humor much at all. Having students pay attention to how an author uses language to create a funny scene and to why they find certain things funny can help them be more active readers. They learn to appreciate tone and style and how authors combine the two to get the effects they want. They also gain a greater understanding of their own literary tastes.

### Preview Prompts

Get students thinking and exploring literary humor by having them think about something they've read that made them laugh. Teachers might ask, "What was funny about the book you read, and why do you think you found it funny? What did the author do to create humor in the book? Did the humor remind you of funny things that have happened to you?"

### Booktalk Activity

Once students have spent some time analyzing why they found a book or story amusing, have them prepare short booktalks in which they use the humor in the book to convince other students to read it.

## Lights! Camera! Action! Laughs!

Kids are familiar with funny movies, and they can use their film knowledge to try their hands at planning their own movies. Having students adapt a favorite book into a film idea encourages them to look at a work of art in a new and fun way.

### Preview Prompts

Here are some suggestions for helping students get into a "movie-making mode." Have students imagine how they would adapt the book they just read into a film. Remind them of common book-to-film adaptations they've probably seen, particularly *Alias Madame Doubtfire* to *Mrs. Doubtfire*. Teachers might ask, "What parts of your book would work in a comedy? What events and characters would you keep the same? What parts would you change? How would you translate the humor in the book into a visual medium?"

### Writing a Script Proposal Activity

Have students write a detailed description of their film idea. Ask them to plot out any changes they would make to events and characters. Remind them to include a list of the famous movie actors and actresses they would like to cast in their movie. Students should also detail where they would film their comedy and sketch out what kinds of sets, props, and costumes they might need.

## Siskel and Ebert Say . . .

Playing the role of critic helps students feel more comfortable about expressing their honest and uninhibited feelings, opinions, and ideas about a book. When students know that their purpose is to discuss whether and why they liked or disliked a book, and to "rate" it for others, they often take a closer look at what really makes a work of literature engaging and worthwhile.

### Preview Prompts

Brainstorm with students to come up with some characteristics that make a book worth reading, concentrating in this case on humor in particular. Teachers ask, "What was your overall impression when you first picked up your book? What made you decide to try it? Was the title catchy? What about the cover and the blurb you read on the back of the book? What did the author do to make the book 'work' for you? Was it as funny as you thought it would be? Why or why not?"

### The Critics' Forum Activity

If possible, pair students who have read the same book to create a "Siskel and Ebert" team. Remind students of how Siskel and Ebert dialogue about the movies they rate, then have them stage a critics' forum where they review their book and rate it from "two thumbs down" to "two thumbs up."

## There Is No Business Like . . . Funny Business!

Have you flipped through the cable television channels lately? It seems like stand-up comedians are on television 24 hours a day. From late night hosts David Letterman and Jay Leno to comedy club favorites like Jeff Foxworthy, Rosie O'Donnell, Robin Williams, Whoopi Goldberg, and Ellen de Generes, people who make their living making other people laugh just keep riding the wave of comic popularity; adolescents are a big part of these comics' audience. Giving students a chance to relate their favorite comedian's act to the humor they read helps enhance the enjoyment of both.

### Preview Prompts

Help spark students' thinking about stand-up comedy with the following prompts: "Do you have a favorite comic or comedian? Tell about your favorite stand-up comics, and why you enjoy their comedy. Who makes you laugh every time you see or hear them? Why do you enjoy their comedy so much? Is their comedy suitable for every-one, or is it for more mature tastes? Who was funny in the book you just read? Does a funny character(s) in your book remind you of your favorite comic? How do you think your favorite comedian would react to that person, and what might your comic say? Explain."

### Stand-up Routines Activity

Once students have begun to make connections between their favorite comedians, book characters, and their own senses of humor, let them develop their own stand-up routines. Encourage them to take on the role of one of their favorite comics. Then have them create and deliver a routine in the style of that comedian that revolves around a scene or series of scenes from the humorous book they read.

## Those Who Laugh Together Stay Together

Humor is often generated out of everyday family disagreements and petty squabbles, as well as what we might call "gender wars." Erma Bombeck and Dave Barry have written humorously about their family trials and tribulations. There are quite a few books on the market exploring why women and men can't seem to communicate. Asking students to examine why domestic turmoil and male-female interaction is ripe with comedic possibilities serves as an excellent discussion starter for how human differences and the stuff of everyday life can be the catalyst for laughter as well as anger or sorrow.

### Preview Prompts

Ask students to quickly jot down some notes about a time when a family situation that seemed serious became absurd, or when they or someone they know had a fight with a member of the opposite sex that in retrospect seemed funny. Teachers might ask, "Why do so many funny things happen in the context of family life? Have you ever been in a fight with someone and suddenly both of you burst out laughing? What made you laugh? In your opinion, what are some of the major areas where boys and girls just don't seem to understand each other?"

### "Boys Are from Mars and Girls Are from Venus Activity"

Have students write a short piece to be included in a class book about a domestic or gender-related situation they found amusing. Alternatively, students can record their stories on audiotape to create a class humor tape.

## The War Between Cats and Dogs

James Thurber often wrote about animals and how they can both amuse and vex their human companions. He often anthropomorphized animals, giving them characteristics that are particularly human in scope. Students can gain an appreciation of Thurber's technique by writing funny stories about animals they know, assigning them human qualities that reflect their personalities, habits, and actions.

### Preview Prompts

Read any one or two of Alexandra Day's "Carl" books such as *Good Dog, Carl*; *Carl's Afternoon in the Park*; or *Carl Goes to Daycare* to your students. These are hysterical children's picture books about a Rottweiler who has a mind of his own. Then get them thinking about their own or a friend's or a relative's pet. Teachers might ask, "What kinds of funny things have you seen this animal do? In what ways does this animal reveal its personality? Have you ever attributed human characteristics to this pet? For example, have you ever said something like, 'Look, Rover's smiling!' or

'Spot does things just to get under my skin,' or 'Rex just likes to chill out in the evenings.' "

### A "Far Side" Activity

Once students have selected a particular anecdote about an animal they know, have them create a children's book or comic strip about that animal. The book or comic strip may tell the particular anecdote or it may describe a series of adventures the pet goes through that show the animal's personality. Remind students that they should illustrate their work with humorous pictures.

## Riddle Me This

Punning is an art that is practiced by few and appreciated by even fewer. People have to be really listening to catch the subtlety of a play on words. Those not paying close attention are the ones who have to ask, "What did I just miss?" By getting students to pay close attention to verbal jests, we help them appreciate "words for words' sakes." That's something that Thurber and other humorists understand very well.

### Preview Prompts

Provide students with some examples of puns, riddles, and plays on words. Then encourage them to volunteer their own, including, if they can, a selection from a book that they have read where the author has made particularly good use of verbal puns and jokes. Record them on the board or on an overhead transparency. Then get students thinking about the following questions: "Why do people enjoy riddles, puns, and word plays? What makes this kind of humor funny? What are some particular words or expressions that lend themselves to humorous word play?"

### Word Play Activity

Suggest that students work in pairs or small groups to create riddle, joke, or word play books. Encourage them to illustrate their books and share them with classmates. Alternatively, students might want to try their hands at creating a word play dialogue such as the famous Abbott and Costello's "Who's on First?" routine.

## Conclusion

James Thurber is usually the only American humorist that middle and high schoolers study in school. His acerbic and literate portraits of life in middle-class America serve as reminders of how silly human beings can be and how honest they can be in their emotions. Individuals often say and do things that inflict sudden pain without realizing that their verbal quips and principled barbs are hurtful. Thurber recognized that blowing petty differences out of proportion to point out how silly they are was a way of turning pain into pleasure. His wisdom is in showing us how the mundane, as well as trivial disagreements, can actually be quite humorous.

Admittedly, Thurber is not for all students. Young adults might instinctively understand what Thurber is saying—that life's little annoyances can cause both grief and glee—but his writing style often gets in their way. Teenagers, however, can understand his message in their own language and in their own terms. They flock to YA literature, where they can appreciate "Thurberesque" angst and satire in a more familiar context. By helping students to recognize the similarities between Thurber's and YA authors' use of humor to explain the human condition, you can also help them begin to recognize the grand continuum of life's pain and joys.

And who knows, they might authentically say, "Hey teach, this is really funny!"

# References

Amory, C. (1987). *The cat who came for Christmas*. New York: Little, Brown, & Company.

Auch, M. J. (1989). *Glass slippers give you blisters*. New York: Holiday House.

Bernstein, B. (1975). *Thurber: A biography*. New York: Dodd, Mead.

Blume, J. (1991). *Are you there God? It's me, Margaret*. New York: Dell.

Camuti, L. J. with Frankel, M. & Frankel, H. (1985). *All my patients are under the bed*. New York: Simon & Schuster.

Conford, E. (1987). *The things I did for love*. New York: Bantam.

Conford, E. (1985). *You never can tell*. New York: Pocket Books.

Danziger, P. (1979). *Can you sue your parents for malpractice?* New York: Delacorte Press.

Danziger, P. (1980). *The cat ate my gymsuit*. New York: Dell.

Danziger, P. (1986). *It's an aardvark-eat-turtle world*. New York: Dell Laurel-Leaf.

Danziger, P. (1990). *Make like a tree and leave*. New York: Delacorte Press.

Danziger, P. (1978). *The pistachio prescription*. New York: Dell.

Danziger, P. (1986). *This place has no atmosphere*. New York: Delacorte Press.

Fine, A. (1988). *Alias Madame Doubtfire*. Boston: Little, Brown, & Company.

Greene, C. C. (1986). *The love letters of J. Timothy Owen*. New York: Harper & Row.

Herriot, J. (1992). *All creatures great and small*. New York: St. Martin's Press.

Herriot, J. (1974). *All things bright and beautiful*. New York: St. Martin's Press.

Herriot, J. (1986). *James Herriot's dog stories*. New York: St. Martin's Press.

Hopper, N. J. (1985). *Whoppers*. New York: Pocket Books.

Klass, S. S. (1987). *Credit-card Carole*. New York: Charles Scribner's Sons.

Morsberger, R. E. (1979). James Thurber: 1894-1961. In L. Unger's (Ed.), *American writers: A collection of literary biographies*. New York: Charles Scribner's Sons.

Pascal, F. (1995). *Love and betrayal and hold the mayo!* New York: Bantam.

Pascal, F. (1995). *My first love and other disasters*. New York: Bantam.

Pinkwater, J. (1989). *Buffalo Brenda*. New York: Macmillan.

Sachar, L. (1992). *Dogs don't tell jokes*. New York: Bullseye Books.

Sachar, L. (1994). *More sideways arithmetic from wayside school*. New York: Scholastic.

Sachar, L. (1989). *Sideways arithmetic from wayside school.* New York: Scholastic.

Sachar, L. (1987). *Sixth grade blues.* New York: Scholastic.

Sachar, L. (1987). *There's a boy in the girl's bathroom!* New York: Alfred A. Knopf.

Sachar, L. (1995). *Wayside school gets a little stranger.* New York: Morrow Junior Books.

Spinelli, J. (1991). *Fourth grade rats.* New York: Scholastic.

Spinelli, J. (1982). *Space station seventh grade.* New York: Dell.

Spinelli, J. (1991). *There's a girl in my hammerlock.* New York: Simon & Schuster.

Spinelli, J. (1986). *Who put that hair in my toothbrush?* New York: Dell.

Springstubb, T. (1989). *With a name like Lulu, who needs more trouble?* New York: Delacorte Press.

Stren, P. (1985). *I was a fifteen-year-old blimp.* New York: Harper & Row.

Townsend, S. (1986). *The Adrian Mole diaries.* New York: Grove Press.

Wersba. B. (1988). *Beautiful losers.* New York: Harper & Row.

Wersba, B. (1989). *The farewell kid.* New York: Harper & Row.

Wersba, B. (1988). *Just be gorgeous.* New York: Harper & Row.

Wersba, B. (1989). *Wonderful me.* New York: Harper & Row.

Zindel, P. (1987). *The amazing and death-defying diary of Eugene Dingman.* New York: Harper & Row.

Zindel, P. (1990). *A begonia for Miss Applebaum.* New York: Bantam Starfire.

## Works of James Thurber

Thurber, J. (1981). *Alarms and diversions.* New York: Harper & Row.

Thurber, J. (1973). *The beast in me and other animals.* New York: Harcourt Brace.

Thurber, J. (1983). The catbird seat. In A. Dube, J. K. Franson, J. W. Parins, & R. E. Murphy's (Eds.), *Structure and meaning: An introduction to literature.* Boston: Houghton Mifflin, pp. 11–17.

Thurber, J. (1939). *Cream of Thurber.* London: Hamish Hamilton.

Thurber, J. (1983). *Credos and curios.* New York: Harper & Row.

Thurber, J. (1956). *Further fables for our time.* New York: Simon & Schuster.

Thurber, J. (1975). *The great quillow.* New York: Harcourt Brace.

Thurber, J. (1992). *Lanterns and lances.* New York: D.I. Fine.

Thurber, J. (1939). *The last flower.* New York: Harper & Brothers.

Thurber, J. (1993). *Let your mind alone!* London: Methuen.

Thurber, J. (1971). *Many moons.* New York: Harcourt Brace.

Thurber, J. (1977). *Men, women, and dogs.* New York: Ballantine Books.

Thurber, J. (1935). *The middle-age man on the flying trapeze.* New York: Harper & Brothers.

Thurber, J. (1969). *My world—and welcome to it.* New York: Harcourt Brace.

Thurber, J. (1965). *The owl in the attic and other perplexities.* New York: Perennial Library.

Thurber, J. (1950). *The seal in the bedroom and other predicaments.* New York: Harper & Brothers.

Thurber, J. (1990). *The 13 clocks*. New York: Dell.

Thurber, J. (1965). *The Thurber album*. New York: Penguin.

Thurber, J. (1966). *Thurber and company*. New York: Harper & Row.

Thurber, J. (1962). *A Thurber carnival*. New York: Samuel French.

Thurber, J. (1979). *Thurber country*. New York: Simon & Schuster.

Thurber, J. (1963). *Thurber's dogs*. New York: Simon & Schuster.

Thurber, J. (1963). *Vintage Thurber, 2 Volumes*. London: Hamish Hamilton.

Thurber, J. (1973). *The white deer*. New York: Harcourt Brace.

Thurber, J. (1990). *The wonderful O*. New York: D.I. Fine.

Thurber, J. (1984). *The years with Ross*. New York: Penguin.

Thurber, J. & Nugent, E. (1983). *Fables for our time and famous poems illustrated*. New York: Harper & Row.

Thurber, J. & White, E.B. (1978). *Is sex necessary? Or why you feel the way you do*. New York: Queen's House.

## Film Cited (Available on Home Video)

Williams, M. G., Williams, R., & Radcliffe, M. (Producers). (1993). *Mrs. Doubtfire*. Beverly Hills, CA: Twentieth Century Fox.

# References

## Children's Literature

Anderson, Hans Christian. (1987). *The little match girl*. New York: Sandcastle Books. (ISBN: 1-555-32317-0)

Grimm, Jacob & Grimm, Wilhelm. (1976). *The complete Grimm's fairy tales*. New York: Pantheon Books. (ISBN: 0-394-49415-6)

MacLachlan, Patricia. (1994). *All the places to love*. New York: HarperCollins. (ISBN: 0-060-21098-2)

Maruki, Toshi. (1980). *Hiroshima no pika*. New York: Lothrop, Lee, & Shepard. (ISBN: 0-688-01297-3)

Perrault, Charles. (1973). *Cinderella*. New York: Bradbury Press. (ISBN: 0-878-88056-9)

San Souci, Robert D. (1989). *The talking eggs*. New York: Dial Press. (ISBN: 0-803-70620-0)

Scieszka, Jon & Johnson, Steve. (1991). *The frog prince continued*. New York: Viking. (ISBN: 0-670-83421-1)

Scieszka, Jon & Smith, Lane. (1992). *The stinky cheese man and other fairly stupid tales*. New York: Viking. (ISBN: 0-670-84487-X)

Scieszka, Jon & Smith, Lane. (1989). *The true story of the 3 little pigs!* New York: Viking. (ISBN: 0-670-82759-2)

Tsuchiya, Yukio. (1988). *Faithful elephants*. Boston: Houghton Mifflin. (ISBN: 0-395-46555-9)

## Young Adult Literature

Adams, Carmen. (1994). *The band*. New York: Avon Books. (ISBN: 0-380-77328-7)

Adams, Nicholas. (1994). *Vampire's kiss*. New York: HarperCollins. (ISBN: 0-061-06177-8)

Alvarez, Julia. (1991). *How the Garcia girls lost their accents*. Chapel Hill, NC: Algonguin. (ISBN: 0-945-57557-2)

Amory, Cleveland. (1987). *The cat who came for Christmas*. New York: Little, Brown, & Company. (ISBN: 0-316-03737-0)

Anaya, Rudolfo A. (1972). *Bless me, Ultima*. Berkeley, CA: Tonatiuh-Quinto Sol International Publications. (ISBN: 0-892-29002-1)

Anaya, Rudolfo A. (1976). *Heart of Aztlan*. Berkeley, CA: Editorial Justa. (ISBN: 0-915-80817-X)

Appleman-Jurman, Alicia. (1988). *Alicia my story*. New York: Bantam. (ISBN: 0-53-28218-2)

Arparicio, Frances R. (Ed.). (1994). *Latino voices*. New York: The Millbrook Press, Inc. (ISBN: 1-562-94388-X)

Ashabranner, Brent. (1986). *Children of the Maya: A Guatemalan Indian odyssey*. New York: Putnam. (ISBN: 0-399-21707-X)

Atkin, Beth S. (1993). *Voices from the fields: Children of migrant farm workers tell their stories*. Boston: Little, Brown, & Company. (ISBN: 0-316-05633-2)

Auch, Mary Jane. (1989). *Glass slippers give you blisters*. New York: Holiday House. (ISBN: 0-823-40752-7)

Avi. (1993). *Nothing but the truth*. New York: Avon Books. (ISBN: 0-380-71907-X)

Balcells, Jacqueline. (1989). *The enchanted raisin*. Swissdale, PA: Latin American Literary Review Press. (ISBN: 0-935-48038-2)

Barrie, Barbara. (1994). *Adam Zigzag*. New York: Delacorte Press. (ISBN: 0-385-31172-9)

Beals, Melba P. (1995). *Warriors don't cry: A searing memoir of the battle to integrate Little Rock's Central High*. New York: Pocket Books. (ISBN: 0-671-86639-7)

Bennett, James. (1994). *Dakota dream*. New York: Scholastic. (ISBN: 0-590-46680-1)

Bierhorst, John. (1990). *The mythology of Mexico and Central America*. New York: William Morrow. (ISBN: 0-688-06721-2)

Bierhorst, John. (1988). *The mythology of South America*. New York: William Morrow. (ISBN: 0-688-06722-0)

Blair, David Nelson. (1992). *Fear the condor*. New York: Lodestar Books. (ISBN: 0-525-67381-4)

Block, Francesca Lia. (1991). *Weetzie bat*. New York: HarperKeypoint. (ISBN: 0-064-47068-7)

Blume, Judy. (1991). *Are you there God? It's me, Margaret*. New York: Dell. (ISBN: 0-440-90419-6)

Borland, Hal. (1985). *When the legends die*. New York: Bantam. (ISBN: 0-553-25738-2)

Boyd, Candy Dawson. (1987). *Charlie Pippin*. New York: Puffin Books. (ISBN: 0-140-32587-5)

Brancato, Robin F. (1990). War of the words. In Don R. Gallo's (Ed.), *Center stage*. New York: HarperCollins, pp. 335–361. (ISBN 0-06-447078-4)

Brancato, Robin. (1988). *Winning*. New York: Alfred A. Knopf. (ISBN: 0-394-80751-0)

Bridgers, Sue Ellen. (1993). *Keeping Christina*. New York: HarperCollins. (ISBN: 0-060-21504-6)

Bridgers, Sue Ellen. (1981). *Notes for another life*. New York: Alfred A. Knopf. (ISBN: 0-394-84889-6)

Brooks, Bruce. (1986). *Midnight hour encores*. New York: HarperCollins. (ISBN: 0-064-47021-0)

Brooks, Bruce. (1984). *The moves make the man*. New York: Harper & Row. (ISBN: 0-060-20679-9)

Brooks, Bruce. (1989). *No kidding*. New York: HarperKeypoint. (ISBN: 0-064-47051-2)

Bunting, Eve. (1991). *Fly away home*. New York: Clarion. (ISBN: 0-395-55962-6)

Buss, Fran Leeper & Cubias, Daisy. (1991). *Journey of the sparrows*. New York: Lodestar Books. (ISBN: 0-525-67362-8)

Cambodia, Louis J. with Frankel, Marilyn & Frankel, Haskel. (1985). *All my patients are under the bed*. New York: Simon & Schuster. (ISBN: 0-671-24271-7)

Cameron, Ann. (1988). *The most beautiful place in the world*. New York: Alfred A. Knopf. (ISBN: 0-394-89463-4)

Campbell, Eric. (1994). *The shark callers*. San Diego: Harcourt Brace. (ISBN: 0-152-00007-0)

Carlson, Lori M. (Ed.). (1994). *Cool Salsa: Bilingual poems on growing up Latin in the United States*. New York: Henry Holt. (ISBN: 0-805-03135-9)

Carlson, Lori M. & Ventura, Cynthia L. (Eds.). (1990). *Where angels glide at dawn: Stories from Latin America*. New York: HarperCollins. (ISBN: 0-397-32424-3)

Carson, Jo. (1989). I am asking you to come back home. In *Stories I ain't told nobody yet*. New York: Theater Communications Group, Inc., p. 93. (ISBN: 1-559-36027-5)

Carson, Jo. (1989). *Stories I ain't told nobody yet*. New York: Theater Communications Group, Inc. (ISBN: 1-559-36027-5)

Carter, Alden R. (1995). *Between a rock and a hard place*. New York: Scholastic. (ISBN: 0-590-48684-5)

Carter, Forrest. (1986). *The education of Little Tree*. Albuquerque, NM: University of New Mexico Press. (ISBN: 0-826-30879-1)

Castañeda, Omar S. (1991). *Among the volcanoes*. New York: Lodestar Books. (ISBN: 0-525-67332-6)

Castañeda, Omar S. (1994). *Imagining Isabel*. New York: Lodestar Books. (ISBN: 0-525-67431-4)

Cheney, Glenn Alan. (1990). *El Salvador: Country in crisis*. New York: Franklin Watts. (ISBN: 0-531-10916-X)

Childress, Alice. (1982). *A hero ain't nothing but a sandwich*. New York: Avon Books. (ISBN: 0-380-00132-2)

Cisneros, Sandra. (1991). *The house on Mango Street*. New York: Random House. (ISBN: 0-679-43335-X)

Cisneros, Sandra. (1991). *Woman hollering creek and other stories*. New York: Random House. (ISBN: 0-394-57654-3)

Coe, Charles. (1990). *Young man in Vietnam*. New York: Scholastic. (ISBN: 0-590-43298-2)

Cofer, Judith Ortez. (1995). *An island like you: Stories of the barrio*. New York: Orchard Books. (ISBN: 0-531-06897-8)

Cohen, Daniel. (1995). *Real vampires*. New York: E.P. Dutton. (ISBN: 0-525-65189-6)

Conford, Ellen. (1987). *The things I did for love*. New York: Bantam. (ISBN: 0-553-05431-7)

Conford, Ellen. (1985). *You never can tell*. New York: Pocket Books. (ISBN: 0-671-66182-5)

Cooney, Caroline B. (1991). *The cheerleader*. New York: Scholastic. (ISBN: 0-590-44316-X)

Cooney, Caroline B. (1991). *The party's over*. New York: Scholastic. (ISBN: 0-590-42553-6)

Cooney, Caroline B. (1991). *The return of the vampire*. New York: Scholastic. (ISBN: 0-590-44884-6)

Cormier, Robert. (1980). *8 plus 1*. New York: Pantheon. (ISBN: 0-394-84595-1)

Cormier, Robert. (1986). *The chocolate war*. New York: Pantheon. (ISBN: 0-440-94459-7)

Cormier, Robert. (1977). *I am the cheese*. New York: Pantheon. (ISBN: 0-394-83462-3)

Covington, Dennis. (1992). *Lizard*. New York: Delacorte Press. (ISBN: 0-385-30307-6)

Crew, Gary. (1993). *Strange objects*. New York: Simon & Schuster. (ISBN: 0-671-79759-X)

Crutcher, Chris. (1991). *Athletic shorts: Six short stories*. New York: Greenwillow Books. (ISBN: 0-688-10816-4)

Crutcher, Chris. (1991). *Chinese handcuffs*. New York: Dell. (ISBN: 0-440-20837-8)

Crutcher, Chris. (1987). *The crazy horse electric game*. New York: Greenwillow Books. (ISBN: 0-688-06683-6)

Crutcher, Chris. (1993). *Staying fat for Sarah Byrnes*. New York: Bantam. (ISBN: 0-440-22009-2)

Crutcher, Chris. (1986). *Stotan!* New York: Dell Laurel-Leaf. (ISBN: 0-688-05715-2)

Curry, Constance. (1995). *Silver rights*. Chapel Hill, NC: Algonquin Books. (ISBN: 1-56512-095-7)

Cushman, Karen. (1994). *Catherine, called Birdy*. New York: Clarion. (ISBN: 0-395-68186-3)

Cushman, Karen. (1995). *The midwife's apprentice*. New York: Clarion. (ISBN: 0-395-69229-6)

Danziger, Paula. (1979). *Can you sue your parents for malpractice?* New York: Delacorte Press. (ISBN: 0-434-96570-7)

Danziger, Paula. (1980). *The cat ate my gymsuit*. New York: Dell. (ISBN: 0-440-41612-4)

Danziger, Paula. (1986). *It's an aardvark-eat-turtle world*. New York: Dell Laurel-Leaf. (ISBN: 0-385-29371-2)

Danziger, Paula. (1990). *Make like a tree and leave*. New York: Delacorte Press. (ISBN: 0-385-30151-0)

Danziger, Paula. (1978). *The pistachio prescription*. New York: Dell. (ISBN: 0-440-96895-X)

Danziger, Paula. (1986). *This place has no atmosphere*. New York: Delacorte Press. (ISBN: 0-385-29489-1)

de Jenkins, Lyll Becerra. (1993). *Celebrating the hero*. New York: Lodestar Books. (ISBN: 0-525-67399-7) de Jenkins, Lyll Becerra. (1989). *The honorable prison*. New York: Puffin Books. (ISBN: 0-525-67238-9)

de Trevino, Elizabeth Borton. (1987). *I, Juan de Pareja*. New York: Farrar, Straus, & Giroux. (ISBN: 0-374-43525-1)

de Trevino, Elizabeth Borton. (1994). *Leona: A love story*. New York: Farrar, Straus, & Giroux. (ISBN: 0-374-34382-9)

Doherty, Berlie. (1994). *Street child*. New York: Orchard Books. (ISBN: 0-531-06864-1)

Dorris, Michael. (1992). *Morning girl*. New York: Hyperion Books for Children. (ISBN: 1-562-82284-5)

Edelman, Bernard. (Ed.). (1985). *Dear America: Letters home from Vietnam*. New York: Norton. (ISBN: 0-393-01998-5)

Fernandez, Roberta. (1990). *Intaglio: A novel in six stories*. Houston, TX: Arte Publico Press. (ISBN: 1-558-85016-3)

Fine, Anne. (1988). *Alias Madame Doubtfire*. Boston: Little, Brown, & Company. (ISBN: 0-316-28313-4)

Flagg, Fannie. (1988). *Fried green tomatoes at the Whistle Stop Cafe*. New York: McGraw-Hill. (ISBN: 0-07-021257-0)

Fleischman, Paul. (1995). *A fate totally worse than death*. Cambridge, MA: Candlewick Press. (ISBN: 1-564-02627-2)

Forrester, Sandra. (1995). *Sound the jubilee*. New York: Lodestar Books. (ISBN: 0-525-67486-1)

Fox, Paula. (1991). *The slave dancer*. New York: Dell. (ISBN: 0-440-40402-9)

Frey, Bradshaw. (Ed.). (1992). *Letters from 'Nam*. New York: Warner Books. (ISBN: 0-446-36346-4)

Friedman, Carl. (1991). *Nightfather*. New York: Persea Books. (ISBN: 0-892-55210-7)

Garland, Sherry. (1995). *Indio*. San Diego: Harcourt Brace. (ISBN: 0-152-00021-6)

Gelman, Rita Golden. (1988). *Inside Nicaragua: Young people's dreams and fears*. New York: Franklin Watts. (ISBN: 0-531-15085-2)

George, Jean Craighead. (1990). *One day in the tropical rain forest*. New York: HarperCollins. (ISBN: 0-690-04767-3)

Gibbons, Kaye. (1987). *Ellen Foster*. New York: Random House. (ISBN: 0-912-69752-0)

Glenn, Mel. (1982). *Class dismissed: High school poems*. New York: Clarion. (ISBN: 0-899-19075-8)

Goodwillie, Susan. (Ed.). (1993). *Voices from the future: Our children tell us about violence in America*. New York: Crown Publishers, Inc. (ISBN: 0-517-59494-3)

Gordon, Sheila. (1990). *Waiting for the rain: A novel of South Africa*. New York: Bantam. (ISBN: 0-553-27911-4)

Greene, Bette. (1991). *The drowning of Stephan Jones*. New York: Bantam. (ISBN: 0-553-07437-7)

Greene, Bette. (1973). *Summer of my German soldier*. New York: Dial Press. (ISBN: 0-553-10192-7)

Greene, Bob. (1989). *Homecoming: When the soldiers returned from Vietnam*. New York: G.P. Putnam's Sons. (ISBN: 0-399-13386-0)

Greene, Constance C. (1986). *The love letters of J. Timothy Owen.* New York: Harper & Row. (ISBN: 0-060-22156-9)

Greene, Patricia Baird. (1993). *The Sabbath garden.* New York: Lodestar Books. (ISBN: 0-525-67430-6)

Hadley, Lee & Irwin, Ann. (1990). *So long at the fair.* New York: Avon Books. (ISBN: 0-380-70858-2)

Hahn, Mary D. (1988). *December stillness.* New York: Clarion. (ISBN: 0-899-19758-2)

Hamilton, Virginia. (1987). *A white romance.* New York: Philomel. (ISBN: 0-399-21213-2)

Haskins, Jim. (1988). *Winnie Mandela: Life of struggle.* New York: G.P. Putnam's Sons. (ISBN: 0-399-21515-8)

Hassler, Jon. (1980). *Jemmy.* New York: Ballantine Books. (ISBN: 0-449-70302-9)

Hentoff, Nat. (1982). *The day they came to arrest the book.* New York: Delacorte Press. (ISBN: 0-385-28218-4)

Hermes, Patricia. (1991). *Mama, let's dance.* Boston: Little, Brown, & Company. (ISBN: 0-316-35861-4)

Herriot, James. (1992). *All creatures great and small.* New York: St. Martin's Press. (ISBN: 0-312-08498-6)

Herriot, James. (1974). *All things bright and beautiful.* New York: St. Martin's Press. (ISBN: 0-029-76660-5)

Herriot, James. (1986). *James Herriot's dog stories.* New York: St. Martin's Press. (ISBN: 0-312-90143-7)

Hicyilmaz, Gaye. (1994). *The frozen waterfall.* New York: Farrar, Straus, & Giroux. (ISBN: 0-374-32482-4)

Hinojosa, Maria. (1995). *Crews.* San Diego: Harcourt Brace. (ISBN: 0-152-92873-1)

Hinton, S.E. (1989). *The outsiders.* New York: Dell. (ISBN: 0-440-96769-4)

Hirshon, Sheryl & Butler, Judy. (1984). *And also teach them to read.* Westport, CT: Lawrence Hill. (ISBN: 0-882-08170-5)

Ho, Min Fong. (1991). *The clay marble.* New York: Farrar, Straus, & Giroux. (ISBN: 0-374-31340-7)

Hobbs, Will. (1992). *The big wander.* New York: Avon Books. (ISBN: 0-380-72140-6)

Hobbs, Will. (1988). *Changes in latitudes.* New York: Atheneum. (ISBN: 0-689-31385-3)

Hobbs, Will. (1991). *Downriver.* New York: Atheneum. (ISBN: 0-689-31690-9)

Hodge, Merle. (1993). *For the life of Laetitia.* New York: Farrar, Straus, & Giroux. (ISBN: 0-374-32447-6)

Hoh, Diane. (1995). *Nightmare hall: The vampire's kiss.* New York: Scholastic. (ISBN: 0-590-25089-2)

Hopper, Nancy J. (1985). *Whoppers.* New York: Pocket Books. (ISBN: 0-671-55420-4)

Houston, Jeanne Wakatsuki & Houston, James D. (1973). *Farewell to Manzanar.* New York: Bantam. (ISBN: 0-553-27258-6)

Huddle, David. (1987). Stopping by home. In Paul Janeczko's (Ed.), *Going over to your place: Poems for each other.* New York: Bradbury Press, pp. 51–56. (ISBN: 0-027-47670-7)

Hughes, Monica. (1990). *Invitation to the game*. New York: Simon & Schuster. (ISBN: 0-663-56260-0)

Hunt, Irene. (1987). *No promises in the wind*. New York: Berkley Publishing Group. (ISBN: 0-425-09969-5)

Hyppolite, Joanne. (1995). *Seth and Samona*. New York: Delacorte Press. (ISBN: 0-385-32093-0)

Janeczko, Paul B. (Ed.). (1987). *Going over to your place: Poems for each other*. New York: Bradbury Press. (ISBN: 0-027-47670-7)

Janeczko, Paul B. (Ed.). (1984). *Strings: A gathering of family poems*. New York: Bradbury Press. (ISBN: 0-027-47790-8)

Jensen, Kathryn. (1989). *Pocket change*. New York: Macmillan. (ISBN: 0-027-47731-2)

Johnson, Angela. (1993). *Toning the sweep*. New York: Scholastic. (ISBN: 0-590-48142-8)

Johnson, Charles. (1991). *Middle passage*. New York: Plume. (ISBN: 0-452-26638-6)

Johnson, Denis. (1985). *Fiskadoro*. New York: Alfred A. Knopf. (ISBN: 0-394-53839-9)

Jones, Adrienne. (1990). *Long time passing*. New York: Harper & Row. (ISBN: 0-060-23055-X)

Jordan, Sherryl. (1992). *Winter of fire*. New York: Scholastic. (ISBN: 0-590-45288-6)

Keller, Helen. (1988). *The story of my life*. New York: New American Library. (ISBN: 0-451-52245-1)

Kirkpatrick, Kathryn. (1995). *Keeping the good light*. New York: Delacorte Press. (ISBN: 0-385-32161-9)

Klass, Sheila Solomon. (1987). *Credit-card Carole*. New York: Charles Scribner's Sons. (ISBN: 0-684-18889-9)

Klause, Annette Curtis. (1990). *The silver kiss*. New York: Bantam. (ISBN: 0-440-21346-0)

Kronenwetter, Michael. (1992). *United they hate: White supremacist groups in America*. New York: Walker. (ISBN: 0-8027-8162-4)

Kuklin, Susan. (1993). *Speaking out: Teenagers take on race, sex, and identity*. New York: G.P. Putnam's Sons. (ISBN: 0-399-22343-6)

Laird, Elizabeth. (1991). *Kiss the dust*. New York: E.P. Dutton. (ISBN: 0-525-44893-4)

Langone, John. (1993). *Spreading poison: A book about racism and prejudice*. Boston: Little, Brown, & Company. (ISBN: 0-316-51410-1)

Lapierre, Dominique. (1985). *City of joy*. Garden City, NY: Doubleday. (ISBN: 0-385-18952-4)

Lasky, Kathryn. (1996). *Memoirs of a bookbat*. San Diego: Harcourt Brace. (ISBN: 0-152-01259-1)

Lasky, Kathryn. (1993). *A voice in the wind*. San Diego: Harcourt Brace. (ISBN: 0-152-94102-9)

Lawrence, Louise. (1991). *Andra*. New York: HarperCollins. (ISBN: 0-060-23685-X)

Le Carre, John. (1992). *The spy who came in from the cold*. New York: Ballantine Books. (ISBN: 0-345-37737-0)

Lester, Julius. (1995). *Othello: A novel*. New York: Scholastic. (ISBN: 0-590-41967-6)

Levine, Ellen. (1993). *Freedom's children*. New York: Avon Flare. (ISBN: 0-380-72114-7)

London, Jonathan. (1995). *Where's home?* New York: Viking. (ISBN: 0-670-86028-X)

Lowry, Lois. (1993). *The giver.* Boston: Houghton Mifflin. (ISBN: 0-395-64566-2)

Lynch, Chris. (1993). *Shadow boxer.* New York: HarperTrophy. (ISBN: 0-060-23028-2)

Marsden, John. (1991). *Letters from the inside.* New York: Bantam. (ISBN: 0-440-21951-5)

Martinez, Max. (1988). *Schoolland.* Houston, TX: Arte Publico Press. (ISBN: 0-934-77087-5)

Mason, Bobbie Ann. (1985). *In country.* New York: Harper & Row. (ISBN: 0-060-15469-1)

McCloud, Bill. (1992). *What should we tell our children about Vietnam?* New York: Berkley Publishing Group. (ISBN: 0-425-13361-3)

McPhee, John. (1994). Survival in the Forty-Ninth. In Arthur N. Applebee, A.B. Bermudez, Judith Langer & J. Marshall's (Senior Consultants), *Literature and language.* Blue Level, 10. Evaston, IL: McDougal, Littell, pp. 269–274.

Medearis, Angela Shelf. (1995). Skin deep. In *Skin deep and other teenage reflections.* New York: Macmillan. (ISBN: 0-02-765980-1)

Meyer, Carolyn. (1994). *Rio Grande stories.* San Diego: Harcourt Brace. (ISBN: 0-152-00066-6)

Meyer, Carolyn. (1993). *White lilacs.* San Diego: Harcourt Brace. (ISBN: 0-152-95876-2)

Miklowitz, Gloria D. (1985). *After the bomb.* New York: Scholastic. (ISBN: 0-590-33287-2)

Mills, Claudia. (1981). *Luisa's American dream.* New York: Four Winds Press. (ISBN: 0-027-67040-6)

Mizell, Linda. (1992). *Think about racism.* New York: Walker. (ISBN: 0-802-77365-6)

Moeri, Louise. (1989). *The forty-third war.* Boston: Houghton Mifflin. (ISBN: 0-395-50215-2)

Mohr, Nicholasa. (1975). *El Bronx remembered: A novella and stories.* New York: Harper & Row. (ISBN: 0-060-24314-7)

Mohr, Nicholasa. (1973). *Nilda.* New York: Harper & Row. (ISBN: 0-060-24332-5)

Moody, Anne. (1968). *Coming of age in Mississippi.* New York: Dell. (ISBN: 0-440-31488-7)

Myers, Walter Dean. (1994). *Darnell Rock reporting.* New York: Delacorte Press. (ISBN: 0-385-32096-5)

Myers, Walter Dean. (1988). *Fallen angels.* New York: Scholastic. (ISBN: 0-590-40942-5)

Naidoo, Beverly. (1989). *Chain of fire.* New York: HarperTrophy. (ISBN: 0-064-40468-4)

Namioka, Lensey. (1994). *April and the dragon lady.* New York: Browndeer Press. (ISBN: 0-15-200886-1)

Nasaw, Jonathan. (1993). *Shakedown street.* New York: Bantam. (ISBN: 0-440-21930-2)

Neufeld, John. (1995). *Almost a hero.* New York: Atheneum. (ISBN: 0-689-31971-1)

Nichols, Grace. (1986). *Whole of a morning sky.* London: Virago. (ISBN: 0-860-68779-1)

Nixon, Joan Lowery. (1988). *Caught in the act.* New York: Bantam. (ISBN: 0-553-05443-0)

Nixon, Joan Lowery. (1994). *A dangerous promise.* New York: Bantam. (ISBN: 0-440-21965-5)

Nixon, Joan Lowery. (1987). *A family apart*. New York: Bantam. (ISBN: 055-3054-325)

Nixon, Joan Lowery. (1988). *In the face of danger*. New York: Bantam. (ISBN: 055-3054-902)

Nixon, Joan Lowery. (1995). *Keeping secrets*. New York: Delacorte Press. (ISBN: 0-385-32139-2)

Nixon, Joan Lowery. (1990). *A place to belong*. New York: Bantam. (ISBN: 0-553-28485-1)

Nunes, Lygia Bojunga. (1991). *My friend, the painter*. New York: Harcourt Brace Jovanovich. (ISBN: 0-152-56340-7)

O'Brien, Robert C. (1975). *Z for Zachariah*. New York: Atheneum. (ISBN: 0-689-30442-0)

O'Brien, Tim. (1990). *The things they carried*. Boston: Houghton Mifflin. (ISBN: 0-395-51598-X)

O'Dell, Scott. (1983). *The castle in the sea*. Boston: Houghton Mifflin. (ISBN: 0-395-34831-5)

Oliver, Mary. (1984). A letter from home. In Paul B. Janeczko's (Ed.), *Strings: A gathering of family poems*. New York: Bradbury Press, p. 58. (ISBN: 0-027-47790-8)

Oneal, Zibby. (1986). *In summer light*. New York: Bantam. (ISBN: 0-553-25940-7)

Pascal, Francine. (1995). *Love and betrayal and hold the mayo!* New York: Bantam. (ISBN: 0-553-40966-2)

Pascal, Francine. (1995). *My first love and other disasters*. New York: Bantam. (ISBN: 0-553-40965-4)

Paterson, Kathryn. (1987). *The great Gilly Hopkins*. New York: Avon Books. (ISBN: 0-380-45963-9)

Paulsen, Gary. (1996). *Brian's winter*. New York: Delacorte Press. (ISBN: 0-385-32198-8)

Paulsen, Gary. (1990). *Canyons*. New York: Delacorte Press. (ISBN: 0-385-30153-7)

Paulsen, Gary. (1985). *Dogsong*. New York: Scholastic. (ISBN: 0-590-43893-X)

Paulsen, Gary. (1988). *Hatchet*. New York: Puffin Books. (ISBN: 0-140-32724-X)

Paulsen, Gary. (1991). *The monument*. New York: Delacorte Press. (ISBN: 0-385-30518-4)

Paulsen, Gary. (1994). *Mr. Tucket*. New York: Delacorte Press. (ISBN: 0-385-31169-9)

Paulsen, Gary. (1993). *Nightjohn*. New York: Dell Laurel-Leaf. (ISBN: 0-440-21936-1)

Paulsen, Gary. (1991). *The river*. New York: Dell. (ISBN: -440-40753-2)

Paulsen, Gary. (1993). *Sisters/Hermanas*. San Diego: Harcourt Brace. (ISBN: 0-152-75323-0)

Paulsen, Gary. (1987). *Woodsong*. New York: Puffin. (ISBN: 0-14-034905-7)

Peck, Richard. (1995). *The last safe place on earth*. New York: Delacorte Press. (ISBN: 0-385-32052-3)

Peck, Robert Newton. (1972). *A day no pigs would die*. New York: Alfred A. Knopf. (ISBN: 0-394-48235-2)

Peel, John. (1993). *Night wings*. New York: G.P. Putnam's Sons. (ISBN: 0-448-40526-1)

Peel, John. (1995). *Tombstones: The last drop*. New York: Pocket Books. (ISBN: 0-671-53530-7)

Pettit, Jayne. (1992). *My name is San Ho*. New York: Scholastic. (ISBN: 0-590-44172-8)

Pfeffer, Susan B. (1995). *Nobody's daughter*. New York: Delacorte Press. (ISBN: 0-385-32106-6)

Philbrick, Rodman. (1993). *Freak the mighty*. New York: Scholastic. (ISBN: 0-590-47412-X)

Pike, Christopher. (1994). *The last vampire*. New York: Pocket Books. (ISBN: 0-671-87264-8)

Pike, Christopher. (1994). *The last vampire 2: Black blood*. New York: Pocket Books. (ISBN: 0-671-87258-3)

Pike, Christopher. (1995). *The last vampire 3: Red dice*. New York: Pocket Books. (ISBN: 0-671-87268-0)

Pike, Christopher. (1996). *The last vampire 4: Phantom*. New York: Pocket Books. (ISBN: 0-671-55030-6)

Pinkwater, Jill. (1989). *Buffalo Brenda*. New York: Macmillan (ISBN: 0-027-74631-3)

Pullman, Philip. (1987). *The ruby in the smoke*. New York: Alfred A. Knopf. (ISBN: 0-394-98826-4)

Pullman, Philip. (1988). *Shadow in the north*. New York: Alfred A. Knopf. (ISBN: 0-394-99453-1)

Pullman, Philip. (1990). *Tiger in the well*. New York: Alfred A. Knopf. (ISBN: 0-679-90214-7)

Pullman, Philip. (1996). *The tin princess*. New York: Random House. (ISBN: 0-679-87615-4)

Qualey, Marsha. (1995). *Hometown*. Boston: Houghton Mifflin. (ISBN: 0-395-72666-2)

Randall, Margaret. (1995). *Sandino's daughters: Testimonies of Nicaraguan women in struggle*. New Brunswick, NJ: Rutgers University Press. (ISBN: 0-813-52214-5)

Read, Piers Paul. (1974). *Alive*. New York: Avon Books.

Reed, Don C. (1995). *The kraken*. Honesdale, PA: Boyds Mills Press. (ISBN: 0-563-97216-6)

Rees, Elizabeth M. (1996). *Plainsong for Caitlin*. New York: Avon Books. (ISBN: 0-380-78216-2)

Rinaldi, Ann. (1994). *Finishing Becca*. San Diego: Harcourt Brace. (ISBN: 0-152-00879-9)

Rinaldi, Ann. (1988). *The last silk dress*. New York: Holiday House. (ISBN: 0-823-40690-3)

Rinaldi, Ann. (1991). *A ride into morning: The story of Tempe Wick*. San Diego: Harcourt Brace. (ISBN: 0-152-00573-0)

Rivera, Tomas. (1986). *The migrant earth*. Houston, TX: Arte Publico Press. (ISBN: 0-934-77055-7)

Rodríguez, Richard. (1993). *Days of obligation: An argument with my father*. New York: Penguin. (ISBN: 0-140-09622-1)

Rosen, Billi. (1989). *Andi's war*. New York: E.P. Dutton. (ISBN: 0-525-44473-4)

Rosen, Michael J. (Ed.). (1992). *Home: A collaboration of thirty distinguished authors and illustrators of children's books to aid the homeless*. New York: HarperCollins. (ISBN: 0-060-21788-X)

Rylant, Cynthia. (1985). *A blue-eyed daisy*. New York: Bradbury Press. (ISBN: 0-027-77960-2)

Rylant, Cynthia & Evans, Walker. (1994). *Something permanent*. San Diego: Harcourt Brace. (ISBN: 0-152-77090-9)

Sachar, Louis. (1992). *Dogs don't tell jokes*. New York: Bullseye Books. (ISBN: 0-679-83372-2)

Sachar, Louis. (1994). *More sideways arithmetic from wayside school*. New York: Scholastic. (ISBN: 0-590-47762-5)

Sachar, Louis. (1989). *Sideways arithmetic from wayside school*. New York: Scholastic. (ISBN: 0-590-42416-5)

Sachar, Louis. (1987). *Sixth grade blues*. New York: Scholastic. (ISBN: 0-590-40709-0)

Sachar, Louis. (1987). *There's a boy in the girl's bathroom!* New York: Alfred A. Knopf. (ISBN: 0-394-88570-8)

Sachar, Louis. (1995). *Wayside school gets a little stranger*. New York: Morrow Junior Books. (ISBN: 0-688-13694-X)

Sanders, Dori. (1991). *Clover*. New York: Fawcett Columbine. (ISBN: 0-449-90624-8)

Scieszka, Jon. (1993). *Your mother was a Neanderthal*. New York: Puffin Books. (ISBN: 0-140-36372-6)

Sebestyen, Ouida. (1994). *Out of nowhere*. New York: Penguin. (ISBN: 0-140-37640-2)

Shorris, Earl. (1994). *Latinos: A biography of the people*. New York: Avon Books. (ISBN: 0-380-72190-2)

Simmen, Edward. (Ed.). (1992). *North of the Rio Grande: The Mexican-American experience in short fiction*. New York: Mentor (Penguin). (ISBN: 0-451-62834-9)

Skarmeta, Antonio. (1987). *Burning patience*. New York: Pantheon. (ISBN: 0-394-55576-7)

Skarmeta, Antonio. (1979). *Chileno!* New York: William Morrow. (ISBN: 0-688-32213-1)

Smith, Lisa J. (1991). *The vampire diaries: The awakening*. New York: HarperCollins. (ISBN: 0-061-06097-6)

Smith, Lisa J. (1992). *The vampire diaries: Dark reunion*. New York: HarperCollins. (ISBN: 0-061-06775-X)

Smith, Lisa J. (1991). *The vampire diaries: The fury*. New York: HarperCollins. (ISBN: 0-061-06099-2)

Smith, Lisa J. (1991). *The vampire diaries: The struggle*. New York: HarperCollins. (ISBN: 0-061-06098-4)

Snyder, Zipha Keatley. (1991). *Libby on Wednesday*. New York: Dell. (ISBN: 0-040-40498-3)

Somonte, Carlos. (1985). *We live in Mexico*. Living Here Series. New York: Franklin Watts. (ISBN: 0-531-03820-3)

Soto, Gary. (1990). *Baseball in April: And other stories*. New York: Harcourt Brace Jovanovich. (ISBN: 0-152-05720-X)

Soto, Gary. (1994). *Jesse*. San Diego: Harcourt Brace. (ISBN: 0-152-40239-X)

Soto, Gary. (1985). *Living up the street: Narrative recollections*. San Francisco: Strawberry Hill Press. (ISBN: 0-894-07064-9)

Soto, Gary. (1992). *Pacific crossing*. New York: Harcourt Brace Jovanovich. (ISBN: 0-152-59187-7)

Soto, Gary. (Ed.). (1993). *Pieces of the heart: New Chicano fiction*. San Francisco: Chronicle Books. (ISBN: 0-811-80068-7)

Soto, Gary. (1990). *A summer life*. New York: Dell. (ISBN: 0-440-21024-0)

Sparks, Beatrice. (Ed.). (1994). *It happened to Nancy*. New York: Avon Books. (ISBN: 0-380-77315-5)

Speare, Elizabeth, G. (1958). *The witch of Blackbird Pond*. New York: Dell. (ISBN: 0-395-07114-3)

Spinelli, Jerry. (1991). *Fourth grade rats*. New York: Scholastic. (ISBN: 0-590-44243-0)

Spinelli, Jerry. (1990). *Maniac Magee*. New York: HarperTrophy. (ISBN: 0-064-40424-2)

Spinelli, Jerry. (1982). *Space station seventh grade*. New York: Dell. (ISBN: 0-440-96165-3)

Spinelli, Jerry. (1991). *There's a girl in my hammerlock*. New York: Simon & Schuster. (ISBN: 0-671-74684-7)

Spinelli, Jerry. (1986). *Who put that hair in my toothbrush?* New York: Dell. (ISBN: 0-440-99485-3)

Springstubb, Tricia. (1989). *With a name like Lulu, who needs more trouble?* New York: Delacorte Press. (ISBN: 0-385-29823-4)

Stevermer, Caroline. (1992). *River rats*. New York: Harcourt Brace Jovanovich. (ISBN: 0-152-00895-0)

Stine, R.L. (1992). *Goodnight kiss*. New York: Pocket Books. (ISBN: 0-671-73823-2)

Stren, Patti. (1985). *I was a fifteen-year-old blimp*. New York: Harper & Row. (ISBN: 0-060-26057-2)

Swindells, Robert. (1985). *Brother in the land*. New York: Holiday House. (ISBN: 0-823-40556-7)

Taylor, Mildred. (1981). *Let the circle be unbroken*. New York: Bantam. (ISBN: 0-803-74748-9)

Taylor, Mildred. (1991). *Roll of thunder, hear my cry!* New York: Puffin Books. (ISBN: 0-140-34893-X

Taylor, Theodore. (1995). *The bomb*. San Diego: Harcourt Brace. (ISBN: 0-152-00867-5)

Taylor, Theodore. (1977). *The cay*. New York: Avon Books. (ISBN: 0-380-00142-X)

Taylor, Theodore. (1993). *Timothy of the cay*. New York: Avon Books. (ISBN: 0-380-72119-8)

Taylor, Theodore. (1994). *Walking up a rainbow*. San Diego: Harcourt Brace. (ISBN: 0-152-94512-1)

Thompson, Kathleen. (1990). *Sor Juana Ines de la Cruz*. Milwaukee, WI: Raintree. (ISBN: 0-817-23377-6)

Tolan, Stephanie S. (1987). *Pride of the peacock*. New York: Ballantine Books. (ISBN: 0-449-70207-3)

Townsend, Sue. (1986). *The Adrian Mole diaries*. New York: Grove Press. (ISBN: 0-394-55298-9)

Unger, Douglas. (1988). *El Yanqui*. New York: Harper & Row. (ISBN: 0-060-15645-7)

Velásquez, Gloria. (1994). *Juanita fights the school board*. Houston, TX: Arte Publico Press. (ISBN: 1-558-85119-4)

Vick, Helen Hughes. (1994). *Walker of time*. Tucson, AZ: Harbinger House. (ISBN: 0-943-17380-9)

Vick, Helen Hughes. (1995). *Walker's journey home*. Tucson, AZ: Harbinger House. (ISBN: 0-571-40000-1)

Vinz, Mark. (1987). Return. In Paul B. Janeczko's (Ed.), *Going over to your place: Poems for each other*. New York: Bradbury Press, p. 114. (ISBN: 0-027-47670-7)

Voigt, Cynthia. (1981). *Homecoming*. New York: Atheneum. (ISBN: 0-689-30833-7)

Voigt, Cynthia. (1987). *Izzy, willy-nilly*. New York: Fawcett Juniper. (ISBN: 0-449-70214-6)

Voigt, Cynthia. (1992). *Orfe*. New York: Atheneum. (ISBN: 0-689-31771-9)

Volavkova, Hana. (Ed.). (1993). *I never saw another butterfly*. New York: Schocken Books. (ISBN: 0-805-24115-9)

Warner, Gertrude Chandler. (1993). *The boxcar children*. New Hyde Park, NY: Learning Links. (ISBN: 0-881-22879-6)

Watkins, Yoko Kawashima. (1996). *My brother, my sister, and I*. New York: Simon & Schuster. (ISBN: 0-689-80656-6)

Wepman, Dennis. (1987). *Benito Juarez*. World Leaders Past and Present Series. New Haven, CT: Chelsea House. (ISBN: 0-877-54537-5)

Wersba. Barbara. (1988). *Beautiful losers*. New York: Harper & Row. (ISBN: 0-060-26363-6)

Wersba, Barbara. (1989). *The farewell kid*. New York: Harper & Row. (ISBN: 0-060-26378-4)

Wersba, Barbara. (1988). *Just be gorgeous*. New York: Harper & Row. (ISBN: 0-060-26359-8)

Wersba, Barbara. (1989). *Wonderful me*. New York: Harper & Row. (ISBN: 0-060-26362-8)

West, Cornel. (1993). *Race matters*. Boston: Beacon Press. (ISBN: 0-807-00918-0)

Westall, Robert. (1996). *Gulf*. New York: Scholastic. (ISBN: 0-590-22218-X)

White, Ryan & Cunningham, Anne Marie. (1991). *Ryan White: My own story*. New York: Dial Press. (ISBN: 0-8037-0977-3)

Wolff, Virginia Euwer. (1993). *Make lemonade*. New York: Scholastic. (ISBN: 0-590-48141-X)

Wolitzer, Meg. (1986). *Caribou*. New York: Bantam Starfire. (ISBN: 0-553-25560-6)

Woodson, Jacqueline. (1994). *I hadn't meant to tell you this*. New York: Bantam. (ISBN: 0-440-21960-4)

Yep, Laurence. (Ed.). (1993). *American dragons: Twenty-five Asian American voices*. New York: HarperTrophy. (ISBN: 0-064-40603-2)

Yep, Laurence. (1992). The lightwell. In Michael J. Rosen's (Ed.), *Home: A collaboration of thirty distinguished authors and illustrators of children's books to aid the homeless*. New York: HarperCollins, p. 12. (ISBN: 0-060-21788-X)

Yep, Laurence. (1989). *The rainbow people*. New York: Harper & Row. (ISBN: 0-060-26761-5)

Yolen, Jane. (1990). *The dragon's boy*. New York: Harper & Row. (ISBN: 0-060-26789-5)

Yolen, Jane. (1991). *Vampires*. New York: HarperCollins. (ISBN: 0-060-26800-X)

Yolen, Jane. (1991). *Wizard's hall*. San Diego: Harcourt Brace. (ISBN: 0-152-98132-2)

Zindel, Paul. (1987). *The amazing and death-defying diary of Eugene Dingman*. New York: Harper & Row. (ISBN: 0-060-26862-X)

Zindel, Paul. (1990). *A begonia for Miss Applebaum*. New York: Bantam Starfire. (ISBN: 0-553-28765-6)

Zindel, Paul. (1983). *The pigman*. New York: Bantam. (ISBN: 0-553-26321-8)

## Classic Literature

Baldwin, James. (1993). Stranger in the village. In Carl Klaus, Chris Anderson, Rebecca Faery's (Eds.),  *In depth: Essayists for our time*. Second Edition. San Diego: Harcourt Brace. (ISBN: 0-1550-0172-8)

Bradbury, Ray. (1953). *Fahrenheit 451*. New York: Ballantine Books. (ISBN: 0-345-34296-8)

Bronte, Charlotte. (1986). *Jane Eyre*. New York: Bantam. (ISBN: 0-553-21140-4)

Carroll, Lewis. (1994). The walrus and the carpenter. In Arthur N. Applebee, A.B. Bermudez, Susan Hynds, Judith Langer, J. Marshall, & D.E. Norton's (Senior Consultants), *Literature and language*. Gold Level, 6. Evanston, IL: McDougal, Littell, pp. 92-95.

Cervantes, Saavedra M. (1957). *Don Quixote*. Translated by Walter Starkie. New York: Mentor (Penguin). (ISBN: 0-451-62684-2)

Chaucer, Geoffrey. (1994). *The Canterbury tales*. Translated by N. Coghill. In Arthur N. Applebee, A.B. Bermudez, Judith Langer, & J. Marshall's (Senior Consultants), *Literature and language*. Purple Level, 12. Evanston, IL: McDougal, Littell, pp. 117-125.

Crane, Stephen. (1957). The open boat. In Robert Anderson, John Malcolm Brinnin, John Leggett, Gary Q. Arpin, and Susan Allen Toth's (1993), *Elements of literature*. Orlando, FL: Holt, Rinehart, & Winston, pp. 464–478. (ISBN: 0-03-075942-0)

Crane, Stephen (1981). *The red badge of courage*. Mahwah, NJ: Watermill Press. (ISBN: 0-893-75606-7)

Defoe, Daniel. (1988). *Robinson Crusoe*. New York: Tom Doherty Associates. (ISBN: 0-812-50482-8)

Dickens, Charles. (1983). *A tale of two cities*. New York: Bantam. (ISBN: 0-553-21176-5)

Eliot, T.S. (1994). The love song of J. Alfred Prufrock. In Arthur N. Applebee, A.B. Bermudez, Judith Langer, & J. Marshall's (Senior Consultants), *Literature and language*. Yellow Level, 11. Evanston, IL: McDougal, Littell, pp. 506-510.

Faulkner, William. (1950). Nobel Prize acceptance speech. In Robert Anderson, John Malcolm Brinnin, John Leggett, Gary Q. Arpin, and Susan Allen Toth's (1993), *Elements of literature*. Fifth Course. Orlando, FL: Holt Rinehart & Winston, p. 601. (ISBN: 0-03-075942-0)

Frank, Anne. (1995). *Anne Frank: The diary of a young girl*. New York: Doubleday. (ISBN: 0-385-47378-8)

Frost, Robert. (1994). The death of the hired man. In Arthur N. Applebee, A.B. Bermudez, Judith Langer, & J. Marshall's (Senior Consultants), *Literature and language*. Yellow Level, 11. Evanston, IL: McDougal, Littell, pp. 541–545.

Frost, Robert. (1989). Out, out—. In Robert Anderson, John Malcolm Brinnin, John Leggett, Janet Burroway, & David Adams Leeming's (Consultants), *Elements of literature*. Third Course. Austin, TX: Holt, Rinehart, & Winston, p. 328.

Frost, Robert. (1994). The road not taken. In Arthur N. Applebee, A.B. Bermudez, Judith Langer, & J. Marshall's (Senior Consultants), *Literature and language*. Yellow Level, 11. Evanston, IL: McDougal, Littell, pp. 541–545.

Golding, William. (1954). *Lord of the flies*. New York: Paragon Books. (ISBN: 399-50148-7)

Hansberry, Lorraine. (1958). *A raisin in the sun*. New York: New American Library. (ISBN: 0-451-16137-8)

Hemingway, Ernest. (1969). *A farewell to arms*. New York: Charles Scribner's Sons. (ISBN: 0-684-71797-2)

Henry, Patrick. (1755). Speech to the Virginia convention. In Robert Anderson, John Malcolm Brinnin, John Leggett, Gary Q. Arpin, and Susan Allen Toth's (1993), *Elements of literature*. Fifth Course. Orlando, FL: Holt Rinehart Winston, pp. 88–90. (ISBN: 0-03-075942-0)

Hughes, Langston. (1958). A dream deferred. In Lorraine Hansberry's, *A raisin in the sun*. New York: New American Library, p. 5. (ISBN: 0-451-16137-8)

Hughes, Langston. (1984). Dreams. In George Kearns's (General Adviser), *Understanding literature*. New York: Macmillan Publishing Company, p. 203. (ISBN: 0-02-192640-9)

Hughes, Langston. (1993). I, Too. In Robert Anderson, John Malcolm Brinnin, John Leggett, Gary Q. Arpin, and Susan Allen Toth's, *Elements of literature*. Fifth Course. Orlando, FL: Holt, Rinehart, & Winston, p. 690. (ISBN: 0-03-075942-0)

Hughes, Langston. (1993). Mother to son. In Robert Anderson, John Malcolm Brinnin, John Leggett, Janet Burroway, Virginia Hamilton, and David Adams Leeming's, *Elements of literature*. Fourth Course. Orlando, FL: Holt, Rinehart, & Winston, p. 232. (ISBN: 0-03-075939-0)

Keats, John. (1986). On first looking into Chapman's Homer. In Meyer Howard Abrams's (Ed.), *The Norton anthology of English literature*. Fifth Edition. Volume Two. New York: Norton, p. 796. (ISBN: 0-3939-5563-X)

King, Martin Luther. (1992). I have a dream. In James Melvin Washington's (Ed.), *I have a dream: Writings and speeches that changed the world*. San Francisco: Harper. (ISBN: 0-0625-0552-1)

Lee, Harper. (1960). *To kill a mockingbird*. New York: Warner Books. (ISBN: 0-446-31078-6)

London, Jack. (1903). *The call of the wild*. In George Kearns's (1984), *Understanding literature*. New York: Macmillan, pp. 493–539. (ISBN: 0-02-192640-9)

London, Jack. (1903). To build a fire. In George Kearns's (1984), *American literature*. New York: Macmillan, pp. 341–351. (ISBN: 0-02-192680-8)

Longfellow, Henry Wadsworth. (1994). Paul Revere's ride. In Arthur N. Applebee, A.B. Bermudez, Susan Hynds, Judith Langer, J. Marshall, & D.E. Norton's (Senior Consultants), *Literature and language*. Green Level, 8. Evanston, IL: McDougal, Littell, pp. 92–96.

Montgomery, Lucy M. (1908). *Anne of Green Gables*. Boston: L.C. Page & Company. (ISBN: 0-448-06030-2)

Noyes, Alfred. (1994). The highwayman. In Arthur N. Applebee, A.B. Bermudez, Susan Hynds, Judith Langer, J. Marshall, & D.E. Norton's (Senior Consultants), *Literature and language*. Red Level, 7. Evanston, IL: McDougal, Littell, pp. 409–413.

Poe, Edgar Allan. (1994). The raven. In Arthur N. Applebee, A.B. Bermudez, Judith Langer, & J. Marshall's (Senior Consultants), *Literature and language*. Yellow Level, 11. Evanston, IL: McDougal, Littell, pp. 236–239.

Raffel, Burton. (Trans.). (1994). *Beowulf*. In Arthur N. Applebee, A.B. Bermudez, Judith Langer, & J. Marshall's (Senior Consultants), *Literature and language*. Purple Level, 12. Evanston, IL: McDougal, Littell, pp. 22–30.

Salinger, Jerome David. (1951). *Catcher in the Rye*. Boston: Little, Brown, & Company. (ISBN: 0-316-76948-7)

Service, Robert. (1994). The cremation of Sam McGee. In Arthur N. Applebee, A.B. Bermudez, Susan Hynds, Judith Langer, J. Marshall, & D.E. Norton's (Senior Consultants), *Literature and language*. Gold Level, 6. Evanston, IL: McDougal, Littell, pp. 132–137.

Shakespeare, William. (1599). *Julius Caesar*. In G. Kearns's (1984), *Appreciating literature*. New York: Macmillan, pp. 438–535. (ISBN: 0-02-192660-3)

Shakespeare, William. (1942). *Othello, the moor of Venice. Romeo and Juliet*. In William Allan Neilson & Charles Jarvis Hill's (Eds.), *The complete plays and poems of William Shakespeare*. New York: Houghton Mifflin. (LCNN: 42-15352)

Shakespeare, William. (1987). *The tempest*. Stephen Orgel (Ed.). Oxford: Oxford University Press. (ISBN: 0-198-12917-3)

Shelley, Mary. (1993). *Frankenstein*. New York: Random House. (ISBN: 0-679-74954-3)

Stafford, William. (1989). Fifteen. In Robert Anderson, John Malcolm Brinnin, John Leggett, Janet Burroway, & David Adams Leeming's (Consultants), *Elements of literature*. Third Course. Austin, TX: Holt, Rinehart, & Winston, p. 281.

Steinbeck, John. (1939). *The grapes of wrath*. New York: Penguin. (ISBN: 0-140-04239-3)

Steinbeck, John. (1965). *Of mice and men*. New York: Bantam. (ISBN: 0-553-12257-6)

Stoker, Bram. (1983). *Dracula*. New York: Bantam. (ISBN: 0-553-21271-0)

Tennyson, Alfred Lord. (1994). The charge of the light brigade. In Arthur N. Applebee, A.B. Bermudez, Susan Hynds, Judith Langer, J. Marshall, & D.E. Norton's (Senior Consultants), *Literature and language*. Red Level, 7. Evanston, IL: McDougal, Littell, pp. 87–88.

Thurber, James. (1981). *Alarms and diversions*. New York: Harper & Row. (ISBN: 0-060-90830-0)

Thurber, James. (1973). *The beast in me and other animals*. San Diego: Harcourt Brace. (ISBN: 0-156-10850-X)

Thurber, James. (1983). The catbird seat. In A. Dube, J.K. Franson, J.W. Parins, & R.E. Murphy's (Eds.), *Structure and meaning: An introduction to literature*. Boston: Houghton Mifflin, pp. 11–17. (ISBN: 0-395-32570-6)

Thurber, James. (1939). *Cream of Thurber*. London: Hamish Hamilton. (LCCN: 40-6648)

Thurber, James. (1983). *Credos and curios*. New York: Harper & Row. (ISBN: 0-060-91018-6)

Thurber, James. (1956). *Further fables for our time*. New York: Simon & Schuster. (ISBN: 0-671-24218-0)

Thurber, James. (1975). *The great quillow*. San Diego: Ballantine Books. (ISBN: 0-156-36490-5)

Thurber, James. (1992). *Lanterns and lances*. New York: D.I. Fine. (ISBN: 1-556-11299-8)

Thurber, James. (1939). *The last flower*. New York: Harper & Brothers. (LCCN: 39-32475)

Thurber, James. (1993). *Let your mind alone!* London: Methuen. (ISBN: 0-749-31158-4)

Thurber, James. (1971). *Many moons*. San Diego: Harcourt Brace. (ISBN: 0-156-56980-9)

Thurber, James. (1977). *Men, women, and dogs*. San Diego: Harcourt Brace.

Thurber, James. (1935). *The middle-age man on the flying trapeze*. New York: Harper & Brothers. (LCCN: 35-29198)

Thurber, James. (1969). *My world - and welcome to it*. San Diego: Harcourt Brace. (ISBN: 0-156-62344-7)

Thurber, James. (1965). *The owl in the attic and other perplexities*. New York: Perennial Library. (ISBN: 0-608-03517-?)

Thurber, James. (1950). *The seal in the bedroom and other predicaments*. New York: Harper & Brothers. (LCCN: 50-9838)

Thurber, James. (1990). *The 13 clocks*. New York: Dell. (ISBN: 0-440-40582-3)

Thurber, James. (1965). *The Thurber album*. New York: Simon & Schuster. (ISBN: 0-671-21015-7)

Thurber, James. (1966). *Thurber and company*. New York: Harper & Row. (LCCN: 64-18067)

Thurber, James. (1962). *A Thurber carnival*. New York: Samuel French. (ISBN: 0-573-61668-X)

Thurber, James. (1979). *Thurber country*. New York: Penguin. (ISBN: 0-140-01769-0)

Thurber, James. (1963). *Thurber's dogs*. New York: Simon & Schuster. (ISBN: 0-671-21031-9)

Thurber, James. (1963). *Vintage Thurber, 2 Volumes*. London: Hamish Hamilton. (LCCN: 64-51597)

Thurber, James. (1973). *The white deer*. San Diego: Harcourt Brace. (ISBN: 0-156-96264-0)

Thurber, James. (1990). *The wonderful O*. New York: D.I. Fine. (ISBN: 1-556-11189-4)

Thurber, James. (1984). *The years with Ross*. New York: Penguin. (ISBN: 0-140-07380-9)

Thurber, James. & Nugent, E. (1983). *Fables for our time and famous poems illustrated*. New York: Harper & Row. (ISBN: 0-060-90999-4)

Thurber, James. & White, E.B. (1978). *Is sex necessary? Or why you feel the way you do*. New York: Queen's House. (ISBN: 0-892-44056-2)

Updike, John. (1994). Ex-basketball player. In Arthur N. Applebee, A.B. Bermudez, Judith Langer, & J. Marshall's (Senior Consultants), *Literature and language*. Blue Level, 10. Evanston, IL: McDougal, Littell, p. 328

Wyss, Johann D. (1991). *The Swiss family Robinson*. New York: Bantam. (ISBN: 0-440-40430-4)

## Films Cited (Each Available on Home Video)

Allen, Lewis M. (Producer). (1966). *Fahrenheit 451*. Universal City, CA: MCA Universal. (ISBN: 0-7832-0197-4)

Anderson, Bill. (Producer). (1960). *Swiss family Robinson*. Burbank, CA: Walt Disney Home Video. (ISBN: 1-55890-053-5)

Avnet, Jon & Kerner, Jordan. (Producers). (1991). *Fried green tomatoes*. Universal City, CA: MCA Universal. (ISBN: 1-55880-952-X)

Borzage, Frank. (Producer). (1991). *A farewell to arms*. Cincinnati, OH: The Congress Video Group. (ISBN: 8-5476-0100-5)

Brooks, Mel. (Producer). (1995). *Dracula: Dead and loving it*. Castle Rock Entertainment: Columbia Tristar Home Video. (ISBN: 0-8001-8403-3)

Coppola, Francis Ford, Fuchs, Fred, & Mulvehill, Charles. (Producers). (1993). *Dracula*. Burbank, CA: Columbia Pictures. (ISBN: 0-8001-2106-6)

Corman, Julie. (Producer). (1993). *White wolves: A cry in the wild II*. New Horizons Home Video. (ISBN: 7-36991-24703-1)

Eberts, Jake & Joffe, Roland. (Producers). (1992). *City of joy*. Burbank, CA: TriStar Pictures. (ISBN: 0-8001-1414-0)

Fullerton-Smith, Jill. (Producer). (1992). *Alive 20 years later*. Burbank, CA: Touchstone Home Video. (ISBN: 1-55890-192-2)

Goetz, William. (Producer). (1944/1972). *Jane Eyre*. Beverly Hills, CA: 20th Century Fox. (ISBN: 0-7939-1247-4)

Gorrie, John. (Director). (1980). *The tempest*. Video Production: BBC-TV/Time-Life, Inc.

Greene, Justis & Fallon, David. (Producers). (1994). *White Fang 2: Myth of the white wolf*. Burbank, CA: Walt Disney Home Video. (ISBN: 1-55890-978-8)

Hansen, Curtis. (Producer). (1994). *The river wild*. Universal City, CA: MCA Universal. (ISBN: 0-7832-1273-9)

Hinds, Anthony. (Producer). (1985). *Horror of Dracula*. Burbank, CA: Warner Brothers. (ISBN: 0-85391-14993-4)

Hines, Gene, Zatolokin, James R., & Rotman, David. (Producers). (1993). *Cliffhanger*. TriStar: Columbia TriStar Home Video. (ISBN: 0-8001-2586-X)

Jacobs, Alan. (Producer). (1993). *Call of the wild*. Cabin Fever Entertainment. (ISBN: 1-56202-938-X)

Kaufman, Robert & Hamilton, George. (Producers). (1979). *Love at first bite*. Melvin Simon Productions: Orion Home Video. (ISBN: 0-85392-60093-9)

Laemmle, Carl, Jr. & Browning, T. (Producers). (1931). *Dracula*. Universal City, CA: MCA Home Video.

Marvin, Niki. (Producer). (1994). *The Shawshank redemption*. Castle Rock Entertainment: Columbia Tristar Home Video. (ISBN: 0-8001-4048-6)

Marx, Frederick, James, Steve, & Gilbert, Peter. (Producers). (1995). *Hoop dreams*. Turner Home Entertainment: New Line Home Video. (ISBN: 0-7806-0565-9)

Murphy, Eddie. & Lipsky, Mark. (Producers). (1996). *Vampire in Brooklyn*. Hollywood, CA: Paramount Pictures. (ISBN: 0-7921-3827-9)

Palmer, Patrick & Schwartz, Robert. (Producers). (1993). *Iron Will*. Burbank, CA: Walt Disney Home Video. (ISBN: 1-55890-756-4)

Powell, MaryKay. (Producer). (1991). *White Fang*. Burbank, CA: Walt Disney Home Video. (ISBN: 1-55890-151-5)

Smith, Russ & Sinise, Gary. (Producers). (1992). *Of mice and men*. Culver City, CA: Metro-Goldwyn-Mayer. (ISBN: 0-7928-1715-X)

Spielberg, Steven, Molen, Gerald R., & Lustig, Branko. (Producers). (1994). *Schindler's list*. Universal City, CA: MCA Universal Home Video. (ISBN: 0-7832-0832-4)

Steel, Dawn. (Producer). (1993). *Cool runnings*. Burbank, CA: Walt Disney Home Video. (ISBN: 1-55890-519-7)

Watts, Robert & Kennedy, Kathleen. (Producers). (1992). *Alive*. Burbank, CA: Touchstone Home Video. (ISBN: 1-55890-156-6)

Williams, Marsha Garces, Williams, Robin & Radcliffe, Mark. (Producers). (1993). *Mrs. Doubtfire*. Beverly Hills, CA: Twentieth Century Fox. (ISBN: 0-7939-8588-9)

Woolley, Stephen. & Geffen, David. (Producers). (1995). *Interview with the vampire: The vampire chronicles*. Geffen Pictures: Warner Home Video. (ISBN: 0-7907-2452-9)

Zeffirelli, Franco. (1996). *Jane Eyre*. Miramax Films.

## Songs Cited

Collins, Phil. (1989). Another day in paradise. In *But seriously*. New York: Atlantic Recording Corporation.

Ford, Tennessee Ernie. (1955). Sixteen tons. In *Sixteen tons*. Nashville, TN: Capital Records.

Hornsby, Bruce. (1986). The way it is. In *The way it is*. New York: RCA Records.

Kapp, Michael. (1973). To dream the impossible dream. In *Man of La Mancha*. Universal City, CA: MCA Records.

## Teachers' Resources

Abrams, Meyer Howard. (1993). Text and writing (*ecriture*). *A glossary of literary terms*. Sixth Edition. Fort Worth, TX: Holt, Rinehart, & Winston. (ISBN: 0-0305-4982-5)

Agee, James & Evans, Walker. (1973). *Let us now praise famous men*. Boston: Houghton Mifflin. (ISBN: 0-395-07330-8)

Allen, Janet S. (1995). Exploring the individual's responsibility in society in *The giver* and *Brave new world*. In Joan F. Kaywell's (Ed.), *Adolescent literature as a complement to the classics*. Volume Two. Norwood, MA: Christopher-Gordon Publishers, Inc., pp. 199–212. (ISBN: 0-926842-43-9)

Allen, Janet S. (1995). *It's never too late: Leading adolescents to lifelong literacy.* Portsmouth, NH: Heinemann. (ISBN: 0-4350-8839-4)

Alvine, Lynne & Duffy, Devon. (1995). Friendships and tensions in *A separate peace* and *Staying fat for Sarah Byrnes*. In Joan F. Kaywell's (Ed.), *Adolescent literature as a complement to the classics*. Volume Two. Norwood, MA: Christopher-Gordon Publishers, Inc., pp. 163–174. (ISBN: 0-926842-43-9)

Bernstein, Burton. (1975). *Thurber: A biography.* New York: Dodd, Mead. (ISBN: 0-396-07027-2)

Berthoff, Ann E. (1981). A curious triangle and the double-entry notebook: Or how theory can help us teach reading and writing. *The making of meaning: Metaphors, models, and maxims for writing teachers.* Portsmouth, NH: Boynton Cook, pp. 41–47. (ISBN: 0-8670-9003-0)

Biedermann, Hans. (1992). Agate. In J. Hulbert's (Trans.), *A dictionary of symbolism.* New York: Facts on File. (ISBN: 0-8160-2593-2)

Booksearch. (1993, April). Books worth teaching even though they have proven controversial. *English Journal, 82* (4), pp. 86-89.

Bradbrook, Muriel Clara. (1984). *Muriel Bradbrook on Shakespeare.* Sussex, England: The Harvester Press. (ISBN: 0-7108-0687-6)

Bushman, Kay Parks & Bushman, John H. (1993). Dealing with the abuse of power in *1984* and *The chocolate war*. In Joan F. Kaywell's (Ed.), *Adolescent literature as a complement to the classics*. Volume One. Norwood, MA: Christopher-Gordon Publishers, Inc., pp. 215–222. (ISBN: 0-926842-23-4)

Carroll, Pamela S. (1993). *Their eyes were watching God* and *Roll of thunder, hear my cry*: Voices of African-American Southern women. In Joan F. Kaywell's (Ed.), *Adolescent literature as a complement to the classics*. Volume One. Norwood, MA: Christopher-Gordon Publishers, Inc., pp. 163–183. (ISBN: 0-926842-23-4)

Censored. (1993, Winter). *ALAN Review, 20* (2).

Chambers, Aidan. (1996). *Tell me: Children reading and talk.* York, ME: Stenhouse Publishers. (ISBN: 1-571-10030-X)

Cole, Pam B. (1995). Bridging *The red badge of courage* with six related young adult novels. In Joan F. Kaywell's (Ed.), *Adolescent literature as a complement to the classics*. Volume Two. Norwood, MA: Christopher-Gordon Publishers, Inc., pp. 21–39. (ISBN: 0-926842-43-9)

Daniel, Patricia L. (1995). Relationships and identity: Young adult literature and the *Tragedy of Julius Caesar*. In Joan F. Kaywell's (Ed.), *Adolescent literature as a complement to the classics*. Volume Two. Norwood, MA: Christopher-Gordon Publishers, Inc., pp. 145–161. (ISBN: 0-926842-43-9)

DelFattore, Joan. (1992). *What Johnny shouldn't read: Textbook censorship in America.* New Haven: Yale University Press. (ISBN: 0-8141-5666-5)

Dorris, Michael. (1994). Rewriting history. *Paper trail: Essays*. New York: HarperCollins, pp. 133–144. (ISBN: 0-0601-6971-0)

Elbow, Peter. (1990). Democracy through language. *What is English?* New York: Modern Language Association, pp. 31–43. (ISBN: 0-8735-2382-2)

Ericson, Bonnie O. (1993). Introducing *To kill a mockingbird* with collaborative group reading of related young adult novels. In Joan F. Kaywell's (Ed.), *Adolescent literature as a complement to the classics*. Volume One. Norwood, MA: Christopher-Gordon Publishers, Inc., pp. 1–12. (ISBN: 0-926842-23-4)

Foerstel, Herbert N. (1994). *Banned in the U.S.A.: A reference guide to book censorship in schools and public libraries*. Westport, CT: Greenwood Press. (ISBN: 0-313-28517-9)

Gilligan, Carol. (1992). Continuing the conversation: Gender and literature. In Nancy McCracken & Bruce Appleby's (Eds.), *Gender issues in the teaching of English*. Portsmouth, NH: Heinemann, p. 111. (ISBN: 0-8670-9310-2)

Haba, James. (Ed.). (1995). *The language of life: A festival of poets*. New York: Doubleday. (ISBN: 0-3854-7917-4)

Heard, Georgia. (1995). *Writing toward home: Tales and lessons to find your way*. Portsmouth, NH: Heinemann. (ISBN: 0-435-08124-1)

Higgins, Jo. & Fowinkle, Joan. (1993). *The adventures of Huckleberry Finn*, prejudice, and adolescent literature. In Joan F. Kaywell's (Ed.), *Adolescent literature as a complement to the classics*. Volume One. Norwood, MA: Christopher-Gordon Publishers, Inc., pp. 37–59. (ISBN: 0-926842-23-4)

Hipple, Ted. (1993). *Catcher* as core and catalyst. In Joan F. Kaywell's (Ed.), *Adolescent literature as a complement to the classics*. Volume One. Norwood, MA: Christopher-Gordon Publishers, Inc., pp. 61–78. (ISBN: 0-926842-23-4)

Hipple, Ted. (1992, November). Have you read? *English Journal, 81* (7), p. 73.

Hipple, Ted. (1990). *Presenting Sue Ellen Bridgers*. Boston: Twayne Publishers. (ISBN: 0-805782-13-3)

Hodges, Margaret. (1992). *Don Quixote and Sancho Panza*. Illustrated by Stephen Marchesi. New York: Charles Scribner's Sons. (ISBN: 0-684-19235-7)

Iser, Wolfgang. (1972). The reading process: A phenomenological approach. *New Literary History, 3*, pp. 279-300.

Johannessen, Larry R. (January, 1996). Conflict with authority: James Hanley's 'The Butterfly.' *Notes Plus, 13* (3), pp. 10-14.

Kaywell, Joan F. (1993). *Adolescents at risk: A guide to fiction and nonfiction for young adults, parents, and professionals*. Westport, CN: Greenwood Press. (ISBN: 0313-29039-3)

Kaywell, Joan F. (1993). Anne Frank's *The diary of a young girl*: World War II and young adult literature. In Joan F. Kaywell's (Ed.), *Adolescent literature as a complement to the classics*. Volume One. Norwood, MA: Christopher-Gordon Publishers, Inc., pp. 13–35.

Kaywell, Joan F. (1995). Using young adult literature to develop a comprehensive world literature course around several classics. In Joan F. Kaywell's (Ed.), *Adolescent literature as a complement to the classics*. Volume Two. Norwood, MA: Christopher-Gordon Publishers, Inc., pp. 111–143. (ISBN: 0-926842-43-9)

Kirby, Dan & Liner, Tom. (1988). *Inside out: Developmental strategies for teaching writing*. Portsmouth, NH: Boynton Cook. (ISBN: 0-86709-225-4)

Lesesne, Teri S. (1993). Exploring the horror within: Themes of duality of humanity in Mary Shelley's *Frankenstein* and ten related young adult novels. In Joan F. Kaywell's (Ed.), *Adolescent Literature as a Complement to the Classics*. Volume Two. Norwood, MA: Christopher-Gordon Publishers, Inc., pp. 187–197. (ISBN: 0-926842-43-9)

Levitt, Phyllis. (September, 1994). Douse the lit matches aimed at literature. *Council Chronicle*. Urbana, IL: National Council of Teachers of English, pp. 1–2.

Lowe, Peter. (1995). *Success talk: Featuring Jimmy Johnson*. Tampa, FL: Peter Lowe International, Inc., Side B.

Macrorie, Ken. (1988). *The I-search paper*. Portsmouth, NH: Boynton Cool. (ISBN: 0-8670-9223-8)

Marshall, Donald G. (1992). Literary interpretation. In Joseph Gibaldi's (Ed.), *Introduction to scholarship in modern language and literature*. New York: Modern Language Association, pp. 159–182. (ISBN: 0-8735-2093-9)

McCracken, Nancy. (1994, Winter). Censorship matters. *The ALAN Review, 21* (2), pp. 39–41.

Mitchell, Diana. (1993). Exploring the American dream: *The great Gatsby* and six young adult novels. In Joan F. Kaywell's (Ed.), *Adolescent literature as a complement to the classics*. Volume One. Norwood, MA: Christopher-Gordon Publishers, Inc., pp. 143–161. (ISBN: 0-926842-23-4)

Mizener, Arthur. (Ed.). (1969). *Teaching Shakespeare*. New York: New American Library. (LCCN: 71-79101)

Moffett, James & Wagner, Betty Jane. (1992). *Student-centered language arts, K–12*. Fourth edition. Portsmouth, NH: Boynton Cook. (ISBN: 0-86709-292-0)

Morsberger, Robert Eustis. (1979). James Thurber: 1894-1961. In Leonard Unger's (Ed.), *American writers: A collection of literary biographies*. New York: Charles Scribner's Sons. (ISBN: 0-684-13662-7)

National Council of Teachers of English. (1986). *Guidelines for the preparation of teachers of English language arts*. Urbana, IL: National Council of Teachers of English. (ISBN: 0-8141-4730-5)

Nilsen, Alleen Pace & Donelson, Ken L. (1994). *Literature for today's young adults*. 4th Edition. Glenview, IL: Scott, Foresman. (ISBN: 0-6734-6652-3)

Okura, Sandra. (1996). Unpublished class handout. Grant High School, Los Angeles Unified School District.

Pennac, Daniel. (1994). *Better than life*. Toronto: Coach House Press. (ISBN: 0-889-10484-0)

Poe, Elizabeth A. (1993). Alienation from society in *The scarlet letter* and *The chocolate war*. In Joan F. Kaywell's (Ed.), *Adolescent literature as a complement to the classics*. Volume One. Norwood, MA: Christopher-Gordon Publishers, Inc., pp. 185–194. (ISBN: 0-926842-23-4)

Probst, Robert E. (1990). *Five kinds of literary knowing*. Albany, NY: Center for the Learning and Teaching of Literature. (Technical Report 5.5)

Randall, Dudley. (1983). Ballad of Birmingham. In X.J. Kennedy's (Ed.), *Literature: An introduction to fiction, poetry, and drama*. Third Edition. Boston: Little, Brown, & Company, pp. 750–751. (ISBN: 0-3164-8876-3)

Reed, Arthea J. S. (1993). Using young adult literature to modernize the teaching of *Romeo and Juliet*. In Joan F. Kaywell's (Ed.), *Adolescent literature as a complement to the classics*. Volume One. Norwood, MA: Christopher-Gordon Publishers, Inc., pp. 93–115. (ISBN: 0-926842-23-4)

Rosenblatt, Louise M. (1995). *Literature as exploration*. New York: Modern Language Association. (ISBN: 0-8735-2568-X)

Rosenblatt, Louise M. (1978). *The reader, the text, the poem: The transactional theory of the literary work*. Carbondale, IL: Southern Illinois University Press. (ISBN: 0-8093-1805-9)

Rosenblatt, Louise M. (1989). Writing and reading: The transactional theory. In J.M. Mason's (Ed.), *Reading and writing connections*. Boston: Allyn & Bacon, pp. 153–176. (ISBN: 0-2051-1855-0)

Samuels, Barbara G. (1993). The beast within: Using and abusing power in *Lord of the flies*, *The chocolate war*, and other readings. In Joan F. Kaywell's (Ed.), *Adolescent literature as a complement to the classics*. Volume One. Norwood, MA: Christopher-Gordon Publishers, Inc., pp. 195–214. (ISBN: 0-926842-23-4)

Sanchez, Rebecca. (December, 1995). Bubble reading: The active read aloud. *Notes Plus, 13* (2), pp. 9-10.

Scholes, Robert E. (1985). The text in the class. *Textual power: Literary theory and the teaching of English*. New Haven: Yale University Press, pp. 18–36. (ISBN: 0-3000-3350-8)

Schwartz, Howard. (1996). *Next year in Jerusalem: 3000 years of Jewish stories*. New York: Viking. (ISBN: 0-670-86110-3)

Simmons, John S. (Ed.). (1994). *Censorship: A threat to critical reading*. Newark, DE: International Reading Association. (ISBN: 0-8720-7123-5)

Sullivan, Jack. (Ed.). (1986). *The Penguin encyclopedia of horror and the supernatural*. New York: Viking. (ISBN: 0-6708-0902-0)

Tchudi, Stephen & Mitchell, Diana. (1989). *Explorations in the teaching of English*. New York: Harper & Row. (ISBN: 0-0604-3466-X)

Tompkins, Gail E. (1994). *Teaching writing: Balancing process and product*. 2nd edition. Englewood Cliffs, NJ: Merrill. (ISBN: 0-6752-0926-9)

Vaughan, Alden T. & Vaughan, Virginia Mason. (1991). *Shakespeare's Caliban: A cultural history*. Cambridge: Cambridge University Press, pp. ix–xxiii. (ISBN: 0-5214-0305-7)

Wilhelm, Jeff. (1996). *"You gotta be the book": Teaching engaged and reflective reading with adolescents.* New York: Teachers College Press. (ISBN: 0-8077-3566-3)

Wilson, Robert F., Jr. (1992). Enframing style and the father/daughter theme in early Shakespearean comedy and late romance. In Maurice Hunt's (Ed.), *Approaches to teaching Shakespeare's The tempest and other late romances.* New York: Modern Language Association, pp. 38–48. (ISBN: 0-8735-2708-9)

# Contributors

**Janet Allen** is an Assistant Professor of English Education at the University of Central Florida in Orlando, Florida. Prior to this, she taught English and reading for 20 years at a high school in Maine. In 1991, she received the Milken Foundation's National Educator Award for her work with at-risk secondary students, and in 1995, she received two undergraduate teaching awards at UCF. She's the author of *It's Never Too Late: Leading Adolescents to Lifelong Literacy* (Heinemann, 1995) and has two new books which will be available in 1996-1997: *Turning Points: Language and Learning with Adolescents* (Richard C. Owen Publishers); and a book co-authored with Kyle Gonzalez, *There's Room for Me Here: Literacy Workshop in the Middle School* (Stenhouse Publishers). She has had articles published in *English Journal*, *Journal of Teacher Research*, and *Teachers Networking*. Allen contributed to Volume Two of *Adolescent Literature as a Complement to the Classics* and wrote on *Brave New World*.

**Pamela Sissi Carroll** is an Assistant Professor of English Education at Florida State University in Tallahassee, Florida. A former teacher of middle and high school English, she currently is engaged in research and instructional projects that encourage prospective and practicing teachers and adolescents to connect with young adult books. She is particularly interested in ways that YA literature can be integrated into the curricula of middle schools, and in ways that the concerns and needs of today's older adolescents are recognized and addressed in contemporary young adult literature. She is a member of the Executive Board of ALAN and SIGNAL, and serves as research editor for *The ALAN Review*. Carroll contributed to Volumes One and Two of *Adolescent Literature as a Complement to the Classics* and wrote on *Their Eyes Were Watching God* and *The Awakening*.

**Kelly Chandler** is a doctoral student in Literacy Education at the University of Maine, where she serves as managing editor of *Teacher Research: The Journal of Classroom Inquiry*. Before beginning graduate school, she taught English at Noble High School in Berwick, Maine. She has published articles in *The ALAN Review*, *Teaching Tolerance*, *The Journal of Maine Education*, and *Teacher Research: The Journal of Classroom Inquiry*.

**Leila Christenbury** is a former high school English teacher and is currently professor of English Education at Virginia Commonwealth University in Richmond. The editor of *English Journal* and of the 1995 *NCTE Books for You*, she is the author of *Making the Journey: Becoming a Teacher of English Language Arts* (1994, Heinemann). Christenbury contributed to Volume One of *Adolescent Literature as a Complement to the Classics* and wrote on *Great Expectations*.

**Pam B. Cole** is a former secondary English teacher at Whitewood High School in Whitewood, Virginia. She received her Ph.D. in Curriculum and Instruction from Virginia Polytechnic Institute and State University. She is currently an Assistant Professor of Middle Grades English Education at Kennesaw State University in Kennesaw, Georgia, where she teaches language arts methods courses and adolescent literature. Cole contributed to Volume Two of *Adolescent Literature as a Complement to the Classics* and wrote on *The Red Badge of Courage*.

**Patricia L. Daniel** taught middle schoolers for 12 years in Oklahoma. She is an Assistant Professor in the Department of Secondary Education at the University of South Florida in Tampa, Florida, where she teaches middle school English language arts methods and adolescent literature. Daniel contributed to Volume Two of *Adolescent Literature as a Complement to the Classics* and wrote on the *Tragedy of Julius Caesar*.

**Bonnie O. Ericson** is a Professor of Secondary Education at California State University, Northridge, where she supervises English student teachers and teaches English methods and literacy across the curriculum classes. She currently edits the "Resources and Reviews" column for *English Journal* and serves on the NCTE Secondary Section Steering Committee. Ericson contributed to Volumes One and Two of *Adolescent Literature as a Complement to the Classics* and wrote on *To Kill a Mockingbird* and *The Odyssey*.

**Ted Hipple** is a professor of English education and adolescent literature at the University of Tennessee-Knoxville. He is also one of the founders of ALAN, a past president, and currently its Executive Secretary. Hipple contributed to Volume One of *Adolescent Literature as a Complement to the Classics* and wrote on *The Catcher in the Rye*.

**Rosemary Oliphant Ingham** is a professor of Education at Belmont University in Nashville, Tennessee, where she teaches courses in children's and adolescent literature. She has contributed the "Horror, Witchcraft, and Occult" sections to both NCTE publications *Your Reading* and *Books for You*.

**Jeffrey S. Kaplan** is Assistant Professor of Educational Foundations in the College of Education at the University of Central Florida in Orlando and Area Campus Coordinator for the COE on the UCF Daytona Beach campus. He teaches undergraduate and graduate education courses with an emphasis in general teaching methods and classroom learning principles. A former middle and high school English teacher, his first love is working with all teachers in using innovative teaching strategies to enhance classroom instruction. His wife, Renee, a talented teacher in her own right, and his daughter, Lauren, a funny and creative middle schooler, are the source of his inspiration.

**Joan F. Kaywell** is Associate Professor of English Education at the University of South Florida, where she won Undergraduate Teaching Awards in 1991 and 1994. She is passionate about assisting preservice and practicing teachers in discovering ways to improve literacy. She donates her time extensively to the NCTE and its affiliate, FCTE. She is currently the President of FCTE, the Adolescent Literature Column Editor for *English Journal*, and a reviewer for *The New Advocate*. She is published in several journals, regularly reviews young adult novels for *The ALAN Review*, and has three textbooks: *Adolescent Literature as a Complement to the Classics, Volumes One and Two* (Christopher-Gordon Publishers, 1993 & 1995) and *Adolescents At Risk: A Guide to Fiction and Nonfiction for Young Adults, Parents, and Professionals* (Greenwood Press, 1993). Kaywell contributed to Volumes One and Two of *Adolescent Literature as a Complement to the Classics* and wrote on *The Diary of a Young Girl* and several classics of world literature.

**Teri S. Lesesne** is an Assistant Professor in the Department of Library Science at Sam Houston State University in Texas, where she teaches courses in children's and young adult literature and coordinates the annual Young Adult Conference. Her columns appear in the *Journal of Adolescent and Adult Literacy, Emergency Librarian*, and *The ALAN Review*. She is a regional coordinator for the Teachers' Choices Committee of the International Reading Association and President of the Texas Council of Teachers of English. Lesesne contributed to Volume Two of *Adolescent Literature as a Complement to the Classics* and wrote on *Frankenstein*.

**John Noell Moore** is an Assistant Professor of English and Curriculum & Instruction at Purdue University in West Lafayette, Indiana. A Phi Beta Kappa graduate of the College of William and Mary and a former high school English teacher, he was a 1994 recipient of an ALAN Foundation Award for Research in Young Adult Literature. He is a member of MLA, NCTE, VATE, and ALAN, and he serves on NCTE's CEE Commission on English Education and English Studies. He has published in *The ALAN Review*, *Virginia English Bulletin*, *The Virginia Quarterly Review*, and *SIGNAL*. His *Interpreting Young Adult Literature: Literary Theory in the Classroom* will be published by Heinemann early in 1997.

**Lois T. Stover** is the Chair of the Educational Studies Department at St. Mary's College of Maryland where she teaches a variety of courses in the Teacher Education Program. She has served as the editor for the "Young Adult Literature" column for *English Journal* and is currently co-editing the 13th edition of *Books for You*, NCTE's booklist for high school readers. She graduated as an English major from the College of William and Mary, received her M.A.T. from the University of Vermont, and her Ed.D. from the University of Virginia. Stover contributed to Volume Two of *Adolescent Literature as a Complement to the Classics* and wrote on *Things Fall Apart* with Connie S. Zitlow.

**Connie S. Zitlow**, a former English and music teacher, is Associate Professor of Education at Ohio Wesleyan University where she directs the Secondary Education Program and teaches reading, young adult literature, and secondary methods courses. She is the co-editor of the *Ohio Journal of the English Language Arts* and is published in *English Journal, Language Arts, Teacher Education Quarterly*, various state journals, and a book on literacy. She reviews books for *The ALAN Review* and the 13th edition of *Books for You* and serves as the Past President of the Ohio Council of Teachers of English Language Arts. Zitlow contributed to Volume Two of *Adolescent Literature as a Complement to the Classics* and wrote on *Things Fall Apart* with Lois T. Stover.

# Subject Index

# Authors and Titles

## Authors

### A

Abrams, Meyer Howard, 72
Adams, Carmen, 189
Adams, Nicholas, 189, 190
Agee, James, 36, 43, 48
Allen, Janet S., 16, 38, 48, 105
Alvarez, Julia, 148
Alvine, Lynne, 33
Amory, Cleveland, 220
Anaya, Rudolfo A., 143, 153
Anderson, Hans Christian, 125
Anderson, Robert, 33
Appleman-Jurman, Alicia, 207
Arparicio, Frances R., 118
Arpin, Gary Q., 33
Ashabranner, Brent, 155
Atkin, Beth S., 143
Auch, Mary Jane, 221
Avi, 165, 190

### B

Balcells, Jacqueline, 153
Baldwin, James, 93, 97, 98
Barrie, Barbara, 5, 16
Beals, Melba P., 53
Bennett, James, 123, 131
Berthoff, Ann E., 78
Biedermann, Hans, 73
Bierhorst, John, 153, 154
Blair, David Nelson, 143
Block, Francesca Lia, 54, 65
Blume, Judy, 222
Borland, Hal, 90

Boyd, Candy Dawson, 176
Bradbrook, Muriel Clara, 95, 95
Bradbury, Ray, 1, 2, 9, 10, 12, 13, 16
Brancato, Robin F, 175, 207
Bridgers, Sue Ellen, 20, 23, 33, 57. 91
Brinnin, John Malcolm, 33
Bronte, Charlotte,123, 128, 131, 132
Brooks, Bruce, 3, 16, 91, 100, 163, 164
Bunting, Eve, 109, 116
Bushman, Kay Parks, 16
Bushman, John H., 16
Buss, Fran Leeper, 143
Butler, Judy, 147

### C

Cameron, Ann, 155
Campbell, Eric, 208
Carlson, Lori M., 142
Carroll, Lewis, 51, 53, 64
Carroll, Pamela S., 48, 51
Carson, Jo, 111, 118
Carter, Alden R., 208
Carter, Forrest, 43, 48
Castañeda, Omar S., 137, 140, 149
Cervantes, Saavedra M., 137
Chambers, Aidan, 111
Chaucer, Geoffrey, 52, 63
Cheney, Glenn Alan, 143
Childress, Alice, 4, 16
Choy, Isabel P., 137
Christenbury, Leila, 93
Cisneros, Sandra, 154, 155
Coe, Charles, 176
Cofer, Judith Ortez, 144, 148

## Titles

# Producers